the
Unofficial
Guide® to
London
1st Edition

Also available from IDG Books Worldwide, Inc.:

Beyond Disney: The Unofficial Guide to Universal Studios, Sea World, and the Best of Central Florida, by Amber Morris and Bob Sehlinger

Inside Disney: The Incredible Story of Walt Disney World and the Man Behind the Mouse, by Eve Zibart

Mini Mickey: The Pocket-Sized Unofficial Guide to Walt Disney World, by Bob Sehlinger

The Unofficial Guide to Bed & Breakfasts in New England, by Lea Lane

The Unofficial Guide to Bed & Breakfasts in the Northwest, by Sally O'Neal Coates

The Unofficial Guide to Branson, Missouri, by Eve Zibart and Bob Sehlinger

The Unofficial Guide to California with Kids, by Colleen Dunn Bates and Susan LaTempa

The Unofficial Guide to Chicago, by Joe Surkiewicz with Bob Sehlinger

The Unofficial Guide to Cruises, by Kay Showker and Bob Sehlinger

The Unofficial Guide to Disneyland, by Bob Sehlinger

The Unofficial Guide to Florida with Kids, by Pam Brandon

The Unofficial Guide to the Great Smoky and Blue Ridge Region, by Bob Sehlinger and Joe Surkiewicz

The Unofficial Guide to Las Vegas, by Bob Sehlinger

The Unofficial Guide to Miami and the Keys, by Bob Sehlinger and Joe Surkiewicz

The Unofficial Guide to New Orleans, by Eve Zibart and Bob Sehlinger

The Unofficial Guide to New York City, by Eve Zibart and Bob Sehlinger with Jim Leff

The Unofficial Guide to Paris, by David Applefield

The Unofficial Guide to San Francisco, by Joe Surkiewicz and Bob Sehlinger with Richard Sterling

The Unofficial Guide to Skiing in the West, by Lito Tejada-Flores, Peter Shelton, Seth Masia, and Bob Sehlinger

The Unofficial Guide to Walt Disney World, by Bob Sehlinger

The Unofficial Guide to Walt Disney World with Kids, by Bob Sehlinger

The Unofficial Guide to Washington, D.C., by Bob Sehlinger and Joe Surkiewicz with Eve Zibart

the Unofficial Guide® to London

1st Edition

Lesley Logan

Every effort has been made to ensure the accuracy of information throughout this book. Bear in mind, however, that prices, schedules, etc., are constantly changing. Readers should always verify information before making final plans.

IDG Books Worldwide, Inc.

An International Data Group Company
919 E. Hillsdale Blvd., Suite 400
Foster City, CA 94404

Copyright © 2000 by Bob Sehlinger

Produced by Menasha Ridge Press

MACMILLAN is a registered trademark of Macmillan General Reference USA, Inc., a wholly owned subsidiary of IDG Books Worldwide, Inc. *UNOFFICIAL GUIDE* is a registered trademark of Macmillan General Reference USA, Inc., a wholly owned subsidiary of IDG Books Worldwide, Inc.

ISBN 0-02-863096-3
ISSN 1521-4907
Manufactured in the United States of America
10 9 8 7 6 5 4 3 2 1
First edition

Contents

List of Maps

About Our Authors and Contributors

Lesley Logan is a freelance writer who has worked in publishing over the years as a nonfiction ghostwriter, publicity copywriter, and editor. She is the writer/editor of a new publication called *The London Newsletter* and is at work on a novel for young adults. She has lived in London as an expatriate for a number of years and has no intention of leaving anytime soon.

Richard Ehrlich, who wrote the Dining chapter, has been writing about food and drink in major United Kingdom magazines and newspapers since 1988. His work appears regularly in *The Independent on Sunday*, *The Guardian*, and *Time Out*. An American, Richard has lived in London since 1974.

Andy Craft, a native Londoner, wrote the Exercise and Recreation chapter as well as sections on British Culture, What the Locals Already Know, and Getting Around London. He is the author of several screenplays, and has worked for PBS in New York City, where he now resides.

Rusty Egan contributed tremendously to the Nightlife section. As a young entrepreneur, he started several successful nightclubs in London in the 1980s, following a career as a pop artist in the band Visage.

Tony Heiberg wrote the Entertainment chapter. He is a freelance writer and has worked as a critic and journalist for a number of magazines on both sides of the Atlantic. He is now working on a novel.

Atalanta Knatchbull assisted on the hotel and shopping chapters as well as provided office support. Her knowledge of London is extensive, and her stories brightened many a morning at the patisserie.

Denise Knestaut researched and wrote several of the entries for the Sightseeing section, as well as all of the London walks. She has lived in London for two years and has created a London Web site for her sixth grade students back in the States.

Acknowledgments

First and foremost I want to thank Tom and Nora Logan without whom nothing, least of all this book, would be possible.

And to Bob Sehlinger and Molly Burns of Menasha Ridge Press, thanks for a wonderful assignment.

Many heartfelt thanks to the legions of anonymous curators, cab drivers, London Transport people, London Tourist Board employees, shopkeepers, waiters, concierges, hotel managers, bellhops, B&B owners, and people on the street who generously gave me tips, information, guided tours, and unfailingly pointed me in the right direction.

I am grateful to all the family and friends who stayed at our house and regaled me with tales from the tourist trail, as well as forced me out onto it. They are too numerous to mention, but they know who they are, and they know they are welcome back anytime. I am especially grateful to the kids who helped me research the children's section of this book: London kids Daisy Knatchbull, Nora Logan, Francesca Bindi Craft, Georgina Godik, Rayana Pharaon, Tom Vereker, Olivia Williams, and the greatly missed Georgina Horlick; and the Americans, Asha Kinney, Maia and Margo Kinney-Petrucha, Gregory and Neal Beeken, Bo and Quinn Wilke, Sophia Logan, JP and Arliss Gussin, Lucia and David Haladjian, Tessa and Sarah Barlow-Ochshorn, and Legoland expert Lily Adler.

For all their help with the research and writing of this book, as well as for their friendship and moral support, I would like to thank: my dear sisters Sheila, Nancy, Lynn, and Sarah Kinney, Ellen and Moshe Adler, Bailey Beeken, Paul Becken, Andy and Diane Craft, Beth Crehan, Leslie Farhangi, Nina Gerli, Donna Heroy, Sarah and Kerry Holmberg, Atalanta Knatchbull, Margaret Logan, Mary Logan, Robert Logan, Charlotte Martin, Chris Marzec, Josie Miguel, Stefan Petrucha, Jill Robinson, Rob Sunderland, Nancy Tuckerman, Arietta Venizelos, David Wilke, and last but certainly not least, Allan Weisbecker.

—*Lesley Logan*

Introduction

London Calling

Let's just get it out of the way, shall we? Dr. Samuel Johnson's quote about his beloved city is as famous as Big Ben: "When a man is tired of London, he is tired of Life, for there is in London all that Life can afford." Only in London could the words of an eighteenth-century writer be put to such persistent modern PR use; it is exactly this easy—some might say surreal—connection between past and present that makes London the powerful draw for tourists that it is and has always been.

London is a historical free-for-all where, against the gorgeous Georgian facade of the Royal Academy, you'll find a series of seriously modern sculpture; where horse-drawn carriages and soldiers on horseback in full regalia barely merit a passing glance from Londoners in their cars; where the Liberty department store on the eighteenth-century Nash-designed Regent Street is housed in a Tudor building straight out of a fairy tale. This wonderful palimpsest of centuries—the layering of post–World War II London over Edwardian elegance, on top of Victorian glory, over eighteenth-century exuberance, under which the medieval and even the Roman city can be appreciated—is, especially to the American eye, a miracle of conservation and civic pride.

But if London were only the sum of its past, it would hardly be the relentlessly hyped city of cool Britannia fame, the scene of a constantly evolving culture of theater, arts, and music, not to mention the birthplace of cutting-edge clothing designers, rock and rollers, and night-clubbers. In 1978, Bette Midler said, "When it's three o'clock in New York, it's still 1938 in London." Today, this remark might be received with some puzzlement, except perhaps by those who expect stores to be open on Sunday and remain open past six and who believe that public transportation ought to run after midnight. Despite its current high prices, London attracts over 25 million visitors a year, swelling its

1

permanent population of 7 million. This is not to say it's a nirvana for visitors —London is no quaint theme park. This city takes a bit of work, and visitors may struggle to reconcile the picture of London carried in their minds against the sometimes dirty, indifferent, and confusing contemporary reality of the place. But the payoff for a little footwork is huge.

London can be many cities to many people. Contrast Dr. Johnson's hymns of worship ("The happiness of London is not to be conceived but by those who have been in it") with Percy Bysshe Shelley's assessment of early nineteenth-century London: "Hell is a city much like London—a populous and smoky city." People may have a wide range of feelings about London, but indifference is usually not one of them. It's the rare English-speaker who comes here without a mental trunk full of preconceptions. Those of us of a certain age had an intimate acquaintance with the bells of St. Clements, London Bridge, and the Drury Lane home of the muffin man before we could even read. When we could finally read, we absorbed the London of Charles Dickens, who captured the nineteenth-century city in all its degradation and beauty, who spent hours each night exploring his city on foot, and who left his unforgettable impressions on the pages of his novels and the psyches of his readers. London has appeared as a character in so much English literature that it is a place we carry in our collective consciousness like a dream.

Waking up to London is another story. To arrive here for the first time is to suddenly confront the fantasy with the fact. The most outstanding fact about London is its sprawling geography—there is nothing so neat as a "downtown" of London. It isn't so much one big city as a series of interconnected villages on a human-size scale and liberally dotted with breathing spaces of greenery. London can take a lifetime to explore fully, and a tourist with only a week to cover the major sights will find it impossible to take it all in. The best approach to London is to decide where your interests lie; you will soon discover that there are few interests known to humanity that London cannot entertain.

We want you to make the best of this best of all possible cities. We want you to not waste one minute getting lost in the Underground or taking a taxi if walking would be quicker. We don't want you to get such a bad case of museum legs that you can't make it to the theater that night, and we definitely don't want you to spend your hard-earned money buying anything that's cheaper back home. London is a great place for visitors —tourism is its second largest industry—and we love the fact that we North Americans can, for the most part, communicate with the locals without needing a course from Berlitz. We hope to identify and address any difficulties you might have in visiting London, so that you can pursue whatever course of entertainment you desire, efficiently and happily. And there's so much to be done. . . .

London has the best museums in the world, the famous as well as some lesser-known ones. There are miles of parklands, offering some of the most beautiful natural scenery to be found in any metropolis. Part of London's charm lies in the sudden deluges from leaden skies that will just as quickly crack open with swords of sunlight. There are also the people of London, a rich concoction of accents, classes, nationalities, and politics, speaking over 200 languages. No matter what moves you—theater, architecture, sports, antiques, markets, designer clothing, contemporary art and old masters, heart-stopping cathedrals, Internet cafes, palaces, poetry readings, elegant casinos, lunatic nightclubs, pubs, bungee jumping, horticulture, witchcraft, fencing, pigeons, boating—there truly is, as the good doctor pointed out almost three centuries ago, "in London all that Life can afford."

About This Guide

WHY UNOFFICIAL?

Most London travel guides follow the usual tracks of the typical tourist, automatically sending them to the well-known sights without any information about how to do it painlessly, recommending restaurants and hotels indiscriminately, and failing to recognize the limits of human endurance in sight-seeing. This guide is different: We understand that in a huge city like London, it is essential for one to discriminate, make plans, whittle the town down to size, and be just a little bit flexible when hours-long lines appear out of nowhere or when the clouds burst and you've forgotten your umbrella.

We'll tell you what we think of certain tourist traps, what the real story is on the famous restaurants and hotels, what the options are if you want to stay off the beaten track, or spend a little less money on one thing so you can spend more on another. We'll complain about rip-offs, we'll advise you on bargains, and we'll steer you out of the madness of the crowds for a break now and then. We also hope to give you the kind of information that will make you love London all the more—some of the endearing eccentricities that make you realize you're definitely not in Kansas anymore.

London is such a complex and sprawling city, so full of fantastic anecdote and incident, that it's hard to edit out the trivia—it's all great stuff, and the more tales you hear, the more you want to know. London is all about history—every building and monument, every alley and lane has a story that has seeped through the mists of time and simply must be passed on. The longer you stay here, the larger London becomes in some ways: Each door that opens reveals ten windows to look through. In the old days a visit to London was a rite of passage for the upper classes of North America, and they used to spend six months at it. You probably haven't got that luxury (unless you're here as an exchange student), so you have to be very efficient and organized if you want to make the most of your time. The majority of overseas visitors only stay for about five to ten days. How much can you squeeze into that time? How much do you *want* to see? What are your priorities, and how can they best be served? Like any worthwhile undertaking, some preparation and strategy is needed to make London reveal its charms to you. We have done the footwork: We've checked out the hotels to find the best deals and the most interesting buildings; Richard Erlich, who has been reviewing the restaurants for years, will give you the benefit of his experience; and we've got the low-down on the nightlife straight from nightclub impresario Rusty Egan and entertainment expert Tony Heiberg. If a museum is dull, or there's a two-hour wait for an attraction that just isn't worth it, we'll tell you why—and we hope in the process to make your visit more fun, efficient, and economical.

We also want to do a little matchmaking between you and London. There are some guidebooks that seem to have missed the great romance of this electrifying city: They may know London well enough, but they don't seem to love it enough. The best guidebooks will try to inspire that love in the reader and the visitor, for we all know how much more pleasure and beauty is to be found in what we adore than in what we merely admire. For us, to know London *is* to love London.

We've tried in this book to anticipate the special needs of older people, families with young children, families with teenagers, solo travelers, people with physical challenges, and those who have a particular passion for literature, sport, architecture, shopping, painting, antiques, or whatever. We can help you customize your trip to accommodate both your personal interests and the amount of time you have to spend in London.

London has hundreds of attractions, and we've tried to sort them into first-rate, special interest, and hype jobs, giving space to only the best. Obviously, even if you visit London dozens of times, you won't be able to see all that we describe to you, and by then you'll have discovered some of your own favourite haunts. But we want you to always have the options of exploring more and more of this endlessly interesting city, and we want to give you the best tips for doing so. We take things easy, the way we think you'll want to, but we don't forgive exploitation or stupidity. If it isn't fun, if it isn't informative, if it isn't a reasonable deal, we don't want you to go. If there's a better alternative, we want you to know. We hope to keep the quality of your visit high and the irritation quotient low.

We've covered attractions in these various ways because we want to make sure you can pick out the ones you'd enjoy most. For those of you who don't wish to do it all yourselves, we've listed a number of good commercial and customized tours on page 262 in Part Nine: "Sight-Seeing and Tours."

Even keeping in mind that your time will be filled, we have included a list of opportunities for exercise. Travel can be pretty hard on the body—airplane stiffness, walking around galleries and streets—and it's wise to get some endorphins going at some point in your visit. Also, London has so many great restaurants and opportunities to try new foods that you may well need a little calorie-corrective run or swim, unless you want to take home more than photos and souvenirs (try a few days of cream teas and you'll see what we mean).

Please do remember that prices and admission hours change constantly; we have listed the most up-to-date information we can get, but it never hurts to double-check times in particular (if prices of attractions change, it is generally not by much). Remember, this is one of the busiest tourist towns in the world, so make your reservations early and reconfirm at least once.

ABOUT UNOFFICIAL GUIDES

Readers care about authors' opinions. The authors, after all, are supposed to know what they are talking about. This, coupled with the fact that the traveler wants quick answers (as opposed to endless alternatives), dictates that travel authors should be explicit, prescriptive, and above all, direct. The authors of the *Unofficial Guide* try to do just that. We spell out alternatives and recommend specific courses of action. We simplify complicated destinations and attractions to allow the traveler to feel in control in the most unfamiliar environments. The objective of *Unofficial Guide* authors is not to give the most information or all of the information but to offer the most accessible, useful information. Of course, in a city like London there are many hotels, restaurants, and attractions that are so closely woven into the fabric of the city that to omit them from our guide because we can't recommend them would be a disservice to our readers. We have included all the famous haunts in here, giving our opinion and experience of them, in the hopes that you will approach (or avoid) these institutions armed with the necessary intelligence.

An *Unofficial Guide* is a critical reference work; we focus on a travel destination that appears to be especially complex. Our authors and researchers are completely independent from the attractions, restaurants, and hotels we describe. *The Unofficial Guide to London* is designed for individuals and families traveling for fun as well as for business, and it will be especially helpful to those hopping "across the pond" for the first time. The guide is directed at value-conscious, consumer-oriented adults who seek a cost-effective but not Spartan travel style.

Special Features

- Vital information about traveling abroad.
- Friendly introductions to London's "villages."
- "Best of" listings giving our well-qualified opinions on everything from yoga classes to views of the Thames.
- Listings that are keyed to your interests, so you can pick and choose.
- Advice to sight-seers on how to avoid the worst crowds; advice to business travelers on how to avoid traffic and excessive costs.
- Recommendations for lesser-known sights that are off the well-beaten tourist path, but no less worthwhile.
- A zone system and maps to make it easy to find places you want to go and avoid places you don't.
- A hotel section that helps you narrow down your choices quickly, according to your needs and preferences.
- A table of contents and detailed index to help you find things fast.
- Insider advice on best times of day (or night) to go places.

WHAT YOU WON'T GET

- Long, useless lists where everything looks the same.
- Information that gets you to your destination at the worst possible time.
- Information without advice on how to use it.

HOW THIS GUIDE WAS RESEARCHED AND WRITTEN

In preparing this work, we took nothing for granted. Each hotel, restaurant, shop, and attraction was visited by trained observers who conducted detailed evaluations and rated each according to formal criteria. Team members conducted interviews with tourists of all ages to determine what they enjoyed most and least during their London visit.

Though our observers are independent and impartial, they are otherwise "ordinary" travelers. Like you, they visited London as tourists or business travelers, noting their satisfaction or dissatisfaction.

The primary difference between the average tourist and the trained evaluator is the evaluator's skills in organization, preparation, and observation. A trained evaluator is responsible for more than just observing and cataloging. Observer teams use detailed checklists to analyze hotel rooms, restaurants, nightclubs, and attractions. Finally, evaluator ratings and observations are integrated with tourist reactions and the opinions of patrons for a comprehensive quality profile of each feature and service.

In compiling this guide, we recognize that a tourist's age, background, and interests will strongly influence his or her taste in London's wide array of attractions and will account for a preference for one sight or museum over another. Our sole objective is to provide the reader with sufficient description, critical evaluation, and pertinent data to make knowledgeable decisions according to individual tastes.

LETTERS, COMMENTS, AND QUESTIONS FROM READERS

We expect to learn from our mistakes, as well as from the input of our readers, and to improve with each new book and edition. Many of those who use the *Unofficial Guides* write to us asking questions, making comments, or sharing their own discoveries and lessons learned in London. We appreciate all such input, both positive and critical, and encourage our readers to continue writing. Readers' comments and observations will be frequently incorporated in revised editions of the *Unofficial Guide* and will contribute immeasurably to its improvement.

How to Write the Author

Lesley Logan
The Unofficial Guide to London
P.O. Box 43673
Birmingham, AL 35243

When you write, be sure to put your return address on your letter as well as on the envelope—sometimes envelopes and letters get separated. Remember, our work takes us out of the office for long periods of time, so forgive us if our response is delayed.

How Information Is Organized: By Subject and by Geographic Zones

To give you fast access to information about the best of London, we've organized material in several formats.

HOTELS

There are many hotels in London that would be unrecognizable as hotels in America. They are small, quirky, and unique. Even the four- and five-star hotels can vary dramatically in room size and amenities, and a midprice-range hotel can have under one charming roof and at a similar price both closet-size attic rooms and magnificent salons with French windows. We have tried to stick to the hotels that are more reliable and consistent in their accommodations, and we have attempted to summarize this somewhat unwieldy and problematic subject in ratings and rankings that allow you to quickly focus your decision-making process. We concentrate on the specific variables that differentiate one hotel from another: location, size, room quality, services, amenities, and cost.

ENTERTAINMENT AND NIGHTLIFE

Visitors frequently try several different clubs or nightspots during their stay in London. Since clubs or nightspots, like restaurants, are usually selected rather spontaneously after arriving, we believe that detailed descriptions are warranted. The best nightspots in London are profiled in Part Six, "Entertainment and Nightlife," beginning on page 206.

RESTAURANTS

We provide plenty of detail when it comes to restaurants. You will probably eat a dozen or more restaurant meals during your stay, and not even you can predict what you might be in the mood for on Saturday night. You can browse through our detailed profiles of the best restaurants in London before dining out.

Geographic Zones

Once you've decided where you're going, getting there becomes the issue. To help you do that, we have divided London into geographic zones, which we briefly describe below to give you an idea of what they're about. These zones are unrelated to and should not be confused with the zones laid out by the London's public transportation system. All profiles of hotels, restaurants, attractions, and nightspots include zone numbers. If you are staying in Knightsbridge, for example, and are interested in a place to eat within walking distance, look at the restaurant profiles for restaurants in Zone 10.

Zone 1: North London: Hampstead, Highgate (NW3, NW8, NW9)

This is an almost suburban area, which can seem to be in the heart of the country when you're standing in Hampstead Heath looking out at a castle-like mansion on a hill, surrounded by old trees and wild grass. Hampstead has always been a salubrious place: during the Black Death of the early 1200s, people fled to Hampstead, and again during the Great Plague of 1665–66. By the eighteenth century, Hampstead had become a fashionable resort for Londoners seeking fresh air and healthy spring water.

The nineteenth century saw an influx of artists, writers, and intellectuals, a community still found here. Hampstead Heath is approximately 800 acres of natural beauty, with a bucolic bounty not often found within miles of a large city. There are views from Highgate and Hampstead across the whole of London, which, along with the charm of the high street, makes this quite a satisfying destination for the discerning tourist. Kenwood House is a stately home on the heath that is well worth a visit.

Zone 2: Bloomsbury and Holborn (WC1, WC2)

Bloomsbury is dominated by the British Museum and the University of London, as well as by many hospitals and institutes of learning. In Holborn, one finds many traces of old London: Dickens's House, Coram's Fields, Dr. Johnson's House, the Silver Vaults, and more are to be found here. There are a number of relatively reasonably priced lodgings here, within walking distance of the West End—a good thing for the club crawlers, as many buses and all trains stop running shortly after midnight. There's a lot of literary history here: the famous Bloomsbury Group of the early 1900s—a tightly related gang of writers and artists that included Virginia Woolf and Lytton Strachey—will always be associated with this area, and is reflected in numerous blue plaques on various buildings.

Zone 3: The City, Clerkenwell, and Barbican (EC1, EC2, EC4)

This is the oldest part of London, where you will find the magnificent St. Paul's Cathedral, winding medieval lanes, and some remnants of Londinium—things that managed to survive the devastating Great Fire of 1666 and the Blitz of World War II. This is also where most of the financial business of London is conducted. It pretty much dies at night and on weekends, but during the day you'll find many good restaurants. The Bank of England Museum and the Lloyd's of London building by Richard Rogers are two other attractions. There are some amusing architectural visions here, such as the grasshopper on the top of the Stock Exchange. The old markets —Smithfield's, Billingsgate, and Leadenhall—are fun to check out.

Zone 4: East End: Spitalsfields, White Chapel (E1)

Besides the Tower of London, Zone 4 offers markets, Victorian architecture, art galleries and churches, and cockney English. The once-thriving Jewish center of London used to be here, and you can still go to the *schwitzes,* the old-style men's steambaths, or get a great piece of smoked fish and latkes from the oldest Jewish deli in London. Some of the schmatta business has survived the general exodus to Golders' Green, but not much. This is where Jack the Ripper stalked his prey and Sweeny Todd made mincemeat of his customers. Here, too, you can get boats to Greenwich, see some of the old Roman wall around London, and visit the Tower Bridge.

Zone 5: South London: South Bank, Lambeth, Brixton

Zone 5 encompasses the great renaissance of buildings on the South Bank—the London Aquarium, the Marriott Hotel, the National Theatre, the Hayward Gallery—as well as the ancient palace of Lambeth, where the archbishop of Canterbury lives; Waterloo Station, from which the Eurostar leaves; and the Old Vic Theatre. There's great nightlife in Brixton, with lots of reggae venues, thanks to its large Caribbean contingent. From the South Bank you get the very best views of the halls of Westminster and Big Ben, and along the promenade you will find outdoor cafes in the summer, where you can lounge and watch the river flow.

Zone 6: Greenwich and The Docklands

Greenwich is chock-full of tourist venues: the National Maritime Museum, two old tea clippers, the Old Royal Observatory, Inigo Jones's Queen's House, the Royal Naval College, and the odd but interesting Museums of Fans and Teapots. You could easily spend a full day seeing Greenwich. The Docklands are of more limited appeal, featuring mainly Canary Wharf, a high-rise office complex, and the much-debated, oft-maligned Millennium Dome.

Zone 7: Soho and the West End (W1)

This is where the nightlife and the theater district are located. Charing Cross bookshops, St. Martin–in-the-Fields, Trafalgar Square, rowdy Leicester Square, Chinatown, the National Gallery, and pubs, pubs, pubs are in this zone. Carnaby Street and Neal's Yard are the alternative lifestyle, clothing, and health therapies areas, and Covent Garden has absolutely everything for everybody. There's also the London Transport Museum, the Trocadero, the Rock Circus, and the Theatre Museum. You might want to stay in a hotel around here, but it can get loud at night, with drunks roaring up and down side streets and tourists as far as the eye can see. Of course, that may be part of its appeal.

Zone 8: Mayfair and Piccadilly (W1, SW1)

This is a very classy zone, in which you can find the most expensive shops in the world—from the designers on New and Old Bond Streets, to the bespoke trade in St. James, to the White House Linen shop, where you can spend thousands on bedclothes. There is every imaginable hotel here, except for inexpensive ones—the Atheneum, Park Lane, Ritz, Brown's, Dorchester, Metropolitan, Claridges . . . the list is impressive. Hatchard's, the oldest bookstore in London is on Piccadilly, as are Fortnum and Mason's, the Burlington Arcade, and the wonderful Royal Academy, whose exhibits are always top-notch. Shepherds' Market is here, which in the 1600s was the site of the riotous saturnalia known as the May Fair and a place for the entertainers of the day—jugglers, fire eaters, boxers, prostitutes—to parade their talents. Today, it is merely a quaint place to take a look.

Zone 9: Victoria and Westminster (SW1)

This zone encompasses the halls of government and power in London: Whitehall, Westminster Abbey, Parliament, and Buckingham Palace. There are plenty of hotels to go along with the preponderance of tourist attractions. Due to the heavy concentration of World War II bombing in this area, there are patches of ugliness here and there where rebuilding went on without much attention to architectural coherence. Much of Westminster simply closes down on the weekend—not the attractions but the eateries, which cater mainly to the business crowd. Pimlico to the south has lots of cheap hotels and bedsits, but may not be the greatest place to be late at night. This zone runs from the seedy to the sublime. There is the most magnificent vista here: the view from Buckingham Palace across St. James's Park toward Westminster Abbey is like something out of a fairy tale.

Zone 10: Knightsbridge and Belgravia (SW1, SW3)

This zone is the stronghold of the very wealthy: expatriate entrepreneurs, British aristocrats, movie stars, rock and roll gods, and sultans coexist peacefully in the splendor of Georgian townhouses or in deceptively simple mews houses within walking distance of Hyde Park, Harrods, and Harvey Nichols. Knightsbridge is mainly about shopping: Sloane Street, Walton Street, and Beauchamp Place have all the trendiest designer shops; the auction house Bonhams is in Knightsbridge Village, as are a large assortment of second-hand designer clothes shops. Knightsbridge has the distinction of having the most consonants in a row in any English word. Belgravia has less to talk about, as it is an enclave of ambassadors and billionaires, with enormous attached mansions, some of which are five houses strung together as one, as in the humble home of the sultan of Brunei. It's a very convenient zone to stay in if you can afford it: You can walk to Oxford Street; the Victoria and Albert Museum; the Natural History Museum; Hyde, Green, and St. James's parks; and Piccadilly. Also, there are buses that go everywhere from Hyde Park Corner.

Zone 11: Chelsea and South Kensington (SW3, SW7, SW10)

South Kensington is known as Albertopolis and Museumland because of the many cultural institutions Prince Albert founded here: The Victoria and Albert and the Natural History Museums, Royal Albert Hall, the Royal Art College, Imperial College, and numerous other learned societies. You can now see the Albert Memorial in all its restored glory; its gold magnificence was camouflaged in black during World War I to confound the bombers. It's also known as Little France, thanks to the Lycee Français and the Institute Français in the middle of town. There are lots of great patisseries, a few good restaurants, and plenty of fine hotels. Chelsea is to the south and is home to the famous King's Road, the once-swinging home to '60s hipsters and '70s punks. In the neighborhoods off King's Road, there are a multitude of blue plaques identifying the many writers and artists who once called Chelsea home: Oscar Wilde, George Eliot, Thomas Carlyle, Dante Gabriel Rossetti, James Whistler . . . the list goes on. Chelsea is very beautiful in areas and is considered a very smart area in which to live—and the property prices reflect this.

Zone 12: West London: Hammersmith, Chiswick, Richmond, Kew (W4)

These are primarily residential areas outside of central London, with only a couple of tourist attractions. Chiswick has Hogarth's House, Chiswick House, and a few good restaurants; Richmond has the huge Park and Wimbledon Common; Hammersmith has its beautiful old bridge that one can walk across, a theater, Olympia Arena, some old pubs, and new strip clubs; and Kew has the gorgeous gardens and Syon House, home to the Butterfly House. Hampton Court, the great Tudor palace on the Thames, is in this zone.

Zone 13: Kensington, Holland Park, Notting Hill (W8, W11)

As a result of King William and Queen Mary moving their royal residence to the then far-flung country village of Kensington in 1689, lots of grand houses were built in this area. As rich attracts rich, the neighborhoods to the west and north, especially in Holland Park, developed into very exclusive places to live. Notting Hill used to be a big Jamaican enclave, but was soon attracting the idle trust-fund kids who were quickly dubbed "trustafarians." It is a very happening place, as its ever-increasing rents attest. This is where the famous Portobello Market is, which is worth a look on Saturday as long as you're not prone to agoraphobia. Attractions: Kensington Palace and Gardens, Leighton House, Linley Sambourne House, Holland Park, and the Kensington Church Street antiques store mecca.

Zone 14: Bayswater, Marylebone, Little Venice, St. John's Wood (NW1, W1, W9, NW8)

At the north border of Hyde Park, Bayswater and Marylebone have an enormous Arab population and a lot of great Middle Eastern restaurants.

Here you'll find the Wallace Collection, Whiteley's Shopping Mall, Regent's Canal Waterbus, Sherlock Holmes Museum, Madame Tussaud's, and two horseback riding stables that take customers for trots around Hyde Park. There are tons of cheap hotels here, some pretty funky, some good value. Paddington Station is the terminus for the train from Heathrow as well as for trains that serve the West Country and South Wales. There's a bit of a sleaze factor, with hookers and drug dealers lurking around Paddington. Farther north is Little Venice, which has a canal running through it with boats that can be taken on Regent's Canal and the Grand Union Canal. St. John's Wood is the home of the American School, where a lot of the expats send their kids and have settled in the many beautiful houses on the many quiet streets. The main attraction is the Abbey Road zebra crossing, where tourists annoy the locals by taking pictures of themselves re-creating the Beatles' famous album cover.

Zone 15: Regent's Park and Camden Town (NW1, NW8)

Regent's Park houses the London Zoo, the London Central Mosque, Regent's Open Air Theatre, and affords some of the most beautiful eighteenth-century vistas in London. Designed in concert with King George IV, this area is architect John Nash's crowning achievement. Camden Town, to the northwest, is a bustling market town, and rivals Portobello Road for good buys and cool stuff. There's a great antiques market and lots of hip clothing and knickknacks, plus plenty of body piercing and tattoos on display. Primrose Hill is another sylvan glade in this zone and is one of the best places to watch the Guy Fawkes' Day fireworks.

Note: Please keep in mind that as of October 2000, all 0171 phone prefixes change to 0207 and all 0181 prefixes become 0208. The remaining seven numbers stay the same.

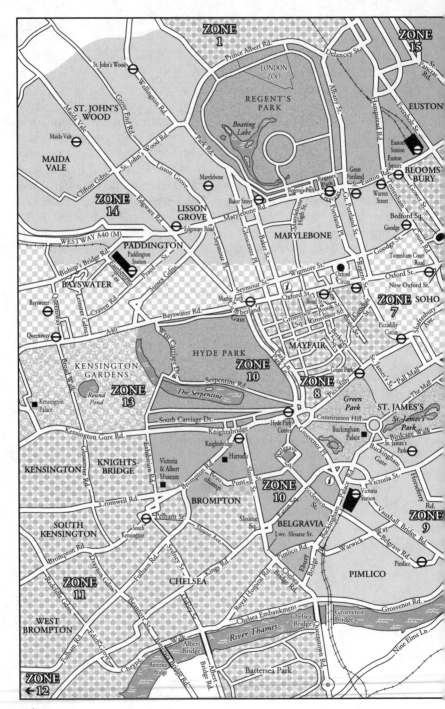

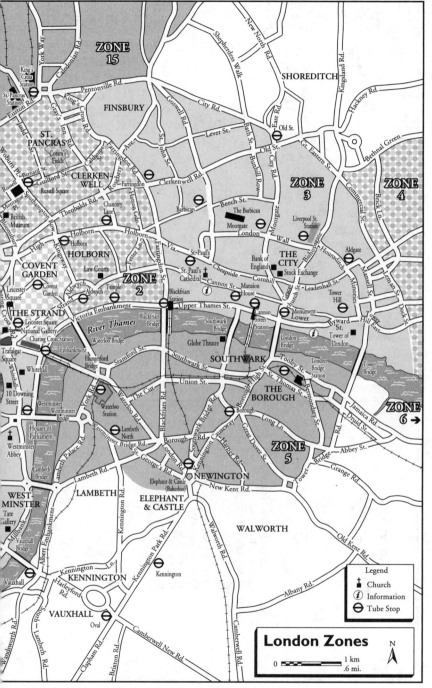

London Zones

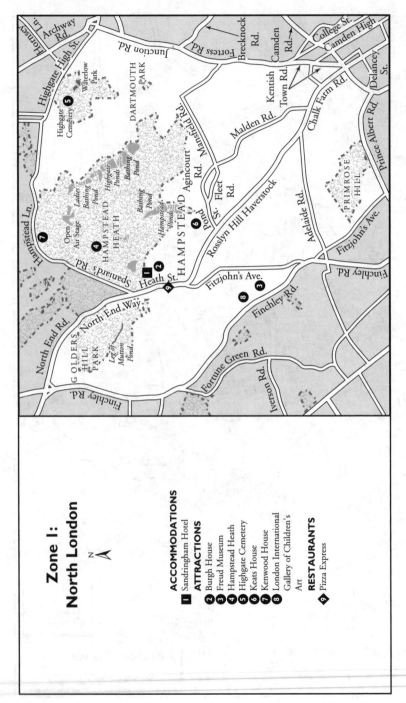

Zone 1: North London

N

ACCOMMODATIONS
1 Sandringham Hotel

ATTRACTIONS
2 Burgh House
3 Freud Museum
4 Hampstead Heath
5 Highgate Cemetery
6 Keats House
7 Kenwood House
8 London International Gallery of Children's Art

RESTAURANTS
9 Pizza Express

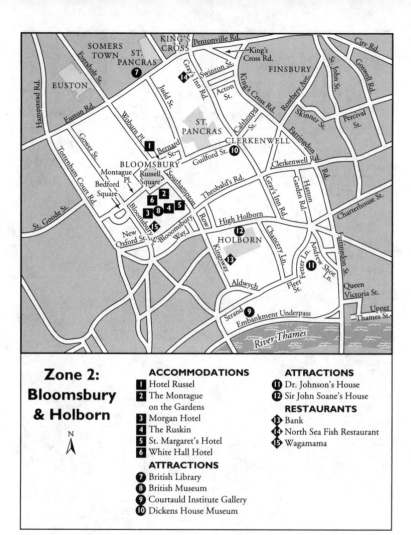

Zone 2:
Bloomsbury
& Holborn

N

ACCOMMODATIONS
1 Hotel Russel
2 The Montague
   on the Gardens
3 Morgan Hotel
4 The Ruskin
5 St. Margaret's Hotel
6 White Hall Hotel

ATTRACTIONS
7 British Library
8 British Museum
9 Courtauld Institute Gallery
10 Dickens House Museum

ATTRACTIONS
11 Dr. Johnson's House
12 Sir John Soane's House

RESTAURANTS
13 Bank
14 North Sea Fish Restaurant
15 Wagamama

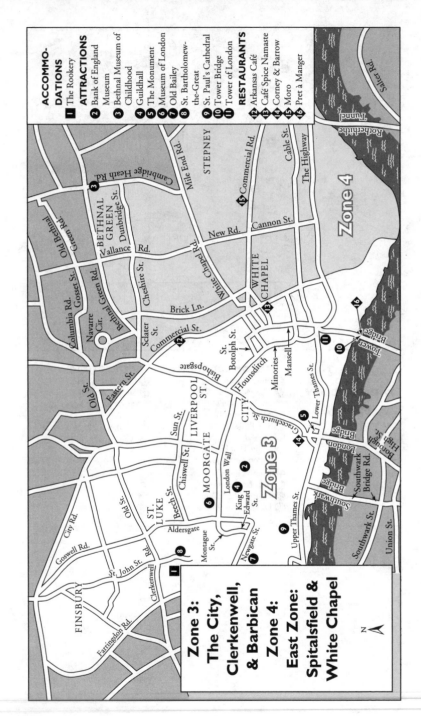

ACCOMMO-
DATIONS
■ 1 The Rookery

ATTRACTIONS
2 Bank of England Museum
3 Bethnal Museum of Childhood
4 Guildhall
5 The Monument
6 Museum of London
7 Old Bailey
8 St. Bartholomew-the-Great
9 St. Paul's Cathedral
10 Tower Bridge
11 Tower of London

RESTAURANTS
12 Arkansas Café
13 Café Spice Namaste
14 Corney & Barrow
15 Moro
16 Pret à Manger

Zone 3:
The City,
Clerkenwell,
& Barbican
Zone 4:
East Zone:
Spitalsfield &
White Chapel

N

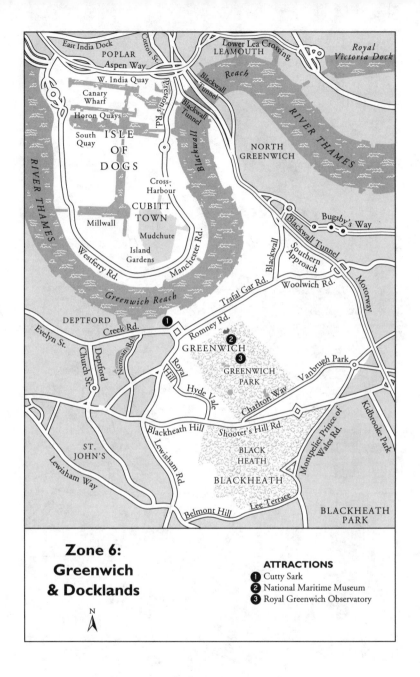

Zone 6: Greenwich & Docklands

N

ATTRACTIONS
1. Cutty Sark
2. National Maritime Museum
3. Royal Greenwich Observatory

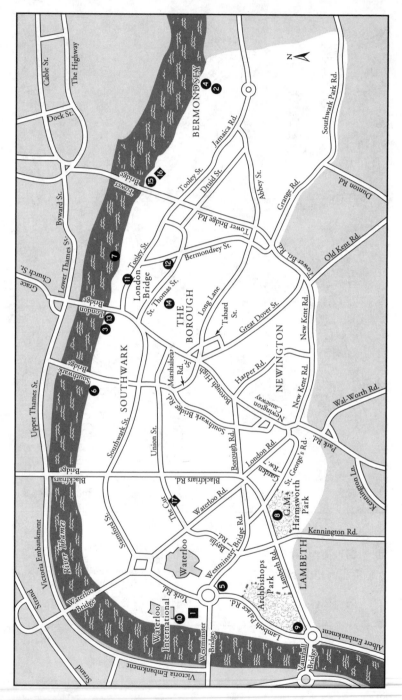

Zone 5:
South Bank

ACCOMMODATIONS

1 London Marriott Hotel,
County Hall

ATTRACTIONS

2 Bramah Tea & Coffee Museum
3 Clink Exhibition
4 Design Museum
5 The Florence Nightingale Museum
6 The Globe Theatre
7 HMS Belfast
8 Imperial War Museum
9 Lambeth Palace

ATTRACTIONS

10 London Aquarium
11 London Dungeon
12 Old Operating Theatre,
Museum, and Herb Garrett
13 Southwark Cathedral
14 Tate Gallery of Modern Art
15 Tower Bridge

RESTAURANTS

16 Blueprint Café
17 Livebait

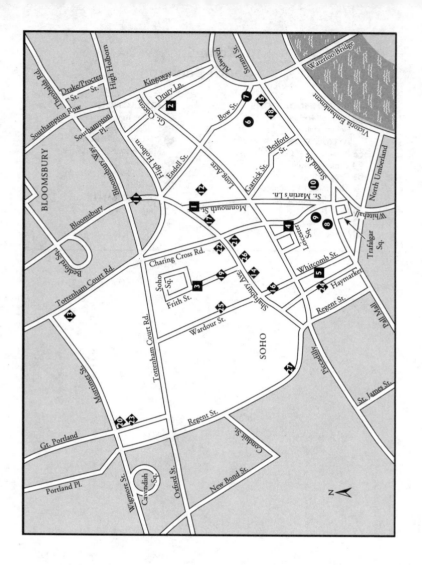

Zone 7:
Soho & West End

ACCOMMODATIONS
1. Covent Garden Hotel
2. The Fielding House
3. Hazlitt's
4. The Hampshire
5. The Pastoria

ATTRACTIONS
6. Covent Garden
7. London Transport Museum
8. National Gallery
9. National Portrait Gallery
10. St. Martin in the Fields

RESTAURANTS
11. Alfred
12. Belgo
13. The Birdcage

RESTAURANTS
14. Café Fish
15. Chez Gerard
16. Chuen Cheng Ku
17. The Ivy
18. Joe Allen
19. Lindsay House
20. Mash
21. Mr. Kong
22. Pollo
23. RK Stanley's
24. Spaghetti House
25. Spiga
26. Teatro
27. Veeraswamy

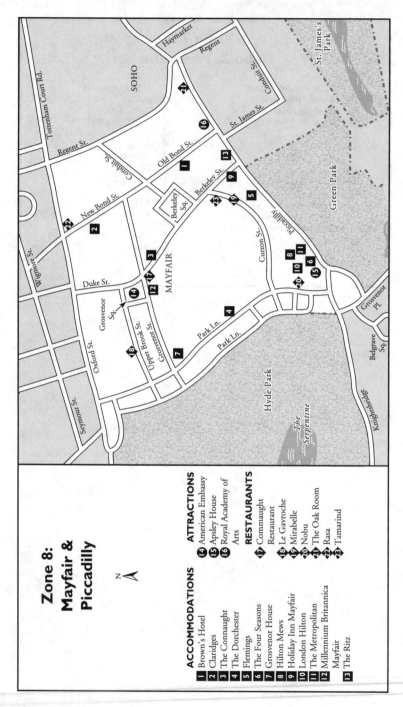

Zone 8:
Mayfair & Piccadilly

N

ACCOMMODATIONS
1 Brown's Hotel
2 Claridges
3 The Connaught
4 The Dorchester
5 Flemings
6 The Four Seasons
7 Grosvenor House
8 Hilton Mews
9 Holiday Inn Mayfair
10 London Hilton
11 The Metropolitan
12 Millennium Britannica
   Mayfair
13 The Ritz

ATTRACTIONS
14 American Embassy
15 Apsley House
16 Royal Academy of
   Arts

RESTAURANTS
17 Connaught
   Restaurant
18 Le Gavroche
19 Mirabelle
20 Nobu
21 The Oak Room
22 Rasa
23 Tamarind

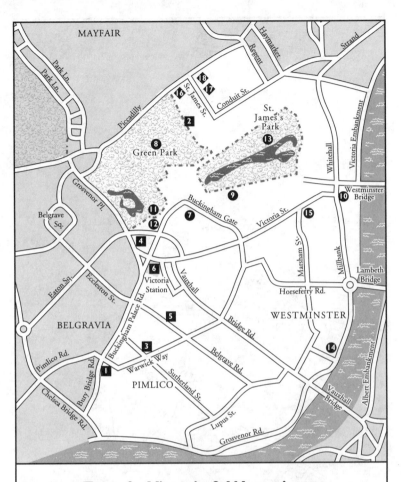

Zone 9: Victoria & Westminster

N

ACCOMMODATIONS
1 Cherry Court Hotel
2 Dukes Hotel
3 Elizabeth Hotel
4 Goring Hotel
5 Quality Hotel
6 The Thistle Victoria

ATTRACTIONS
7 Buckingham Palace
8 Green Park
9 Guards Museum

ATTRACTIONS
10 Houses of Parliament and Big Ben
11 Queen's Gallery
12 Royal Mews
13 St. James's Park
14 Tate Gallery
15 Westminster Abbey

RESTAURANTS
16 Le Caprice
17 Matursi
18 Quaglino's

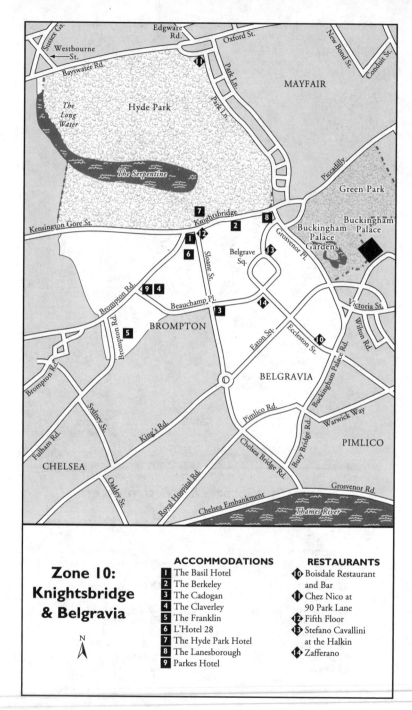

**Zone 10:
Knightsbridge
& Belgravia**

N

ACCOMMODATIONS
1 The Basil Hotel
2 The Berkeley
3 The Cadogan
4 The Claverley
5 The Franklin
6 L'Hotel 28
7 The Hyde Park Hotel
8 The Lanesborough
9 Parkes Hotel

RESTAURANTS
10 Boisdale Restaurant and Bar
11 Chez Nico at 90 Park Lane
12 Fifth Floor
13 Stefano Cavallini at the Halkin
14 Zafferano

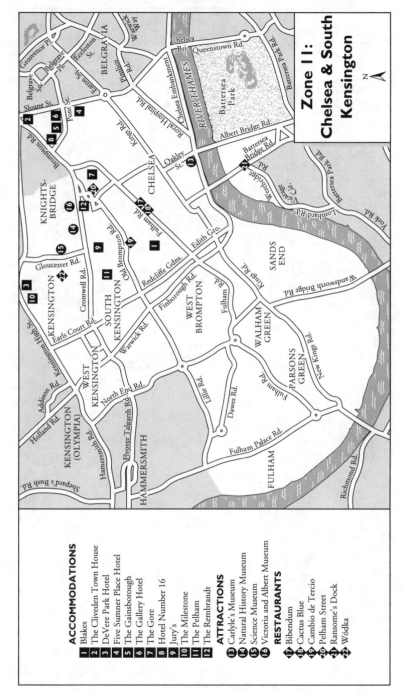

Zone 11:
Chelsea & South Kensington

ACCOMMODATIONS
1. Blakes
2. The Cliveden Town House
3. DeVere Park Hotel
4. Five Sumner Place Hotel
5. The Gainsborough
6. The Gallery Hotel
7. The Gore
8. Hotel Number 16
9. Jury's
10. The Milestone
11. The Pelham
12. The Rembrandt

ATTRACTIONS
13. Carlyle's Museum
14. Natural History Museum
15. Science Museum
16. Victoria and Albert Museum

RESTAURANTS
17. Bibendum
18. Cactus Blue
19. Cambio de Tercio
20. Pelham Street
21. Ransome's Dock
22. Wódka

27

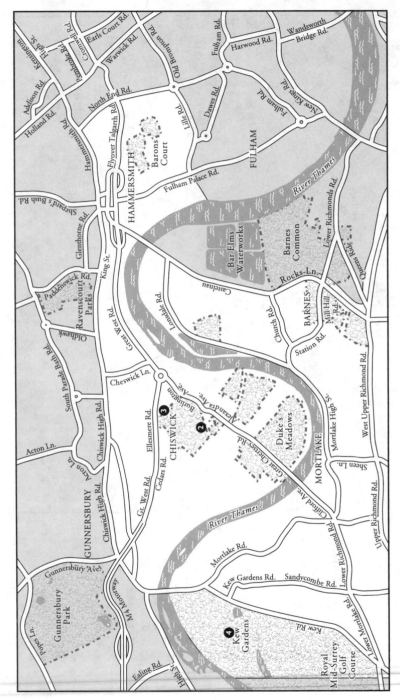

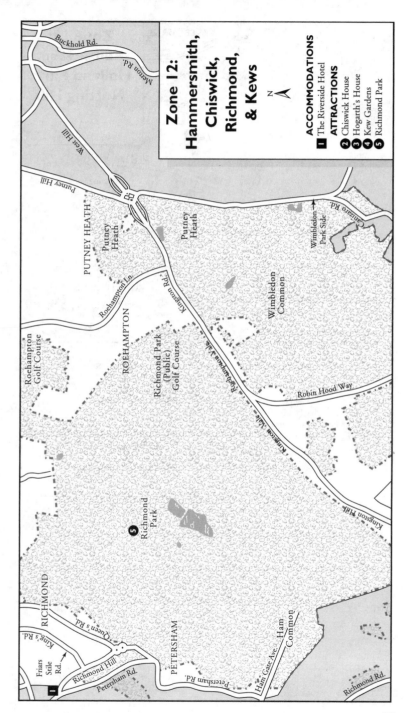

Zone 12:
Hammersmith,
Chiswick,
Richmond,
& Kews

N

ACCOMMODATIONS
■ The Riverside Hotel

ATTRACTIONS
❷ Chiswick House
❸ Hogarth's House
❹ Kew Gardens
❺ Richmond Park

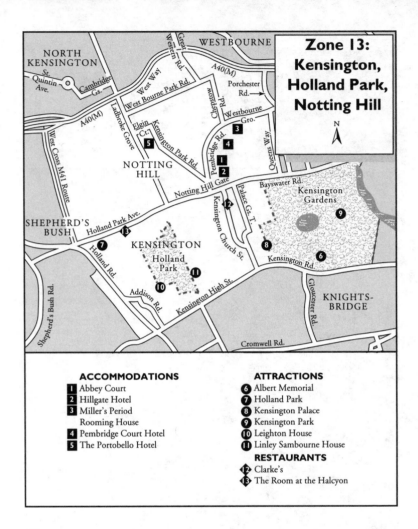

ACCOMMODATIONS
1 Abbey Court
2 Hillgate Hotel
3 Miller's Period
   Rooming House
4 Pembridge Court Hotel
5 The Portobello Hotel

ATTRACTIONS
6 Albert Memorial
7 Holland Park
8 Kensington Palace
9 Kensington Park
10 Leighton House
11 Linley Sambourne House

RESTAURANTS
12 Clarke's
13 The Room at the Halcyon

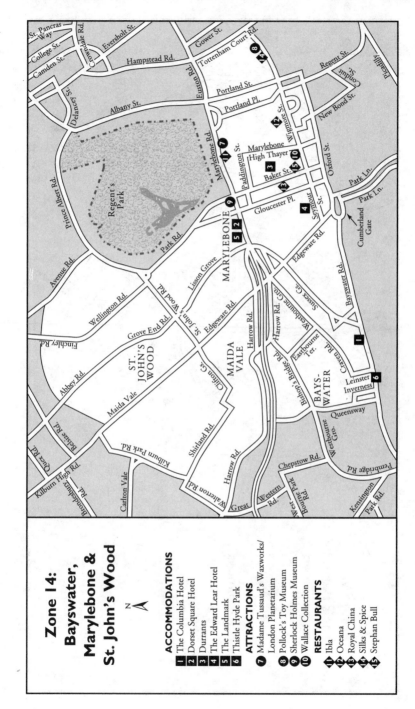

Zone 14:
Bayswater,
Marylebone &
St. John's Wood

N

ACCOMMODATIONS
1 The Columbia Hotel
2 Dorset Square Hotel
3 Durrants
4 The Edward Lear Hotel
5 The Landmark
6 Thistle Hyde Park

ATTRACTIONS
7 Madame Tussaud's Waxworks/
   London Planetarium
8 Pollock's Toy Museum
9 Sherlock Holmes Museum
10 Wallace Collection

RESTAURANTS
11 Ibla
12 Oceana
13 Royal China
14 Silks & Spice
15 Stephan Bull

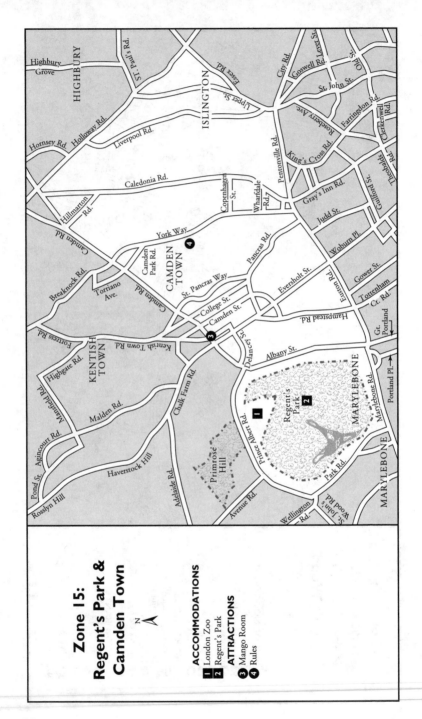

Zone 15:
Regent's Park &
Camden Town

N

ACCOMMODATIONS
1 London Zoo
2 Regent's Park

ATTRACTIONS
3 Mango Room
4 Rules

An Overview of London

There are so many ways to appreciate London, and it offers something for every mood, desire, and interest. Music, sports, architecture, theater, fashion, antiques, gardens, nightlife . . . the list of what London has to offer goes on and on. It's an amazing place today, but it takes on even more amazing dimensions when you know what it was yesterday. A bit of the history of this town on the Thames is just as useful for the discerning visitor as a street map. So, here we go.

The Long Life of an Ancient City

London's history, perhaps because it is situated on the banks of a wide river cutting through a large island, is initially one of invasion and conquest. Because of England's system of monarchy, her later history is one of bloody factionalism and revolving persecutions. As the empire began to take shape, the blood was shed on foreign soil, as the idea of England's sovereignty was propped up by the exploitation of foreign continents and by the misery of the impoverished workers in London. But throughout all of it, the history of the city of London has been the history of commerce: This port city has beckoned to artisans and sailors, farmers, prostitutes, and wheelers and dealers of all shades of corruption for two millennia. London shows no signs of flagging in its appeal as we head into the twenty-first century.

Some of the highlights from London's past can be found in the Museum of London, where you can wander from the prehistoric banks of the Thames all the way through to the Millennium Dome, seeing the everyday sights of London's long life that you won't find anywhere else, such as the underground heating system of Roman Londinium or an Anderson Shelter from the days of the Blitz. The museum's overall style is nostalgic and cheerful, although you do get to look into a cell of Newgate Prison. It's a great overall experience for the young and the old, the well-informed and the merely curious students of London.

When Rome Ruled Londinium

Julius Caesar's famous remark about how Britons were simply not good slave material was sour grapes: In 55 and 56 B.C., he tried to subdue England two times and failed both times. In A.D. 43, the Romans again sent an army to conquer the island and built a bridge over the Thames at the narrowest crossing, near the present London Bridge. Soon, Londinium grew into a thriving port of commerce, as luxury goods from all over the Roman empire arrived and were exchanged for corn, iron, and—Julius Caesar notwithstanding—slaves. Roman historian Tacitus wrote that Londinium was "famed for commerce and crowded with merchants," a description that remained accurate for the next 2,000 years (and beyond, one assumes). Roadways, the most ubiquitous and long-lasting feature of Roman rule, soon headed in every direction from this trading post and were well traveled by Romans and Britons in search of adventure and wealth. After enjoying a period of Pax Romana, the Roman rule became increasingly unbearable to the local tribes. Queen Boudicca of the Iceni tribe led a violent revolt, invading Londinium, massacring everyone in sight, and burning the camp to the ground. The revolution was short-lived, however; Londinium was rebuilt with a huge wall around it, the remains of which can be seen around the Barbican area. A piece is preserved near the Museum of London.

In 410, the sun was setting on the Roman empire and the troops were withdrawn, leaving the sprouts of the newly adopted Christian faith behind. London then went into a decline; when new invaders arrived, they superstitiously stayed away from the Roman ruins, which were soon buried, not to be rediscovered until after the Blitz of World War II.

The Saxon's Lundenwic

After the Saxons came over the North Sea in about 450 to settle in southeast England, London slowly began its rise from the Roman ashes to again become a trading post, called Lundenwic. King Ethlebert, after presiding over a pagan society, became a Christian convert and the first cathedral of St. Paul was built. The Saxon kings spent most of the next five centuries fighting Viking invaders and fortifying their kingdom, whose capital was at Winchester. London has King Alfred to thank for rebuilding it after Danish invaders left it in ruins and for lighting a few candles in those Dark Ages. The tenth century saw a new prosperity as neighborhoods and parishes were formed on the banks of the Thames River. In the eleventh century, the Danes finally won the day, and England was forced to accept the Danish King Canute as its leader. He put London on the map as the capital of the kingdom, and by the time Edward the Confessor took the scepter in 1042,

London was poised on the brink of a great architectural leap forward. Westminster Abbey and the Palace at Westminster gave the raucous commercial port a dignity that was soon complemented by the construction of the White Tower, the tallest building at the Tower of London.

William the Conqueror

In 1066 at the Battle of Hastings, a Norman army led by William conquered the Saxon armies, and with that victory spelled a new dawn for London. William decided to have his coronation in Westminster Abbey, a tradition unchanged since that time. He saw that London was perfectly placed to be a rich capital and located the impressive stronghold of the White Tower on the Thames to show the inhabitants of this headstrong city just who was in charge. He was also a smart politician, however, and granted freedoms to the Saxon-dominated church and the local governors that ensured a pleasant and profitable back-scratching for all concerned. London grew rich under the watchful eye of the monarchs, who knew the key to their power lay in the wealth and acquiescence of London's merchants and churchmen. In 1180, William Fitzstephen, in the preface to his *Life of Thomas à Becket,* sang high praises of London: "It is blessed by a wholesome climate . . . in the strength of its fortifications, in the nature of its site, the repute of its citizens, the honour of its matrons; happy in its sports, prolific in noble men. . . . I can think of no other city with customs more admirable. . . . The only plagues of London are the immoderate drinking of fools and the frequency of fires." True, but he forgot that other plague of London: the plague.

A Vibrant Medieval Port

Medieval London was a crazy conglomeration of streets, alleys, markets, outdoor brothels, bear-baiting pits, pubs, and theaters. The vibrancy of the streets was matched in energy by the jostling for power among the court, the burgesses, and the church. In 1215, the Magna Carta, which attempted to limit the excesses and power of the king and establish personal rights and political freedom for the nobility, was signed by King John, who was forced to do so by rebellious barons and the newly created lord mayor of London. Soon, Parliament and the House of Commons were created, and England became a place of liberty and justice for at least a few more than before. Though the Magna Carta was designed to free the aristocracy from the despotism of a monarch, they had placed in it the fateful word *freemen,* and so signaled at least theoretical rights for the common people.

The port was thriving, with houses and warehouses lining the river banks, and the power of the guilds and merchants grew apace. The position of

London as a window on the world, crowded with thousands of people living in appalling sanitary conditions, led to the first outbreak of plague. The Black Death of 1348 came across from the European continent, which was reeling from the disease. Nearly half of England's population succumbed to the plague, which was carried by rats who multiplied in the filthy streets and fetid sewers. The general unrest and loss of labor led to the ill-advised poll tax imposed in 1381 by a financially strapped court—a shilling a person, regardless of income or situation. The Peasant's Revolt, led by Jack Straw and Wat Tyler, put every future monarch on notice that Londoners had a breaking point that should be avoided. After a riotous spree of looting, burning, and murder the rebels were overcome and order was restored by a young King Richard II, but the point was taken—and the poll tax was quietly dropped.

A new intellectual age dawned around this time when Geoffrey Chaucer wrote *The Canterbury Tales* in the 1390s, and William Caxton set up his printing press at Westminster in 1476. The numerous and wealthy monasteries became centers for teaching and learning, and literacy began creeping into the middle and upper classes, setting the scene for the Renaissance culture of the Tudor era.

Tudor London

The War of the Roses between the fractious factions of the House of Plantagenet—York and Lancaster—provided William Shakespeare with a superabundance of material for his tragedies. As he wrote in *Richard III:*

> *England hath long been mad, and scarred herself;*
> *The brother blindly shed the brother's blood,*
> *The father rashly slaughtered his own son,*
> *The son, compelled, been butcher to the sire:*
> *All this divided York and Lancaster.*

The bloody dynastic feud for the throne had relatively little effect on the daily lives of Londoners scrambling for a living, but when Richard III allegedly smothered the two young princes, the rightful heirs to the throne, in the Tower of London, the citizenry grew restless; few regretted the end of Richard's reign. Next came the Tudor dynasty, whose heirs were at least as ruthless when it came to insulting relatives as any of the previous Plantagenets had been.

Henry VIII married his brother's widow, Catherine of Aragon, to keep the peace with Spain. After 20 years of marriage and one daughter, Mary, Henry fell in love with Anne Boleyn and decided he had to marry again in order to have a male heir. He cast off his wife, alienating the Catholic Church in Rome, which refused to grant him an annulment. Not one to take no for an answer, and a man who willingly threw out baby *and* bath with the bathwater, Henry reformed the church in England, styling himself as the supreme head of the church in England. He had two powerful churchmen, Sir Thomas More and Bishop John Fisher, beheaded for refusing to go along with his program. Then he went on a serial marital spree that left in its wake a total of six wives; as the nursery rhyme goes, "two beheaded, two divorced, one died, and one survived." The most radical expression of this religious overhaul was in the dissolution of the monasteries, in which Henry took for the Crown all the property of the Catholic cathedrals, churches, priories, convents, and monasteries in England. He destroyed huge numbers of beautiful gothic and medieval buildings, redistributing them among the new loyal-to-Henry aristocracy, creating new streets, houses, and courtyards where there had once been wealthy Catholic establishments. Resistant nuns and clergy were hung, drawn, and quartered; the army of crippled, diseased, and homeless who had been supported by the charity of the churches were thrown to their own resources, and the streets of London resounded with the cries of their misery.

After Henry VIII died, syphilitic and obese, the six-year reign of the child king Edward didn't amount to much more than a vicious power struggle among his courtiers and further religious persecutions. When Bloody Mary, Henry's first daughter, became queen a bit after Edward's early death, she put her half-sister Elizabeth in the Tower of London, and it was the turn of the Protestants to have their property seized and be hung or burnt alive. The daily spectacle at Smithfields of burning heretics finally disgusted even the Londoners accustomed to gruesome public punishments. Another turn of the dynasty and Elizabeth returned England to its Protestant base, forestalling any Catholic overthrow by having her cousin, Mary Queen of Scots, executed at the Tower. (The Tower of London, incidentally, is probably as haunted a place as you can find in ghost-ridden London. Heads rolled like billiard balls there, innocent souls were racked and tortured regularly, and their tormented specters are well known to the people who remain there past nightfall. However, you'd be hard-pressed to sense so much as a shiver of the supernatural in daylight, during the tourists' mad realm.)

The Elizabethan Flowering of London

What were the good citizens of London doing while all the royal kin-killing kerfuffle and musical thrones were being played out? Well, while the aristocrats built over-the-top estates from the remains of the monasteries, and Hyde Park became a happy hunting ground for King Henry, the ordinary Londoner was going about the usual: earning and eating, fornicating and frolicking, marrying and burying. William Shakespeare arrived in London in 1586, joining Ben Jonson, Christopher Marlowe, John Donne, and others of the day's glitterati in the boom years of English letters, helping record the uproar that was London. The city now had a population of 200,000 people, up from 50,000 in the 1300s, and more arrived every day. The great era of exploration was under way, as the English plied the oceans in search of riches, returning with sugar, spice, coffee, and tobacco. Sir Thomas Gresham started the Royal Exchange from its humble beginnings as a coffee house and made London the known world's most important financial center, a position it maintained into the early twentieth century.

Although Queen Elizabeth could be as dangerous a friend (and cousin) as she was a foe, she was devoted to the welfare of her kingdom and understood that her greatest power lay in the love her subjects had for her—she had an instinctive gift for good public relations. Perhaps the greatest gift she gave the nation was her much vaunted "virginity": By not marrying a foreign prince, she kept England solidly English for 45 prosperous years. By the end of her long reign, the memories of those ugly battles of succession faded.

Roundheads and Restoration

The Gunpowder Plot—in which a group of Catholic conspirators, including Guy Fawkes, were thwarted in their plan to blow up King James, his ministers, and Parliament at the Palace of Westminster—rather appropriately opened London's apocalyptic seventeenth century. King James died in 1625, leaving a somewhat backwards son, Charles I, on the throne.

Although London was the wealthiest city in the world at the time of Charles I's reign, he simply could not let well enough alone. Insisting on the divine right of kings, a philosophy that was anathema to the Parliament and businessmen of London, he started a civil war. The monarchist Cavaliers were defeated by the Puritan Roundheads, and Charles I was beheaded outside his beloved Banqueting Hall, designed by Inigo Jones. (The king's last walk is still commemorated on the last Sunday in January.) Although the majority of London had been on the side of the Commonwealth, 18 years of dour Puritan reign during Oliver Cromwell's rule, during which all fun was canceled, left the city gasping for a breath of fresh air. The diarist John Evelyn wrote at Cromwell's death that "it was the joyfullest funeral I ever saw, for there were none that cried but dogs." In 1661, London warmly welcomed the exiled Charles II back from France, "shouting with inexpressible joy" and watching undismayed when Charles ordered the exhumation of the three-year-old corpses of Cromwell and two cronies for the dubious purpose of hanging and beheading them publicly for the murder of his father. Perhaps the citizens thought it fitting punishment for closing the theaters, brothels, and gambling houses.

1660s: Plague and Fire

Charles II barely had time to adjust his crown when disaster struck. In early 1665, the first cases of a second major round of the bubonic plague were seen in London. Samuel Pepys, the great diarist, first heard of the outbreak in April, writing, "Great fear of the sickness here in the city, it being said that two or three houses are already shut up. God preserve us." The hot summer saw the outbreak burst into an epidemic, with affected houses painted with red crosses and shut up with a guard outside—people trapped inside died either of the plague or starvation. By September, red crosses bloomed everywhere, and the rattle of the death cart was heard in the streets with its mournful accompaniment, "Bring out your dead!", a wretched parody of the cries of the apple or mussel sellers that had been silenced by the calamity. John Evelyn wrote on September 7, "I went all along the city and suburbs from Kent street to St James's, a dismal passage and dangerous, to see so many coffins exposed in the streets thin of people, the shops shut up and all mournful silence, as not knowing whose turn might be next."

It was not humanity's finest hour: The stricken were prevented from leaving their homes, or if they had escaped London, from traveling on roads. They were often pelted with rocks and dung at the outskirts of villages. Con artists and quacks sold phony cures, and the rich and powerful jumped ship like the rats who were carrying the plague. The problem was that no one had figured out that it was the rats'—or, more accurately, the fleas on the rats—fault. Mistaking the disease as airborne, someone decided that the very cats and dogs who could have helped control the rats had to be destroyed and, in killing 60,000 animals, certainly added to the disaster. The horror and pain of the disease was unspeakable, dispatching an estimated 100,000 by the time this epidemic began to abate, around Christmas 1665. The king returned to London in February to survey—in safety, he thought—the melancholy scene of a decimated London still smelling of rotted flesh. But the rough hand of fate hadn't finished with London yet.

On September 2, 1666, a baker's oven in Pudding Lane was left unbanked. Its sparks, teased out of the chimney by a stiff wind, fired like tinder the dry wood of summer-baked houses and ignited the city in a matter of hours. Pepys was called by a servant to look at it at three in the morning, and being used to little local fires in the cramped wooden alleys and byways of London, he "thought it to be on the back side of Mark Lane at the furthest . . . I thought it far enough off, and so went back to bed."

The lord mayor also brushed the fire off, saying "a woman might piss it out," and no measures were taken to control the conflagration until it was too late. Amazingly, only a handful of people lost their lives, one of them a servant in the house of the baker where the fire had started. John Evelyn describes a ghastly picture of the event, two days after it started: "The burning still rages, and it was now gotten as far as the Inner Temple; all Fleet Street, the Old Bailey, Ludgate Hill, Warwick Lane, Newgate, Paul's chain, Watling Street, now flaming, and most of it reduced to ashes; the stones of St Paul's flew like grenados, the melting lead running down the streets in a stream, and the very pavements glowing with fiery redness, so as no horse nor man was able to tread on them, and the demolition had stopped all the passages, so that no help could be applied."

King Charles finally stepped in and did what the lord mayor should have done sooner: His navy blew up the houses in the way of the fire, creating a break in its path. After four grim days, the driving wind died down and the fire finally ended. In its wake lay an unrecognizable London, suffering untold losses in its architecture, treasures, books, and art. In all, 436 acres of London had been consumed by the fire: 13,200 houses, 87 parish houses and many of their churches, 44 merchants' halls, the Royal Exchange, the magnificent medieval Guildhall, and St. Paul's Cathedral. It was, if nothing else, an opportunity to rebuild the city along straight and reasonable lines, obliterating the medieval maze of streets that had contributed to the tragedy.

But this was not to be. Although both John Evelyn and the young Christopher Wren submitted designs for a new London with wide thoroughfares and sensible squares and circuses, the urgent need for housing and the legal problems of ownership of land assured that the rebuilding followed the original "plan" of medieval London somewhat faithfully. The main difference was that the lanes were widened to a mandatory 14 feet, and the buildings were made of stone. This was Wren's great opportunity, as he rebuilt 51 of the ruined churches, including, of course, St. Paul's Cathedral. Despite the loss of many of those edifices during World War II, Wren's name will forever be associated with the glory of that age, as London rose like a phoenix from the ashes of the fire into the magnificence of the eighteenth century.

Georgian London

To most London connoisseurs, the 1700s remain the very apex of the city's greatness: In architecture, literature, theater, painting, sculpture, the building of stately homes and parks, philosophy, and sciences there can be no other century to rival the verve and creativity of the eighteenth. The names of the artists, thinkers, and artisans of the day have come to define their disciplines: William Hogarth, Sir Joshua Reynolds, Thomas Gainsborough (painting); Jonathan Swift, Henry Fielding, Oliver Goldsmith (literature); David Garrick (theater); Alexander Pope (poetry); John Nash, Robert Adams (architecture); Edward Gibbon (history); John Gay (opera); David Hume (philosophy); Captain James Cook (exploration); Adam Smith (economics); James Watt (technology); and the naturalized British subject, composer George Frederic Handel. Of course, you can hardly mention London and the eighteenth century in the same breath without a bow to the looming figure of the formidable writer and lexicographer Dr. Samuel Johnson and his biographer and friend, James Boswell. There are countless other figures who made major breakthroughs in technology, medicine, and science in this robust century. There was something in the air it would seem, and not just the stench of the tanneries, slaughterhouses, and privies. London grew from 650,000 souls to close to a million in the 100-year span of this period. The small villages north and west of the city were embraced by London's expansion; near the bucolic hamlet of Knightsbridge, a country house was bought and grandly rebuilt by the duke of Buckingham, later to go to King George III as a private royal residence.

The 12-year reign of Queen Ann left her name to a wildflower and a style of furniture. In 1714 came the Hanover succession from Germany. Georges I through IV presided over the acquisition of imperial lands from Canada to Australia and the ignominious loss of the wealthy American colonies to the war of independence. They saw the rise of a new technology that revolutionized the cotton and wool trade of England. They watched as the Bastille was stormed, igniting the French Revolution, and managed to keep their crowns on while across the channel others were losing their heads. They continued to prefer the German language while ruling an English-speaking kingdom. Due to this oddity the position of prime minister came to be; thanks to the madness of King George and the dissolute lifestyle of the prince regent the policy-making powers of the monarch were carefully whittled away by an increasingly powerful Parliament.

The expansion and progress of London were attended by an increase in crime, corruption, drinking, and poverty. Dr. Johnson, famed for his remark that "when a man is tired of London, he's tired of life," wrote a poem about London that exposes this dark underbelly:

Here malice, rapine, accident, conspire,
And now a rabble rages, now a fire;
Their ambush here relentless ruffians lay,
And here the fell attorney prowls for prey;
Here falling houses thunder on your head,

And here a female atheist talks you dead. . . .
Prepare for death if here at night you roam,
And sign your will before you sup from home. . . .

Tired of life, indeed!

There was an increasing polarization—due to the incipient Industrial Revolution—of London's society into owners and workers, rich and poor. The coarseness and insensitivity to the less fortunate on the part of the wealthy was truly shocking. Their entertainment included outings to the insane asylums for a laugh, and attendance at public executions. There was one law for the rich and one for the poor; the criminals who weren't executed for the slightest offense were made to endure a grueling and often fatal passage to the new penal colony in Australia. It was only by the most repressive of measures that the revolution in France did not spread to London's gates, especially after the Gordon Riots of 1780, in which the Newgate Gaol was stormed and 300 were left dead. There were a few reformers and progressive thinkers, most memorably Jonathan Swift, who with his "Modest Proposal" of solving the problem of the Irish poor by feeding their babies to the rich, refined a tradition of savage English satire and social commentary that found many talented exponents in the Victorian century.

Victorian London

Queen Victoria's reign started in 1837, after the unlamented last gasp of Georgian rule by the grotesque George IV. He may have been the patron of John Nash, who developed Regent's Park and filled the city with white stucco-covered houses, but other than that George IV didn't do much for London. Princess Victoria was a woman of only 18 years when she became queen and gave her name to an age of change and reaction, reform and wretchedness, empire and exploitation.

There is another name so completely identified with nineteenth-century London that it has become an adjective describing it: Charles Dickens. He is never far from the hearts and minds of the London dweller: His face appears—appropriately for one who wrote so much about money's awful power—on the £10 note. It is the London of Dickens we tend to think of when we envision the nineteenth century: poor Bob Cratchit freezing in Scrooge's office; the convict Magwitch and Pip fleeing on the Thames under cover of a pea soup fog; Oliver Twist asking for more food in the orphanage. Dickens was an insomniac who walked the streets of London for hours every night, and in his travels he picked up the sounds and secrets of the city as no one ever had or has since. He is as much the voice of nineteenth-century London as Pepys and John Evelyn were of the seventeenth. Through his deeply compassionate reporting and fiction, Dickens opened up the eyes of the middle class to the misery of the poor. He helped steer England toward a more humane course, as reformers worked to abolish the slave trade, put limits on child labor, allow women to keep their own property, extend voting rights, and open the first state schools.

The Industrial Revolution didn't so much flower as detonate in the nineteenth century; its effects were not entirely salutary. The gulf widened between rich and poor, the landscape and atmosphere were degraded, and as people in the country lost their self-sustainability, they trickled into a city already bursting at the seams with immigrants from the far reaches of the empire. But with all that cheap labor available, London grew at an amazing rate. New houses were built in every direction, with formerly quiet outlying villages becoming part of London's urban scene. The first underground trains began operation, sewers were built, transatlantic cable laid, the first police force was established, train tracks originating in London criss-crossed the country, omnibuses were pulled through the streets by huge work horses, streets were gas-lit, and roads were laid all over the city. Museums, monuments, learned societies, and public libraries flourished. The Great Exhibition of 1851, organized by Victoria's husband, Prince Albert, showed the world that London was a city of cosmopolitan suaveness and culture, firmly looking to the future.

That Karl Marx wrote *Das Capital* while living in this two-faced city has a certain poetic logic. The terrible contrast between the shiny new city, with its shops and theaters, hotels and townhouses, and the unmitigated squalor of the East End slums in many ways defined the Victorian Age. It's interesting to see how rosy with nostalgia that era has come to be: Look at the industry that has sprung up around all things Victorian in the last 20 years. It couldn't have been all that much fun to be alive then: the sexual hypocrisy, claustrophobic class system, sexism, racism, xenophobia, and social Darwinism must have been about as easy to deal with as a night out with Jack the Ripper. Yet it was a time in which enormous changes took place, in which terrible injustices were at last redressed, and a time of unforgettable literature and indelible heroes. Let's face it, any age that could produce Florence Nightingale, Oscar Wilde, Lewis Carroll, and Mary Shelley's *Frankenstein* can't be all bad.

World War I

Queen Victoria made a perfect exit in January 1901, keeping her era clearly defined by century. And now the twentieth century dawned with poor old Bertie, prince of Wales, at last out from under his mother's long shadow to lend his own name of King Edward to a new age. It was a short reign—

only a decade, a mere fraction of his mother's 64 years on the throne—but it was distinctive enough to earn the title of the Edwardian Age—England's last age to be described in terms of the monarch. It was a clear cusp between the centuries, a time of speeded-up progress. Motor cars became common, corsets came off, women demonstrated for the vote and smoked in public, and people started to challenge a number of tired Victorian verities. As a well-known sensualist of the time, King Edward helped usher in a more permissive era in which free love, divorce, and bohemian living arrangements were practiced without the terror of ostracism from an uptight moral majority. The famous, free-thinking Bloomsbury Group formed around this time, in which artists and writers who lived in the then shabby-genteel neighborhood of the British Museum redefined not only their artistic disciplines but also their relationships. Virginia Woolf's famous quote, "In or about December 1910, human character changed," underscores the leap made in thought and behavior by this new generation.

In 1914, London and the British empire enjoyed the zenith of their world power. The British pound sterling was as safe as gold and was the currency of international commerce all over the globe. There was peace and prosperity. Social activists were kept busy working to get the vote for women, get children out of the factory and into a classroom, and force legislation that would make the government responsible for its neediest citizens. But the shadow of the German zeppelins loomed above London. Despite the efforts of pacifists like George Bernard Shaw, England was plunged into the ghastly war fought across the English Channel that came close to wiping out an entire generation of young Englishmen. When it was over in 1918, the whole social order changed. It was a completely different London, filled with emancipated working women and powered by electricity, that faced the modern era.

The Long Weekend: 1918–1939

There is a sense, as there is in America of the 1920s, of this period between the World Wars as being a last gasp of glamour for London. There is something to that, despite the ugly rumblings from the black-shirted British fascists led by Nazi-sympathizer Sir Oswald Mosley; despite the economic depression that left millions unemployed; and in spite of the terrible losses of life, limb, and hope of World War I. It may be that we view this interlude with an acute awareness of how much was soon to be buried under the Blitz, which makes the frivolity of that time seem all the more poignant.

The country embraced the work of humorist P. G. Wodehouse to help them shake off the blues of the war and depression. To this day, people still love Wodehouse's version of London between the wars: gin-soaked parties with bright young things, dim right honourable, creaking lords and terrifying aunts, the Drones Club, and of course the unflappable Jeeves and his young master Bertie Wooster. They inhabit a hilarious fictional world that reveals what made London laugh between cataclysms. Noel Coward, Cecil Beaton, Virginia Woolf, George Orwell, Nancy Mitford, W. H. Auden, and T. S. Eliot are a few of the artists whose work also captures the feeling of the time and still resonates for us.

London gave Hollywood a run for its money with its own studios, making movies with such luminaries as Sir Laurence Olivier, Peggy Ashcroft, Charles Laughton, and Alfred Hitchcock. Agatha Christie and Dorothy Sayers fed the increasing demand for murder mysteries. The West End was alive with plays, from melodramas to social realism. But nothing cooked up in the imagination could even come close to the real-life drama of the big story of 1936: the abdication of King Edward VIII for the "woman I love," the American divorcée, Mrs. Wallis Simpson. It was the year of three kings, but the one who is best remembered is the one that got away, the man who spent the rest of his life as the duke of Windsor, in jet-setting exile from England's green and pleasant land. Although the event was billed as a grave constitutional crisis, it was clear that the monarch of England was becoming increasing irrelevant to the citizenry, except as gossip and newsreel fodder. The citizens were mainly concerned with their own lives, as they joined trade unions, built suburban communities, and tried to figure out the map of the Underground. In 1931, this tangled web was simplified into the sleek, art-deco design we know and love, and the population of 8 million began using it to escape the brown-fogged city to ever-more distant reaches of residential London.

Meanwhile, across the English Channel, Europe was increasingly threatened by Adolf Hitler, dismissed in the early days as a twisted clown by most intelligent Londoners and admired by a shameful number of dim-witted English aristocrats and hate-filled fascists. They would all come to despise his name, as his Luftwaffe rained destruction on London, and Europe's fleeing Jews came to town with stories of concentration camps and genocide.

The Blitz: "Our Finest Hour"

World War I, the "war to end all wars" couldn't live up to that promise for long: Only two decades after the armistice was signed, London was once again anxiously watching the skies over Whitehall, though this time it wasn't the lumbering zeppelins but the significantly more deadly Messerschmitts, Stukas, and the unpiloted "doodle-bugs" that spelled disaster. The attack started in earnest on a sunny day on September 7, 1940, when hundreds of fighter planes and bombers buzzed up the Thames and destroyed docks, gas works, and power stations. The Luftwaffe went on to bomb London nightly for 76 consecutive nights, dropping over 27,000 high explosives and thousands more incendiaries. The Blitz was on. Children were hurriedly sent to the countryside or to America, but the royal family made a point of staying in town, even after nine bombs dropped on Buckingham Palace. People sheltered in the Underground stations in staggeringly large numbers, sleeping on the ground or in bunk beds placed on the tracks and platforms. Above ground, civilians coped with bombed-out streets, nightly fires, disrupted railways, power and water failures, the destruction of their homes, and, most terribly, the deaths of their friends, neighbors, and family. Novelist Nancy Mitford described the scene vividly in a letter to a friend:

I find my nerves are standing up to the thing better now—I don't tremble quite all the time as I did. . . . NOBODY can have the slightest idea of what it is like until they've experienced it. As for the screaming bombs they simply make your flesh creep but the whole thing is so fearful that they are actually only a slight added horror. The great fires everywhere, the awful din which never stops, & wave after wave after wave of aeroplanes, ambulances tearing up the street & the horrible unnatural blaze of lights from search-lights etc.—all has to be experienced to be understood. Then in the morning the damage—people ring one another up to tell one how their houses are completely non-existent. . . . People are beyond praise, everyone is red eyed and exhausted but you never hear a word of complaint or down-heartedness. It is most reassuring. (Selina Hastings, Nancy Mitford *[London: Hamish Hamilton, 1985], p. 134.)*

The bombardment put to the test the famous English stiff upper lip, and London's amazing rise to the challenge earned the admiration of the rest of the country and the world. Prime Minister Winston Churchill was the voice of the people during those dark days, author of such unforgettable war cries as "we shall defend our island, whatever the cost may be, we shall fight on the beaches, we shall fight on the landing grounds, we shall fight in the fields and in the streets, we shall fight in the hills; we shall never surrender," and "Let us therefore brace ourselves to our duties, and so bear ourselves that, if the British Empire and its Commonwealth last for a thousand years, men will still say, 'This was their finest hour.'"

And so it was. Despite the thousands killed, the millions wounded and made homeless, the destruction of hundreds of thousands of dwelling places and buildings, and the nearly total destruction of the city and the East End, London carried on. The people lived in corrugated steel caves called Anderson shelters (to be replaced later by the heavier Morrison shelters) buried three feet under ground. The homeless were sheltered by hotels—when the East End was first bombed, a huge crowd marched to the Savoy and demanded to be admitted, which they were—as well as by the not-completely-invulnerable Underground stations. Brigades of men and women pulled all-night duties to put fires out in likely targets such as Westminster Abbey and St. Paul's Cathedral, saving some of the precious treasures of London's past. When the war finally ended, it could be well said of the Blitzed Londoners that, again in the words of Churchill, "Their will was resolute and remorseless, and as it proved, unconquerable."

Sunset of the Empire

In 1948, England lost the jewel of her colonial crown when India became independent, and over the next decade it continued to lose colonies around the world, as well as much of the shipping and manufacturing business that made her rich. The 1950s were spent cleaning up the wreckage of the Blitz and continuing to live under strict food rationing. There was a grayness in the city: Grim gaps of bomb sites yawned among the old Victorian buildings that were still black with coal grime and sagging under the weight of the years. People abandoned the city for the suburbs, whose spread was contained by the public lands of the Green Belt on the outer perimeters of London. Yet London was buoyant; the welfare state of the Labour government helped people rebuild their lives and gave them a sense of security unknown up to that time. Heathrow Airport was opened in 1946, followed by Gatwick Airport three years later; the city was quickly rebuilt with modern glass and steel towers (Samuel Johnson and Charles Dickens would weep with confusion if they time-traveled back to their old haunts); and domestic labor-saving devices were new, plentiful, and affordable.

The most influential of these was certainly the television, on which people watched the colorful coronation of Queen Elizabeth II in 1953 from the comfort of their own armchairs. The prime minister, Harold Macmillan, said in 1959, "Most of our people never had it so good."

The Festival of Britain celebrated the centennial of Prince Albert's Great Exhibition, and it was on the site of it that the South Bank Arts Centre came to be. The fog lifted, thanks to antipollution measures, and the future looked as bright as the sky on a clear day. A new age was indeed coming, and it was a doozy. A quarter of the map of the world had been colored with empire pink after the war; by the mid-1960s England had lost almost all of her colonial possessions.

The Swinging Sixties and Punk Seventies

Whatever England may have lost in her empire, London certainly tried to make up for by becoming ground zero of the 1960s' "youth quake." The quintessential '60s figures of the Beatles and James Bond joined the thinner ones of Twiggy and Julie Christie in making all things British very hip. England was swinging like a pendulum, and London, as always, was the epicenter of the groove. Movies such as *A Hard Day's Night, Blow Up, To Sir with Love,* and *A Man for All Seasons* were worldwide hits. The comedy of Spike Milligan gave way to Monty Python. Michael Caine, Vanessa and Lynn Redgrave, Oliver Reed, and Terrence Stamp were among the many English stars who could pull off a Hollywood blockbuster as well as do Pinter in the West End. Peter Sellers's Inspector Clouseau made him a superstar—a word and concept born in the bright light of the '60s. Fashion designers of Carnaby Street and the King's Road started the miniskirt and bell-bottom trends (Mary Quant ruled), and fashion photographers like David Bailey became as famous as their subjects. The Rolling Stones, The Kinks, Cream, The Yardbirds, Marianne Faithfull, Led Zeppelin, The Who . . . London's bands in the '60s were a veritable Debrett's Peerage of rock and roll. Twentysomething rock stars and their birds got their clothes at Granny Takes a Trip and Biba, drove around in Bentleys, and bought stately old piles in the country from hard-up toffs. *Hair* was performed in the West End; the Rolling Stones put on a free concert in Hyde Park, home to political demonstrations and love-ins. Drugs, sex, and rock and roll became a way of life for the new generation.

No one did sex, drugs, and rock and roll better than the glam rockers and punks of the 1970s. Green mohawk hairdos, safety pins piercing cheeks, very high platform shoes, and in-your-face attitudes were the usual for the King's Road, where designer Vivian Westwood and Malcolm McLaren (later manager of The Sex Pistols) had a punk-rock clothing shop—still there with the fast backward-moving clock outside—under a series of interesting names ("Sex" was one, and "Too Fast to Live, Too Young to Die" another). Feminism had many local, brilliant exponents, with Angela Carter writing in south London and Aussie expat Germaine Greer lecturing around the city. The literature of the day was pretty dark: Martin Amis's *Dead Babies* was a savage and chilling portrait of young people in 1970s London that opened the door to many imitators. *A Clockwork Orange,* filmed by Stanley Kubrick in 1972 from the novel by Anthony Burgess, was a surreal prediction of a London gone viciously mad in the not-too-distant future. And when The Sex Pistols recorded a little ditty called "God F— the Queen," that forecast must have seemed to have come quite true to the older generation. The IRA started bombing London in the 1970s, and in 1979 killed Lord Mountbatten, former admiral of the fleet and cousin to the queen. Squatters took over entire buildings that were earmarked for renovation; value added tax was introduced; and a Women's Year Rally coincided with the election of Margaret Thatcher as leader of the Conservative Party. By the time Sid Vicious of The Sex Pistols had (allegedly) stabbed his girlfriend and then overdosed himself in New York City, people were exhausted and disillusioned with the '70s, and it seemed as if it might be time to get on to more upbeat pastimes. Like making money, that old-time London passion.

The Thatcher Years

When Margaret Thatcher was made prime minister in 1979 she announced the somewhat astonishing goal of returning to Victorian values. And did she ever deliver, most alarmingly. She axed 40,000 civil service jobs and wrested control of London Transport away from the Greater London Council (GLC) and sold it to private investors. The gap between rich and poor became wider, as a very Victorian economic and social Darwinism took shape. After fighting constantly with the Labour-based GLC over social services and privatization, in 1986 she simply abolished the GLC altogether. People in the city were suddenly making gobs of dough (as they were on Wall Street across the pond), property prices were sky-high, and the materialistic yuppie came to define the era in both England and the United States.

In 1981, the so-called fairy tale wedding of Diana Spencer and Charles, prince of Wales, was watched by millions on television. Diana bewitched the media and was soon the most famous woman in the world, putting an uncomfortable spotlight on the lives of the royals. The couple's marital problems later came to sell many a tabloid and upset the queen mightily.

London in the 1980s also saw race riots in Brixton, the first cases of AIDS, strikes by tube and steel workers, and a ban on smoking on the Underground after a fire at King's Cross killed 31 people. More disaster prevention was instituted with the Thames Barrier, which ensured that London would never be flooded again. Homelessness rose most disturbingly as Thatcher dismantled the socialist safety net, and the real estate boom took its toll on government housing. In 1989, Thatcher closed out her decade nicely by resigning, and John Major took over as another Conservative prime minister.

Cool Britannia

The '90s started with the historical joining of the French and English sides of the new tunnel beneath the English Channel, linking Paris and London with a three-hour train ride. The local fears that hordes of foreigners would breach London by rail never quite materialized, although the train surely had a part to play in the huge upsurge of tourism in the 1990s.

In 1992, the queen suffered her famous "annus horribilis" (you've got to love a queen who thinks everyone still understands Latin). A fire at Windsor Castle caused extensive damage, two of her sons were going through horrendously public marital scandals, and she started paying taxes for the first time in her life. Not one to leave books unbalanced—this is a woman who lived through the Blitz and food rationing—the queen decided to pay for the repair of Windsor Castle by opening Buckingham Palace to the public for two months a year. They're now raking in so much money that there's enough left over to upgrade the Queen's Gallery, which will let us see even more of the royal treasures. This tends to keep everyone but the most die-hard antimonarchists quiet.

The '90s saw the *Big Issue* launched, the magazine that helps the homeless earn money and tries to keep a conscience alive in the city. It also saw the premier of the runaway television hit, *Absolutely Fabulous*, which neatly and hilariously skewered the hypocrisies of the day. The two royal divorces, between Charles and Diana and Andy and Sarah (Fergie) may or may not have had anything to do with the mad cow disease that rocked the British beef industry, but they did tend to keep the media eye on London. By the time the Britpop explosion signaled the start of "Cool Britannia," everyone in the world knew that London was again the place to be. The Spice Girls, Oasis, All Saints, and Robbie Williams put British music back at the top of the charts. London Fashion Week became one of the hottest tickets in Europe, rivaling even Milan and Paris as the place to show new collections. Unfortunately, London's bright young designers, like Stella McCartney, Galliano, and Alexander McQueen, all seemed to move on to Paris pretty quickly, but there will always be Vivian Westwood and Zandra Rhodes to keep the scene alive.

In May 1997, Tony Blair of the Labour Party was voted in as prime minister, signaling an end to the Conservative Party's 18-year run. Blair ran on a platform of finding the "third way" between the policies of Tory and Labour, and he has succeeded in annoying both parties. The same year also saw the tragedy of Princess Diana's death in a car crash in Paris, and the resulting week of completely un-British mourning: a spasm of national grief that had Buckingham Palace doing backflips to appease the people who found fault with how the royal family was responding. People stood in line for days to sign the condolence book at St. James Palace, while a sea of flowers numbering in the millions were left at the gates of Kensington Palace. It was a London no one had ever seen before and will likely ever see again. London has recovered enough to have dislodged plans to build a memorial garden to Diana in Kensington Gardens, and the first anniversary of her death passed quietly enough.

Next up for London is the opening of the Millennium Dome, the much-maligned and -hyped exhibition to celebrate the turning of the century and the next millennium. Whether the city will continue on its buoyant path as the coolest city in Europe remains to be seen, but what is certain is that London will *always* remain a fascinating, fast-paced, infuriating, and fun-filled tourist destination of choice. So come on over, you're gonna love it here.

British Culture: Queues, the Weather, and a Stiff Upper Lip

A FOREIGN TRIBE

The most wonderful thing about coming to London is the opportunity for English-speaking transatlantics to learn more about a foreign culture than could be possible in any European city with a language barrier. Which is not to say that there won't be communication problems, but at least you'll know the words, if not the meaning behind them. The great misunderstandings are not in language but in nuance. This is a society based on the oblique and the tacit, with an intrinsic orderliness based on the old class system. You'll never understand it, so just be polite and go along with the program. They're not going to change a hair for you.

George Bernard Shaw said that it is impossible for one Englishman to open his mouth without inviting the disdain of another. When the British meet each other for the first time they know instantly from each other's accent how they may feel toward their new acquaintance: superior (relief), or inferior (depressed). In these days of Cool Britannia some people would very much like to believe that this is no longer true, and though that question is open to argument, it is certain that as a foreigner, you will never have to go through that process of having your class and social status sized up, judgements made, and conclusions drawn. You will be treated as an unknown, perhaps a novelty, and if you are American, with a curious combination of envy, contempt, and admiring amusement.

The primary exposure most Brits have to Americans comes from the export of American culture via Hollywood, and they may check you out to see if the stereotype matches up with the real thing. You, of course, are free to do likewise. But you will probably not find Mary Poppins, Bertie Wooster, Jeeves, James Bond, Miss Marple, or Austin Powers. You will find that they Are Not Amused by any attempts to claim some kind of special kinship with them—this is essentially an island culture, insulated for centuries against all comers, and still in some ways quite impenetrable by outsiders. This gives them their strength, eccentricity, and quiet assumption of superiority. The wonderful thing about us transatlantics is how we buy into this assumption in an automatic, reflexive way. Americans, it has been observed, can go weak before an English accent—and it doesn't even have to be a "posh" one because we've somehow trained ourselves to think of the English as indeed superior in intelligence and experience—it could be thought of as the Masterpiece Theatre complex, except that it existed long before television. Americans visiting London have admitted that they start to feel ashamed of their accents and slightly contemptuous when they hear other Americans speaking. Don't fall into that trap—they're just different; the language lures us into thinking we are not apples and oranges, or as the British say, chalk and cheese.

GET IN LINE: THE ENGLISH ART OF QUEUING

All the rumors are true: The British queue for everything. Even soccer hooligans queue for tickets and beer. To jump the queue is the height of bad manners, and to do so is to invite certain tut-tutting, muttered comments, and possibly even an open challenge. In fact, it is such a violent breach of etiquette that it is about the only time the British will break another taboo, the one that prohibits raising one's voice in public (markets, pubs, and soccer stadiums notwithstanding). Raising one's voice attracts attention and may possibly give someone *the wrong idea,* whatever that is. However you may be tempted, do *not* jump the queue.

Also, always stand to the right when riding on escalators—the locals hate it when tourists stand two abreast and clog up the path, even if they have no intention of passing you.

WEATHER REPORTS

The old saw about how everyone talks about the weather but no one does anything about it is not entirely true in London. The passion that the British have for talking about the weather amounts nearly to an interactive hobby. They will even go so far as to discuss it vigorously with complete strangers. Part of the reason may be the basically mild but changeable weather. London often goes through four seasons in one day, except for winter when cold, gray, and damp are the standard. The casting of aspersions on the abilities of the forecasters is a tried and true ice breaker and will pave the way for inquiries from the Brits about the extreme and interesting weather (tornadoes, blizzards, hurricanes, and so on) of America. As everyone must know by now, the famous London fogs of the past were a result of the coal burned in London, and a bona fide "pea-souper" hasn't been sighted since the early '60s, after the Clean Air Act of 1956 put a stop to industrial pollution. The idea of it raining constantly in London is also a myth, although there isn't one Londoner who doesn't own at least one umbrella (called a brolly), nor will you find too many tourists who haven't been forced to buy a rain poncho or umbrella on short notice.

AT YOUR SERVICE, SORT OF

A recent study concluded that the British complain more about poor service than any other country. However, it also concluded that this is because they have more to complain about. Good service is something this erstwhile "nation of shopkeepers" are doing their best with. They have only recently realized that it's okay to enjoy good food: the deprivations and sacrifices of the postwar years have cast a long shadow. The old-fashioned British Rail sandwich (inedible, of dubious content, and possibly poisonous) is mercifully a thing of the past. There's good fast food all over London now, and extra-virgin olive oil is no longer considered a foreign delicacy. However, they will not put iced water and a basket of bread on the table as a matter of course (worse, they may charge you a pound). They will not rush to take your order or bring you your bill. They will not take kindly to complaint — it's not so much that the customer is always wrong, but that the customer overestimates his or her importance. They subscribe to a theory of blame and will deluge the dissatisfied with unwanted information about *why* the food took so long to arrive or *how* the trains got to be so late. What they will *not* do is say, "I'm sorry, let me fix that for you right away." Don't take it personally. It's a British thing.

THE GREAT BRITISH RESERVE

This is alive and well, stiffening the upper lip and continuing to define "Englishness." You will see it manifested in the advertising, where wit and word play take precedence over volume, sloganeering, and repetition. It is in the weather forecasts ("Today will be rather damp, with a possibility of patchy fog and maybe a spot of drizzle in between clear intervals") and on the tube at rush hour, where instead of mouthing off at an annoying commuter who refuses to move down in the carriage, muttered "excuse me's," irritated coughs, and great flappings of newspapers pass for expressions of anger and frustration. This quietude can be almost soothing to an American accustomed to the chattering hordes of compatriots asking personal questions and offering the usual too much information, but it can take a bit of getting used to at first and might leave the visitor feeling a little out in the cold.

However, this reserve is not to be taken for granted. Road rage is a big problem in traffic-choked London, but luckily the gun laws are stringent enough that it results in shouting matches and fisticuffs rather than more serious consequences. There is nothing quite so terrifying as standing on the terraces at a soccer game, trapped among 10,000 grown men singing with one voice, "You're shite and you know you are!" Not for them the cozy familiarity of the seventh-inning stretches and the lilting tones of "Take Me Out to the Ballgame."

A similar contradiction to the stereotype is found at the prime minister's question time in the House of Commons. This has to be seen to be believed. Barely veiled or even naked insults are hurled by members of Parliament at one another, while howls of derision and guffaws of braying laughter render the institution more like a high school classroom whose teacher has stepped out than a hallowed hall of government. There is something rather invigorating about this cacophony, and it gives you an idea of the healthy self-regard in which the English hold themselves. The great paradox is that they yield to no one, except for the monarch.

To Do or Not to Do: That Is the Culture

There was an article in *The Spectator* magazine a few years ago about how the staff would try to think up the worst possible advice to put in a tourist guide to London. They came up with, among others, "Introduce yourself and shake hands all around in your train compartment," and "Try out the famous echo in the British Library Reading Room." As funny as we find this concept, we will resist temptation and give you the following dos and don'ts guaranteed to be 100% valid.

- Don't call people by their first names unless expressly asked to—it is considered normal to use no names when addressing people.
- Don't expect people to introduce you around. One can spend an entire evening with a group of people who neither introduce themselves nor their friends to you.
- Don't try to intervene in football arguments—it's a very serious subject, one no outsider can comprehend properly. Remember at games that the hooligans mean business.
- Don't take it personally when people act as if you're not there; or correct your pronunciation; or look at you as if you're daft when

asking directions to "Lye-cester Square"; or act slightly exasperated by your inability to read your *A to Zed*; or try to run you down in the street. You'll get a lot of this—get used to it.

- Don't brag about how much sunlight you get at home; this will not endear you to anyone.
- Don't tell anyone that their accent is "cute." It is you who have the accent, and it is not considered remotely cute by the British.
- Don't gloat about the American Revolution. Again, not cute.
- Do watch out for queues and take your place in them.
- Do be courteous, be very courteous—it's much more appreciated than friendliness.
- Do remember that this is a country of rules, rules, rules—and they aren't just making them up as they go along, thought it sometimes seems they are.
- Do avoid arguments along lines of common sense—you won't win.
- Do be patient in restaurants and stores; use your vacation as an opportunity to slow down and practice your manners.
- Do learn to enjoy being called "love" and "darling" and "sweetheart" by certain strangers.
- Do prepare for your visit by reading as much as you can on London; try to listen more than you speak. This is a very interesting place, and the people are fascinating. Make the most of your visit.

Divided by a Common Language: A British-English Glossary

Thanks to the cross-pollination of television shows and films (in London it is films that are viewed at the cinema, not movies or flicks at the movie theater) the British are more hip to our lingo than they may let on, but if your exposure to Brit-speak has been limited to watching some shows on PBS, you may need a bit of a leg up. We have provided a short glossary of some words you may not have caught on *Prime Suspect* or *Pride and Prejudice*.

American	English
At the airport:	
bill	bank note
wallet	billfold/purse
telephone booth	telephone box/kiosk

Divided by a Common Language: A British-English Glossary (continued)

American	English
On the road:	
baby carriage/stroller	pram/buggy
back-up lights	reversing lights
dead-end road	cul-de-sac
delivery truck	van
divided highway	dual carriageway
detour	diversion
gas	petrol
hood (car)	bonnet
license plate	number plate
minivans	people carriers
sedan car	saloon car
subway	Underground or tube
overpass	flyover
one-way ticket	single journey
pull-off	lay-by
round-trip ticket	return ticket
station wagon	estate car
truck	lorry
trunk	boot
underpass	subway
(pedestrian, under streets)	
windshield	windscreen
At the hotel:	
antenna	aerial
apartment hotel	service flats
apartment building	block of flats, mansion flats
baby crib	cot
baggage room	left luggage office
bathe (verb)	bath (bathing— short "a" sound)
bathrobe	dressing gown
cot	extra bed or camp bed

Divided by a Common Language: A British-English Glossary (continued)

American	English
At the hotel (continued):	
call (on the telephone)	ring
call collect	reverse charges
closet	cupboard/wardrobe
comforter/quilt	eiderdown/duvet
connect (on the telephone)	put through
elevator	lift
first floor	ground floor
second floor	first floor
long-distance call	trunk call
make a reservation	book
milk in coffee/tea or not	white or black
outlet/socket	power point
rent	let
vacuum	Hoover
washcloth	face flannel
In a restaurant or food store:	
buffet	sideboard
broiled	grilled
bun (hamburger)	bap
can (of food)	tin
candy	sweets
check	bill
cookie	biscuit
cotton candy	candy floss
cracker	savoury biscuit
dessert	pudding
diaper	nappy
downtown	town center/high street
druggist/drugstore	chemist/chemist's shop
eggplant	aubergine
eraser	rubber
French fries	chips

Divided by a Common Language: A British-English Glossary (continued)

American	English
In a restaurant or food store (continued):	
hamburger meat	mince
hardware store	ironmonger
lima bean	broad bean
molasses	black treacle
potato chips	crisps
pit	stone
popsicle	ice lolly
raisin	sultana
smoked herring	kipper
zucchini	courgette
At the theatre:	
aisle	gangway
balcony	gallery/upper circle
intermission	interval
mezzanine/loge	dress circle
movie theater	cinema
movie	film
In the markets and on the high street:	
liquor store	off license
news stand	newsagent
notions	haberdashery
panties	knickers
panty hose	tights
raincoat	macintosh (or mac)/kagool
rest room	public convenience/loo/ w.c./lavatory
sneakers	trainers or plimsolls
scotch tape	cellotape
shorts (underwear)	pants
sweater	jumper
undershirt	vest
vest	waistcoat

Divided by a Common Language: A British-English Glossary (continued)	
American	**English**
In sickness and in health:	
acetaminophen (Tylenol)	paracetamol
emergency room	casualty
Band-Aids	plasters
funny bone	crazy bone
pimples	spots
rubbing alcohol	surgical spirit

Part Two

Planning Your Visit to London

Airline Deals

British Airlines and Virgin Atlantic are the two biggest transatlantic air carriers in and out of London, with American Airlines and Delta right behind. I prefer British Air because it has a lot of daily flights in and out of Heathrow Airport. I prefer Heathrow because there are so many transportation options to central London (more on this on page 161 in Part Four, "Arriving and Getting Oriented"). Both airlines engage in occasional price wars, and there are always packages available that are worth looking into. If you find a low fare from American Airlines, call British Air and see if they'll match it. Of course, whomever you have a frequent-flier program with may be your best choice—you can rack up a fair number of miles on a round trip to London.

One way to go about getting a cheap flight is to call a flight consolidator, who can find very good deals. Global Discount Travel Services usually has amazing prices, and you still may be able to collect your frequent-flier miles. Call (800) 497-7132, or visit their Web site at *www.lowestfare.com*. Another cheap airfare Web site is Microsoft's Expedia (*www.expedia.com*), where you can find some excellent deals. Delta encourages booking through its Web site, at *www.deltaairlines.com*.

Winter is London's off-season, and that's when some hotels offer impressive air and land packages, which are discussed on page 79 in Part Three, "Hotels."

Average Temperatures and Rainfall in London (Daytime):		
Month	**Temperature (°F)**	**Rainfall (inches)**
January	40	2.1
February	40	1.6
March	44	1.5
April	49	1.5
May	55	1.8
June	61	1.8
July	64	2.2
August	64	2.3
September	59	1.9
October	52	2.2
November	46	2.5
December	42	1.9

The Weather

London measures its mild weather in degrees Celsius (Centigrade) rather than Fahrenheit, so you might want to memorize a few conversions. You can check out the weather from the United States before you go. Call (900) WEATHER and dial the first four letters of your destination city (LOND), and you'll get a recording of current temperatures, current weather conditions, and the forecast for the next few days. If you're online, go to the Weather Channel Web site at *www.weather.com* or check CNN weather at *www.cnn.com*.

Convert temperatures (approximately) from Celsius to Fahrenheit by doubling Celsius and adding 30. Here are some more exact numbers:

- 3°C = 26.7°F
- 1° = 30.2°
  0° = 32.0° (temperature of freezing)
  1° = 33.8°
  5° = 41.0°
 10° = 50.0°
 15° = 59.0°
 20° = 68.0°
 25° = 77.0°
 30° = 86.0°
 37° = 98.6° (normal human body temperature)

What to Bring

What to bring on your trip to London depends on the weather, which we've mapped out seasonally, but there are a few things that you might appreciate having handy at all times of the year:

- this book
- £50 to £100 (use your ATM bank card to stock up when you get here, it's the best way to avoid money-changing commissions)
- money belt
- good backpack or shoulder bag
- small, collapsible umbrella
- folding rain poncho
- currency converter
- portable electrical transformer from American 110 V to British 220 V—if you bring your own hair dryer or electric toothbrush (check amps to make sure it can handle your appliances—hair dryers are notorious for blowing out transformers)
- small map of Central London and a portable street atlas, such as *London A to Zed*
- camera and lots of extra film (like everything else, film is expensive here)
- sugar substitute (it's not as readily available in restaurants as it is in the United States)
- favorite snacks (American snacks are not always easy to find and often can't be found anywhere)
- books on London that relate to your interests
- good walking shoes
- passport-size photos for travel card

CLOTHING

London is a city where people dress with a degree of decorum—at least in Central London, where you'll probably be spending most of your time. This neatness is something of a tradition and may have to do with the fact that the majority of schools, private and public, have uniforms. If you happen across a wedding, you'll see how seriously Londoners take their clothing: Formal suits and amazing hats are de rigueur at most British nuptials, even at civil ceremonies at town hall. Harrods, which has a ridiculously high opinion of itself, actually has a dress code, as does the Ritz Hotel. Teenagers and twentysomethings have their own styles (which I dare not go into as I am past the age of getting it), but you may need to discuss the dress codes with your teenager before they pack. No blue or black jeans at the Ritz; no cut-offs or offensive-wear (it's completely and mysteriously up to their discretion) at Harrods.

Natives can pick out the average American tourist at 200 paces from his or her inevitable expensive sneakers, sweatshirt, blue jeans, or, God forbid, track suits, so you may want to try a bit of camouflage. Bring at least one or two good outfits for stepping out to restaurants and the theater; smart casual is what you want to aim for. This is not Paris, where urban chic is the style on the street and the average American suburbanite can feel hopelessly dowdy. London is more about being neat and presentable than being fashionable (except for various pockets of poshness to which you will most likely not be invited). In the same way the British tend to consume their meals in restaurants and don't eat on the streets, they tend to leave the workout clothes at the gym and dress more properly in public. You can look good and still be sensibly comfortable for sight-seeing.

When to Go

The best time to go to London is whenever it's possible for you. If you want more than anything to see this remarkable city but can't afford the high-season airfare, then by all means go in the winter, when the fares drop by as much as 75%—if you book sufficiently in advance and look around for the good deals. Other considerations might include what special events you're eager to see—perhaps Wimbledon or the Chelsea Flower Show—or which attractions you're most interested in. Some of your choices may be closed if you go in the winter. Although the winter is dark and dreary, it's free of the swarms of tourists that you find in the summer. Let's take it season by season:

Summer For many of us, summer is the *only* option because of our children's summer vacation and the slowdown in our work lives. Summer in London, though unpredictable, is often quite gorgeous—Henry James was probably thinking of England, his adopted home, when he declared the two most beautiful words in the English language to be summer afternoon. However, one thing these summer afternoons can't promise is heat—three consecutive days of 75° and sun is considered a heat wave. However, the global warming trend is upsetting London's traditional brisk summer, and 1999 saw record-breaking heat that upset many tourists: air conditioning is relatively rare in shops, restaurants, and many hotels; it's nonexistent in buses and trains.

At night the temperature of even a hot day will drop, and, generally speaking, a fan will suffice to cool a hotel room.

During each season in London, you should plan your clothing in layers, as the weather can change dramatically in one day. *Don't* pack only shorts and T-shirts, which you may not even get a chance to wear. Be sure to bring socks, a sweater or two, trousers ("pants" here are underpants, also known as knickers), a light jacket, and a rain poncho. The most crucial piece of clothing is a good pair of walking shoes, decent-looking ones that would not be out of place in the Ritz.

In the summer you can count on all the museums and attractions being very crowded. Busloads of tourists are constantly bearing down on the most popular attractions, and the decent hotels are often completely booked by April or May. Unless the global economy goes completely into the toilet (or the "loo" as it's called here), a summer visit to London can require nerves of steel and the planning capabilities of Winston Churchill.

On the plus side, summer in London means that the parks are at their most fragrant and riotously floral and that all the stately homes and palaces are open (many have an April–October season); buskers (street performers) are everywhere on the streets; there are carnivals, street fairs, and more outdoor dining than makes sense in a country whose weather is so variable. Private garden squares are open to the public on one Sunday in June. The Royal Parks have green-and-white-striped lawn chairs ready for hire, and stables lay on extra horses for rides in the parks. The locals take off on holiday, so the streets are relatively free to accommodate the stampedes of tourists. I repeat—*always* book your hotel well in advance for summer visits.

Fall   I much prefer the autumn to the summer in London for many reasons, the most important being that most of the hordes of tourists clear out. Also, since even in summer London's weather may tend toward the fall-like, it is reassuring to have the weather match the calendar. Because of London's mild climate, many flowers in the parks last all the way into November, and to see their radiance blending with the hues of the changing leaves is wonderful. The sunny days are mood-lifting, and the briskness in the air invigorating. The main thing to remember is that most of the stately homes and palaces close October 30, so come before then if these sights are on the top of your list. (Buckingham Palace closes at the end of September or in the first week of October.) November can get as cold as 45°F, but not much below that. Bring gloves and a hat for the windy days. The days get shorter and shorter.

Winter   There is a beautiful old English folk song heard at Christmas called "In the Bleak Midwinter" ("ground as hard as iron, water like a stone"), which plays in many Londoners' minds as they wake up to the darkness that returns around 4 p.m., and the ancient trees in the parks have shed their leaves, standing like skeletons again a leaden sky. I personally don't mind the bleakness much, as it doesn't include temperatures below freezing very often and because the museums are so warm and inviting in the winter. The airline deals are fantastic, the hotels are cheaper, there aren't tourists everywhere (just busloads of uniformed school children flooding the museums), and your choice of plays at the half-price ticket booths expands considerably. All in all, an economical time to make a cultural holiday. No one does Christmas quite like the English. They aren't constrained by Thanksgiving a month earlier and start their decorating and selling in the first couple of weeks of November. There are the Oxford Street and Regent Street Christmas lighting ceremonies, and there's a Santa Parade when he arrives at Harrods the first week of November. (The decorations of Oxford and Regent streets are getting tackier and more commercial every year—go to Marylebone High Street, Bond Street, or St. Christopher's Place for the more appealing Christmas lights.) There are scores of wonderful Christmas concerts at churches and cathedrals—check *Time Out* or *What's On* for where and when. What you won't find much of is snow, which may be a relief for some of you Northerners. But there is plenty of rain, and it's the cold kind. The best news is that after December 21, the days start getting longer.

Spring   Spring starts early in London. Carpets of crocuses cover Hyde Park as early as February, with daffodils not far behind. It's a fine time to visit: The stately homes reopen at the end of March or April, and the parks and gardens come into bloom. The weather is still quite brisk, though. Early May can be downright nippy, even though the cafes start putting tables on the street around then. London starts coming back to its outdoor life, with the London Marathon, boat races on the Thames, and the Chelsea Flower Show. The weather can be fantastic, with not as much rain as in winter, but it's the foolish optimist who ventures out without an umbrella.

Gathering Information

Lucky for you, the British Tourist Authority is ready to help with your vacation. They have the following offices in the United States and a central toll-free number for information: (800) GO-TO-BRITAIN. (In London the number is (0181) 846-9000.) They have brochures, maps, and a booklet that they will be happy to give you. Make a point of calling, writing, or going in for these goodies.

In Chicago: no phone calls, write or walk in: 625 N. Michigan Ave., Suite 1510, Chicago, IL 60611

In New York: (212) 986-2200 or (800) 462-2748; 555 5th Ave., 7th Fl., New York, NY 10176. There is a bookstore next door to the office, which has many London-related items of interest.

You can also take advantage of the following Web sites for the very latest information on what's going on in London:

- London Calling: *www.london-calling.co.uk*
- Time Out: *www.timeout.co.uk*
- Tourism Information: *www.londontourism.com*
- Train Information: *www.railtrack.co.uk*
- Sunday Times: *www.sundaytimes.co.uk*
- The Telegraph: *www.telegraph.co.uk*
- Buckingham Palace: *www.royal.gov.uk*
- Miscellaneous Tourist Info: *www.LondonTown.com*

A site called Virtual London (*www.virtual-london.com*) has a lot of valuable information on tourist attractions, shopping, hotels, and more, as well as related links.

There is a BritRail Pass that you can purchase in the United States—it isn't available in England—and the British Tourist Association may invite you to purchase one if you're planning on lots of overnight sight-seeing from London. This is not always the best deal, however. An adult second-class pass costs $250 for 8 days, $380 for 15 days, $485 for 22 days, and $565 for one month. This is a bargain only if you plan to do a lot of traveling around the United Kingdom. Consider your plans carefully before springing for one. Call British Rail toll-free in the United States at (800) 677-8585 for fares and information; or in England at (0345)-484-950.

Special Considerations

PASSPORT, VISAS, AND CUSTOMS

You must have a valid passport to enter England—if you have one be sure to check the expiration date at least a month before going. Call your local passport office or Washington, D.C. for information and guidelines on renewing or getting your first passport: (202) 647-0618. You don't need a visa for a vacation; you will be allowed in for up to 90 days. Make a copy of the information page of your passport and keep it in your luggage, in case your passport gets lost or stolen. It will expedite replacement considerably if you have that on hand.

WHAT YOU MAY AND MAY NOT BRING INTO THE UNITED KINGDOM

You can bring in, duty-free, a carton of cigarettes, a few bottles of wine, perfume, toilet water, and other items up to a value of £136 (about $225).

You may not bring in controlled drugs (any medication you have should be in its original bottle with your name on it), firearms and/or ammunition, plants and vegetables, fresh meats, or any kind of animals.

See page 160 for more details about customs.

ELECTRICITY

The electricity supply is 240 volts AC, which will blow out any American 110-V appliance you may have. Electric lamps are the only items that don't require a transformer. Check to be sure your laptop computer has a built-in transformer, or buy one at the airport or at a Dixons when you arrive. Razors, hair dryers, boom boxes, cell phone rechargers—all will need to be plugged into a transformer. Since the British outlets are made for large three-prong plugs, you will also need to get an adapter, available at any iron mongers (hardware store), chemists (drug store), supermarket, or gadget store. *Don't plug anything in until you've checked the voltage on the transformer!* It should be set to "Input AC 110 volt, output AC 220 volt." You'll know by the pop, flash, and smoke if you got it wrong.

POUNDS, PENCE, AND TRAVELER'S CHECKS

The British are going slowly into this European Union business, taking a wait-and-see attitude toward the Euro Unit. At this writing, they are still using pounds (£), and the pound converts to about 1.67 dollars. The pound is a unit divided into 100 pence, abbreviated "p." One p is called a penny. Gone are the days of the shilling, the tuppence, and the farthing; what we lose in quaintness we make up for in manageability.

There are no longer any £1 notes. There are red 50s, purple 20s, brown 10s, and green 5s. Coins are divided into £2, £1, 50p, 20p, 10p, 5p, 2p, and 1p. Coins cannot be changed into foreign cash, so spend them while you're in London; better still, donate them on your way home to the brilliant UNICEF Change Collection scheme that most airlines sponsor.

Go to your bank before you leave and buy about £100 worth of British pound sterling notes so you will have plenty on hand to pay for transportation from the airport and maybe even that first meal. Request 20s, as 50s can sometimes be hard to break.

See Part Four, "Arriving and Getting Oriented," for details on ATMs, changing money, and using your credit cards.

VALUE ADDED TAX (VAT)

VAT is one of the great frustrations of shopping in London. It is a 17.5% tax slapped on everything from hotel rooms to lipstick—the only exceptions are food and books, yet these are still very expensive. There are ways to get this tax refunded, which we'll tell you about in Part Eight, "Shopping in London." Most everything has the VAT added into the sticker price, except for some small shops and various services. Check before you book a hotel whether the quoted price includes VAT. It can make a huge difference in your bill, obviously.

UNITED STATES EMBASSY

The embassy is housed in Mayfair at 24 Grosvenor Square, London, W1A1AE, (0171) 499-9000. This is where you will go if your passport gets lost or stolen or if you have some emergency. The embassy's Web site is at *www.usembassy.org.uk*. The hours are 8:30 a.m.–5:30 p.m. Passports are handled from Monday to Friday, 8:30–11a.m.; and Monday, Wednesday, and Friday, 2–4 p.m. The Passport Office is on 55 Upper Brook Street, around the corner from the main entrance (tube: Marble Arch or Bond Street).

TRAVELING WITH CHILDREN

In planning your vacation, remember that children get jet-lagged, too, and plan your first day so you all can recover from it. Our attractions are rated according to suitability for children, but bear in mind that all children have different interests and differing levels of tolerance for museums and attractions. See Part Ten, "Children's London."

DISABLED ACCESS IN LONDON

London may be more wheelchair- and disabled access–ready than many cities in Europe, but it still has some insurmountable problems in many of its attractions. In America one can count on wheelchair access and disabled rest rooms in public buildings; in London you need to call ahead or use any of the following excellent references:

- *Access in London.* This is the best book on the subject, researched by disabled people and updated regularly. It is published by the Access Project and is available at various bookstores and in the London Museum Giftshop; you can also call or write to order it: Access Project, 39 Bradley Gardens, London W13 8HE, phone (0181) 858-2375. You can also try *www.amazon.com* or another online bookstore to get hold of it.

- *Access to the Underground,* a brochure published by London Transport, is available at tube stations or by writing the London Transport Unit for Disabled Visitors, 172 Buckingham Palace Rd., London SW1 9TN.
- *Information for Wheelchair Users Visiting London* is a pamphlet that you can find in any tourist office in London.
- *Artsline* will give information on access to galleries and museums. Call (0171) 388-2227.
- *Holiday Care Service* offers advice on disabled-friendly lodging: (0129) 377-4535.
- *Tripscope* gives advice and information on transport for the elderly and disabled throughout the United Kingdom and London. Most amazingly, they have a real live human answering the phone. Call (0181) 994-9294.

EASING JET LAG

Jet lag is a very real problem as any long-distance traveler can tell you. The number of time zones passed through is directly proportional to how much jet lag you'll suffer—visitors from Lost Angeles will feel worse than the New Yorkers. The common wisdom is that you will have roughly one day of symptoms for each hour of time difference. Though some people don't experience jet lag at all (or so they say), most of us do to varying degrees. The symptoms include fatigue, muscle and headaches, changes in appetite, sleep disturbances, irritability, forgetfulness, confusion, and dizziness. Of course these symptoms could also describe middle age, but jet lag is much more pronounced. There are a number of confusing remedies —eating a certain kind and amount of food on either end of your trip, taking homeopathic remedies every hour on the plane, digesting a number of vitamins, and so on. For me, and I learned this through many painful flights between Hong Kong and New York, the best remedy is to try to reset your internal clock as soon as possible. The main thing to remember on the plane is to drink lots and lots of water, but *no* alcohol, and eat sparingly. Sleeping on the plane is not always an option, but do try. When you arrive, change your watch immediately and try to forget what time it is "for you." Your time is the time of wherever you are, and you've got to get on it as soon as possible. The best way to reset your clock is to get as much sunlight as possible—not always easy in London. I advise my friends to use their first day to take an open-top bus tour, not just for the great introductory overview of the city but also for the generous helping of sunlight you get. Exercise is also advised; a walk in the park helps stretch muscles that are achy from hours of immobilization on a plane.

A relatively new jet lag solution is the hormone melatonin. It is a controversial supplement, and the strict scientific rules for its use are so complicated that only a trip of 12 time zones could really merit trying to follow it. Melatonin cannot be bought in England, but it is easily found in the United States in health food stores, vitamin shops, and pharmacies. It is often used as a sleep aid, which can be helpful in the first few days of your trip, when your body clock tells you it's 7 p.m. but it's really after midnight, and you have a full day of sight-seeing planned for the next day. Take two to three milligrams for sleep—more than that will leave you groggy in the morning.

Calendar of Special Events

London has a huge number of traditional and modern events each month, so many that we had to try to narrow them down to the most interesting and important. When you arrive in London, pick up a *Time Out* magazine for the full selection, dates, and times.

January

London Parade   January 1. A big, brash spectacle with giant balloons, marching bands, clowns, vintage cars, and more, much in the style of the big Fifth Avenue parades in the United States. Starting at Parliament Square at noon, the parade follows Whitehall, Trafalgar Square, Lower Regent Street, and Piccadilly, ending up at Berkeley Square at 3 p.m. Lots of spillover fun can be had in Hyde Park later that day. (0181) 566-8586.

Charles I Commemoration   Last Sunday of January. The English Civil War Society, dressed in authentic seventeenth-century uniforms complete with arms, follows the route King Charles I took on January 30, 1649, before he lost his head. They march from St. James's at 11:30 a.m., down the mall, through the Horse Guards, to the Banqueting House. It's an amazing sight.

London International Boat Show   Mid-January, lasting about ten days. The biggest boat show in all of Europe. A must for even the most casual water bug. Order tickets from (0121) 767-4600.

February

Chinese New Year Celebrations   Chinese New Year changes every year, but is always in either late January or early February. The celebration is usually on the first Sunday after the first day of the New Year. London's Chinatown is located in Soho, around Garrard Street. It comes alive with bright decorations, red streamers, and the Lion Dance. Great food everywhere. Call the Hong Kong Government Office at (0171) 499-9821.

Great Spitalfields Pancake Race   Shrove Tuesday (changes yearly, check calendar—it can also fall in early March). Starts at noon at the Old Spitalfields Market or in Soho on Carnaby Street. Here's fun: Teams of people running down Carnaby Street and Spitalfields flipping pancakes as they go. Why not? If you want to join in, call a few days before, (0171) 375-0441.

March

The Daily Mail Ideal Home Exhibition   Mid-March through April, Earls Court Exhibition Centre, SW5. Enormous display of every possible gadget, knick-knack, or consumer item one could attach to or use in a home. Tickets from (0990) 900-090.

Head of the River Boat Race   End of March (usually the Saturday before the Oxford and Cambridge Boat Race). Starting at Mortlake and ending at Putney, this is a smaller affair than the mighty Oxford and Cambridge race, but no less interesting to observe from the banks of the Thames—the Surrey Bank above Chiswick Bridge is a good viewing station, or you can park yourself in any of the riverside pubs along the way. Call the Amateur Rowing Association at (0181) 748-3632 for date and starting time.

Oxford Vs. Cambridge Boat Race   Saturday in late March or early April. The big magilla, held since 1829. These teams of eight battle the current, rowing upriver from Putney to Mortlake. Be prepared for crowds on the bridges, banks, and riverside pubs. Call Cambridge University Boat House at (0122) 346-7304.

April

Chaucer Festival   Early April. A parade of people dressed in medieval finery (or approximations thereof) prance from Southwark to the Tower of London, where the festivities include jugglers, minstrels, food, and fun. Call (0122) 747-0379.

London Harness Horse Parade   Easter Monday, Battersea Park. This competition of magnificent "working" horses drawing carriages and carts make this parade a treat unlike any. Battersea Park is a beautiful place in which to enjoy it. Call (0173) 323-4451.

London Marathon   Mid-April, Sunday. Starts at Greenwich Park and ends at Buckingham Palace. 35,000 competitors means if you want in, you'd better apply early. Entries close in October. Call (0171) 620-4117.

May

Chelsea Flower Show   Two weeks in May, Chelsea Royal Hospital. The *ne plus ultra* of London's spring affairs, you'd better get tickets in advance and prepare to be jostled. Go early in the morning to see the amazing flora and fauna and garden accoutrements, the great passion of even the city-dwelling English. Call Ticketmaster at (0171) 344-4343; more information at (0171) 630-7422.

May Fayre and Puppet Festival   Second Sunday, St. Paul's Church Garden and Covent Garden. A procession, service at St. Paul's, and then hours of Punch and Judy shows and family fun. Call Alternative Arts at (0171) 375-0441 for information.

Royal Windsor Horse Show   Mid-May, Home Park, Windsor Castle. A wonderful day out for everyone, equestrians or not. Besides the jumping and showing competitions, there are amazing Pony Club games, booths galore, and a few carnival rides, all conducted under the impressive, hulking presence of Windsor Castle. Call (0175) 386-0633.

June

Beating Retreat: Household Division   Early June, Buckingham Palace. Floodlit nighttime spectacle of all the queen's horses and all the queen's men. Tickets available from March, book early. Call the Household Division at (0171) 839-5323.

Trooping the Colour   Early June, Horse Guards Parade, Whitehall. This is the queen's unofficial birthday party, during which she inspects her troops, who parade before her. There is a procession to Buckingham Palace, where the air force flies overhead and a gun salute is fired. Tickets are awarded by ballot; call (0171) 414-2479 for details. Check in Hyde Park during the preceding Saturdays—you may catch a rehearsal.

Kenwood Lakeside Concerts   Every Saturday night until September, Hampstead Heath. A 50-year-old tradition of open-air classical concerts. Laser shows, fireworks displays, and the Heath at sundown—enchanting. For tickets call (0171) 973-3427.

Royal Academy Summer Exhibition   From early June to mid-August, Royal Academy, Piccadilly. For over 200 years, the Royal Academy of Art has been showing the work of contemporary artists in its summer exhibitions, many of which have caused scandals in their day. You can browse and/or buy. Call (0171) 439-7438.

Royal Ascot   Mid-June, Ascot Racecourse, Berkshire. Made famous to Americans by the scene in the movie *My Fair Lady,* Ascot brings out all of social London. It's almost more entertaining to dish the outfits and hats than watch the races. For information call (0134) 462-2211.

Wimbledon Lawn Tennis Championships   Late June to early July, Wimbledon, Southwest London. This is where all true tennis fans want to be, and everyone else loves the strawberries and cream. Tickets are hard to come by, so make plans in advance if possible. Tickets for Centre and Number One Courts are awarded by ballot. Call (0181) 946-2244 for information.

July

BBC Henry Wood Promenade Concerts (the Proms)   Mid-July through September, Royal Albert Hall, Kensington Gore, SW7. Known affectionately as the "Proms," it's eight weeks of a variety of orchestral concerts, from classical to contemporary. You can stand for a small fee, or get a seat for significantly more. The last night is the big extravaganza. Call to get a copy of the BBC Proms Guide (0191) 222-0381. For more information call (0171) 765-5575.

Gay Pride Day   First week of July. Parade through London followed by fun on Clapham Common. Though not as huge and outrageous as the ones in New York and San Francisco by any means, it's getting bigger and splashier each year. Call (0171) 737-6903 for more details.

August

Opening of Buckingham Palace   Early August through October. While the queen's away, the tourists will play. Lines and lines of camera-laden hoi polloi wait to take the grand tour through Queen Elizabeth's townhouse while she summers in Scotland. Tickets can be ordered in advance by calling (0171) 321-2233 or bought at the ticket booth in Green Park.

Notting Hill Carnival   End of August, Ladbroke Grove and Portobello Road. It's the biggest street fair in all of Europe, held on a rather slim street, so be ready to stand shoulder to shoulder to enjoy the Caribbean flavor of steel bands and wild partying. Call (0181) 964-0544 for exact date.

September

Great River Race   Early September, starting on the Thames at Richmond. You have never seen such a collection of boats. Over 200 traditional crafts—including such diverse specimens as whalers, Viking longboats, Chinese dragon boats, and canoes—race from Ham House in Richmond at 2:30 p.m., finishing at Island Gardens, across from Greenwich Pier about three hours later. Call the London Tourist Board for more information at (0171) 971-0027.

Horse of the Year Show   End of September, Wembley Arena, Wembley. In a country that takes its horses seriously, this event features the finest creatures and most gifted riders. It doesn't get any better than this. Get your tickets early from the Wembley Arena Box Office at (0181) 900-1234.

Open House Weekend   Mid-September. Finally, a chance to get in to look inside (for free!) more than 500 of the more amazing houses and buildings usually off-limits to the likes of us commoners. Call (0181) 341-1371 for information.

October

Costermongers Pearly Harvest Festival   First Sunday in October, St. Martin–in-the Fields, Trafalgar Square. An old cockney tradition celebrating the apple ("coster") harvest that starts with a service at the church and displays a Pearly King or Queen decked out in a costume bombarded with white buttons. Musical merry-makers everywhere. Service starts at 3 p.m. Call (0171) 930-0089 for details.

Trafalgar Day Parade   Third Sunday in October, Trafalgar Square. Big, traditional, military-style parade commemorating Lord Nelson's sea victory at the Battle of Trafalgar in 1805. Marching bands, Sea Cadets. Call (0171) 928-8978.

November

Bonfire Night and Guy Fawkes' Day Firework Displays November 5, all over London. Guy Fawkes was the Catholic conspirator who gave his name to history to commemorate the narrowly averted Gunpowder Plot to blow up King James I and Parliament. To find out the best displays and the best places to see them, consult *Time Out* or call the London Tourist Board at (0171) 971-0026.

London to Brighton Veteran Car Run First Sunday of November. Come to Hyde Park to see the array of vintage cars that will drive to Brighton. Call (0175) 368-1736 for time and exact place.

Lord Mayor's Show Mid-November. This is an event that goes back 700 years, which is old even by England's standards. The lord mayor rides through the city in a let-them-eat-cake-type gilded carriage (which can be seen at the Museum of London during the rest of the year) followed by a retinue of floats, bands, and military marchers. Call for details at (0171) 332-1906.

Remembrance Day November 11. At the 11th hour on the 11th day of the 11th month, all of England falls silent in remembrance of those who died in the two World Wars. Red poppies are bought and worn by an enormous number of Londoners to show respect for the soldiers who gave their lives for England. On the nearest Sunday to the 11th, there is a service for the war dead at the Cenotaph in Whitehall.

December

Christmas Lights and Tree Late November and December, central London. Various Christmas lighting ceremonies take place on Regent, Oxford, Bond, and Jermyn streets, among others. These often involve some flavor-of-the-month celebs. Check *Time Out*. The real fun is the tree-lighting ceremony in Trafalgar Square, which is followed by caroling around the tree each evening, between 4 and 10 p.m.

Olympia International Show Jumping Champions Mid-December, Grand Hall, Olympia. This is a fun-filled exhibition, rivaling even the Wembley Show for sheer excitement. Lots of trade booths provide plenty of Christmas-shopping opportunities for horse-lovers. Call the box office for tickets at (0171) 373-3113.

Part Three

Hotels

Selecting Accommodations

Your accommodations can make or break a vacation or business trip. Traveling is stressful, touring around London is certainly tiring, and nothing takes the edge off like sinking into a warm, comfortable, hospitable room—that doesn't cost an arm and a leg—after a long day.

London hotels are notorious the world over for their high prices and questionable value for money. But then, everything in London costs more, so why should hotels be any different? The standards for hotels are different in the United States: When you're paying enough, you can safely assume a variety of goods and services, such as bellhops, concierge, 24-hour room service, a health club, king-size beds, full business facilities, minibar, cable TV, and so on. Because many hotels in America are part of a chain, they tend to have standardized properties with predictable amenities. Not so in London. You can go from crash pads to castles in one neighborhood, even on the same street, maybe even in the same hotel. In a typical townhouse conversion hotel, you can have a room on the first floor with a balcony and French windows looking onto a garden square, and for the same price get a room on the top floor with small windows, a slanted ceiling, and a view of the brown-bricked backs of white-fronted houses. Even the chains that do operate here can have wildly varying properties with unvarying prices.

Note: Please keep in mind that as of October 2000, all 0171 phone prefixes change to 0207 and all 0181 prefixes become 0208. The remaining seven numbers stay the same.

WHAT TO EXPECT

Here are some important facts to remember and resign yourself to regarding London hotels:

1. Expect small rooms. Even in expensive hotels, the size tends to be smaller than a standard chain hotel in America, land of the large.
2. Certain amenities are not a given. Air conditioning is not always available, neither are minibars, safes, cable TV, health facilities, or even private bathrooms.
3. If the price is really low, say £30 a night, the likelihood is high that the hotel is going to be pretty funky, and you'll be sharing a bathroom. Budget hotels can be abysmal. I have included a couple of places costing £45 that I have checked out that are clean and reasonably bearable.
4. A four-star hotel can cost exactly the same as a five-star inn; check prices, ask for discounts, and don't take it for granted that a four-star will cost less, it will just offer less.
5. When you're looking for a discount you're better off calling a hotel directly and making a deal with the reservations managers rather than booking through a travel agent.
6. Take advantage of the weekend break rates at the five-star hotels, and spend the weekdays at a moderately priced one.
7. Don't expect the level of service you would get in a moderate-to-expensive hotel in the United States in comparable London hotels. It's pretty much only the five-star hotels here that have the customer-is-always-right-what-can-I-do-for-you-right-away-sir-yes-ma'am kind of service.
8. Always check to see if breakfast is included in your price. Also, it's very important to know if service and the 17.5% Value Added Tax (VAT) are also reflected in the price. These two add-ons can be a considerable addition to your bill.

BEST OF BRITAIN

The hotels listed here are those that I think are very English, with the best kind of British atmosphere and charm. It seems a shame to come to London and not get to enjoy traditional English style. I've included a few plain, chainlike moderate hotels, but I have concentrated on the ones that don't remind me of America. There are so many hotels in London with pleasing sitting rooms that have gas fires, antiques, and deep sofas, who serve an authentic cream tea and massive English breakfast—they simply must be experienced to get the full flavor of London. Of course, some of the standard chain hotels might well have features that may make the most sense for you, such as wheelchair access, fitness club, frequent-flier mile tie-ins, good incentive packages, and the price and location you prefer. I have my own preferences as to neighborhoods, but they may not be yours.

NEIGHBORHOODS FOR HOTELS

There are a number of excellent neighborhoods to stay in. Here are my favorite top five and why:

1. **Zone 11.** South Kensington: Easy walk to Hyde Park and Kensington Gardens, three museums, Harrods, Albert Hall, Christies' Auction House, and Chelsea; three Underground lines, many buses; lots of French bakeries, restaurants for every budget, a small-town feeling in the big city. Downside: a bit expensive for smallish quarters (although that could be said of most hotels in London).
2. **Zone 8.** Mayfair and Piccadilly: Hyde Park, Green Park, St. James's Park, Bond Street shopping, art galleries everywhere, the Royal Academy, walk to West End, good transportation. Downside: extravagantly expensive—look for deals at the (few) moderately priced choices.
3. **Zone 7.** Soho and the West End: Nightlife, theaters, restaurants, National Gallery, Covent Garden, bookstores on Charing Cross, better people-watching and nightlife than anywhere else. Downside: noise and fumes.
4. **Zone 2.** Bloomsbury: British Museum, bookstores, walk to West End and Soho; easy commute to Lincoln's Inn and the City. Downside: a little desolate here and there.
5. **Zone 1.** Hampstead: Fresh air, the Heath, the feeling of country. Downside: need to commute to everything on the dreaded Northern Line.

Cheap but Not Always Cheerful
Hotel Neighborhoods

- Bayswater
- Earl's Court
- Victoria

Out There

There's something to be said for staying well out of central London, but not all of it is good. The public transportation can be dreadful and downright unapproachable at rush hours. Many of the outer areas of London are lacking in amenities like a wide choice of restaurants, convenience stores, and entertainment. There are also parts of outer London that are aesthetically unpleasing, downright grotty, or dully suburban. Whatever hotels you may find may be less expensive, but will rarely—with some exceptions in Richmond and in Hampstead—offer the standard of service that the central London hotels will.

Having said that, there *are* good bed-and-breakfast deals to be had in areas far from the sound and fury and pollution of London, which have tube and rail services that can get you into the middle of town in 30 to 40 minutes or less. People can get more house for their money out there, and so you may find a bed-and-breakfast with a garden, your own private entrance, perhaps a basement apartment or your own floor, cleanish air, and blessed quiet. The innkeepers probably will leave you quite alone, as personal reserve is still one of the great British traditions.

CALL FOR DEALS

Almost every hotel in London, except for the already cut-rate ones, will have some kind of saver scheme, be it a weekend reductions, a package that includes breakfast and a free night, annual shop sales reduction, a summer season, a low season, a Christmas season, a corporate rate, a half-price scheme, a no-reason lowered rate, and so on. They want you to come to London, and they want you to stay in their hotel. There is also the possibility of last-minute rooms, in which a hotel with an empty room will agree to a huge reduction just to fill it. This is not an option for everyone—it requires flexibility—but it can spell big savings.

Rule Number One in making any of these deals is to talk to the reception manager—she or he is the only person who can agree to making deals. Chat with the manager, and see what can be arranged—service is their business, and they do aim to please. But remember that some hotels don't need to make deals—check out the listings and see how many rooms a hotel has. Chances are that the more rooms there are, the more empty rooms they will have. Often, the rooms that remain empty are the junior, executive, or superior suites. To get one of those for the price of a standard double is a worthy coup, and you will be very happy in such a room, especially in the grand hotels.

BED-AND-BREAKFASTS

Bed-and-breakfasts are big in Britain, and in London there are some drop-dead gorgeous homes that are open to you through agencies—you won't believe your luck. The price, with a few exceptions, includes breakfast and is per person per night. There is often a minimum stay required. You may be asked to pay a booking fee and to place a deposit in sterling or credit card.

Some excellent companies are:

The Bulldog Club   (phone (0171) 371-3202, fax (0171) 371-2015). Only the crème de la crème of houses are included in this exclusive group. There are about 30 properties available, and the criteria are that the guests have a reasonably separate area from the host family's quarters, it is within a five-minute walk to public transportation, there will be amenities such as tea and coffeemaking facilities and bathrobes, and it will be in a very fine and beautifully decorated house. Prices range from £105 for two people to £85 for a single. You pay an annual fee of £25 to join the "club," which is the best money you'll spend in London.

Uptown Reservations   (phone (0171) 351-3445, fax (0171) 351-9383, Web *www.fenet.co.uk*. Another very high-tone agency, with fine houses of a breathtakingly high standard in good central neighborhoods as well as in outer London's leafy zones. Singles are a mere £65 a night, family room is £110.

London Homestead Services   (phone (0181) 541-0044 or (0181) 541-4455, fax (0181) 549-5492). This service has about 200 homes in the London area, many of which are pretty far out of central London, where you can get a double room for as little as £16. Naturally, rooms cost more in central London.

London First Choice Apartments   (phone (0181) 575-8877, fax (0181) 933-5778, Web *www.lfca.co.uk*). LFCA has a large assortment of hotels, serviced and nonserviced apartments, and bed-and-breakfasts. See the Web site for more information.

SERVICED AND SELF-SERVICED APARTMENTS

A serviced apartment can be a good alternative to a hotel room, with commensurate prices and much more room—to be able to close a door on your traveling companion(s) once in a while can be a great luxury. The best ones will offer everything a hotel does, some even provide meals. You may get a

24-hour concierge, cable TV, laundry, and daily maid service; you may even get a washer/dryer in the apartment, secretarial services, membership to a health club, a fully equipped kitchen, and more. When you factor in the costs of eating all your meals in restaurants, a hotel costs considerably more than its nightly rate. An apartment can save you wads of dosh, as they say here, by allowing you to make some of your meals yourself.

Holiday Apartments Ltd.   (phone (0171) 235-2486, fax (0171) 235-1222) Holiday has the most wide-ranging selection of first-rate properties, from studios to five bedrooms, all over the London area. With stringent inspections at least once a year, they are not reluctant to drop any properties whose quality is slipping. They are creative, helpful, and responsive to your needs.

London First Choice Apartments   (phone (0181) 575-8877, fax (0181) 933-5778, Web *www.lfca.co.uk)*. This service also has a selection of serviced apartments, ranging from £108 per night for a two-person studio apartment, to £197 for a four-person two-bedroom flat. Prices for what they call "prestige apartments" are higher.

Manors & Co.   (phone (800) 454-4385 in the United States or (0171) 487-4333 in London, fax (0171) 486-6770) Manors & Co. will send you a beautiful color brochure of its selection of high-end apartments in good neighborhoods, from studios to five-bedroom pads.

Home From Home   (phone (0171) 584-8914, fax (0171) 823-8433, Web *www.homefromhome.co.uk)*. With over 200 properties in London, Home From Home can be dialed from America toll-free at (800) 748-9783 for a brochure.

LONDON'S LUXURY HOTELS

If you can afford the $500+ a night that the following hotels charge, you don't need much in the way of direction from me. You will know that a luxury hotel will have pretty much the same high standards of service found in five-star hotels all over the world. One word of caution about London's five-stars, however: The styles vary to a large degree, from the stark minimalism of the Hempel to the Georgian excesses of the Lanesborough or the art deco insouciance of Claridges. They will also vary in size: There are a few rooms at the world-famous Browns that, despite the tasteful furnishings, can be rather cramped. Views are never a given, even when you're paying $600 a night; and business amenities are not always part of the package. So, buyer beware: If you are splurging on a five-star hotel, question the reservations clerk closely as to what they offer, and make a point of requesting a good view, a spacious room, and a good location on your floor. As I said, in the converted townhouse variety of hotel, the first floor (first above the ground floor, that is) rooms in the front will have the balconies and the French windows, and the top floors will have tiny windows and angled ceilings.

The majority of the following hotels are in Zone 8, the Mayfair and Piccadilly area. In the hotel listing, you will find somewhat more moderately priced establishments (except for the extended profile on Brown's), but the fact is that this is a very expensive hotel neighborhood, frequented by movie stars on studio tabs and assorted millionaires with expense accounts.

You can, however, call any of the following hotels and look into a discount. There are a number of possibilties: low season rates, applicable in January and February; summer discounts; weekend break rates; upgrading to a bigger room; paying for your room in advance in dollars; executive discounts; and frequent-flier tie-ins. Call directly and talk to the reservations manager to work out a deal—many of the good hotels have toll-free numbers in the United States. A few of these luxury hotels are owned by chain groups, such as Savoy, Forte, Intercontinental, and Hilton. Chains may offer any number of promotional deals, from holiday discounts to packages that include meals. Some of these otherwise astronomically priced hotels have single rooms at surprisingly good rates—the room may be small, but you'll have the best of comfort and service you can imagine. Many will upgrade you to a junior suite if there's one available. Remember that no hotel likes an empty room. All the prices quoted below are for standard doubles and I have calculated and included the 17.5% VAT, which adds up to a sizable dollop on top of a sizable basic rack rate—the more expensive hotels just don't have the nerve to include it in quoted prices. Some think the best way to experience these hotels is to have tea or a meal there, and save your money on a less pricey pad.

The Berkeley   Wilton Place, SW1, phone (0171) 235-6000, fax (0171) 235-4330 (tube: Knightsbridge). Right off Knightsbridge by Hyde Park Corner, this hotel has a fitness center, two excellent restaurants, and well-appointed spacious rooms. 157 rooms, starting at £370.

Blakes   33 Roland Gardens, SW7, phone (0171) 370-6701, fax (0171) 373-0442 (tube: South Kensington). Completely gorgeous hotel in South Kensington, catering to rock stars, models, actors, and so on. Although less expensive than the others in this class, you can still fracture your credit card between the tariff and the very fine restaurant. The rooms are exuberantly and individually decorated in styles ranging from expensive bordello to country squire to Raj's field tent. Good value for a five-star hotel, even though some of the rooms are smallish. 51 rooms, starting at £260.

Brown's Hotel   30–34 Albemarle St., W1, phone (0171) 493-6020, fax (0171) 493-9381 (tube: Green Park). Victorian gentlemen's club atmosphere and beautiful antique furnishings, nothing showy or over-the-top about this place except for its prices. Some of the rooms can be surprisingly small, although cozy, and there is no air conditioning. They serve an excellent afternoon tea in one of the three lovely sitting rooms. 118 rooms, starting at £411. (See profile for more information.)

Claridges   Brook Street, W1, phone (0171) 629-8860, fax (0171) 499-2210 (tube: Bond Street). Bold decor evokes Jazz Age glamour and royal luxury. People of serious substance stay here. Fantastic, albeit expensive tea in impressive surroundings, with a likely chance to see a society wedding. Rooms and baths are quite deluxe and start at £394. 196 rooms.

The Connaught   16 Carlos Place, W1, phone (0171) 499-7070, fax (0171) 495-3262 (tube: Bond Street). Grand country-house is the style here, and perfect service is the watchword. It's been around since 1897—Chalres DeGaulle made it his wartime headquarters, and Cecil Beaton and David Niven called it home. It attracts so many regulars that it's almost a club—make reservations well in advance of your visit. 90 rooms, starting at less than £352.

The Dorchester   53 Park Lane, W1, phone (0171) 629-8888, fax (0171) 409-0114 (tube: Marble Arch). One of London's grandest establishments, this hotel is right across from Hyde Park and walking distance to some of the toniest shops in London. Restaurants and the health club are of the highest standards, as are the rooms and the decor. You can see where your money is going at this hotel. 244 rooms, starting at £346.

The Four Seasons   Hamilton Place in Park Lane, W1, phone (0171) 499-0888, fax (0171) 493-6629 (tube: Hyde Park Corner). Owned by the Four Seasons Group, promotional packages are often available. The decor is opulent without being ostentatious; they provide excellent service and food. 220 rooms, starting at £358.

Grosvenor House   Park Lane, W1, phone (0171) 499-6363, fax (0171) 493-3341 (tube: Hyde Park Corner). Old and fabulous, this hotel houses the splendid restaurant Nico at 90, among other fine eateries. It's a bit formal, but very luxurious, and is owned by the Meridien group. 586 rooms, starting at £288.

The Halcyon Hotel   81 Holland Park, W11, phone (0171) 727-7288, fax (0171) 229-8516 (tube: Holland Park). What a charmer this one is, in this fashionable neighborhood, a stone's throw from Richard Branson's huge pied à terre. Exquisitely decorated and well sited for a stroll in Holland Park, this 43-room hotel attracts the rich and famous in droves. Your £275 for a standard double *includes* VAT—always give hotels extra credit when they have the decency to include the VAT in their quoted prices, and this is the only one in this class who does.

The Hyde Park Hotel   66 Knightsbridge, SW1, phone (0171) 235-2000, fax (0171) 201-3633 (tube: Knightsbridge). A grand old hotel, bought by the Mandarin Group, in the most marvelous location. Rooms facing north on Hyde Park are the ticket—the hotel also faces Knightsbridge, one of the noisiest, busiest streets in London. Complete Edwardian elegance, with a good restaurant overlooking the park. 200 rooms; doubles on the park (there are approximately 30) start at £376.

The Landmark   222 Marylebone Rd., NW1, phone (0171) 631-8000, fax (0171) 631-8033 (tube: Marylebone). Tucked between Oxford and Baker streets, The Landmark gives good value for money because it's out of the Mayfair-Piccadilly high-rent district. There's an impressive atrium in which to eat, a fitness center and pool, and good-sized rooms. Modern refurbishment in an old building. All 298 rooms are double and start at £340.

The Lanesborough   Hyde Park Corner, SW1, phone (0171) 259-5599, fax (0171) 259-5606 (tube: Hyde Park Corner). You'd never guess to look at the elaborately Georgian interior that gurneys used to be rolled around these floors instead of room service carts. This former hospital is now a formal hotel, full of charm and mahogany-paneled splendor, with an Oriental theme—decor restaurant of high quality. There's a butler call button in all the rooms, need I say more? 95 rooms starting at £364 for a standard double.

London Hilton   22 Park Lane, W1, phone (0171) 493-8000, fax (0171) 208-4140 (tube: Green Park). The place where Elizabeth Taylor reportedly spent more than one of her wedding nights, the London Hilton has successfully made the transition from the James Bond era to today with all five stars firmly intact. It isn't a picturesque building on the outside, but it does have the greatest views of Hyde Park available and huge rooms. If you want to check the view but not pay the £329 for a room, stop in for a drink on the twenty-eighth floor restaurant. Half of the 449 rooms overlook the park. If you want to be near the Hilton, try the Hilton Mews around back, a slightly less expensive but charming alternative.

The Metropolitan   Old Park Lane, W1, phone (0171) 447-1000, fax (0171) 447-1100 (tube: Hyde Park Corner). Minimalist to a fault, this is where the renowned Met Club is housed, a private club that was at the top of the social ladder when it opened in 1997, and is still formidable. Guests at The Metropolitan can get in, a big plus for young social types. It has a state-of-the-art gym. Its sister hotels, The Halkin in Belgravia (5 Halkin St. in Belgravia, 41 rooms from £300) and Myhotel in Bloomsbury (11–13 Bayley St., Bedford Square, phone (0171) 667-6000, 76 rooms from £185) are also shrines to cool beige, beech, and blank walls. 155 rooms from £300 to £1,527.

The Ritz   150 Piccadilly, W1, phone (0171) 493-8181, fax (0171) 493-2687 (tube: Green Park). What can you say about a synonym for luxury and extravagance? Before you think it's just plain out of the question, call and see what kind of deals they may have. They have a lot of rooms to fill. If all you want is tea, call well in advance of your trip to make a reservation —weekends can be booked as much as a month ahead. The decor is Versailles on Piccadilly, and the comfort is sumptuousness itself. The rooms facing Green Park are the best, sharing the view with such worthy mansions as Spencer House. Individually decorated rooms, 131 in all, start at £320 and go up, up, up.

The Savoy   1 Savoy Hill, Strand, WC2, phone (0171) 836-4343, fax (0171) 240-6040 (tube: Charing Cross). I don't think the Savoy has changed much since it was Frank Sinatra's favorite hotel in foggy London town. It is still a gorgeous place: Like Claridges, it maintains the Jazz Age decor of its salad days, and its service is impeccable. It's located right in the thick of things, perfect for theatergoers. Rooms, 207 in all, start at £382. £1,100 will get you a one-bedroom suite. The only rooms overlooking the Thames are junior suites plus. I believe Frank took the penthouse suite.

Hotel Ratings

Star Ratings   To distinguish properties according to relative quality, tastefulness, state of repair, cleanliness, and size of standard rooms, we have grouped hotels in classifications denoted by stars. Star ratings in this guide apply to London properties only and do not necessarily correspond to ratings awarded by the department of tourism, automobile clubs, or other travel critics. Star ratings are presented to show the difference we perceive between one property and another. They are assigned without regard to location, or whether a property has restaurants, recreational facilities, entertainment, or other extras.

What the Star Ratings Mean		
★★★★★	Superior	Tasteful and luxurious by any standard
★★★★	Extremely Nice	Above average in appointments and design; very comfortable.
★★★	Nice	Average but quite comfortable
★★	Adequate	Plain but meets all essential needs
★	Budget	Spartan, not aesthetically pleasing, but clean

Numerical Ratings   In addition to stars (which delineate broad categories), we also employ a numerical rating system. Numerical ratings apply to room quality only and describe the property's standard accommodations. In addition to standard accommodations, many hotels offer luxury rooms and special suites that are not rated in this guide. Our rating scale is 0–100, with 100 as the best possible rating and zero (0) as the worst. To use the ratings, consider this: Rooms at the Hilton Mews, Pembridge Court Hotel, and The Franklin Hotel are all rated as four stars (★★★★). In the supplemental numerical ratings, the Hilton is rated an 86, the Pembridge an 84, and the Franklin a 79. This means that within the four-star category, the Hilton and Pembridge are comparable and both have better rooms than the Franklin.

Value Ratings   We also provide a Value Rating to give you some sense of quality received for the pound spent. As before, the ratings are based on the quality of room for the money and do not consider location, services, or amenities.

Our value rating scale is as follows:

A An exceptional bargain
B A good deal
C Fairly priced (You get exactly what you pay for)
D Somewhat overpriced
F Significantly overpriced

We would remind you that the purpose of the value ratings is to give you a relative sense of room quality received for pounds spent. A ★★½ room at £100 may have the same value rating as a ★★★★ room at £180, but that does not mean that the rooms will be of comparable quality. Regardless of whether it's a good deal or not, a ★★½ room is still a ★★½ room.

For each hotel we also provide the London geographic zone where the property is located.

HOW THE HOTELS COMPARE

Here's a list of the hotels we profile organized by overall rating. To find a particular hotel listed in this table, look through the alphabetical section of profiles later in the chapter.

If you use subsequent editions of this guide, you will notice that many of the ratings and rankings change. In addition to the inclusion of new properties, these changes also consider guest room renovations or improved maintenance and housekeeping. A failure to properly maintain guest rooms or a lapse in housekeeping standards can negatively affect the ratings.

Finally, before you begin to shop for a hotel, take a hard look at this letter we received from a couple in Hot Springs, Arkansas:

> *We cancelled our room reservations to follow the advice in your book [and reserved a hotel room highly ranked by the Unofficial Guide]. We wanted inexpensive, but clean and cheerful. We got inexpensive, but [also] dirty, grim, and depressing. I really felt disappointed in your advice and the room. It was the pits. That was the one real piece of information I needed from your book! The room spoiled the holiday for me aside from our touring.*

Needless to say, this letter was as unsettling to us as the bad room was to our reader. Our integrity as travel journalists, after all, is based on the quality of the information we provide our readers. Even with the best of intentions and the most conscientious research, however, we cannot inspect every room in every hotel. What we do, in statistical terms, is take a sample: We check out several rooms selected at random in each hotel and base our ratings and rankings on those rooms. The inspections are conducted anonymously and without the knowledge of the management. Although unusual, it is certainly possible that the rooms we randomly inspect are not representative of the majority of rooms at a particular hotel.

Another possibility is that the rooms we inspect in a given hotel are representative, but that by bad luck a reader is assigned a room that is inferior. When we rechecked the hotel our reader disliked, we discovered our rating was correctly representative, but that he and his wife had unfortunately been assigned to one of a small number of threadbare rooms scheduled for renovation.

The key to avoiding disappointment is to snoop around in advance. We recommend that you ask for a photo of a hotel's standard guest room before you book, or at least get a copy of the hotel's promotional brochure. Be fore-warned, however, that some hotel chains use the same guest room photo in their promotional literature for all hotels in the chain; a specific guest room may not resemble the brochure photo. When you or your travel agent call, ask when your guest room was last renovated. If you arrive and are assigned a room inferior to that which you had been led to expect, demand to be moved to another room.

How the Hotels Compare				
Hotel	Overall Quality	Room Quality	Value	Zone
The Gore	★★★★★	100	A	11
The Rookery	★★★★★	98	B	3
Covent Garden Hotel	★★★★★	95	B	7
The Basil Street Hotel	★★★★★	94	A+	11
Dorset Square Hotel	★★★★★	93	B	14
Goring Hotel	★★★★★	90	B	9
Dukes Hotel	★★★★½	94	B	9
The Cliveden Town House	★★★★½	90	C	11
The Pelham	★★★★½	90	B	11
Brown's Hotel	★★★★½	89	C	8
London Marriot Hotel at County Hall	★★★★½	85	C	5
The Milestone House	★★★★½	84	C–	11
11 Cadogan Gardens	★★★★½	83	B	11
The Hampshire Edwardian Radisson	★★★★½	83	D	7
The Thistle Victoria	★★★★½	83	A	9
Hilton Mews	★★★★	86	C	8
Miller's Period Rooming House	★★★★	85	B	13
L'Hotel 28	★★★★	84	A	10
Pembridge Court Hotel	★★★★	84	A+	13
Abbey Court	★★★★	83	A	13
Hotel Number Sixteen	★★★★	83	A	11
The Montague on the Gardens	★★★★	82	C	2
The Portobello Hotel	★★★★	82	C	13

How the Hotels Compare (continued)

Hotel	Overall Quality	Room Quality	Value	Zone
The Sandringham	★★★★	82	B	1
Durrants	★★★★	81	A	14
The Cadogan Hotel	★★★★	80	C	11
Millenium Britannia Mayfair	★★★★	80	C	8
The Franklin Hotel	★★★★	79	B–	10
The Rembrandt Hotel	★★★★	79	C	11
Thistle Hyde Park	★★★★	79	B	14
Hazlitt's Hotel	★★★½	96	B	7
Parkes Hotel	★★★½	83	B	10
Flemings	★★★½	78	B	8
The Claverley	★★★½	77	A	10
The Gallery	★★★½	77	B	11
Holiday Inn Mayfair	★★★½	77	C	8
Jury's	★★★½	77	C	11
Quality Hotel	★★★½	77	A	9
White Hall Hotel	★★★½	77	B	2
The Columbia Hotel	★★★½	75	A	14
The Edward Lear Hotel	★★★½	75	A	14
Morgan Hotel	★★★½	75	A	2
The Gainsborough	★★★½	73	B+	11
Hotel Russell	★★★½	72	B	2
Five Sumner Place Hotel	★★★	73	A	11
Riverside Hotel	★★★	70	B	12
The Pastoria Radisson Edwardian	★★★	68	D	7
DeVere Park Hotel	★★★	66	A	11
St. Margaret's Hotel	★★★	64	A	2
Elizabeth Hotel	★★★	63	A	9
Hillgate Hotel	★★★	62	A	13
The Fielding Hotel	★★½	65	A	7
Ruskin Hotel	★★½	58	B+	2
The Cherry Court Hotel	★★	55	B	9

Hotels by Zone

**Zone 1: North London: Hampstead and Highgate
(NW3, NW8, NW9)**
Sandringham Hotel

Zone 2: Bloomsbury and Holborn (WC1, WC2)
Hotel Russell
The Montague on the Gardens
Morgan Hotel
The Ruskin
St. Margaret's Hotel
White Hall Hotel

Zone 3: The City, Clerkenwell, and Barbican (EC1, EC 2, EC4)
The Rookery

Zone 5: South London: South Bank and Lambeth, Brixton (SE1)
London Marriott Hotel, County Hall

Zone 7: Soho and the West End (W1)
Covent Garden Hotel
The Fielding Hotel
Hazlitt's
The Hampshire
The Pastoria

Zone 8: Mayfair and Piccadilly (W1, SW1)
Brown's Hotel
Flemings
Hilton Mews
Holiday Inn Mayfair
Millennium Britannia Mayfair

Zone 9: Victoria and Westminster (SW1)
Cherry Court Hotel
Dukes Hotel
Elizabeth Hotel
Goring
Quality Hotel
The Thistle Victoria

Hotels by Zone (continued)

Zone 10: Knightsbridge and Belgravia (SW1, SW3)
The Basil Hotel
The Cadogan
The Claverley
L'Hotel 28
The Franklin
Parkes Hotel

Zone 11: Chelsea and South Kensington (SW3, SW5, SW7)
The Cliveden Town House
The Milestone
Five Sumner Place Hotel
The Gainsborough
The Gallery Hotel
The Gore
Hotel Number 16
Jury's
DeVere Park Hotel
The Pelham
The Rembrandt

Zone 12: West London: Hammersmith, Chiswick, Richmond, Kew (SW14)
The Riverside Hotel

Zone 13: Kensington, Holland Park, Notting Hill (W8, W11)
Abbey Court
Hillgate Hotel
Miller's Period Rooming House
Pembridge Court Hotel
The Portobello Hotel

Zone 14: Bayswater, Marylebone, Little Venice, St. John's Wood (NW1, W1, W9, NW8)
The Columbia Hotel
Dorset Square Hotel
Durrants
The Edward Lear Hotel
Thistle Hyde Park (formerly Whites Hotel)

Hotel Profiles

All prices include the 17.5% Value Added Tax (VAT)

ABBEY COURT			£93–£115
Overall: ★★★★	Room Quality: 83	Value: A	Zone 13

Abbey Court is a lovely old Victorian house in a white-stucco front neighborhood around the corner from Portobello Road. It's a real beauty, and at a very good price, too. It's quite popular with antiques dealers, not only because they can walk to Kensington Church Street and all the other antiques warrens along Portobello, but also because it has plenty of really fine old furniture, art, and decorations to admire. It's comfortable and homey, as well as being elegant and serene—it feels like you're visiting a rich aunt's house who has very good taste. There are plenty of good old books, some first editions, which you can (carefully) borrow to read. Downstairs there's a small conservatory where breakfast is served (continental breakfast is included), and an honor bar is set out all day. A tiny little patio off the conservatory has a small pool with goldfish. Newspapers are ordered for you, free, and there are plenty of English magazines in each room. You can get a reduction for stays longer than a week. Except for the fact that there's no elevator, this is truly a four-star townhouse hotel at three-star prices.

SETTINGS & FACILITIES

Location: Notting Hill Gate
Nearest Tube Station: Notting Hill Gate
Quietness Rating: A in back, B in front (quiet street)
Dining: Small breakfast room
Amenities: Newspapers, bathrobes, biscuits, and bottled water, associated with nearby health club, breakfast included, honor bar
Services: Receptionist does work of concierge, 24-hour room service, bellhop, laundry

ACCOMMODATIONS

Rooms: 22
All Rooms: Telephone, television, hair dryer, trouser press, bathrobe, heated towel racks, Jacuzzi baths
Some Rooms: Four-poster beds
Bed & Bath: Italian marble bathrooms with tubs that have Jacuzzi jets, shower, and heated towel racks. The beds are excellent, some are old brass bedsteads and there are a few four-posters.

Favorites: The four-poster rooms are the biggest and the nicest.
Comfort & Decor: The decor is quite fine, with good antiques and nice prints all around, fantastic mirrors, and nice wallpaper. It's a pleasure to see how well-appointed it is, and for me, that spells comfort. However, there is no elevator for the five floors. Beautiful stairway, though.

RATES, RESERVATIONS, & RESTRICTIONS

Deposit: Credit card, 48-hour cancellation policy
Credit Cards: All major
Check-in/Out: 1 p.m., /11:30 a.m.
Pets: Not allowed
Elevator: No
Children: Yes
Disabled-friendly: No lift

20 Pembridge Gardens, W4
(0171) 221-7518
fax (0171) 792-0858
abbey@telinco.co.uk
www.telinco.co.uk/abbeycourt

THE BASIL STREET HOTEL   £150+

Overall: ★★★★★	Room Quality: 94	Value: A+	Zone 11

For 85 years, The Basil Street Hotel has been attracting loyal customers with its homey (a very extraordinary home) comfort and elegance. It's the kind of hotel you want to hang around in; there are a few common sitting areas that are so comfortable, so pleasing to the eye, and so well-appointed that you may not be tempted outside to nearby Harrods, Hyde Park, the museums of South Kensington, Harvey Nichols, or the designer boutiques of Sloane Street. This is not an ostentatious hotel by any means, but if you look at the art on the wall—check out the paintings on glass on the way to the dining room—or the pieces of furniture, the carpets, and the bric-a-brac, you may imagine yourself in a very fine stately home or a museum. They aim for the country-house feeling, and it is maintained even against all the noise and hubbub on the streets outside. There are sitting alcoves, looking out over the roofs of Knightsbridge, that have desks supplied with writing paper, evoking a gentler time before email. It's a feminine place in many ways, but it is in no way frilly—compared to some of ye-olde-

English-country-house imitation decor in so many hotels in London, it's positively restrained. Probably because it's the real thing. It offers some of the best value for the money you will find in this part of town, if not in all of central London.

SETTINGS & FACILITIES

Location: Knightsbridge
Nearest tube station: Knightsbridge
Quietness Rating: C on lower floors; B+ on higher floors.
Dining: Dining room was given award by the Automobile Association. It's a very lovely, traditional sort of dining room, with live classical music most nights. There's also a warm and comfy sitting room for excellent afternoon teas.

Amenities: Women's Club (The Parrot Club) into which men only can go if accompanied by a woman, and which provide office services for businesswomen; ironing rooms on each floor; parking spaces available at a reasonable charge; smoking and nonsmoking rooms.
Services: Concierge, bellhop, laundry

ACCOMMODATIONS

Rooms: 93
All Rooms: Cable television, hair dryer, bathtubs, writing desk, comfortable sitting chair
Some Rooms: Air conditioning, bay windows, glass-fronted cabinets
Bed & Bath: Bathrooms range from irreproachable to irresistable: Some simply enormous, some paneled in pine wainscoting. Beds are quite comfortable.

Favorites: Singles are among the largest in London. Beautiful bay windows in some rooms. You can't go too wrong at the Basil, whatever room you get.
Comfort & Decor: Exquisite antiques and a huge collection of mezzotints, fine carpets, superior furniture, and really good pieces of porcelain and lamps. High ceilings, good closet space. Functional and roomy layout in all rooms (by London standards, anyway.)

RATES, RESERVATIONS, & RESTRICTIONS

Deposit: Credit card, 24-hour cancellation policy
Credit Cards: All major
Check-In/Out: mid-day/noon
Pets: Not allowed
Elevator: Yes
Children: Yes

Disabled-friendly: Limited
Basil Street, Knightsbridge, SW3
(0171) 581-3311
in U.S. (800) 448-8355
fax (0171) 581-3693
The Basil@aol.com

BROWN'S HOTEL   £295–£425

Overall: ★★★★½	Room Quality: 89	Value: C	Zone 8

This five-star hotel has something of a reputation among Americans as *the* English Hotel to stay in, and I am including it because so many people want to stay here. It is normal to see at least one celebrity during a typical stay: I've seen Johnny Depp and Annie Leibovitz. The service is excellent and good-natured in that arch English way, and the food, though sky-high in price, is simple and good. Especially at teatime: The afternoon cream tea is excellent, and the ambience of the sitting room is great. The history of the place is pretty remarkable: Alexander Graham Bell made the first telephone call in Britain from here, Rudyard Kipling wrote from here, and Theodore Roosevelt got married while a guest at Brown's. Lord Byron's valet, James Brown, started the hotel in 1837, with funds apparently acquired through his wife's connection as maid to Lady Byron. His wife, Sarah, and he had learned a thing or two from living in the "mad, bad, and dangerous to know" lordship's household, and the hotel was a success from the start. After the Browns sold it in 1859, the next owner made it the first hotel in London to have an elevator, telephone, and electricity. It grew from 1 townhouse to 11, which is why you'll find the configurations of the rooms so completely unpredictable. Brown's is all about service: With 118 rooms, it has 160 in staff. Yes, the prices are very steep, so be sure to talk to reception about deals. The location is excellent, by the way.

SETTINGS & FACILITIES

Location: Mayfair
Nearest Tube Station: Green Park
Quietness Rating: A
Dining: Fine dining (and expensive, too) at award-winning 1837 Restaurant features English fare, with the greatest wine list in London. Breakfast in dining room, and afternoon teas in The Draw-ing Room. St. Georges' Bar for drinks and cigars.
Amenities: Fitness room, afternoon teas, business center
Services: Concierge, 24-hour room service and valet, laundry, business support

ACCOMMODATIONS

Rooms: 118
All Rooms: Minibars, multiline phones, voice mail, sitting area, writing desks, cable TV, air conditioning.
Some Rooms: Sitting areas with sofa, working fireplaces, four-poster beds, French doors
Bed & Bath: Superior. Heated towel racks, Moulton Brown toiletries, bathrobe, and slippers. Queen- or king-size beds.
Favorites: Mayfair and Royal suites. First-floor rooms are the best, with high ceilings and big windows. Avoid the rooms at the top—they are low-ceilinged, and some of the junior suites are small.
Comfort & Decor: This is a five-star hotel, so you will find the comfort factor high, although some of the rooms are not as large as one would expect, and some are downright cramped. The decor is English country-house traditional, very comfy and unpretentious, with some fine pieces of furniture, carvings, and art here and there. Carved fireplace in the reception, paneling, cut glass, and the stained-glass windows in the stairwells and elsewhere are all exquisite.

RATES, RESERVATIONS, & RESTRICTIONS

Deposit: Credit card, 24-hour cancellation policy
Credit Cards: All major
Check-In/Out: 2 p.m./noon
Pets: Not allowed
Elevator: Yes
Children: Yes

Disabled-friendly: Yes, though limited
30–34 Albemarle St., W1
(0171) 493-6020
fax (0171) 493-9381
brownshotel@brownshotel.com
www.brownshotel.com

THE CADOGAN HOTEL			£195–£365
Overall: ★★★★	Room Quality: 80	Value: C	Zone 11

This is the hotel at which Oscar Wilde was arrested. Its other famous association is with Lillie Langtry, the Jersey songbird more well-known these days for her long-term affair with the prince of Wales (later King Edward) than her singing. The two of them represent a time and place in Victorian London that the Cadogan Hotel has tried to evoke in its decor and atmosphere. It is impossible not to feel some connection with that time when you walk in the door and see the leaded windows, the William Morris–style wallpaper, and the stately and elegant drawing room that sports a notice asking people to leave their mobile phones and laptop computers outside. Terribly civilized. The restaurant is quite grand-looking and is reputed to have an excellent menu, but there are tons of great restaurants within walking distance of the hotel. The rooms aren't breathtaking, but they're attractive, each individually decorated, with some enjoying a good amount of space and views of the greenery of Cadogan Place across the street. Hotel guests have access to these widely coveted gardens that have a tennis court, also at your disposal.

SETTINGS & FACILITIES

Location: Knightsbridge
Nearest Tube Station: Knightsbridge or Sloane Square
Quietness Rating: A in the interior, B/C on Sloane and Pont streets side
Dining: Restaurant has two rosettes from the Automobile Association

Amenities: Drawing room and a bar with leaded windows, health club affiliation, access to gardens and tennis
Services: Concierge, 24-hour room service, bellhop, laundry

ACCOMMODATIONS

Rooms: 65
All Rooms: Telephone, voice mail, satellite TV, air conditioning, hair dryer, trouser press, writing desk
Some Rooms: Sitting rooms, two bathrooms, view of gardens
Bed & Bath: High standard of both
Favorites: The large studio in the

front with two bathrooms is lovely, as are some of the luxury doubles. Try the Oscar Wilde Room.
Comfort & Decor: Beautiful William Morris wallpaper and wood wall-paneling in halls. All rooms are individually decorated nicely. The comfort is of a high standard.

RATES, RESERVATIONS, & RESTRICTIONS

Deposit: Credit card
Credit Cards: All major, though they prefer to not take AMEX
Check-In/Out: noon/noon
Pets: Small dogs allowed
Elevator: Yes
Children: Yes

Disabled-friendly: Yes, though there are limits on wheelchair access
75 Sloane St., SW1
(0171) 235-7141
fax (0171) 245-0994
info@thecadogan.u-net.com

THE CHERRY COURT HOTEL   £45

Overall: ★★	Room Quality: 55	Value: B	Zone 9

The Cherry Court Hotel has the cheeriest exterior of all the many budget/ backpacker hotels and hostels in this neighborhood. There are flowers in the window sills, and a wooden and gold sign has been carefully hung. The best thing about the hotel (it's really more of a rooming house, minus a dining room) besides the price and the ensuite toilets and showers is the friendliness and goodwill of the owners, the Patels. They've been here for 17 years and are committed to constant improvements, one of which includes turning the back patio into a rose garden and making a small breakfast room that opens onto it. The rooms are small and utilitarian, some are a bit sadsack, but to the traveler on a serious budget they offer a clean place to sleep where you don't have to share a toilet with strangers.

SETTINGS & FACILITIES

Location: Victoria
Nearest Tube Station: Victoria
Quietness Rating: A
Dining: No
Amenities: Fruit basket and cereal

bar for breakfast, though that may be upgraded in the future
Services: Helpful management, daily cleaning

ACCOMMODATIONS

Rooms: 11
All Rooms: Telephone, five-channel TV
Bed & Bath: Small beds and bathrooms, which are showers and toilet in a small closet, but all are clean and adequate
Favorites: Rooms in the back

Comfort & Decor: This is a backpacker's rooming house. The rooms are small, the beds are serviceable. The decor has been upgraded recently, and there are nice shades of blue carpets and wallpapers in the hallways, which are fresh and clean.

RATES, RESERVATIONS, & RESTRICTIONS

Deposit: Credit card
Credit Cards: All major
Check-In/Out: 1 p.m./11 a.m.
Pets: Not allowed
Elevator: No
Children: Yes
Disabled-friendly: Two rooms on ground floor, and three steps outside

23 Hugh St., SW1
(0171) 828-2840
fax (0171) 828-0393
info@cherrycourthotel.co.uk
www.cherrycourthotel.co.uk

THE CLAVERLY £75–£215

Overall: ★★★½	Room Quality: 77	Value: A	Zone 10

This inn is an award-winner for Best Bed and Breakfast Hotel in Central and Greater London. It is clean, well decorated, has a charming breakfast room much larger than most of its competition's, and has a selection of rooms that range from sweet to fabulous. The single rooms all have large three-quarter beds. Smoking is allowed only in the sitting room downstairs, not in the rooms. The breakfast is big and hearty, the location is perfect, and the service is friendly and unstuffy, but completely professional. Harrods is around the corner, South Kensington museums and restaurants a four-minute walk away, and Hyde Park can be accessed in minutes. The traditional English style of decor, the sunlight in the front rooms, and the relatively reasonable price will delight the discerning tourist.

SETTINGS & FACILITIES

Location: Knightsbridge
Nearest Tube Station: Knightsbridge
Quietness Rating: A
Dining: Breakfast in room or breakfast room
Amenities: Sitting room with carved fireplace and complimentary papers and magazines; breakfast room with waiter service, full English breakfast included in price, airport transfer and taxis.
Services: Concierge, bellhop, laundry, faxing

ACCOMMODATIONS

Rooms: 29
All Rooms: Cable TV, hair dryers
Some Rooms: Four-poster bed, balcony, pull-out sofa, writing desk, sitting area, walk-in closet
Bed & Bath: Beds are new. Bathtubs in 85% of rooms; the rest have shower stalls. All the bathrooms have been recently renovated and are in pristine condition.
Favorites: Number 12 is the best junior suite with balcony, French windows, and awesome four-poster bed. Junior suite number 33 has a walk-in closet. Single, number 35, in the rear of the building is pretty good, too, with a large bed and a charm not defeated by the view of the backs of houses.
Comfort & Decor: Individually decorated, all the rooms are attractive and clean and some are downright luxurious. The hotel has a great collection of portraits and drawings on the wall, and curtains in the magnificent English style.

RATES, RESERVATIONS, & RESTRICTIONS

Deposit: Credit card; 48-hour cancellation policy
Credit Cards: All major
Check-In/Out: 1 p.m./11:30 a.m.
Pets: Not allowed
Elevator: Yes
Children: Yes

Disabled-friendly: No wheelchair access
13–14 Beaufort Gardens, SW3
from U.S. (800) 747-0398;
(0171) 589-8541
fax (0171) 823-3410

THE CLIVEDEN TOWN HOUSE   £155–£400

Overall: ★★★★½	Room Quality: 90	Value: C	Zone 11

As you might guess from the sister townhouse of the world-famous Cliveden, former country house of the Astors, the Cliveden Town House is quite grand. However, it isn't pretentious or over the top in any way; it's got the feeling of a really beautiful home. The rooms are not numbered but named after theatrical legends — Laurence Olivier, Edmund Kean, Edith Evans, George and Ira Gershwin, the Redgraves, Noël Coward, and so on. The lovely drawing room has a welcoming, comfortable atmosphere, and opens onto a nice-sized garden square that makes a wonderful place to sit in good weather. As you walk in the door, there are two urns on either side, each filled with apples, only the first of many appealing touches in this hotel townhouse. The rooms all have Cliveden teddy bears on the beds, there are gas fires in all but the single rooms. A self-service tea is set out each day at 4 p.m., and a complimentary bottle of champagne is uncorked at 6 p.m. The toiletries are made by Penhaligons for Cliveden, one of the little features that help justify the price. You should ask about deals; they are extremely accommodating here. The single rooms are okay, but if you can afford it, step up to a double — even the standard doubles are quite big and have fireplace and sofa. You're within a short walk of Sloane Square and Knightsbridge, but you'd swear you were in the country when you're in a room with a garden view.

SETTINGS & FACILITIES

Location: Knightsbridge/Chelsea
Nearest Tube Station: Knightsbridge or Sloane Square
Quietness Rating: A
Dining: Dinner on request, but it's not a dining room with waiters hovering. Breakfast room is delightful and bright.

Amenities: Private dining room, drawing room, smoking room, afternoon tea, honor bar, breakfast room, garden
Services: Concierge, complimentary chauffeur service into city each weekday, 24-hour room service, laundry, baby-sitting

ACCOMMODATIONS

Rooms: 35
All Rooms: Telephone, voice mail, fax and modem line, air conditioning, satellite TV, VCR, stereo CD
Some Rooms: View onto gardens, fireplace
Bed & Bath: Mattresses made specifically for Cliveden, baths are superior as would be expected

Favorites: Any of the deluxe junior suites overlooking gardens; the doubles are quite fine, too
Comfort & Decor: Highest standard of comfort, the decor is elegance itself, light but sumptuous

RATES, RESERVATIONS, & RESTRICTIONS

Deposit: Credit card
Credit Cards: All major
Check-In/Out: 2 p.m./11 a.m.
Pets: Dogs allowed on certain conditions
Elevator: Yes
Children: Yes

Disabled-friendly: No, too many stairs
26 Cadogan Gardens, SW3
(0171) 730-6466
fax (0171) 730-0236
stephen.colley@clivedentownhouse.co.uk
www.clivedentownhouse.co.uk

THE COLUMBIA HOTEL			£60–£116
Overall: ★★★½	Room Quality: 75	Value: A	Zone 14

This is probably one of the best deals in the area—there may be cheaper rooms to be had, but not with the amenities and friendliness of the Columbia. It looks out on Hyde Park and is well located for buses and the tube. The rooms are plain hotel style, but they're clean and fairly roomy. The hotel is comprised of five Victorian houses strung together, so as with all such buildings, there will be great disparity among the size and shapes of the rooms. Unfortunately, the first floor, with its elegant high ceilings and huge windows, is mostly conference rooms, but there are many park view rooms in the remaining floors. The only problem is that it's noisier on the park. This is a good budget hotel, and one that can accommodate families, pets, and even automobiles (parking on a first-come, first-served basis). Queensway, a few minutes' walk away, has lots of great restaurants (not to mention a skating rink and bowling alley). The staff is friendly and helpful.

SETTINGS & FACILITIES

Location: Lancaster Gate (Bayswater)
Nearest Tube Station: Lancaster Gate
Quietness Rating: C in front, A in back

Dining: Breakfast and dinner
Amenities: Dining room, bar
Services: 24-hour reception desk, laundry

ACCOMMODATIONS

Rooms: 100
All Rooms: Shower and toilet, telephone, BBC TV, hair dryer
Some Rooms: View over park, connecting rooms, four beds in one room

Bed & Bath: Clean and satisfactory, mostly showers
Favorites: Big rooms
Comfort & Decor: Very plain and simple hotel style

RATES, RESERVATIONS, & RESTRICTIONS

Deposit: Credit card, 24-hour cancellation policy
Credit Cards: All major, except DC
Check-In/Out: 2 p.m./11:30 a.m.
Pets: Allowed
Elevator: Two
Children: Yes

Disabled-friendly: One disabled room, and a bedroom for deaf or hearing disabled
95–99 Lancaster Gate, W2
(0171) 402-0021
fax (0171) 706-4691
columbiahotel@btinternet

COVENT GARDEN HOTEL   £205–£350

Overall: ★★★★★	Room Quality: 95	Value: B	Zone 7

Another smash hit by the Firmdale Group, who also own the Pelham Hotel and the Dorset Square Hotel. The Covent Garden is more spacious than the Pelham and offers even more than its four-star rating would lead you to believe, and in fact it perches between a four- and five-star hotel, leaning heavily into the upper range, with more square footage, both in the size of the beds and the size of the rooms and hallways. They have anticipated the needs of the tourist and the business person, offering such amenities as cell phones and VCRs. There is a fitness room, which is tiny and only has one treadmill and one bike—more than you'll find in many hotels in London, anyway. But the outstanding thing about this hotel is the decor—it is the most delightful place imaginable, where the decoration is just plain appealing, not trying to be traditional English or stylishly modern. It's just a place where all the possessions and talents of the designer come together effortlessly and pleasingly. It is also a superb location: Monmouth Street is a relatively quiet street in Seven Dials, but is within skipping distance of Soho, Covent Garden, Bloomsbury, and the theaters of the West End. No wonder so many movie stars call this hotel home. Of course, they can afford it.

SETTINGS & FACILITIES

Location: Covent Garden
Nearest Tube Station: Covent Garden
Quietness Rating: A, but perhaps C on weekend nights
Dining: Brasserie Max is a modern-style dining room with good food

Amenities: Two drawing rooms, one very large, with working fireplaces, restaurant, honor bar with snacks, personal safe, cell phone for rent at £10 a day, small workout room
Services: Concierge, 24-hour room service, valet, bellhop, laundry

ACCOMMODATIONS

Rooms: 50
All Rooms: U.S.-size queen and king beds (even in singles), air conditioning, telephones with extra line, modem with U.S.-style socket, voice mail, cable TV, VCR and movies to watch, CD player and CDs to borrow, cell phone for rent, writing desk, bathtubs, umbrella
Some Rooms: Ornamental fireplace, four-poster bed, sofa and sitting area, roof terrace
Bed & Bath: Bathrooms are splendid, all gray marble and perfection. The beds are huge, outfitted in 100% cotton sheets, and covered with the most beautiful duvets and pillows.
Favorites: Number 304 is a deluxe double with a blue theme, gorgeous

four-poster bed, and an ornamental fireplace with two big chairs in front of it. The terrace suite is preferred by the many movie stars who stay here; it has its own little patio overlooking the roofs of the West End, a library, a sofa, and a sweetly appointed queen-size bed. The walls have been painstakingly painted with a sponge effect in red ... stunning (as are all the rooms, really).
Comfort & Decor: Comfort is of a very high quality indeed, with all of your possible needs accounted for. The decor is sublime—Tim and Kit Kemp are geniuses at interior decoration, neatly blending traditional antiques with their own brand of quirky great taste, creating an atmosphere of delight.

RATES, RESERVATIONS, & RESTRICTIONS

Deposit: Credit card, 24-hour cancellation policy
Credit Cards: All major
Check-In/Out: 1 p.m./ 11 a.m.
Pets: Not allowed
Elevator: Two
Children: Yes

Disabled-friendly: Yes, big elevators and wide hallways
10 Monmouth St., WC2
(0171) 806-1000
fax (0171) 806-1100
covent@firmdale.com
www.firmdale.com

DEVERE PARK HOTEL   £95–£155

| Overall: ★★★ | Room Quality: 66 | Value: A | Zone: 11 |

This is a decent, inexpensive hotel in a very expensive neighborhood—it looks out on Kensington Palace. It is very simple, perhaps even Spartan, but clean. The rooms on the front do have the wonderful views of the palace and across Hyde Park, and in the summer the trees make you feel as if you're in a bird's nest, but there are some downsides. The first floor rooms have wonderful high ceilings and good windows, but the noise from the very busy street below is intense during the day—at night it's not too bad, just a bus or two going by. Breakfast is included in the price, and it's taken in the moderately priced Brasserie Restaurant, a bright and cheery room off the lobby. No amenities to speak of, but it's a very good deal.

SETTINGS & FACILITIES

Location: Hyde Park Gate
Nearest Tube Station: Gloucester Road or Kensington High Street
Quietness Rating: C in front, A in back rooms

Dining: Yes, moderately priced Brasserie
Amenities: Breakfast included in Brasserie
Services: Concierge, bellhop, laundry

ACCOMMODATIONS

Rooms: 93
All Rooms: Telephone, five channels of TV, tea and coffee
Some Rooms: High ceilings, French windows
Bed & Bath: Satisfactory
Favorites: Those on first floor, although they are the noisiest

Comfort & Decor: Single rooms are very small, and the doubles are small double beds. Americans accustomed to big beds should get a family room, which has two doubles and a fold-out couch, or a twin, which has two single beds. Decor is hotel-style, very plain and unfashionable, but clean.

RATES, RESERVATIONS, & RESTRICTIONS

Deposit: Credit card, 24-hour cancellation policy
Credit Cards: All major
Check-In/Out: 2 p.m./ noon
Pets: Not allowed
Elevator: Yes
Children: Yes

Disabled-friendly: No wheelchair access
60 Hyde Park Gate, Kensington, W8
(0171) 584-0051
fax (0171) 823-8583

DORSET SQUARE HOTEL £115–£230

Overall: ★★★★★	Room Quality: 93	Value: B	Zone 14

Once again, the Firmdale Group has created a home away from home in this excellent hotel that looks out on two acres of gardens, seeming to be far from the bustle of nearby Baker Street and Marylebone Road. It's within walking distance of Regent's Park and Oxford Street. The rooms are all beautifully decorated, and the luxury of the common areas is perfect. All the possible amenities of a good hotel are here, with the Potting Shed Restaurant and bar providing fine meals and wines, 24-hour room service, and business support facilities. Each room is individually decorated and is of a decent size, with some magnificent four-poster rooms with garden views. The staff is extremely attentive and can organize anything you need, but most interestingly, you can hire a chauffeur-driven Bentley for business or pleasure. Check out their Web site to see all their properties. Ask about weekend rates and other promotions.

SETTINGS & FACILITIES

Location: Marylebone
Nearest Tube Station: Baker Street
Quietness Rating: A in garden rooms, B in front
Dining: Potting Shed Restaurant serves excellent food and wines

Amenities: Potting Shed Restaurant and Bar, business support, chauffeured Bentley available
Services: Concierge, 24-hour room service, valet, bellhop, laundry

ACCOMMODATIONS

Rooms: 50
All Rooms: U.S.-size queen and king beds (even in singles), air conditioning, telephones with extra line, modem with U.S.-style socket, voice mail, cable TV, VCR on request, cell phone for rent, fabulous antiques and art
Some Rooms: Four-posters, fireplace, sitting room, garden views

Bed & Bath: Superb
Favorites: Any of the rooms looking out on the garden, but especially number 202, which has a sitting room and fireplace
Comfort & Decor: Top of the line, as is usual in the Firmdale establishments. The decor is delightful.

RATES, RESERVATIONS, & RESTRICTIONS

Deposit: Credit card
Credit Cards: All major
Check-In/Out: 1 p.m./noon
Pets: Not allowed
Elevator: Yes
Children: Yes

Disabled-friendly: Limited
39 Dorset Square, Marylebone, NW1
(0171) 723-7874
fax (0171) 724-3328
dorset@firmdale.com
www.firmdale.com

DUKES HOTEL   £217–£365

Overall: ★★★★½	Room Quality: 94	Value: B	Zone 9

Behind a charming courtyard, in one of the most appealing areas of central London is the extremely deluxe Dukes Hotel. Outside this Edwardian building remain gas lamps lit by hand every night. Inside, you'll find a sumptuous hotel with penthouses that promises the highest standards in service and accommodation. It's expensive and caters to the kind of clientele who likes its cognac to be 100 years old and doesn't flinch at outrageous prices for it. It's an intimate, clubby kind of place, but not stuffy or intimidating. The location is great: right by St. James's Park and Piccadilly; you couldn't ask for a more central yet quiet spot to enjoy London. And if you're feeling particularly flush, check out Penthouse One, with the views of all the glory that is London. Go have tea or drinks here even if you can't afford to stay.

SETTINGS & FACILITIES

Location: St. James
Nearest Tube Station: Green Park
Quietness Rating: A
Dining: Private dining room can be booked

Amenities: Bar with exceptional cognacs and wines; health club with massage and personal trainer available
Services: Concierge, butler, valet, secretarial services, 16-hour room service

ACCOMMODATIONS

Rooms: 64
All Rooms: Telephone, satellite TV, air conditioning, private bar, writing desks
Some Rooms: Oversize (7'x7') "Emperor" bed; sitting rooms; views of Big Ben, Westminster Abbey, parks, and Parliament; exceptionally large space (penthouse is 700 square feet)
Bed & Bath: Magnificent marble bathrooms with bathrobes. Beds that you'd be proud to call your own

Favorites: The penthouses are more like flats, absolutely huge and unimaginably luxurious. But even the standard doubles and the deluxe singles are very big for London (190 and 140 square feet, respectively). You can't go too wrong in any of the rooms here.
Comfort & Decor: Highest standards of comfort, and completely pleasing decor—not overdone or too much, just serene and elegant

RATES, RESERVATIONS, & RESTRICTIONS

Deposit: Credit card
Credit Cards: All major
Check-In/Out: 2 p.m./ noon
Pets: Not allowed
Elevator: Yes
Children: No children under age five
Disabled-friendly: Limited

35 St. James Place, SW1
In U.S. (800) 381-4702;
(0171) 491-4840
fax (0171) 493-1264
dukeshotel@compuserve.com
www.dukeshotel.co.uk

DURRANTS	£87.50–£250

Overall: ★★★★	Room Quality: 81	Value: A	Zone 14

A hotel that has been run by the same family since 1921, Durrants has a lot going for it, not least of all its proximity to the Wallace Collection and Regent's Park. But mainly, it's a hotel that gives very good value for money. The prices quoted are inclusive of VAT, and the cost of £130 for a double room is quite good. The rooms are more spacious than comparably priced places, and they certainly are more lovely. The decor is made up of all genuine antique pieces, mixed with clean and bright soft furnishings—the rooms have a very homey but sophisticated feel to them. The atmosphere in the hotel is that of a leather-chaired gentleman's club with oil paintings and gas fires. There's a tiny room called The Pump Room, into which women used to not be allowed, which gave license for the hotel to feature paintings of nudes on its walls. Breakfast (an expensive breakfast) is served by waiters in a very charming breakfast room, and the restaurant on the other side of the lobby is of a good quality. It's a great location for shopping on Oxford and Bond streets, going to Regent's or Hyde Park, and running in and out of the free Wallace Collection any time of the day.

SETTINGS & FACILITIES

Location: Marylebone
Nearest Tube Station: Bond Street
Quietness Rating: A
Dining: The restaurant has the best booths in the world, and decent food besides

Amenities: Pump Room, lounges with fireplaces, bar downstairs
Services: Concierge, 24-hour room service, bellhop, laundry, airport transfer, baby-sitting

ACCOMMODATIONS

Rooms: 92
All Rooms: Telephone, TV, hair dryer, trouser press, writing desks
Some Rooms: Minibars, sitting chairs
Bed & Bath: New mattresses in all rooms, newly remodeled bathrooms that are nice and relatively spacious
Favorites: Suite number 305 is a two-room pleasure: The sitting room has lots of conversation areas and is beautifully decorated with Staffordshire dogs and old portraits
Comfort & Decor: All top-notch, the antiques warm up the unostentatious cleanliness of the hotel decor. There's an effortlessness that is very appealing, and the comfort is part of this.

RATES, RESERVATIONS, & RESTRICTIONS

Deposit: Credit card, noon day before arrival hour cancellation policy
Credit Cards: All major, except DC
Check-In/Out: 2 p.m./noon
Pets: Not Allowed
Elevator: Two
Children: Yes; baby-sitting and cribs can be arranged

Disabled-friendly: One room with wheelchair access and porters to help; call ahead
George Street, W1
(0171) 935-8131
fax (0171) 487-3510

THE EDWARD LEAR HOTEL			**£39.50–£105**
Overall: ★★★½	Room Quality: 75	Value: A	Zone 14

The Edward Lear Hotel is a fine and simple place, and the price is right. It offers many more amenities than comparative hotels, such as telephone and satellite TV, and the owners throw down the challenge that if you can find a cheaper hotel that offers the same facilities, they will refund you double the difference. It's clean, well run, and provides a good breakfast in its price. Only 100 yards from Oxford Street and within a short walk of Hyde Park, the Edward Lear Hotel is popular among budget travelers. Once lived in by its namesake, the famous Victorian artist and poet, the decoration includes some of his drawings and limericks, which are cheerful and charming. The exterior has greenery spilling from every window, which gives it just one more nice homey touch.

SETTINGS & FACILITIES

Location: Marble Arch
Nearest Tube Station: Marble Arch
Quietness Rating: B in back, C in front

Dining: Breakfast room
Amenities: Full English breakfast, two lounges
Services: Breakfast

ACCOMMODATIONS

Rooms: 30
All Rooms: Telephone, satellite TV, radio, tea and coffee
Some Rooms: Shower/toilet
Bed & Bath: Rooms without toilets and showers ensuite do have them nearby and they are clean; beds are satisfactory

Favorites: Rooms in back, triples with shower/toilet
Comfort & Decor: Plain, cheerful, clean, and decorated with Edward Lear's marvelous drawings and non-sense poems and limericks. Smallish rooms.

RATES, RESERVATIONS, & RESTRICTIONS

Deposit: VISA, MC; 24-hour cancellation policy
Credit Cards: VISA, MC
Check-In/Out: 1 p.m./11 a.m.
Pets: Not allowed
Elevator: No
Children: Yes

Disabled-friendly: No
28/30 Seymour St., W1
(0171) 402-5401
fax (0171) 706-3766
edwardlear@aol.com
www.edlear.com

11 CADOGAN GARDENS			£58–£288
Overall: ★★★★½	Room Quality: 83	Value: B	Zone 11

This is a perfectly delightful hotel tucked away behind Sloane Street in the expanses of red-bricked Victorian townhouses. It was built in the 1860s, has been a hotel for 40 years, and has a certain quiet, non-hotel charm. It has held on to all of its oak-paneled walls, which are perfectly set off by the William Morris–style wallpaper. The antiques are of a very high standard, and the walls are filled with fascinating portraits of people from the past few centuries—worthies on every wall. The drawing room has a genuine clubby feeling to it, and one could get extremely comfortable sitting there before the fireplace with a book. Number Eleven is popular for its brand of discreet, effcient service. The hotel has a rare feature: a decent gym room in the lower ground floor, with a couple of Stairmasters, a treadmill, two bikes, and a whole lot of weight equipment. All the rooms are different—in size, in decor, in views. The overall impression of the hotel is so positive that whatever room you end up in will no doubt suit you just fine.

SETTINGS & FACILITIES

Location: Knightsbridge/Chelsea
Nearest Tube Station: Sloane
Square
Quietness Rating: A
Dining: A dining room is planned

Amenities: Drawing room, exercise
room, aromatherapy, massage
Services: Concierge, 24-hour room
service, bellhop, laundry

ACCOMMODATIONS

Rooms: 62
All Rooms: Telephone, satellite TV,
safes, hair dryers, excellent antiques
Some Rooms: Writing desk, views, air
conditioning
Bed & Bath: Bathrooms are marble
and provide Moulton Brown toiletries;
beds are comfortable, many single
rooms have double beds
Favorites: The ones in front with the

view of the garden are nice, but the
best is definitely the biggest suite in
the hotel: It's more like a stately flat,
with high ceilings, four-poster bed,
limited kitchenette, big windows,
and plenty of room for a family of
four.
Comfort & Decor: Exquisite decor
with a feeling of a graceful bygone age;
extremely comfortable

RATES, RESERVATIONS, & RESTRICTIONS

Deposit: Credit card
Credit Cards: All major
Check-In/Out: 1 p.m/noon
Pets: Not allowed
Elevator: Yes

Children: Yes
Disabled-friendly: Will accommodate
11 Cadogan Gardens
(0171) 730-7000
fax (0171) 730-5217

ELIZABETH HOTEL			£45–£115
Overall: ★★★	Room Quality: 63	Value: A	Zone 9

This is one of those inexpensive hotels that is in everybody's guidebook
because it's cheap, it's clean, and it's in a nice old building across from a beautiful garden square, to which guests have access. It is very busy, and you may
find yourself on hold quite a bit while making reservations. You will definitely want to book ahead for this inn. The rooms are not impressive, but
the common areas are quite nice, with really interesting prints all over the
place, and a very nice breakfast room. English breakfast is included. Rumor
has it that this may be closing down to be renovated into a four-star hotel in
the future, so be sure to call or email well in advance if you're counting on a
budget deal. Most of the rooms have a bathroom, but make sure you ask for
one when booking. The house is historic: The father of Lord Mountbatten,
last viceroy of India, lived here. Winston Churchill lived down the street.

SETTINGS & FACILITIES

Location: Victoria
Nearest Tube Station: Victoria
Quietness Rating: A in back, B in the front
Dining: Attractive breakfast room

Amenities: Breakfast room, public phone, car parking can be arranged nearby, access to gardens
Services: Breakfast included in price

ACCOMMODATIONS

Rooms: 38
All Rooms: Beds, wash basins
Some Rooms: Ensuite toilet and shower, TV, bay window and balcony
Bed & Bath: Spartan but clean
Favorites: The rooms on the front

with the bay windows and balcony with view of the garden square across the street
Comfort & Decor: Very nice common areas, enlivened by beautiful prints of historic figures and of England

RATES, RESERVATIONS, & RESTRICTIONS

Deposit: One night's rate for all reservations
Credit Cards: All major, except AMEX
Check-In/Out: 12:30 p.m./10:30 a.m.
Pets: Not allowed
Elevator: Yes

Children: Yes
Disabled-friendly: No
37 Eccleston Square, SW1
(0171) 828-6812
fax (0171) 828-6814
elizabeth@argyll-hotels.com

THE FIELDING HOTEL			£73–£120
Overall: ★★½	Room Quality: 65	Value: A	Zone 7

The Fielding is like a college dormitory: completely untilitarian and inoffensive. It even manages a small amount of charm; certainly the exterior is pretty, with its ivy-covered leaded windows, and the fact that it sits on a pedestrian court with nineteenth-century lamps in the shadow of the Royal Opera House is extremely attractive. It's all cheap pine and hard beds, but you don't share bathrooms, and everything is as clean and simple as you could ask for at the price. The superior double rooms in front are a bit nicer than the double suite, which actually costs more. The Fielding is around the corner from Covent Garden, and is within walking distance of the City, the British Museum, the Thames, and Piccadilly. It's a good location at a very low price.

SETTINGS & FACILITIES

Location: Covent Garden
Nearest Tube Station: Covent Garden
Quietness Rating: A

Dining: Breakfast room
Amenities: Breakfast at a very low price, honor bar
Services: Helpful reception desk

ACCOMMODATIONS

Rooms: 24
All Rooms: Telephone, five-channel TV with remote control, toilet
Some Rooms: Sitting area, writing desk
Bed & Bath: Hard beds, clean bathrooms with showers only

Favorites: Superior doubles in the front of the building have the most space and light
Comfort & Decor: Somewhere between utilitarian and spartan, with an unfortunate shade of orange paint in the halls and stairways

RATES, RESERVATIONS, & RESTRICTIONS

Deposit: One night's rate, 72-hour cancellation policy
Credit Cards: All major
Check-In/Out: noon/11:30 a.m.
Pets: Not allowed
Elevator: No

Children: No children under age 12
Disabled-friendly: No
4 Broad Court at Bow Street, WC2
(0171) 836-8305
fax (0171) 497-0064

FIVE SUMNER PLACE HOTEL			£88–£147
Overall: ★★★	Room Quality: 73	Value: A	Zone 11

Five Sumner Place has those most formidable of qualities: good value for money and good location. It is on the small side, as one would expect from a Victorian town house, but it makes much of its size, and the prices are good for the neighborhood. It was twice awarded the British Tourist Association Best Small Hotel prize and would probably have won it more often except they stopped giving out these awards. It is modest but comfortable and extremely clean and well kept. A couple of good rooms at the front have a scenic Mary Poppins–type view of a white row of town houses. Breakfast is served in the conservatory, which doubles as a sitting area at other times. The owners made a conscious decision to forego cable television, the thinking being that as the place is so intimate, it wouldn't do to have some jet-lagged wide-eyed traveler staying up till 3 a.m. watching CNN or MTV at high volumes. (It also assumes that as one is in London, one ought to be riding the tube, not staring at one.) There are a lot of repeat customers, so book well ahead. You may get a 10% discount during January and February.

SETTINGS & FACILITIES

Location: South Kensington
Nearest Tube Station: South
Kensington
Quietness Rating: A
Dining: Breakfast; tons of restaurants
and a 24-hour grocery nearby

Amenities: Daily newspapers,
magazines, conservatory
Services: Concierge services, laundry,
bellhop, tea, and coffee

ACCOMMODATIONS

Rooms: 13
All Rooms: Telephone, television, radio
Some Rooms: Refrigerator
Bed & Bath: Very good bed and
showers, some baths
Favorites: Numbers 4 and 6 have
balconies. Number 5 is a surprisingly
spacious-feeling single

Comfort & Decor: It's not luxury,
but it's not spartan either; the decor is,
in some rooms, very comely, and in all
rooms, clean and fresh. Some of the
original moldings from 1848 have been
beautifully preserved.

RATES, RESERVATIONS, & RESTRICTIONS

Deposit: Credit card; 14-day cancella-
tion policy
Credit Cards: All major, except DC
Check-In/Out: 11 a.m./11 a.m.
Pets: Not allowed
Elevator: Yes
Children: No children under age six
Disabled-friendly: Two ground-floor
rooms; no wheelchair access

5 Sumner Place, South Kensington,
SW7
(0171) 584-7586
fax (0171) 823-9962
no.5@dial.pipex.com
ds.dial.pipex.com/no.5

FLEMINGS	£188–£240

Overall: ★★★½	Room Quality: 78	Value: B	Zone 8

Flemings is seven old houses strung together in the way that so many London hotels are made, with the result that the rooms are of all different shapes
and sizes, mostly of the smaller variety. It's a friendly place, with good service and a very homey atmosphere. The junior suites are quite lovely, as are
the common sitting areas. The decoration is an interesting pastiche of periods, a kind of art deco meets Victorian, which is more attractive than it
sounds. The hotel has a good restaurant and a bar downstairs, and the rooms
are equipped with all the comforts and amenities you could want (except
for a minibar).

SETTINGS & FACILITIES

Location: Mayfair
Nearest Tube Station: Green Park
Quietness Rating: A in back, B in front (double-glazed windows)
Dining: Flemings Restaurant serves European food with a good wine selection; the Claridge Bar is downstairs, and tea is served in the lounges

Amenities: Restaurant, bar, modem connections for British and American plugs, bathrobes, apartments available as well as rooms
Services: Concierge, 24-hour room service, bellhop, laundry

ACCOMMODATIONS

Rooms: 121
All Rooms: Telephone, satellite TV, air conditioning, hair dryer, trouser press, tea and coffee, in-house movies, writing desk
Some Rooms: Four-poster bed
Bed & Bath: Bathrooms are made of marble and are nicely appointed; beds are on the small side—ask for a twin put together for a king, doubles are

only good for one or two very thin and short people.
Favorites: The junior suites
Comfort & Decor: Victorian paneled wood, art deco cast-iron sculptures, nice art on the wall, great smell in the hotel. Small rooms, but very comfortable, and they aim to please.

RATES, RESERVATIONS, & RESTRICTIONS

Deposit: Credit card, 4 p.m. day of arrival cancellation policy
Credit Cards: All major
Check-In/Out: 2 p.m./noon
Pets: Not allowed
Elevator: Yes
Children: Yes

Disabled-friendly: Limited, but possible
10 Half Moon St., W1
(0171) 493-2088
fax (0171) 499-1817
reservations@flemingsmayfair.co.uk

THE FRANKLIN HOTEL			£176–£350

Overall: ★★★★	Room Quality: 79	Value: B–	Zone 10

The Franklin Hotel is a small, elegant hotel situated on (and with access to) Egerton Gardens, which is a beautiful expanse of greenery wild with bright blooms in the spring. Its almost sylvan peace is uncompromised by the fact that the bustling Brompton Road lies mere steps away. The magnificent Catholic Oratory church is a neighbor, and you should get a White-Card museum pass so you can visit the nearby Victoria and Albert a few times a day. The atmosphere is serene, with antique furniture and art beautifully decorating the sitting rooms. The two sitting rooms look onto the garden, and a fire is kept blazing while you read the complimentary newspapers. It has a clean Georgian feel to it, and though the rooms may be on the small side, they are perfectly appointed.

SETTINGS & FACILITIES

Location: Border of Knightsbridge and South Kensington
Nearest Tube Station: South Kensington
Quietness Rating: A in garden facing rooms, B in front
Dining: Breakfast only

Amenities: Honor bar in separate leather-chaired room, access to gardens, breakfast in breakfast room or bedroom, nonsmoking rooms
Services: Concierge, 24-hour room service, butler, valet

ACCOMMODATIONS

Rooms: 50
All Rooms: Direct-dial phones, modem lines, optional fax, cable TV, minibar, hair dryers, clothes press, heated towel racks
Some Rooms: Garden view and entrance, four-posters, sitting areas, two TVs, bay windows
Bed & Bath: Good beds; all baths are marble and include power-showers

Favorites: There are two rooms that are split-level with lots of room, number 24 and number 26. Number 1 has the entrance to the gardens and a four-poster. Number 5 has a long view of the gardens; number 19 is just about two rooms, with a wall dividing the bedroom and the sitting room.
Comfort & Decor: Excellent decor, very pleasing to the eye; very comfortable

RATES, RESERVATIONS, & RESTRICTIONS

Deposit: Credit card; 48-hour cancellation policy
Credit Cards: All major
Check-In/Out: Whenever possible/noon
Pets: Not allowed
Elevator: Yes
Children: Yes
Disabled-friendly: Steps in front, but help can be arranged

28 Egerton Gardens, Knightsbridge, SW3
In U.S. (800) 473-9487;
(0171) 584-5533
fax in U.S. (800) 473-9489;
(0171) 584-5449
booking@thefranklin.force9.co.uk
www.hotelmk.com/uk/franklin/
 franklin.html

THE GAINSBOROUGH   £76–£200

Overall: ★★★½	Room Quality: 73	Value: B+	Zone 11

This is very similar to its sister hotel across the street, The Gallery, except that it's slightly less expensive, which makes for a very good value. There are no large sitting rooms, but the hotel is extremely serviceable and well decorated. It has been redone recently, and the smallish rooms are comfortable and tasteful. You can feel quite at home here without spending all your money on lodgings—not an easy feat in London. The staff is helpful and friendly. There is a hearty breakfast included in the price, set out each day in the bright room off the lobby that becomes a tea room/bar in the afternoon. Walk out of the hotel and you'll see the magnificent Natural History Museum—one of three museums on your doorstep. Very good location.

SETTINGS & FACILITIES

Location: South Kensington
Nearest Tube Station: South Kensington
Quietness Rating: A in back, C in front and lower floors
Dining: Breakfast room and snack/sandwich room service
Amenities: Breakfast room and bar, fax in lobby, discount at two fitness clubs nearby
Services: Concierge, room service, laundry, breakfast, bellhop

ACCOMMODATIONS

Rooms: 49
All Rooms: Telephone, cable TV, tea and coffee, safe, hair dryer, trouser press
Some Rooms: French windows, balcony, bigger TVs, air conditioning
Bed & Bath: Beds are a bit hard. Singles all have shower stalls in the bathrooms, and doubles have shower/tub combinations. Very nicely decorated bathrooms.
Favorites: Number 112 has a balcony and French windows and seems a little bigger than the others
Comfort & Decor: Rooms are small, but everything is clean and nicely presented. The decor is subdued, individual in each room, but homey

RATES, RESERVATIONS, & RESTRICTIONS

Deposit: Credit card; 24-hour cancellation policy
Credit Cards: All major
Check-In/Out: 1 p.m./noon
Pets: Not allowed
Elevator: Yes
Children: Yes
Disabled-friendly: Wheelchair access planned, call ahead

7–11 Queensberry Place, SW7
In U.S. (800) 270-9206;
(0171) 957-0000
fax (0171) 957-0001
gainsborough@eeh.co.uk
www.eeh.co.uk

THE GALLERY £135–£235

Overall: ★★★½	Room Quality: 77	Value: B	Zone 11

This is a very good, moderately priced hotel in the heart of South Kensington, with the imposing Natural History Museum at the end of the street, the tube a two-minute walk away, and Kensington Gardens/Hyde Park a five-minute walk away. The rooms are not big, except for the totally fabulous suite, number 502 (a mere £235), which has a private garden terrace! There is a very good breakfast room (breakfast is included), with a well-stocked buffet. Upstairs you'll find a pleasant sitting room with a bar and a chess board. Newly refurbished, the decor is attractive; everything shines and sparkles, especially the mahogany and marble bathrooms. They have no packages or deals available at present, as their prices are already relatively low.

SETTINGS & FACILITIES

Location: South Kensington
Nearest Tube Station: South Kensington
Quietness Rating: A in back, C in front
Dining: Breakfast room; room service of sandwiches and snacks

Amenities: Minibars, cable TV, clothing press, tea and coffee, safes, writing desk, fitness club nearby, music in bar on occasion, fax in lobby
Services: Concierge, 24-hour room service

ACCOMMODATIONS

Rooms: 36
All Rooms: Cable TV, hair dryer, safes
Some Rooms: Air conditioning, fax, couches, Jacuzzi
Bed & Bath: Excellent on both counts. Baths in doubles and suites, shower stalls in singles.
Favorites: Number 502, a penthouse suite with a huge bed, a private garden

terrace, a dining table, two couches, and three phone lines. Beautiful and perfect for a business person.
Comfort & Decor: Care has been taken to ensure all comforts, and the decor is individual and restful, a bit on the plain side, but clean and pleasing to the eye

RATES, RESERVATIONS, & RESTRICTIONS

Deposit: Credit card; 24-hour cancellation policy
Credit Cards: All major
Check-In/Out: 1 p.m./noon
Pets: Not allowed
Elevator: Yes
Children: Yes

Disabled-friendly: No wheelchair access
8–10 Queensberry Place, SW7
In U.S. (800) 270-9206;
(0171) 915-0000
fax (0171) 915-4400
gallery@eeh.co.uk
www.eeh.co.uk

THE GORE   £130–£287

Overall: ★★★★★	Room Quality: 100	Value: A	Zone 11

There are not enough superlatives in the thesaurus to cover the wonder of The Gore—it is everything one would ever want in a London hotel and more. Even its brochure is delightful. The Gore was the brainstorm of two antiques dealers who had started their hotel career with the wonderful Hazlitt's in Soho. They bought this fine old mansion on Queen's Gate, steps from Kensington Garden, in which to hang 4,500 prints and paintings and house the most amazing antiques ever seen in one place outside of the Victoria and Albert Museum. They even have their own style Bed of Ware in the Tudor Room: a sixteenth-century bed that could easily find a home in a museum, in a room that could be part of a National Trust property. Even the single rooms are extraordinary, with beds from the nineteenth-century, each one distinct and delightful, and the paintings and drawings on the walls will arouse covetousness in the most casual of art lovers. The bathrooms alone are to die for. There is a restaurant, Bistrot 190, that serves excellent food and good breakfasts at very reasonable prices and has a marvelous atmosphere, very bright and cheerful. There is also a more formal and serious gastronomic experience awaiting the guest in the lower ground floor of The Gore. London hotels don't come quirkier, more brilliantly decorated, or more lovingly maintained than this one—unless it's one of The Gore's sister hotels—Hazlitt's in Soho and The Rookery in the City. The Gore's location is superb, right on the park, minutes from South Kensington, the Albert Hall, and Kensington High Street, not to mention walking distance to Portobello Road and Kensington Church Street if you find your appetite is hopelessly whetted for antiques shopping. A word of caution: The beds are genuine Victorian antiques, and some of the larger guests have a problem with the size. If you are extremely tall or particularly overweight, the beds may pose a problem to you. Talk to the concierge about your needs.

SETTINGS & FACILITIES

Location: South Kensington/ Kensington border
Nearest Tube Station: Gloucester Road
Quietness Rating: A in back and top floors, B in lower front floors
Dining: Two restaurants, Bistrot 190 and Restaurant 190. The first is informal but with an excellent menu, and the second is more formal and expensive. Both are excellent restaurants.
Amenities: Use of two nearby fitness centers
Services: Concierge, 24-hour room service, bellhops, laundry

ACCOMMODATIONS

Rooms: 48
All Rooms: Minibars, limited cable TV, antiques and art, genuine Victorian beds, fans, writing desks,
Some Rooms: Stained-glass windows, French doors and balconies, sitting areas, fireplace
Bed & Bath: The beds may be too small for some people used to king-size modern hotel beds. Try the twin bedded rooms if you can't fit into a double with your partner. The bathrooms are amazing: Many of them have the old-fashioned loo chair around the toilet—a genuine "throne." In one of the suites, there is a shower head as big as a dinner plate.
Favorites: The Tudor is astonishing: a Victorian re-creation of an Elizabethan gallery, complete with huge stone fireplace (using gas) and stained glass of the queen herself. Carved lintels of heads and gargoyles are not for the faint of heart. The bed is a treasure from the sixteenth century. Miss Ada's room (number 207) has a lovely Victorian theme and the aforementioned enormous shower head. It's masculine and mahogany, with a very good double bed and a bust of Queen Victoria at the foot of it. You can sleep in an antique rococo bed once owned by Judy Garland in the Venus Room, a very feminine and well-named room. The Dame Nelly suite is wonderful, and as for singles, number 108 has an ornate bed and airy atmosphere.
Comfort & Decor: There is a sense of perfect comfort throughout the hotel, and the decor is endlessly fascinating, although a radical minimalist may run screaming from its portals. Like the Victorian decorating scheme it has so perfectly re-created, there is something everywhere to look at and love.

RATES, RESERVATIONS, & RESTRICTIONS

Deposit: Credit card, 48-hour cancellation policy
Credit Cards: All major
Check-In/Out: 1 p.m./11:30 a.m.
Pets: Not allowed, exceptions made for guide dogs and perhaps well-behaved lap dogs
Elevator: Yes
Children: Yes
Disabled-friendly: Wheelchair access is planned
189 Queen's Gate, SW7
(0171) 584-6601
fax (0171) 589-8127
reservations@gorehotel.co.uk

GORING HOTEL   £188–£340

Overall: ★★★★★	Room Quality: 90	Value: B	Zone 9

The Goring is a lovely hotel, pure elegance and comfort a few steps from Victoria Station and within easy reach of the wonders of Westminster Abbey and Buckingham Palace. It has the great benefit on being on a tiny street where most of the traffic belongs to the hotel; in the back there's a lawn that is a real oasis of peace, even though you can only look at it. Sometimes that's enough, especially when St. James's Park is so nearby. The hotel is justifiably proud of having remained in the same family since 1911, and it does indeed call to mind a fine country club of the early 1900s. It doesn't have any Victorian frippery, just a cool Edwardian elegance and comfort, from the bright yellow and marble of the beautiful lobby to the lounge tables that look like they've seen quite a few bridge games in their day. There's a finely carved fireplace and a wall of windows through which you can view the garden, and drinks and light food are served there all day. The dining room is of a high quality, as are the rooms themselves. Strangely, but appealingly, there are adorable stuffed sheep in the rooms, which also have lovely furniture and excellent bathrooms outfitted with Penhaligon's toiletries. The Goring plays to a lot of repeat customers—generations of them—and it's easy to see why. Special weekend rates are available.

SETTINGS & FACILITIES

Location: Victoria
Nearest Tube Station: Victoria
Quietness Rating: A/B (double-glazed windows)
Dining: Beautiful dining room, plus Garden Bar and drawing room for teas and lights meals
Amenities: Dining room, a very attractive and capacious drawing room and bar, a splendid expanse of lawn out back to admire, complimentary membership in nearby health club
Services: Concierge, 24-hour room service, bellhop, laundry

ACCOMMODATIONS

Rooms: 75
All Rooms: Individual temperature control (including air conditioning), telephone, cable TV, hair dryer, writing desk
Some Rooms: Balcony overlooking garden, fax
Bed & Bath: Beautiful wood and marble bathrooms, and good-sized beds in all the rooms
Favorites: There are a few rooms with

balconies that overlook the garden. These are fantastic, and quite a rarity in London (or any big city for that matter).
Comfort & Decor: The decor is extremely well done, a kind of Georgian elegance and cheerfulness that is quite pleasing. All the common areas and the individual rooms are bright and warmly welcoming.

RATES, RESERVATIONS, & RESTRICTIONS

Deposit: Credit card
Credit Cards: All major
Check-In/Out: Noon/noon
Pets: Dogs and birds not allowed (since 1911, when apparently, judging from the posted restriction, many people traveled with birds in hand)
Elevator: Yes
Children: Yes

Disabled-friendly: Yes
Beeston Place, SW1
(0171) 396-9000
fax (0171) 834-4393
reception@goringhotel.co.uk
www.goringhotel.co.uk (An excellent Web site, be sure to visit it)

THE HAMPSHIRE EDWARDIAN RADISSON			£330–£430
Overall: ★★★★½	Room Quality: 83	Value: D	Zone 7

Housed in a magnificent building right on Leicester Square behind the half-price ticket booth, The Hampshire is a five-star hotel run by the Radisson Group. It has all the amenities you'd expect from a five-star inn, though, as with so many of London's hotels, not quite as much space as you would want in some of the standard rooms. The rooms are well appointed, and there's a kind of Oriental theme in the decor—check out the grandfather clock in the lobby. The lobby is gorgeous, with walnut paneling everywhere, offering a quiet sitting place far from the madding crowds of Leicester Square, yet with them still in view. There's a bar attached, a restaurant, and Oscar's Wine Bar with seating right on the square from which you can watch the milling crowds. There's a fitness room with two treadmills, a bike, and a stepper. The hotel has a large American clientele and is responding to their customers' requests. The four-poster bedrooms are beautiful, and all the junior suites are a very good size. Telephones are everywhere, and you'll find plenty of closet space. Some of the rooms have views over Trafalgar Square and Leicester Square. Ask about the theater packages and other Radisson-related deals.

SETTINGS & FACILITIES

Location: Leicester Square
Nearest Tube Station: Leicester Square
Quietness Rating: Triple-glazing in all the windows on the Leicester Square side makes those desirable rooms quiet, but beware of the Carnival Fair that comes to the square occasionally —you may want to be in the back.

Dining: Apex Bar and Restaurant, and Oscar's Wine Bar, good food, ambience
Amenities: Room safes, small fitness room, bathrobes, telephones in bathrooms, fully air conditioned
Services: Concierge, 24-hour room service, bellhop, laundry, business support

ACCOMMODATIONS

Rooms: 124
All Rooms: Minibar, telephones with modem lines, satellite TV, in-house movies, hair dryer, bathrobe, tea and coffee, trouser press, writing desk
Some Rooms: Four-posters, views, floor-to-ceiling windows
Bed & Bath: High quality

Favorites: Number 705 is a four-poster suite with a view over Trafalgar. Any of the junior suites is great.
Comfort & Decor: Good, five-star hotel style comforts, and interesting decor, mixing eighteenth-century reproductions with Oriental artwork. Nice, soft furnishings.

RATES, RESERVATIONS, & RESTRICTIONS

Deposit: Credit card, 24-hour cancellation policy
Credit Cards: All major
Check-In/Out: 2 p.m./11 a.m.
Pets: Not allowed
Elevator: Yes
Children: Yes

Disabled-friendly: Yes
Leicester Square, WC2
In U.S., (800) 333-3333;
(0171) 839-9399
fax (0171) 930-8122
www.radissonedwardian.com

HAZLITT'S HOTEL   £152–£293

Overall: ★★★½	Room Quality: 96	Value: B	Zone 7

Hazlitt's Hotel was the first triumph for the creators of The Gore and The Rookery. Hazlitt's, which happens to be author Bill Bryson's favorite home away from home, is a perfect evocation of another time, with handsome antiques and decor in the Georgian style. For those allergic to Victoriana, Hazlitt's is the perfect alternative to The Gore, and it is in the heart of Soho, where sleepy London tends to stay awake. It is not fancy or awe-inspiring like The Gore or The Rookery: It is simple, without an elevator and only a tiny sitting room for communal amenities. It's more like staying at a particularly well-appointed rooming house from days gone by. The house was built in 1718, and the floors sag and droop as you would, too, if you'd been trod on for close to 300 years. The rooms themselves are luxuriously comfortable, with beautiful antique bedsteads and cotton sheets. Busts sculpted by one of the owner's relatives grace many of the bathrooms and rooms, and genuine antique prints adorn the walls—but not too much: The period verisimilitude is strict, and the house of a writer like William Hazlitt in that period would not have been overdone. And Hazlitt's does draw the writers like flies to honey. In the sitting room is a bookcase with signed copies of books written by guests, and it's an impressive collection: Seamus Heaney, Ted Hughes, Vikram Seth, Jostein Gaardner, Susan Sontag, Dava Sobel, and scores of others. Of course, the brilliant Bill Bryson's books are there; in his *Notes from a Small Island,* he sent the phones ringing off the hook with his mention of his favorite hotel in London. Hazlitt's attracts a loyalty —or eccentricity—hardly ever met with: One of the regulars paid for double-glazing to be put on the windows of his favorite room. This is not to say that you will like Hazlitt's: it's for a particular type of person, one who likes the noise and action of the present-day West End, as much as the atmosphere of long-ago Soho. Book way, way in advance.

SETTINGS & FACILITIES

Location: Soho
Nearest Tube Station: Tottenham Court
Quietness Rating: C–D in front during weekend nights, A–B in back at all times

Dining: No
Amenities: Writing desks and modems, cotton sheets, continental breakfast at extra charge
Services: Receptionist, bellhop, laundry, 24-hour room service

ACCOMMODATIONS

Rooms: 23
All Rooms: Telephone, satellite TV, bathtubs, antiques, writing desks
Some Rooms: Ornamental fireplace, four-posters, high ceilings
Bed & Bath: Superb on both counts. Victorian tubs; one bathroom has a dinner-plate–size Victorian shower head. Beds are comfortable, big and cotton-sheeted.
Favorites: The suite on the ground

floor, the double-glazed Jonathan Swift room, and a small room in the back. Really, there are no rooms here that aren't charming and inviting; the high ceilings are found on the first and second floors.
Comfort & Decor: Top-notch comfort (unless you require an elevator), and the decor is superb, very pleasing to the eye and soul

RATES, RESERVATIONS, & RESTRICTIONS

Deposit: Credit card, 48-hour cancellation policy
Credit Cards: All major
Check-In/Out: 2 p.m./noon
Pets: Not allowed
Elevator: No

Children: Yes
Disabled-friendly: No
6 Frith St., Soho Square, W1
(0171) 434-1771
fax (0171) 439-1524
reservations@Hazlitts.co.uk

HILLGATE HOTEL			£78–£104
Overall: ★★★	Room Quality: 62	Value: A	Zone 13

Here's a good budget hotel within a short walk of Portobello Road and Kensington Church Street—perfect for antiques hunters who want to spend all their money on treasures instead of hotels. It's also a short walk to Kensington Gardens and Hyde Park, and the tube is very near. It is comprised of three buildings put together, and it is on a very nice street off the busy Notting Hill Gate—apparently there's not too much noise from it. It's undistinguished aesthetically, but clean and serviceable, with a couple of nice touches, like the huge crystal chandelier. There are two video games and a chocolate vending machine in the honesty bar/lounge, which, along with the breakfast room, has piped-in pop music. Continental breakfast is included in the price, and the breakfast room is a good size and pleasant enough. Good value for money here.

SETTINGS & FACILITIES

Location: Notting Hill Gate
Nearest Tube Station: Notting Hill Gate
Quietness Rating: A in back, B in front

Dining: Breakfast room, honor bar
Amenities: Breakfast included, satellite television in bar, video games
Services: Reception acts as concierge, laundry

ACCOMMODATIONS

Rooms: 66
All Rooms: Ensuite shower/tub and toilet, telephone, five-channel TV, hair dryer
Bed & Bath: Utilitarian, clean, and serviceable
Favorites: Take the double or twin room if you're alone, take the twin if you're with a spouse (double beds are small)
Comfort & Decor: Serviceable comfort, plain and forgettable decor. Like a college dorm.

RATES, RESERVATIONS, & RESTRICTIONS

Deposit: Credit card, 48-hour cancellation policy. A two-night minimum stay is required on weekends.
Credit Cards: All major
Check-In/Out: 1 p.m./10:30 a.m.
Pets: Not Allowed
Elevator: Two
Children: Yes
Disabled-friendly: Steps outside, small lifts
6–14 Pembridge Gardens, Kensington, W2
(0171) 221-3433
fax (0171) 229-4808
hillgate@lth-hotels.com
www.accomodata.co.uk.htm

HILTON MEWS	£89–£450

Overall: ★★★★	Room Quality: 86	Value: C	Zone 8

This is not a moderately priced hotel exactly, but it is less than the big Hilton and it's right around the back from it. The neighborhood is extremely posh, and the hotel itself is very attractive and beautifully appointed. There are 72 rooms with all the amenities you could possibly want, and you are welcome to use all the facilities at the big Hilton: beauty salon, fitness center, treatment rooms, business support. And of course, Hyde Park and Piccadilly with all their various delights are nearby.

SETTINGS & FACILITIES

Location: Mayfair
Nearest Tube Station: Green Park
Quietness Rating: A
Dining: Small, 32-seat restaurant, and lounge for tea and drinks
Amenities: All the facilities at the big

Hilton (fitness, beauty, hair stylist, restaurants) are at your disposal
Services: Concierge, 24-hour room service, bellhop, laundry, rental computers and printers, business support

ACCOMMODATIONS

Rooms: 72
All Rooms: Two-line telephone, modem, voice mail, cable TV, in-house movies, air conditioning, trouser press, hair dryer, tea and coffee
Some Rooms: Mayfair Suite has lounge and private street entrance
Bed & Bath: Top-notch

Favorites: The more expensive doubles are quite nice
Comfort & Decor: Upscale hotel-style, with more than a touch of jolly olde England, and all the comforts of a Hilton

RATES, RESERVATIONS, & RESTRICTIONS

Deposit: Credit card, 4 p.m. day of arrival cancellation policy
Credit Cards: All major
Check-In/Out: 2 p.m./noon
Pets: Not allowed
Elevator: Yes
Children: Yes

Disabled-friendly: No, stairs in lobby
2 Stanhope Row, Park Lane, W1
In U.S. (800) 774-1500;
(0171) 493-7222
fax (0171) 629-9423
www.hilton.com

HOLIDAY INN MAYFAIR	£100–£250

Overall: ★★★½	Room Quality: 77	Value: C	Zone 8

In the United States, the name Holiday Inn has the connotation of a budget to moderate kind of a place, which is why I had to gasp when I saw a Holiday Inn rack rate of £250! But hang on, that's not what you'll end up paying if you are smart and join the Priority Club or take advantage of any of the many packages and deals available here. They don't even have a tariff card to give out because there are so many possible combinations of discounts and promos that you could end up paying a mere £100 a night. And that would be a very good deal, because the neighborhood is fabulous, the rooms have pretty much everything you want, and it's a hotel you would be proud to call home—for a few days, anyway. Okay, so it's not dripping with traditional charm, but it's attractive, well decorated with nice pictures and good furniture, very comfortable, and has everything that the other hotels have, often more. If you want to stay in beautiful Mayfair, gave them a call or email them to see if you can get a good rate.

SETTINGS & FACILITIES

Location: Mayfair
Nearest Tube Station: Green Park
Quietness Rating: A in back,
B in front (double-glazed windows)
Dining: Nightingale's Restaurant
serves international cuisine

Amenities: Bar, very small fitness
room
Services: Concierge, 24-hour room
service, bellhop, laundry

ACCOMMODATIONS

Rooms: 184
All Rooms: Telephone, modem lines
and Internet access, cable TV, minibar,
air conditioning, hair dryer, trouser
press, tea and coffee, in-house movies,
writing desk
Some Rooms: Suites have two
rooms, two bathrooms, two TVs

Bed & Bath: Bathrooms are fine; beds
are comfortable
Favorites: The suites and executive
rooms, which have the most space
Comfort & Decor: Hotel-style, but
not at all drab: Major refurbishment has
been on-going and plans are that it will
continue. This is a very good Holiday Inn.

RATES, RESERVATIONS, & RESTRICTIONS

Deposit: Credit card, 6 p.m. day of
arrival cancellation policy
Credit Cards: All major
Check-In/Out: 2 p.m./1 p.m.
Pets: Not allowed
Elevator: Yes
Children: Yes

Disabled-friendly: Two disabled
rooms available
3 Berkeley St. W1
(0171) 493-8282
fax (0171) 629-2827
HI-PriorityClubEMEA@hiw.com

HOTEL NUMBER SIXTEEN   £85–£196

Overall: ★★★★	Room Quality: 83	Value: A	Zone 11

Number Sixteen is an exceptional place, and everybody knows it, so you'd better look sharp if you want to book a room. It's modestly displayed—with no waving banners or lights outside, it's discretion itself. Number Sixteen is more like a big bed-and-breakfast than a hotel; it has the feel of a warm home, thanks to the prettiness of the decor and the kindness of the staff. And the location is primo. Four Victorian townhouses were connected to make Number Sixteen, stringing together enough room in the back to create a sweet little garden with a fountain; there is a conservatory from which to enjoy the view in the winter. The lower ground-floor rooms look out to the garden, which manages to make the molelike feeling of being in the lower ground actually quite pleasant. The rooms are all decorated differently with an individual theme, and instead of numbers have names: Terrace, Olive, Berry, Studio, and so forth. They are all attractive, nothing grand or showy, just comfy English-style. The downstairs drawing rooms are quite fine, with a library and sitting room that feature an honor bar, as well as the aforementioned conservatory. Ask about deals; they sometimes have a winter discount.

SETTINGS & FACILITIES

Location: South Kensington
Nearest Tube Station: South Kensington
Quietness Rating: A/B
Dining: Breakfast; scores of restaurants nearby
Amenities: Breakfast is included in price; you choose what you want and where you want to eat it, or it will be brought to your room as a matter of course; access to health club nearby
Services: Concierge, laundry

ACCOMMODATIONS

Rooms: 42
All Rooms: Telephone, minibar, room safe, BBC TV, hair dryer
Some Rooms: Balconies, French doors
Bed & Bath: Beds are comfortable; some bathrooms have shower stalls only, all have bathrobe and basket of Moulton Brown toiletries

Favorites: Terrace, Fawn, and Berry
Comfort & Decor: The decor is very Edwardian-feeling, very English country home, not trendy or spiffy, but relaxing and charming. A very comfortable place to hang your hat. Singles are small.

RATES, RESERVATIONS, & RESTRICTIONS

Deposit: Credit card, 48-hour cancellation policy
Credit Cards: All major
Check-In/Out: 3 p.m./11 am
Pets: Not allowed
Elevator: Yes
Children: Yes

Disabled-friendly: Four ground-floor rooms, three stairs outside
16 Sumner Place, South Kensington, SW7
In U.S. (800) 592-5387;
(0171) 589-5232
fax (0171) 584-8615

HOTEL RUSSELL   £139–£204

Overall: ★★★½	Room Quality: 72	Value: B	Zone 2

This is a grand old edifice looking out on Russell Square, a stone's throw from the underground Piccadilly line, which, along with the A2 Heathrow Express that leaves from across the street, makes this hotel a good Heathrow airport connection. It's got a lot of space, unlike so many hotels in London, plus all the services one expects from a four-star hotel. The decor is a bit tired, but it's perfectly suitable plain hotel style. The hotel attracts a business crowd due to all the conference facilities, and so are used to demanding customers. As part of the Forte Group, it knows how to cater to the international traveler. The restaurants are good and quite convenient, and it's close to the West End, the City, and of course, the British Museum. It's a magnificent building to look at—one of the great Victorian hotel palaces.

SETTINGS & FACILITIES

Location: Bloomsbury
Nearest Tube Station: Russell Square
Quietness Rating: C in front (double-glazing), A in back
Dining: Fitzroy's Doll Bar-Restaurant serves European and British food, Virginia Woolf's Brasserie serves burgers, pastas, and so on. The King's Bar and Lounge has a club atmosphere (fireplace, red leather) and drinks

Amenities: Three eating and drinking places, full business support, executive floor with lounge and continental breakfast. Guest relations manager has database with guest history—your preferences and needs—to help with repeat visits.
Services: Concierge, 24-hour room service, bellhop, laundry, conference-ready

ACCOMMODATIONS

Rooms: 329
All Rooms: Telephone, cable TV, hair dryer, trouser press, tea and coffee
Some Rooms: Minibar, writing desks, bathrobes, balcony
Bed & Bath: Perfectly serviceable, some bathrooms are quite big
Favorites: Number 347 is a suite with a sitting room and French doors in both rooms looking out

onto Russell Square. Ask about the French window rooms.
Comfort & Decor: It's your basic hotel style, but in the old-fashioned way—huge hallways, high ceilings, and big rooms. No precious touches, just good hotel rooms. The common areas are appealing, with a beautiful Victorian lobby that has a lovely grand staircase.
Price: Ask about discounts and packages.

RATES, RESERVATIONS, & RESTRICTIONS

Deposit: Credit card, before 2 p.m. day of arrival cancellation policy
Credit Cards: All major
Check-In/Out: 2 p.m./noon
Pets: Not allowed
Elevator: Three
Children: Yes
Disabled-friendly: As a Grade II building, they can't alter structure for built-in ramps, but they can help a lot

Russell Square, WC1
(0171) 837-6470
fax (0171) 837-2857
hotelrussell@ukbusiness.com
www.forte-hotels.com

JURY'S			£155–£175
Overall: ★★★½	Room Quality: 77	Value: C	Zone 11

The best things about Jury's are the location and the lobby. The rooms run a fairly wide gamut from much too small and dull to rather grand, with French windows looking out on the white stucco town houses of Queen's Gate. This hotel provides all the services you want from a hotel, including an airport shuttle bus for a fee. Jury's has a nonsmoking floor, and a great reading room with a fireplace. All the restaurants, shops, and public transportation of South Kensington are at your doorstep, as are Hyde Park and the museums. This is a large enough corporation that it offers deals—call reservations to ask about them, and definitely get an upgrade—I saw a couple of so-called doubles that were very small.

SETTINGS & FACILITIES

Location: South Kensington
Nearest Tube Station: South Kensington
Quietness Rating: B
Dining: Copplestone's Restaurant; Kavanaugh's Irish Pub

Amenities: Elegant lobby and reading room for tea and drinks
Services: 24-hour room service, business services, same-day laundry

ACCOMMODATIONS

Rooms: 156
All Rooms: Satellite television, tea/coffee-making facilities, trouser press
Some Rooms: Minibars only in suites, modem only in suites

Bed & Bath: Clean if boring
Favorites: Executive suite looking out on Queensgate and Manson Place
Comfort & Decor: Comfortable, if small; decor is standard dull hotel chain–style

RATES, RESERVATIONS, & RESTRICTIONS

Deposit: Credit card, 24-hour cancellation policy
Credit Cards: All major
Check-In/Out: 2 p.m./11 a.m.
Pets: Not allowed
Elevator: Yes
Children: Yes

Disabled-friendly: Yes
109–113 Queen's Gate, South Kensington, SW7
(0171) 589-6300
fax (0171) 581-1492
ruth_vaughan@jurys.com

L'HOTEL 28	£170–£194

Overall: ★★★★	Room Quality: 84	Value: A	Zone 10

This is essentially a bed-and-breakfast owned by the neighboring Capitol Hotel, and it only has 12 rooms. Speak up early if you want to book here—it's very popular among the cognoscente. It's located 50 meters from Harrods and 250 from Hyde Park, with Sloane Street right down the way. The rooms are all quiet and simple, in a French country style that may come as a relief to those who find the English traditional too floral. Pine furniture, neutral colors, accented by elegant artwork and bibelots make it a restful aesthetic experience. The staff is friendly and helpful—reception will act as concierge and help out wherever needed. Best of all, there are three rooms and one suite that come with gas fireplaces—these are the rooms that need booking well ahead. The price, for the area and the quality, is extremely good. All the rooms are double, with no extra charge for the second person.

SETTINGS & FACILITIES

Location: Knightsbridge
Nearest Tube Station: Knightsbridge
Quietness Rating: A, double-glazing
throughout
Dining: Le Metro is a wine bar that
serves breakfast, lunch, and dinner. Very
cool modern style.

Amenities: Continental breakfast
included in price, can be served in
room; fax and iron on request
Services: Concierge, breakfast room
service only, laundry

ACCOMMODATIONS

Rooms: 12
All Rooms: Minibar, telephone, cable
TV, in-house movies, hair dryer, tea and
coffee, writing desk, ceiling fan
Some Rooms: Fireplace
Bed & Bath: 100% Egyptian cotton
Fretta sheets. Perfect bathrooms

Favorites: Number 302, a room with
a fireplace, and the suite
Comfort & Decor: Dedicated to
comfort and simplicity of decor. It's a
French country look, with knotty pine
furniture, neutral colors, and ceramics.
A good feeling pervades.

RATES, RESERVATIONS, & RESTRICTIONS

Deposit: Credit card, 72-hour cancel-
lation policy
Credit Cards: All major
Check-In/Out: 1 p.m./noon
Pets: Not allowed
Elevator: Yes
Children: Yes

Disabled-friendly: Limited: there is
one ground-floor room
28 Basil St., SW3
In U.S. (800) 926-3199;
(0171) 589-6286
fax (0171) 823-7826
Lhotel@capitalgrp.co.uk

LONDON MARRIOT HOTEL AT COUNTY HALL			£250–£329
Overall: ★★★★½	Room Quality: 85	Value: C	Zone 5

This hotel has the largest rooms of any Marriott in London, and it has all
the amenities you'd expect from the chain, but with one major difference:
it's located in the old County Hall building right on the Thames and has
spectacular, postcard-perfect views of Parliament, Big Ben, and the tower
of Westminster Abbey. You may feel a bit cut off from a sense of a neighborhood: Waterloo Station is in the rear, and across the bridge is Westminster, which tends to roll up the sidewalks at night and on weekends, but it
doesn't matter, as the South Bank has plenty to look at and the stroll along
the river path is wonderful. The hotel has a 25-meter pool (!) and an excel-

lent gym, which unfortunately you have to pay £25 to use, and beauty and health treatments are available. There are some delightful eating and lounging areas, which you should visit even if you don't stay here—the view is magnificent, especially at night. The Library has been preserved from when it was part of the County Hall and the books are all the original volumes. There are wood-paneled walls everywhere and all kinds of gorgeous architectural features in this historical, listed building. And the beds are huge. Ask for deals and promotions, as the price is steep.

SETTINGS & FACILITIES

Location: South Bank
Nearest Tube Station: Westminster or Waterloo
Quietness Rating: A
Dining: County Hall Restaurant has English cuisine and an oyster and seafood bar, plus great views of the Thames—be sure to make reservations; Library Lounge has tea and snacks; Leaders Cocktail Bar
Amenities: Restaurant, lounge, bar, views of Parliament and Big Ben, health club with pool, disabled rooms, valet parking at good rates for London
Services: Concierge, 24-hour room service, valet parking, bellhop, laundry

ACCOMMODATIONS

Rooms: 195
All Rooms: Telephones, voice mail, cable TV, air conditioning, minibar, queen-size beds, hair dryer, tea and coffee, trouser press, iron and ironing board, personal safes
Some Rooms: Separate sitting rooms, views on river
Bed & Bath: Excellent bathrooms, beds are queen- or king-size
Favorites: River-view superior rooms
Comfort & Decor: Comfort is high, decor is high-standard hotel type, with some unfortunate choices in fabrics

RATES, RESERVATIONS, & RESTRICTIONS

Deposit: Credit card, 4 p.m. day of arrival cancellation policy
Credit Cards: All major
Check-In/Out: 2:30 p.m./noon
Pets: Not allowed
Elevator: Yes
Children: Yes
Disabled-friendly: Six disabled rooms of a very high standard
County Hall, SE1
In U.S. (800) 228-9290;
(0171) 928-5200
fax (0171) 928-5300
www.marriotthotels.com

THE MILESTONE HOUSE   £205–£528

Overall: ★★★★½	Room Quality: 84	Value: C–	Zone 11

A five-star hotel at four-star prices, The Milestone is a relatively new purchase by an owner determined to offer the best in services to international travelers and business people. It is beautifully decorated, especially the common areas, and although all the rooms may not suit all tastes, they are all carefully and imaginatively put together, with good antiques and fine, soft furnishings. Comfort and convenience are of an unusually high standard here, and the location is wonderful for park lovers: directly across the street from Kensington Gardens. Some of the rooms have excellent views of the palace. There is a specially designed room for disabled guests. The hotel offers the very latest in business support systems, not to mention a snooker table that turns into a conference table. The lounge is a fine place to hang out, and there's a bar that has a leathery pub atmosphere.

SETTINGS & FACILITIES

Location: Kensington
Nearest Tube Station: High Street Kensington
Quietness Rating: A in back, B in front (double-glazing on all but corner room 102 with leaded windows protected by landmark status)

Dining: Chenistons Restaurant
Amenities: Sleeping sound machines on request, sitting room, bar, breakfast room, health club
Services: Concierge, 24-hour room service, business amenities

ACCOMMODATIONS

Rooms: 57
All Rooms: Telephone, voice mail, cable TV, air conditioning, minibars, modem stations, in-house movies, CD players, UK/US video players
Some Rooms: Video-conferencing cables, pop-up TVs, electronic blinds, Jacuzzi, fireplaces, four-posters, faxes
Bed & Bath: Excellent, the highest quality

Favorites: Number 509 has bay windows and a park view; and number 106 has the most panoramic view of Kensington Gardens. Number 102 suite has two fireplaces, red velvet sofas, crystal chandeliers, leaded glass windows, the works.
Comfort & Decor: Very beautifully decorated by owner and extremely comfortable in all ways.

RATES, RESERVATIONS, & RESTRICTIONS

Deposit: Credit card, 24-hour cancellation policy
Credit Cards: All major
Check-In/Out: 2 p.m./noon
Pets: Not allowed
Elevator: Yes
Children: Yes

Disabled-friendly: Specially designed disabled room and entrance
1 Kensington Court, W8
(0171) 917-1000
fax (0171) 917-1010
www.themilestone.com

MILLENNIUM BRITANNIA MAYFAIR
£180–£305

Overall: ★★★★	Room Quality: 80	Value: C	Zone 8

The 319-room Millennium Britannia Mayfair faces Grosvenor Square, a most peaceful and dignified old part of London, with the glaring exception of the modern American embassy at one end. It's a perfect hotel for people who have a problem with noise, yet a few blocks in any directions and you're in the middle of Piccadilly, Park Lane, or Oxford Street. The neighborhood is full of magnificent buildings from all different periods, and walking around is a delight. The hotel has most of the amenities of a four-star deluxe hotel—it even has a Japanese restaurant next door that is associated with the hotel. The fitness room is no more than a couple of bikes, a treadmill, a stepper, and some weight machines, but for London that's not bad. The rooms are all a good size, and the decor is pleasing if unadventurous, in a safe hotel style. There are various promotions that you should certainly try for—the rack rate is high, although perfectly in keeping with the posh neighborhood. The hotel has been refurbished extensively since 1996 and it looks quite fresh. There's an Executive Lounge that businesspeople will find attractive.

SETTINGS & FACILITIES

Location: Mayfair
Nearest Tube Station: Green Park or Bond Street
Quietness Rating: A
Dining: Restaurant, Shogun Japanese Restaurant, two bars
Amenities: Two restaurants, two bars, 24-hour fitness room, business center, 24-hour valet, free modem access in rooms, reduced rate at National Car Park
Services: Concierge, 24-hour room service and valet, bellhop, laundry

ACCOMMODATIONS

Rooms: 319
All Rooms: Telephones with free modem access, cable TV, in-house movies, air conditioning and individual climate control, minibar, writing desk
Some Rooms: Tea and coffee, trouser press, fax, safe

Bed & Bath: Marble baths with phone in them, good-sized beds
Favorites: The Millennium Rooms are the best size before you get into suites; overlooking the Square is nice
Comfort & Decor: Decor is uninspired, but of a good hotel standard

RATES, RESERVATIONS, & RESTRICTIONS

Deposit: Credit card, 2 p.m. day of arrival cancellation policy
Credit Cards: All major
Check-In/Out: 2 p.m./noon
Pets: Not allowed
Elevator: Three
Children: Yes

Disabled-friendly: Yes, but limited
Grosvenor Square, W1
(0171) 629-9400
fax (0171) 629-7736
sales.britannia@mill-co.com
www.mill-cop.com

MILLER'S PERIOD ROOMING HOUSE   £155–£170

Overall: ★★★★	Room Quality: 85	Value: B	Zone 13

Miller's Period Rooming House is becoming one of London's worst-kept secrets: it opened in 1997 and has been quietly drawing strength from the numbers of people who love it and keep coming back, and the newspapers and magazines who keep writing about it. Martin Miller, of *Miller's Antique Guide,* and Kay Raveden have created an eccentric and beautiful "rooming house" in Notting Hill Gate, filled to bursting in the common areas with sublime antiques (there's a covered sedan chair, or is it a puppet theater, in the front hall, and an old sled on the wall, to name only two of the first things to hit your eyes). The drawing room is wonderful, with a fireplace that is stunningly well carved and still more antiques — the Millers have clearly spent years successfully scavenging in markets like Portobello and Bermondsey and many a country auction. The seven rooms are all named after English Romantic poets and have lines from the poems of these masters on the back of each door. The Coleridge room has an old model of the HMS *Bounty,* and the "Rime of the Ancient Mariner" is quoted on the door. Long stays will get a discount. Book well in advance. The house is on a busy stretch of Westbourne Grove, not a tremendously charming a neighborhood, but there are lots of restaurants, and Planet Organic down the street has a great juice bar.

SETTINGS & FACILITIES

Location: Notting Hill Gate
Nearest Tube Station: Bayswater
Quietness Rating: B/C
Dining: Breakfast only
Amenities: Amazing drawing room with coffee and tea and a fireplace, all lit up with candles at night
Services: Reception acts as concierge, limited room service (from local restaurants), laundry

ACCOMMODATIONS

Rooms: 7
All Rooms: Telephone, voice mail, satellite television, wonderful antiques
Some Rooms: Four-poster, even more wonderful antiques
Bed & Bath: Beds are of good quality, and the bathrooms are of a high standard
Favorites: All rooms are different and very cool. Try the red Coleridge Room or the lighter Tennyson Room.

Comfort & Decor: Comfort is fine, except for the lack of a lift and the possibility of a hot day or two without air conditioning. The decor has to be seen to be believed. The Millers have spent their time amassing the most amazing antiques and they have spread them wildly and well all over this wonderful rooming house.

RATES, RESERVATIONS, & RESTRICTIONS

Deposit: Credit card, seven days' cancellation policy
Credit Cards: All major
Check-In/Out: 2 p.m./11 a.m.
Pets: Not allowed
Elevator: No
Children: Yes

Disabled-friendly: No
111A Westbourne Grove, W2
(entrance on southeast side of Hereford Road)
(0171) 243-1024
fax (0171) 243-1064
millersuk@dial.pipex.com

THE MONTAGUE ON THE GARDENS	£119–£410

Overall: ★★★★	Room Quality: 82	Value: C	Zone 2

A four-star deluxe hotel, The Montague on the Gardens is part of the Red Carnation Group, who also own the five-star Milestone in Kensington. It features the same type of sumptuous, well-crafted interior design that uses fabric as wallpaper in places and cleverly combines fine antiques with bold patterns and pleasing colors. It provides all the services one would expect of a four-star hotel and then some. There's a garden in the back that you can enjoy while sitting on the patio off the Terrace Bar, and the restaurant is of very good quality at reasonable (for London) rates. It's also across the street from the British Museum, and within walking distance from the West End. The delightful decor of the rooms can't conceal their small size, but it does tend to divert one's attention from it. The Montague is made from eight Grade II townhouses strung together, so the rooms are all of different sizes and shapes. Some of the suites are comprised of three different levels, which might be good if you have a need for privacy from your roommate, but it has less floor space that you might have if it were all on one floor. There are a couple of deluxe kings that are spacious (numbers 319 and 317). Ask about promotional deals. It's a bit pricey for the neighborhood—unless you simply *have* to be near the West End or the British Museum and want a full-service hotel.

SETTINGS & FACILITIES

Location: Bloomsbury
Nearest Tube Station: Russell Square
Quietness Rating: A in garden rooms; B on street
Dining: Blue Door Bistro is a three-star restaurant serving breakfast, lunch, and dinner, with a very pleasing and elegant interior
Amenities: Smoking and nonsmoking rooms, bar, restaurant with piano

music, bathrobes, in-room express checkout via TV system, executive room with business-related amenities, mobile phones for rental, fax machines on request, healthy guest rooms featuring a Nordic exercise bike
Services: Concierge, 24-hour room service, bellhop, laundry, business support

ACCOMMODATIONS

Rooms: 104
All Rooms: Telephone, voice mail, cable TV, in-house movies, air conditioning, hair dryer, writing desk, trouser press, tea and coffee
Some Rooms: Minibars, fax lines, CD players and CD selection
Bed & Bath: Beautiful beds, most with elaborate canopies over the head, and handsome duvets and curtains. The bathrooms are first-rate.

Favorites: Number 219, The Duchesse, is a fine suite that has a sky painted on the ceiling
Comfort & Decor: They aim to please here, so the comfort factor—even adjusting for the size of the rooms—is particularly high. The decor is quite impressive, if a bit over the top in places. Not for those who love minimalism.

RATES, RESERVATIONS, & RESTRICTIONS

Deposit: Credit card, 24-hour cancellation policy
Credit Cards: All major
Check-In/Out: 2 p.m./noon
Pets: Large pets not allowed (small pets conditional)
Elevator: Yes
Children: Yes
Disabled-friendly: Ramps for main stairs, and the people here are very

helpful, but since it's a Grade II listed building, they can't create total wheelchair access
15 Montague St., Bloomsbury, WC1
In U.S. (800) 424-2862;
(0171) 637-1001
fax (0171) 637-2516
hbarnard@montague.red-
carnationhotels.com
www.redcarnationhotels.com

MORGAN HOTEL £52–£98

| Overall: ★★★½ | Room Quality: 75 | Value: A | Zone 2 |

Make your reservation well in advance (months) to get a room at this extremely popular family-run bed-and-breakfast/budget hotel. Practically on the doorstep of the British Museum and within walking distance of the West End, this is the place discerning cheapskates love to go. It's an easy, informal sort of a place, run by a family who seem to do absolutely everything themselves, and pretty nicely, too. The breakfast room is the jewel here: It's done up in booths and decorated with an extraordinary collection of English ceramics, some very interesting pieces. Lots of greenery and photos are on the wall. Clearly, someone here has the taste to make a budget place look inviting and interesting, or maybe it's because they got started on decorating the place when they opened it over 20 years ago, when you could still get a deal in Portobello Road. All the rooms have a private shower and toilet.

SETTINGS & FACILITIES

Location: Bloomsbury
Nearest Tube Station: Tottenham Court
Quietness Rating: A in back, B+ in front (double-glazed windows)

Dining: Breakfast, which is included in price
Amenities: Breakfast in delightful dining room
Services: Bellhop

ACCOMMODATIONS

Rooms: 21 hotel rooms, and 4 apartment flats
All Rooms: Telephone, TV (BBC and CNN), hair dryer
Some Rooms: Tea and coffee, air conditioning, writing desk, bath, TV and VCR in apartments
Bed & Bath: Highest cleanliness and comfort
Favorites: Number 1 is of a good size, with lots of drawers. Room B is a favorite; and Flat 1 is a really nice apartment, with eat-in kitchen, nice decoration, and good space
Comfort & Decor: The decor is superior to most of the local B&Bs in this price range, with really interesting pictures on the wall and a fine collection of English porcelain. The family is well versed in making you comfortable.

RATES, RESERVATIONS, & RESTRICTIONS

Deposit: Credit card, 72-hour cancellation policy
Credit Cards: Most major
Check-In/Out: Noon/10:30 a.m.
Pets: Not allowed

Elevator: No
Children: Yes
Disabled-friendly: No elevator
24 Bloomsbury St., WC1
(0171) 636-3735

PARKES HOTEL			£130–£265
Overall: ★★★½	Room Quality: 83	Value: B	Zone 10

You'll find pristine evocation of English elegance at this hotel, a mere stone's throw from Harrods on a tree-lined dead-end street off the busy Brompton Road. It's not at all stuffy, but it does seem to have high standards for decor and service. There are plenty of maids and bellhops, and very friendly they are, too. There is no restaurant, but they do have a breakfast room with full English breakfast for £5, and you can get room service. But the best thing is that all the rooms have kitchens, so you can feast from Harrods Food Halls without any difficulty. Parkes doesn't offer any deals, and it stays pretty solidly booked.

SETTINGS & FACILITIES

Location: Knightsbridge
Nearest Tube Station: Knightsbridge
Quietness Rating: A
Dining: Breakfast room
Amenities: Sitting room, complimentary newspaper, kitchens
Services: Concierge, room service, bellhops, laundry, chauffeur service and airport transfer

ACCOMMODATIONS

Rooms: 33
All Rooms: Kitchens, cable TV and in-house movies, tea and coffee, hair dryer, iron, minibar, double bed, trouser press, safe, baths
Some Rooms: Fax, writing desk, sitting area, chandeliers, fireplaces (electric)
Bed & Bath: Excellent
Favorites: Number 32 is a front-facing junior suite, and number 37 is a fine one-bedroom suite with huge crystal

chandeliers, high ceilings, and French windows in the bedroom and the sitting room. They are switching some things around, making smaller suites out of the three-bedroom ones, so the room numbers may change. The doubles are a bit small, but the junior suites are a good size.
Comfort & Decor: Pains have been taken to make the rooms comfortable, and the decor is well composed and pleasant

RATES, RESERVATIONS,& RESTRICTIONS

Deposit: Credit card; 48-hour cancellation policy
Credit Cards: All major
Check-In/Out: 2 p.m./noon
Pets: Allowed by arrangement
Elevator: Yes
Children: Yes

Disabled-friendly: No wheelchair access, lots of stairs and small hallways
41 Beaufort Gardens
(0171) 581-9944
fax (0171) 581-1999
reception@parkeshotel.com

THE PASTORIA RADISSON EDWARDIAN   £205–£260

Overall: ★★★	Room Quality: 68	Value: D	Zone 7

These Radisson hotels are just a bit too standard for my taste, however, they offer many deals, frequent-flier tie-ins, and all the service and amenities that Radisson Hotels offer all over the world. You will know what to expect with them, which for many people is important when traveling abroad. The hotel is very used to an American clientele, and in response to the overwhelming demand, is now putting air conditioning in every room. The visitors at this four-star hotel can use the fitness room at the five-star Hampshire across the street. The four-star rating is stretching it a bit: The rooms are very small, and the singles in back are awful; but certainly every basic need is attended to in the rooms. The location is great for action-seekers: right on Leicester Square, which is host to hordes of people all weekend—buskers, carnivals, tourists, drunks, you name it. You'll either love or hate staying on the square; noise-phobics need not apply. Of the six floors, you'll find the high front rooms are the most quiet and bright. There's a small restaurant attached called Flicks Brasserie.

SETTINGS & FACILITIES

Location: Leicester Square
Nearest Tube Station: Leicester Square
Quietness Rating: C in low front floors, A in back; double-glazing throughout

Dining: Flicks Brasserie serves burgers, salads, and pasta
Amenities: Small sitting area, in-house movies
Services: Concierge, 24-hour rooms service, bellhop, laundry

ACCOMMODATIONS

Rooms: 58
All Rooms: Telephone, satellite TV, in-house movies, writing desk, tea and coffee
Some Rooms: Trouser press, chairs
Bed & Bath: Standard and clean

Favorites: The singles are not great, very small and cramped—for the extra money get a double
Comfort & Decor: As you'd expect: inoffensive decor, good beds, and reasonable comfort in small rooms

RATES, RESERVATIONS, & RESTRICTIONS

Deposit: Credit card, 72-hour cancellation policy
Credit Cards: All major
Check-In/Out: 2 p.m./11 a.m.
Pets: Not allowed
Elevator: Yes
Children: Yes

Disabled-friendly: Very limited, small elevator and hallways
3 St. Martin's St., Leicester Square, WC2
In U.S. (800) 333-3333;
(0171) 930-8641
fax (0171) 925-0551
www.radisonedwardian.com

THE PELHAM   £170–£410

| Overall: ★★★★½ | Room Quality: 90 | Value: B | Zone 11 |

The Pelham Hotel is a five-star hotel at four-star prices. And it has charms that other five-stars do not: Each room is unique and exquisitely decorated by the deft hand of the owner, and the size (46 bedrooms and suites) guarantees the guest the most punctilious and personal service. The atmosphere is of a luxurious townhouse, with all the amenities you could desire. There are two sitting rooms with fireplaces, mahogany paneling, artfully arranged flowers, stunning furniture, and deep, comfy chairs and sofas. Even the hallways are admirable, as the wallpaper has been cunningly placed with stripes running horizontally to make them seem larger. The views in the front are of the town of South Kensington, and there's not much more to look at out of the rear windows except for the French Lycee playground. The location is excellent, with the museums of South Kensington just steps away, three underground lines across the street, buses to all over stopping in front of the hotel, and the shops of Knightsbridge a five-minute walk. The staff is friendly, helpful, and knowledgeable. They can get you anything you need at any time—baby-sitter, massage therapist, tickets, tours, airport transfer (for a goodly fee). On Wednesdays they have a champagne get-together in the sitting room. Call about the special deals they offer in summer and winter and holidays. Breakfast is included with some rooms.

SETTINGS & FACILITIES

Location: South Kensington
Nearest Tube Station: South Kensington
Quietness Rating: A in rear, C in front (the front has double-glazing twice, which works very well)
Dining: Kemp's Restaurant has an excellent menu that changes every few weeks. The room is quite comfortable and as beautiful as you'd expect from this exquisite hotel.
Amenities: Sitting rooms with fireplaces, champagne and hors d'oeuvres on Wednesdays, honor bar and coffee and tea in back sitting room
Services: 24-hour room service, concierge, laundry, anything you can think of

ACCOMMODATIONS

Rooms: 46
All Rooms: Satellite TV, two telephones, mobile phone, voice mail, minibar, sitting area
Some Rooms: Video, sofa, balcony, four-poster
Bed & Bath: Twin, double, king (which can be turned into twin) very comfortable; all private bathrooms, big tubs, good showers, granite and mahogany decor
Favorites: Number 101: front luxury double, with French doors leading to balcony; number 204 deluxe double pleasingly decorated; number 409 luxury double, and number 406, a new deluxe, with walk-in wardrobes, two sinks in bathroom, and shower cubicle as well as tub; rooms 405 and 305 are also new and distinguished.
Comfort & Decor: The comfort factor is what we'd all like to achieve in our own homes, and the decor is like stepping into the pages of *Architectural Digest*.

RATES, RESERVATIONS, & RESTRICTIONS

Deposit: Credit card, 48-hour cancellation policy
Credit Cards: All major, except DC
Check-In/Out: 1 p.m./noon
Pets: Not allowed
Elevator: Yes
Children: Yes
Disabled-friendly: Yes, except stairs into hotel must be negotiated with concierge assistance.
15 Cromwell Place, SW7
In U.S. (800) 553-6674;
(0171) 589-8288
fax (0171) 584-8444
pelham@firmdale.com
www.firmdale.com

PEMBRIDGE COURT HOTEL   £115–£185

Overall: ★★★★	Room Quality: 84	Value: A+	Zone 13

This is an excellent townhouse hotel within perfect reach of Portobello Road, a very happening part of town. You only need slip out the back of the house and through an alley and you're there. The atmosphere of this Victorian house is bright and friendly, with the resident cats, Churchhill and Spenser, adding a lovely homey touch—they roam freely and if they take a liking to you, may hang out in your room with you. The rooms are of a decent size—some bigger than others—and decorated in an ingenious way: antique gloves, dresses, belts, fans, and other accessories are beautifully framed and hung all around. There's a very pleasant sitting room with a library and fireplace, and downstairs you'll find a wonderful bar/restaurant called Caps that used to be open to the public until the success of the hotel made the owners decide to keep it as a private place for guests only. It's got a great nautical feel to it, with some very cool antiques. The bar will stay open as long as you need, though they try to close it at 11 p.m. or midnight. Breakfast is included in the price—full English breakfast that is. There's nothing precious or pretentious about this place, just good value and good vibrations in a beautiful setting.

SETTINGS & FACILITIES

Location: Notting Hill Gate
Nearest Tube Station: Notting Hill Gate
Quietness Rating: A
Dining: The Caps Restaurant has a limited but fine menu

Amenities: Full English breakfast included, bar/restaurant, sitting room, arrangements with nearby health club, fax on request
Services: 24-hour room service, limited menu, bellhop, laundry

ACCOMMODATIONS

Rooms: 20
All Rooms: Telephone, satellite TV, writing desk, trouser press
Some Rooms: Air conditioning
Bed & Bath: Bathtubs in all but four rooms (which have showers), some four-poster beds, all of high standard

Favorites: They're all different, but they're all good. If you want a lot of space, look for the ground-floor room, or any of the suites. The rooms at front have marvelous large windows.
Comfort & Decor: High rating in comfort, and the decor is charming

RATES, RESERVATIONS, & RESTRICTIONS

Deposit: Credit card, 48-hour cancellation policy
Credit Cards: All major
Check-In/Out: 2 p.m./noon
Pets: Dogs allowed as long as you don't leave them cooped up in the room

Elevator: Yes
Children: Yes
Disabled-friendly: Steps in front
34 Pembridge Gardens
(0171) 229-9977
fax (0171) 727-4982
reservations@pemct.co.uk

THE PORTOBELLO HOTEL			£115–£260
Overall: ★★★★	Room Quality: 82	Value: C	Zone 13

This is a trendy place with corporate accounts held by a number of modeling, music, and film agencies. It's in an old Victorian terrace house, and the rooms are each completely different from one another, and admirably so. The rooms in the rear look out over a communal garden into which you may not go, but which provides a sublime view. It has a lot of charm, with whimsical and traditional decor blending nicely. There's a sitting room that looks out over the garden and a small breakfast room on the lower ground floor. Continental breakfast is included in the price and is sent to your room. The ambience is pleasant, especially if you get one of the larger rooms—the singles are cell-like, despite the gracious decor, and not a place to do more than sleep in. The most imposing room, number 16, features a big round bed and a balcony on the garden, with an antique copper bathtub right in the room—great for romance. Number 13 has a huge, high four-poster bed that requires a footstool to get into. Book ahead, for these rooms are coveted by all who've been here. It's within walking distance of Portobello Road, which makes it a good hotel for committed Portobello and Kensington Church Street shoppers, but it's not terribly well situated, public transportation–wise, for general sight-seeing.

SETTINGS & FACILITIES

Location: Notting Hill Gate
Nearest Tube Station: Notting Hill Gate
Quietness Rating: A
Dining: Very small breakfast room
Amenities: Tiny basement restaurant with a few tables for breakfast; drawing room with fireplace and view on gardens; health club facilities four-minute walk away
Services: Concierge, 8 a.m.– 4 p.m. room service, continental breakfast sent to room, laundry

ACCOMMODATIONS

Rooms: 24
All Rooms: Telephone, satellite TV
Some Rooms: Balcony, couches, mini-bar, air conditioning, four-poster
Bed & Bath: Beds are divinely comfy; baths range from a huge clawfoot tub to tiny shower stalls, but all are clean and user-friendly
Favorites: Of course number 16, with the balcony overlooking the garden and the big round bed is everyone's favorite. I also like the Asian-style number 46, also with a garden view. The single number 38 is very small, but has a good feeling to it. The first-floor rooms with the large French windows have a spaciousness that is quite fine.
Comfort & Decor: The decoration here is extraordinarily wonderful, ranging from traditional English antiques to exotic Asian treasures. Comfort is as high a priority as style.

RATES, RESERVATIONS, & RESTRICTIONS

Deposit: Credit card, 48-hour cancellation policy
Credit Cards: All major
Check-In/Out: After noon/ noon
Pets: Not allowed for a long stay
Elevator: Yes, but only to third floor
Children: Yes

Disabled-friendly: No
22 Stanley Gardens, W11
(0171) 727-2777
fax (0171) 792-9641
reception@portobello-
    hotel.demon.co.uk
www.portobellohotel.demon.co.uk

QUALITY HOTEL			£84–£119
Overall: ★★★½	Room Quality: 77	Value: A	Zone 9

This is a very good deal. The hotel is one of those standard hotel-type places, without a whole lot of charisma or glamour, but the rooms are tidy, of a good size, and with everything you want. The decor and interior is plain, but reasonably attractive. It has a small restaurant and a self-service coffee area. It's the kind of place that has an automatic shoe shiner near the public telephones, a video slot machine in the bar, and a condom dispenser in the ladies room. But it's also the kind of place that has a marble-floored lobby, with plants in the windows. There's a fax/Internet laptop in the lobby for your use, a sitting area, and a bar that opens at 5 p.m. Apparently, guests can get a key to Eccleston Square, a charming garden with benches and flora across the street. You can also walk to many of the great sights of London, such as Westminter Abbey and Buckingham Palace. The rooms are all a good size and have satellite TV and minibar. There are many promotional deals done in conjunction with the Choice Hotels Europe Group, which has over 3,000 hotels worldwide. This is one of the better deals in London, and these hotels provide similar value for money in all their hotels.

SETTINGS & FACILITIES

Location: Victoria
Nearest Tube Station: Victoria
Quietness Rating: A/B
Dining: Connaught's Brasserie serves delicious breakfast, lunch, and dinner
Amenities: Dining room, bar, airport transfer, key to private gardens across the street
Services: Reception functions as concierge, limited room service, bell-hop, laundry

ACCOMMODATIONS

Rooms: 107
All Rooms: Telephone, satellite TV, ceiling fans, trouser press, tea and coffee, writing desk
Some Rooms: Minibar, teletext TV; some triples have two rooms
Bed & Bath: Good solid moderate hotel style
Favorites: Go for a premier double or triple
Comfort & Decor: All comforts, standard hotel-style, inoffensive and restful

RATES, RESERVATIONS, & RESTRICTIONS

Deposit: Credit card
Credit Cards: All major
Check-In/Out: In 2 p.m., out noon
Pets: Large pets not allowed (small pets allowed conditionally)
Elevator: Yes
Children: Yes
Disabled-friendly: Steps outside, but people to help
82–83 Eccleston Square SW1
(0171) 834-8042
fax (0171) 630-8942
admin@gb614.u-net.com
www.choicehoteleurope.com

THE REMBRANDT HOTEL	£165–£215

Overall: ★★★★	Room Quality: 79	Value: C	Zone 11

The three main reasons to stay at the Rembrandt are location, location, location. It's across the street from the Victoria and Albert and a hop, skip, and jump from the Science Museum, the Natural History Museum, and Harrods. It is also a four-minute walk from the South Kensington Tube Station, which has the Piccadilly (which goes to Heathrow), Circle, and District lines. The A1 Heathrow bus stops within yards of it; there are three useful buses within shouting distance, and taxis are a breeze to hail. It has a pleasant feeling to it, with a big lobby that has a fireplace, bar service, and plenty of couches to go around. It is a four-star hotel with most of the services you'd expect. The staff is plentiful and courteous, if not overawed by one's personage: I once had a cleaning person vacuum around my feet as I sat in the lobby having tea with some friends. The rooms are nice enough and very clean, but without much character. Reservationists usually advise Americans to go for the double executive room since they're accustomed to lots of space. The Rembrandt attracts a lot of conferences and a business crowd, as well as tourists. Ask about upgrading rooms.

SETTINGS & FACILITIES

Location: South Kensington, on the border of Knightsbridge
Nearest Tube Station: South Kensington
Quietness Rating: A at the rear and top floors; C/D front lower floors (double-glazing is not 100% effective, but the traffic roar quiets down at night)
Dining: The Masters Restaurant serves traditional breakfast, lunch, and dinner

Amenities: Lobby with bar and fireplace, big dining room and small conservatory, tour bus pick-up, health club with pool (£5 charge), conference rooms, professional business services
Services: Concierge, 24-hour room service, bellhops, laundry, fax and Internet in lobby, baby-sitting

ACCOMMODATIONS

Rooms: 195; two floors nonsmoking
All Rooms: Telephone, cable TV, in-house movies, minibar on request, tea and coffee, hair dryers, writing desks
Some Rooms: Air conditioning, trouser press, bidets, sitting area
Bed & Bath: Beds are so-so, bathrooms are clean and spacious by London standards. Jacuzzi baths on request for executive doubles.
Favorites: Executive double front rooms on first floor facing Victoria and

Albert Museum—you can admire the statues that you can't see from street level through tall windows. The only drawback is daytime street noise.
Comfort & Decor: The lobby is appealing, with a fireplace and plenty of seating, as well as a bar, but the rooms are somewhat dull, if clean. The decor could be described as unimaginative but safe hotel style.

RATES, RESERVATIONS, & RESTRICTIONS

Deposit: Credit card, 48-hour cancellation policy
Credit Cards: All major
Check-In/Out: 2 p.m/noon; express check-out available
Pets: Not allowed
Elevator: Two
Children: Yes

Disabled-friendly: Yes; but with three front stairs to be negotiated; doormen will gladly help
11 Thurloe Place
(0171) 589-8100
fax (0171) 225-3476
rembrandt@sarova.co.uk

RIVERSIDE HOTEL   £60–£115

| Overall: ★★★ | Room Quality: 70 | Value: B | Zone 12 |

Richmond is a very beautiful town, and it would behoove anyone who wanted to see a bit of the lovelier nearby parts of the Thames to take a trip out there on the tube or rail. If you wanted to be sure of comparatively clean air, you might even want to stay there. A five- to ten-minute walk from the tube along Richmond High Street is the Riverside Hotel, a Victorian building right smack dab on the Thames, with pretty views and easy access to all the shops and amenities of Richmond. Richmond has a lot to enjoy: a historic theater, an arts center, nearby golf course, swimming pools, tennis and squash courts, plenty of pubs and restaurants and shops, not to mention the huge park. The hotel is well priced and well located, and the owners are willing and able to help you find your way to and from central London. It's a homey place, and it's recently been refurbished and upgraded. Some of the rooms are smaller than others, as is the case with the old Victorian conversions, so discuss exactly what you need with the owners when booking. June and July are very busy times, so be sure to book well in advance. Full English breakfast is included. Ten percent discount applies for stays of over a week.

SETTINGS & FACILITIES

Location: Richmond
Nearest Tube Station: Richmond (or BritRail)
Quietness Rating: C in front, A in back, double-glazed windows in front

Dining: Breakfast and dinner
Amenities: Breakfast and dinner room, bar
Services: Helpful reception, one-day laundry service

ACCOMMODATIONS

Rooms: 22
All Rooms: Shower and toilet, telephone, satellite TV, hair dryer, tea and coffee
Some Rooms: View over river, balcony, garden access, four-poster bed
Bed & Bath: Clean and satisfactory,

about half have shower stalls only
Favorites: Big rooms, and balcony rooms with river view—the Riverside Room is the best
Comfort & Decor: Eclectic decor, all rooms different, some small

RATES, RESERVATIONS, & RESTRICTIONS

Deposit: Credit card, 48-hour cancellation policy
Credit Cards: All major, except DC
Check-In/Out: 2 p.m./11 a.m.
Pets: Allowed by arrangement
Elevator: No

Children: Yes, younger than 5 stay free
Disabled-friendly: No
23 Petersham Rd., TW10
(0181) 940-1339
fax (0181) 948-0967
riversidehotel@yahoo.com

THE ROOKERY   £165–£270

Overall: ★★★★★	Room Quality: 98	Value: B	Zone 3

The Rookery is the latest hit by the talented team of Peter McKay and Douglas Blain who brought you The Gore and Hazlitt's. It's in Clerkenwell, a short distance from the City, which makes it perfect for the businessperson. It's not the usual area for tourists to stay, but it is definitely a viable choice, especially if you have an interest in the "real" historic London. Dr. Johnson would find himself completely lost in the postwar City of London, but you should be able to navigate from St. Paul's to the Old Bailey (both of which are visible from some of the hotel's windows). But this hotel isn't about the neighborhood, interesting as it is, it's about the amazing work done restoring the seven eighteenth-century townhouses and turning them into an intimate hotel you'd love to be able to call home. All the modern conveniences are there, but they pale next to the glories of the past carefully culled from auction houses, flea markets, and antiques markets. Like Hazlitt's, the exterior gives no hint of what wonders lie within: The old brick buildings are nondescript, located down a little lane and through an alley that cows used to cross making their fatal way to the Smithfield Meat Market. Look for lanterns and a discreet sign—no waving banners here. There are two common areas: a library and a conservatory that looks out onto a little garden. The rooms are of a decent size, and the bathrooms are utterly unique. A great choice for the businessperson, the antiques freak, or one in search of a very good representation of old London. Sticking to the period theme, there is no elevator for the four floors.

SETTINGS & FACILITIES

Location: Clerkenwell
Nearest Tube Station: Farringdon
Quietness Rating: A
Dining: No
Amenities: Conservatory, meeting rooms, personal safes in each room; you can take your breakfast in the lounge or in your room
Services: Concierge, 18-hour room service, bellhop, laundry

ACCOMMODATIONS

Rooms: 33
All Rooms: Telephones, statellite TV, fans on request, hair dryer, writing desk, personal safe
Some Rooms: Views, four-poster
Bed & Bath: Amazing
Favorites: The Rook's Nest has a view of St. Paul's and the Old Bailey , and if you squint your eyes to remove the modern eyesores, you can really get the measure of Old London town
Comfort & Decor: Of the highest quality on both scores, except for the lack of an elevator. The decor will make you drool.

RATES, RESERVATIONS, & RESTRICTIONS

Deposit: Credit card
Credit Cards: All major
Check-In/Out: 1:30 p.m./11:30 a.m.
Pets: Not allowed
Elevator: No
Children: Yes

Disabled-friendly: No
Peter's Lane, Cowcross Street, EC1
(0171) 336-0931
fax (0171) 336-0931
reservations@rookery.co.uk

RUSKIN HOTEL   £42–£85

Overall:★★½	Room Quality: 58	Value: B+	Zone 2

The Ruskin Hotel has been run by the same Spanish family for the past 22 years, and it has very much the feel of an inexpensive hotel in Barcelona. It also has the loyalty of many customers who return again and again. Unlike many of the budget bed-and-breakfasts in London, the Ruskin has an elevator to all floors, accepts all major credit cards, and has an absolute sense of cleanliness and friendliness. The owner is not interested in customers who want to argue about services and room size, but is happy to welcome the kind of sensible souls who welcome a square deal that's across the street from the British Museum (the rooms in front have a view of the side of it). The sitting room has a beautiful painting from 1801 by John Ward, a painter for the duke of Bedford, whose estate still owns all the land around here. The house is quite old, having started out as a private house, then became a warren of offices where Sir Arthur Conan Doyle was reputed to have worked on his Sherlock Holmes stories. For a no-frills B&B/budget hotel, the Ruskin is a good bet.

SETTINGS & FACILITIES

Location: Bloomsbury
Nearest Tube Station: Russell Square
Quietness Rating: A in back, B in front (double-glazed windows help)
Dining: Breakfast room

Amenities: Breakfast included in a nice breakfast room, generous portions served by waiters
Services: Se habla español, and can manage a few other languages as well

ACCOMMODATIONS

Rooms: 33; 6 with shower and toilet
All Rooms: Telephones, hair dryers, tea and coffee
Some Rooms: Garden views, bathrooms
Bed & Bath: Both communal and private bathrooms are in good shape; the beds are comfortable, though the doubles might be a squeeze for large Americans
Favorites: Number 102 is a family room that is pleasant enough

Comfort & Decor: The exuberance of the many plants and flowers on the outside may betray the utilitarian decor within: strip lights over beds, naughahyde, fake wood, and plastic furniture, plus pink walls that mimic but don't quite match the Mediterranean concept of pink walls. Sensitive souls might shrivel at the decor, frankly, but if you can close your eyes to it, you might find time to admire certain features like friezes and the sitting room mural.

RATES, RESERVATIONS, & RESTRICTIONS

Deposit: One night nonrefundable, unless they can re-let room
Credit Cards: All major
Check-In/Out: 1 p.m./ 11:30 a.m.
Pets: Not allowed
Elevator: Yes

Children: Yes
Disabled-friendly: Yes
23–24 Montague St., WC1
(0171) 636-7388
fax (0171) 323-1662

ST. MARGARET'S HOTEL   £45–£57

Overall: ★★★	Room Quality: 64	Value: A	Zone 2

This is one of those places that you can't help but like, even if it has no frills. What it lacks in amenities and style, it more than makes up for in good intentions, friendliness, amazingly low prices, and a very fine dining room overlooking some lovely gardens. (You are welcome to enjoy the gardens at any time.) It has the feeling of a penzione, appropriately, as the owners are Italian. The senior Marazzis started it when they arrived in London after the war, and their son and his bride, who was trained as a teacher, took it over. Mrs. Marazzi's daughter is now entering the family business, which makes it a real family affair and a labor of love. It's informal, but very clean, and although most of the single rooms don't have ensuite bathrooms, the shared conveniences are spotless. It's a big place, and they renovate rooms one after another, so there are always improvements being made. This is the kind of inexpensive hotel that people continue to come to time and time again, for the friendliness, the British Museum around the corner, the relative spaciousness of many of the rooms, and the sensible cost. Be warned, though, this is a low-cost, bed-and-breakfast-type hotel—if you're looking for elegance and three- or four-star service, you need to pay a lot more than the £56.50 they're charging. Also be warned that there is no elevator and lots of stairs.

SETTINGS & FACILITIES

Location: Bloomsbury, off Russell Square
Nearest Tube Station: Russell Square
Quietness Rating: A
Dining: A bright and very pleasant dining room overlooking gardens for breakfast only (which is included with price)

Amenities: Breakfast in dining room, tea and coffee served anytime, safe in office, fax available for use
Services: 24-hour receptionist who will help you with what you may need

ACCOMMODATIONS

Rooms: 64; 12 with ensuite bathrooms, more planned for future. No singles have toilets at present.
All Rooms: TV, phone
Some Rooms: Ensuite bathrooms, hair dryers, French doors and high ceilings, view of gardens
Bed & Bath: Beds are reasonably comfortable, baths are spotless in both communal bathrooms and ensuite
Favorites: Number 53 is a room that looks over the garden and features a glassed-in conservatory. Book this one

well in advance as it is the favorite of regulars. Number 40 is a fine family room with enough space for four to sleep comfortably, as is number 45. Rooms on the first floor all have high ceilings and long French windows.
Comfort & Decor: The decor is rather utilitarian, but would offend only the very sensitive souls or those used to the Ritz. It feels like a place your sensible, thrifty grandma would put together for you.

RATES, RESERVATIONS, & RESTRICTIONS

Deposit: One night's charge, £6 administration fee for cancellation at any time
Credit Cards: All major
Check-In/Out: Check in whenever room is available; out at noon
Pets: Not allowed
Elevator: No

Children: Yes
Disabled-friendly: There are two rooms on ground floor, but there are steps to reception. Not good for wheelchairs, as there are no porters.
26 Bedford Place, Russell Square, WC1
(0171) 636-4277
fax (0171) 323-3066

THE SANDRINGHAM   £70–£150

Overall: ★★★★	Room Quality: 82	Value: B	Zone 1

If you want to stay out of the pollution and noise of central London, The Sandringham is the place for you. Located in beautiful Hampstead Village with all its restaurants, shops, and historic sights, The Sandringham is a short walk from the Heath, and a 15- to 20-minute tube ride from Leicester Square. The only drawback is that the Northern Line is not one of the Underground's finest achievements, but if you avoid rush hours, you should be okay. There's a walled garden in the back of the hotel, and some of the rooms look out on it. The breakfast room is elegant and peaceful, and all the rooms are individually decorated and quite attractive. Be sure to book ahead—this hotel has a loyal following, especially among nonsmokers; it's one of the few nonsmoking hotels in London.

SETTINGS & FACILITIES

Location: Hampstead Village, north London
Nearest Tube Station: Hampstead
Quietness Rating: A
Dining: Breakfast and afternoon tea in pretty dining room overlooking the garden
Amenities: Home-baked breads, walled garden
Services: Limited 24-hour room service, laundry

ACCOMMODATIONS

Rooms: 17
All Rooms: Telephone, BBC TV, hair dryer, ensuite bathrooms
Some Rooms: Two rooms on top share a bathroom; desks, garden views, decorative fireplace
Bed & Bath: Very high standard
Favorites: Doubles with garden view, junior suite
Comfort & Decor: Well-decorated with art and furniture, extremely comfortable and gracious

RATES, RESERVATIONS, & RESTRICTIONS

Deposit: Credit card, 48-hour cancellation policy
Credit Cards: All major, except DC
Check-In/Out: Midday/11 a.m.
Pets: Allowed by arrangement
Elevator: No
Children: No children under eight years of age
Disabled-friendly: No
3 Holford Rd., Hampstead, NW3
(0171) 435-1569
fax (0171) 431-5932
sandingham.hotel@virgin.net

THISTLE HYDE PARK (FORMERLY WHITE'S HOTEL) £195–£425

Overall: ★★★★	Room Quality: 79	Value: B	Zone 14

If you really want to be on Hyde Park, but don't want to shell out the kind of dough the five-stars on Park Lane charge, this is one of the many hotels along Bayswater that can solve your problem. As a Thistle hotel, it has all the amenities you can safely expect from a good hotel group: room service, a restaurant, newspaper at your door, packages and promotions, business facilities, minibars. What it doesn't have is loads of charm, but that may be made up for by its location, and if you get a good deal. There's a good sitting room with leather chairs and a piano, and a conservatory that looks out across Bayswater to Kensington Gardens and Hyde Park. The traffic of Bayswater's four lanes can be stiff in the daytime, but it becomes relatively quiet at night—the higher the floor, the quieter the room and the more stunning the view.

SETTINGS & FACILITIES

Location: Lancaster Gate (Bayswater Road)
Nearest Tube Station: Queensway
Quietness Rating: High floors and in back A; low floors and front, C
Dining: The restaurant offers white linen service (and prices)

Amenities: Restaurant, fax in reception, fitness center 20-minute walk away, piano in sitting room
Services: Concierge, 24-hour room service, bellhop, laundry

ACCOMMODATIONS

Rooms: 54
All Rooms: Telephone, minibar, cable TV, air conditioning, hair dryer, clothes press, safe
Some Rooms: Balcony, park views, sitting area
Bed & Bath: Good beds, perfect baths

Favorites: Number 405 is a big room that gets lots of light, is very quiet, and has the most spectacular views over Kensington Gardens and Hyde Park. Any on the park are nice.
Comfort & Decor: Good comfort and decor is of the up-market hotel style

RATES, RESERVATIONS, & RESTRICTIONS

Deposit: Credit card, noon on day of arrival cancellation policy, except for group bookings
Credit Cards: All major
Check-In/Out: 2 p.m./noon
Pets: Not allowed
Elevator: Yes
Children: Yes, and near one of the

playgrounds in Kensington Gardens
Disabled-friendly: Planning a wheelchair ramp
Lancaster Gate, W2
(0171) 262-2711
fax (0171) 262-2147
hydepark@thistle.co.uk
www.thistlehotels.co.uk

THE THISTLE VICTORIA (FORMERLY GROSVENOR THISTLE)   £195–£295

Overall: ★★★★½	Room Quality: 83	Value: A	Zone 9

This is one of those massive, grand Victorian hotels that make your eyes pop when you enter it, and by the time you reach the middle of the vast dome with the huge chandelier pending from it, you've unconsciously straightened your posture. It was built to accommodate the visitors coming to see the Great Exhibition of 1851, and it was built to impress. There are stained-glass windows around, wrought-iron staircases, columns, marble floors and walls, carved busts on the interior and exterior walls (the exterior is in its own class altogether), potted plants, and huge windows. The whole place underwent a £3 million, 8-month-long refurbishment in 1996, and it shows. All the rooms are in excellent shape, the common areas are perfect, and the Galleria, which rings the huge lobby one level up, is one of the finest hotel sitting areas in London. It's a Thistle hotel, so it provides all the services one can expect from a hotel group with global standards: modems, fax on requests, cable TV, nonsmoking floors, complimentary newspapers, business support, and so on. It's near Victoria, Westminster Abbey, and Buckingham Palace, a central location that is also rather noisy during the day. The rear rooms have unfortunate views over Victoria Station, but they are very quiet. There are two sections: the "new" wing, built in the 1870s, has more standardized size rooms, the old wing was built at a time when the guest would require a couple of rooms plus one for the maid or valet, so there have been conversions there that have left the sizes of rooms rather disparate. If you're visiting with a group or taking more than one room, ask for the new wing so there are no disappointing comparisons. Ask about the Leisure Breaks and Pound for Dollar promotions.

SETTINGS & FACILITIES

Location: Victoria
Nearest Tube Station: Victoria
Quietness Rating: A in back, C in front, D in lower floors with huge windows, but that doesn't stop people from requesting these rooms again and again
Dining: Very stately dining room, big enough for the whole hotel; Harvard Bar; Galleria and lounge for tea and meals
Amenities: See above, plus modems in some rooms, many different pillows available, newspaper
Services: Concierge, 24-hour room service, bellhop, laundry

ACCOMMODATIONS

Rooms: 364
All Rooms: Telephone, cable TV, hair dryer, trouser press, tea and coffee, in-house movies, writing desk
Some Rooms: Minibar, modem, four-poster and half-tester (half a four-poster, with canopy) beds, huge windows, and high ceilings
Bed & Bath: 100% cotton sheets on the bed, and you can request pillows of all kinds. The bathrooms are perfect.
Favorites: The big rooms at the front in the old wing with the big windows—noisy, but gorgeous
Comfort & Decor: High quality, all rooms individually decorated in nice colors and furniture

RATES, RESERVATIONS, & RESTRICTIONS

Deposit: Credit card
Credit Cards: All major
Check-In/Out: 2 p.m./noon
Pets: Dogs allowed conditionally
Elevator: Yes
Children: Yes
Disabled-friendly: No, many steps
Buckingham Palace Road
(0171) 834-9494
fax (0171) 630-1978
www.thistlehotels.co.uk

WHITE HALL HOTEL			£155–£175
Overall: ★★★½	Room Quality: 77	Value: B	Zone 2

This is a pleasant and well-appointed hotel literally in the shadow of the British Museum (which just doesn't look quite as magnificent from the back—the bricks have not been stuccoed over) with an exquisite and large garden in the back to relax in. There's a glassed-in (air-conditioned) conservatory in the gardens that can be used for afternoon teas or private functions. The rooms are as small as most London hotel rooms, but if you require space, ask for the lower ground (basement) rooms—some have more space for the same price as an upstairs room. The ambience is pleasing, and although all the furniture is reproduction, the decor still has a certain cleanliness and orderliness that is attractive. There are some really lovely touches, such as the elaborate molding in every room that has been painstakingly painted, the stencils on the walls, the glass and brass elevator, and the sumptuous curtains. They have a number of money-saving schemes—be sure to negotiate for a deal.

SETTINGS & FACILITIES

Location: Bloomsbury
Nearest Tube Station: Russell
Square
Quietness Rating: A on garden in
back; B+ in front (double-glazing helps)
Dining: Breakfast, lunch, and dinner in
the gorgeous English Garden Restaurant; The Museum Wine Bar is attached
to hotel, but with a separate entrance

Amenities: Gardens, minibar, TV with
BBC and Sky News, in-house movies,
buffet breakfast, smoking and nonsmoking rooms, daily newspaper
Services: Concierge, 24-hour rooms
service, bellhop, laundry, fitness center
two minutes' walk

ACCOMMODATIONS

Rooms: 50
All Rooms: Telephone, TV, minibar,
trouser press, tea and coffee, hair dryer,
writing desk, computer modem
Some Rooms: Four-poster beds,
balcony, garden view, French doors,
sofa-bed
Bed & Bath: Bathrooms are in perfect
condition; beds are okay, some are
wonderful, such as the four-poster
Favorites: Number 109 has four-
poster bed and a balcony on the gardens; number 106 has a sofa-bed and

also a balcony on the gardens. All the
rooms on the first floor have high
ceilings and French doors.
Comfort & Decor: Decor is quite
rich and handsome, and there is a
surprising amount of light for a period
conversion building. Care has clearly
been taken to make this hotel visually
gratifying, although it lacks a certain
authenticity (not a lot of real antiques).
It is comfortable enough, even though
rooms are of the usual smallish variety.

RATES, RESERVATIONS, & RESTRICTIONS

Deposit: Credit card, 24-hour cancel-
lation policy
Credit Cards: All major
Check-In/Out: 2 p.m./11 a.m.
Pets: Not allowed
Elevator: Yes

Children: Yes
Disabled-friendly: Limited
2–5 Montague St., WC1
(0171) 580-2224
fax (0171) 580-5554

Part Four

Arriving and Getting Oriented

Entering the Country

After you land, try to make a speedy exit from the plane and walk quickly toward the immigration area, without looking like a pushy horror if possible (the English hate that). The walk from plane to immigration may be very long, so try to keep your carry-on luggage light and easy to handle. You should have been issued an arrival card on the plane: Make sure it has been filled out, and stick it in your passport along with your customs form. Arrival cards must be completed by each passport holder in your family, but only one customs form per family is necessary.

IMMIGRATION

Keep your eyes on the signs and make sure you are heading for the right immigration line. If you have been traveling in First or Business class, you can usually head straight for the Fast Track line and show your Fast Track Pass or boarding ticket. There are two other lines: EU Passport Holders and All Other Nationalities. Sometimes these lines will be marked A and B, with the definitions listed below that, so look sharp to know where you're supposed to be. Unless you have a European or U.K. passport, you head for the Other Nationalities line. Have your passport ready, as the line can move pretty swiftly. You may be asked pointed questions about what you're doing here and where you're staying. Answer honestly and solemnly; immigration is a serious business in this country with National Health Service and other quality-of life-attractions. Nationals from the United States, Canada, Australia, New Zealand, South Africa, Japan, or Switzerland can get in without a visa as long as they are on vacation. Anyone carrying another passport should check with the British consulate in their country.

CUSTOMS

Next, you will be sent into the luggage hall to collect your bags. Grab a free trolley, and after you have retrieved your luggage, follow signs for customs. The Goods to Declare exit is red, the Nothing to Declare exit is green, and the European Union exit (anyone arriving from the continent) is blue.

If you have to pay duty, you can pay in pounds sterling or by Master-Card or Visa. You have rights, which Her Majesty's customs officers are supposed to make perfectly clear to you, such as offering help in repacking bags if they make you unpack them, the right to appeal on the spot to a senior officer against a proposed search, and claiming compensation if they have damaged any of your property. If you want to appeal a written tax or duty decision, let the officer know at the time. If you don't do so at the time, you must write to them within 45 days; they will give you a leaflet that explains how to appeal. If you have any complaints about how you were treated, you can get free service from the Adjudicator's Office, Haymarket House, 28 Haymarket, London, SW1 4SP, phone (0171) 930-2292, fax (0171) 930-2298. The phone number for Customs and Excise is (0171) 620-1313. Be prepared to be held in a queue—this is the government, after all.

The customs hall is often unstaffed, or there will be only one or two people there. Assuming you have nothing to declare, march quickly through the appropriate exit. There is a large two-way mirror in some of the airports here, and someone will definitely be looking through it. If you are stopped— occasionally random checks are carried out—*never* make jokes about the contents of your bags. You are almost certain to be arrested, detained, and possibly deported. This is a nation that has had its share of terrorist bombings, and the officials are extremely and understandably jumpy. *Never* leave your bags unattended: They can and will be removed and destroyed quite swiftly.

The guidelines for what you can bring into England are divided into two categories: one for goods bought within the European Union, and the other for items purchased outside the EU. This would be your category as a North American traveler. The likelihood of you having specially bought large jewels or luxury goods to bring into London is remote, but you may want to save some money by bringing in your own instruments of vice. So, you may bring in, duty-free:

- 200 cigarettes, 100 cigarillos, 50 cigars, or 250 grams of tobacco
- 2 liters of table wine and 1 liter of alcohol over 22% by volume (most spirits) and 2 liters of alcohol under 22% by volume (fortified or sparkling wine or liqueurs) *or* 2 more liters of table wine
- 50 milliliters of perfume
- Other goods up to a value of £145 (about $250)

You may not bring in controlled drugs (any medication you have should be in its original bottle with your name on it), firearms and/or ammunition, obscene material, threats to public health and the environment, plants and vegetables, fresh meats, or any kind of animals. There are strict quarantine laws here. These are in the process of being overturned by animal lovers who have organized a "passport for pets" scheme, which will replace the six-month law that has frustrated many animal owners for years.

If you have any questions about import and export issues, contact the Excise and Inland Customs Advice Centre, HM Customs and Excise, Dorset House, Stamford Street, London, SE1 9NG, Phone (0171) 202-4227, fax (0171) 202-4131.

Make sure you have some English pounds to pay for your transportation from the airport. The exchange rate at the airport bureaux de change is murderous, so don't even think about it. I'm not a big supporter of traveler's checks, as you often get hit with a charge to cash them, but if you feel happiest with them, try to get British pound sterling checks, as very few, if any, stores or restaurants here will take American dollar traveler's checks. My opinion is that to get the best exchange rate, and to avoid worry about carrying wads of cash, use the ATMs (known here as "Cashpoints") that abound in London. Most of them are on the Cirrus or MacPlus system and will get money straight from your checking account at home. If you only have a credit card, make sure before you leave that you have a four-digit PIN for use in the Cashpoints. There are usually no letters on the machines, so memorize your PIN numerically. There are plenty of ATMs in all the airports.

Getting into London
From Gatwick Airport (phone (0129) 353-5353)

It's a long and painful drive into London from Gatwick, so don't bother with a taxi or bus. By far the best way is the Gatwick Express (phone (0990) 301-530), which leaves every 15 minutes and takes you right to Victoria Station, where you can take a taxi, tube, or bus to your final destination. The train is in the North terminal; follow signs and take the escalator down to the platform. The Gatwick Express is on the left and is clearly marked. You're encouraged to pay on board the train to avoid the long and pointless line at the airport ticket office. They take most credit cards and cash. The fare is £10.20 one way, half price for children between the ages of 5 and 15, and free for children under age 5.

Thameslink, another train line, also stops at Gatwick and is convenient if you're staying in north London, as it stops at King's Cross. These tickets must be purchased at the ticket office, and the trains don't run as frequently as the Gatwick Express.

From Heathrow Airport (phone (0181) 759-4321)

By Taxi   Heathrow has a number of excellent options for getting into London. The most expensive is the taxi, which can run from £35 for a no-traffic, west London drop off, to upward of £60 for a bad-traffic central or north London destination. There are also car services known as "minicabs." They are normal-sized cars, but the name differentiates them from the black cabs. They don't run on a meter; they are slightly, sometimes quite a lot cheaper than the black cabs; and they are not allowed to cruise the roads looking for fares. You can call a minicab service before you leave, and it will be waiting for you in the arrivals hall—the black cab queue can be long at times. If a minicab driver offers you a ride, don't take it—legitimate minicab drivers know that they're supposed to be booked by phone. Airport Transfers (phone (0181) 691-3400) charges a flat rate of £22 to or from central London. You can book a minicab by email at LPHCA@btinternet.com or on their Web site at *www.lphca.co.uk*. Driving time varies with traffic, but it will generally take between 45 minutes and an hour to most central London locations.

By Bus   The Airbus takes only slightly more time than a cab, but only costs £7 one-way for an adult, £3.50 for children between 5 and 15 years of age and students under age 26 with ID. It's free for children under age five. There are the A1 and the A2, which leave from each terminal at half-hour intervals every day between 6 a.m. and 8 p.m. (the A2 stops running an hour later). The buses are double-deckers and are a nice way to get your first look at the city. Depending on traffic, it can take between 50 to 90 minutes to get from Heathrow to central London. These buses are very convenient for certain hotels along the route.

The A1 goes east along the Cromwell Road, with stops at Earl's Court, South Kensington, Harrods in Knightsbridge, Hyde Park Corner, and ends at Victoria Station.

The A2 runs north–east, stopping at the Kensington Hilton on Holland Park Avenue, Notting Hill Gate, Queensway, Paddington Station, Marble Arch, and ends up at Russell Square in Bloomsbury.

By Underground   The Piccadilly line originates at Heathrow and is a fast and inexpensive way to get into the city, with convenient stops— Hammersmith, Earl's Court, South Kensington, Chelsea, Knightsbridge, Hyde Park Corner, Piccadilly, Leicester Square, Bloomsbury, King's Cross, Finsbury Park, and even beyond to the northern suburbs. This is a great option if you aren't carrying a lot of baggage and it's not rush hour. Be careful about the train—there are some trains on which you have to get out and change trains at Acton Town, which is a pain and can add a sizable chunk of time on your trip. Buy the correct ticket—you'll be going to Zone One (not to be confused with this book's zones, it's an Underground definition)—and hold onto it. You need it when you leave the underground. If you have the wrong ticket, you can be fined £10 on the other end. You can take the Underground into town and then hail a taxi on the street to get you to your hotel for a fraction of what a taxi would cost straight from the airport. Barring delays or train changes, it takes about an hour to get from Heathrow to Piccadilly Circus. The Underground is the least expensive option and the best bet for large groups of travelers.

By Heathrow Express Train   (0845-600-1515) This is a relatively new service and is being heavily promoted within Heathrow, but there are a few kinks still to be ironed out. It's the fastest way into London—at 100 miles an hour it takes only 15 minutes, and it leaves every 15 minutes. The standard round-trip fare is £20 (£10 one-way). The first-class price of £40 round-trip apparently makes it the most expensive public transport in the world per mile and minute traveled, even more than the Concord. The general consensus in England is that only fools and filthy rich foreigners go first class on trains, and you'd be really silly to pay an extra £10 for a 15-minute ride; but the £10 standard price is pretty good, especially as children under age 15 ride for half price, under age 5 ride free.

There's absolutely no downside to taking this train to Heathrow, and the best thing of all is that they have started a service to check your luggage at Paddington with 27 airline desks!

From Stansted Airport (phone (0127) 968-0500)

This is a relatively new airport and functions quite smoothly. As it's 35 miles outside of London, a taxi is prohibitively expensive; luckily, the train is reasonably priced and very fast. Just follow signs down one floor to the train platform and catch the train to Liverpool Street, which is a major rail hub and tube station. Journey time is 45 minutes, and the fare is £10 one-way. Trains run every 30 minutes.

From Luton Airport (phone (0158) 240-5100)

Luton deals mostly with British charter flights or cut-rate budget airlines, so there seems to be no incentive to be efficient or pleasant. Getting into London from Luton is a major hassle; it can take up to 90 minutes in traffic. Greenline Buses travel between Victoria Station in London and Luton for £7.20. Call (0181) 688-7261 for times.

From London City Airport (phone (0171) 646-0000)

This is the closest airport to central London, but it deals mostly with European short hops. It is a good, well-run airport, and the transportation is quite convenient: a taxi ride to the City of London runs about £15; and buses leave every 20 minutes or so for Canary Wharf and Liverpool Street at a cost of only about £3 to £5.

By Eurostar (phone (0123) 361-7575)

This is a fast, though not necessarily cheap, way to get from the heart of Paris or Brussels to London's Waterloo Station. Prices are dependent on the day of the week and time of the day you travel, and can range from £79 round trip to £160. Waterloo Station is on the south side of the Thames across from Westminster and is served by the Underground's Northern line, buses, and taxis (taxis are reasonably priced for a trip to central London). The great advantage of the Eurostar over the plane or ferry is that it is absolutely the fastest, most convenient way to get to and from the continent: three hours from London to the Gare du Nord in Paris. Don't forget your passport and to fill out an arrival card for immigration at Waterloo Station. The train travels at 185 miles per hour on French soil, but must slow down in England because the British didn't spring for the high-speed track. The plan is to lay the track down as soon as possible (we won't be holding our breath) at which point the train will switch stations to St. Pancras.

By Car from the Continent

Renting a car on the European continent to drive into Britain is expensive and a bit risky. There is compulsory insurance, and the European car will have the steering wheel on the wrong side of the car, which will make driving in England much more difficult. Driving in London is pretty hair-raising, even for those who are used to driving on the left, so our advice is to drop your car off at the airport or in the suburbs and take public transportation into town. There are car rental companies at all the major ports, most of whom will allow you to drop off at other locations, though there may be a drop-off fee. It's important to buy a good road atlas of Great Britain if you plan to drive from any of the ports (Dover, Folkestone, Newhaven, Southampton, Harwich, or Ramsgate) into London.

Getting Oriented in London

POST CODES

London is divided into post codes, which instantly identify an area to those in the know. You'll see the post code on maps, street signs, and addresses. This system is very helpful for the tourist, who may want to stay in the same post code as a particular museum, or for the business traveler who may want to be near the office. These are not arbitrary: They represent compass directions: W1 is west, WC is west central, just as E1 is east and EC is east central. The closer a code is to central London, the lower the number—all "1s" abut central London. As the numbers get higher, the farther away from the action they will be. These post codes can encompass more than one "town" and vice versa; SW1 includes Victoria, Pimlico, and Westminster, and what we consider Chelsea can reach into districts SW3, SW7, and SW10. You'll quickly figure it out, and you'll have your own favorite post codes before you know it.

Grasping London's Geography   The most important feature of London's geography is the rolling Thames River. It snakes through the city, bending around boroughs and post codes, and though it may not be the great and busy highway through London that it once was, it is still the major artery. Starting in the east, the Thames is slowed down at the hairpin turn around the Isle of Dogs, with Greenwich on the south side of the river. Canary Wharf is on the Isle of Dogs, and at the next bend of the river is the East End. The river straightens out for the section that includes the Tower of London, Tower Bridge, and the City of London. To the south of this portion of the river is Southwark, turning into the South Bank as you go west. Following the river westward, it slows down again for another curve; on this curve, along Victoria Embankment, you'll see the Temple, Cleopatra's Needle, Big Ben, the Houses of Parliament, and at Lambeth Bridge, on the opposite bank is Lambeth Palace. Radiating north from this important stretch of the river is Soho, then Bloomsbury, and slightly northwest will be Regent's Park. Come back down to the river and follow it past Westminster and Pimlico to Chelsea, where it will continue to flow west through Fulham, Hammersmith, and Chiswick, toward Richmond and Hampton

Palace. North of Chelsea you'll find South Kensington, Hyde Park, Bayswater, and Marylebone, and run into Regent's Park again. North of that is Hampstead Heath.

Hyde Park is another good landmark to help get a handle on London's geography. It is surrounded by central London: On the north is Bayswater, east lies Marble Arch and Mayfair, southeast is Belgravia and Knightsbridge, southwest is South Kensington, and west is Kensington and Holland Park.

London is a huge city, but it is divided into enough discrete areas that you can start to differentiate between parts of it rather easily, using the river and Hyde Park as baselines. Study the map of the whole city, see how the zones intersect; look at the tube map, bearing in mind that it's highly stylized, but it can help you get a grip on this vast metropolis. Look especially at the yellow Circle line, which circles around Central London. The tube map was streamlined from a mess of meandering lines into what you see now. It works and it's readable, but it's not geographically exact. For instance, if you look at the tube map, the distance between Lancaster Gate to Paddington Station looks significant; in fact, it is only a three-minute walk. However, a walk from Marble Arch to Lancaster Gate looks pretty easy on the tube map, but it would take about 15 minutes. Use the street map to determine distance, not the tube map.

The *A to Z Book* (called the *A to Zed*) is essential to you, as it is to any Londoner. There are other street atlases, by Collins and by Nicholson, which are also fine, but the *A to Z* is the most commonly used. It's not for tourists only—in fact, Londoners probably rely even more on these maps than tourists do, because they know how devilishly devious the streets here are. Not only are there streets of the exact name in different post codes but there is also a peculiar habit of major arteries changing names as they wind through various areas. Thus the A4 from Heathrow becomes the Great West Road, then Talgarth Road, then Cromwell, Thurloe Place, Brompton Road, Knightsbridge, and Piccadilly, all without making a single turn.

Some of the major thoroughfares in London are of rather ancient vintage—old Roman commercial routes of strict design—and all the streets, mews, alleys, dead-ends, cul-de-sacs, terraces, and crescents that later made a mess of Rome's plans were often cowpaths, driveways, back passageways to a high street, or a footpath between neighbors and pubs. This city was never brought to heel by planners in the way New York and parts of Paris were, which is what makes it so much fun to explore. For seeing the best of London by foot, there is nothing better than to just get lost. Indeed, it is highly unlikely that you won't do so unintentionally at least once when you're here. But as long as you carry an *A to Z* book and persist in one direction or another, you are bound to eventually hit some major landmark . . . or a taxi.

In Covent Garden (12–14 Long Acre phone (0171) 836-1321) there's a fantastic shop called Stanford's that has every map known to London. Here you can find walking maps, cycling maps, backstreet maps for avoiding the large thoroughfares, and maps of the old city. For your purposes, it is best to get the big picture with a fold-out map that is relatively simple, listing the major attractions and streets, and keep the pocket street atlas for narrowing down your route.

Things the Locals Already Know
GETTING THE LOW-DOWN ON WHAT'S UP

For the latest information on current plays, movies, art exhibits, clubs, fairs, museum tours, lectures, walking tours, or whatever, pick up a *Time Out* magazine. It's more thorough than its competitor, *What's On,* although *What's On* is a little simpler to read. On Thursday, the *Evening Standard* newspaper includes a magazine, *Hot Tickets,* which is the least expensive of the three and is quite comprehensive.

If you want to get a copy of *Time Out* before you leave, you could try emailing them at net@timeout.co.uk, or calling (0171) 813-6060 (Distribution Department). Check out their Web site at *www.timeout.com.* If you're in a big city, try a newsstand that carries foreign newspapers and magazines; they might carry the weekly *Time Out.* If you're a confirmed London lover, you could order a yearly subscription at the cost of £140.

TIPPING

In many restaurants, there is a service charge of between 12% and 15% added on—make sure you examine your menu and your bill to see if it has already been added. If service is not included, it will be mentioned in some way on the bill. Ten to fifteen percent is considered the normal range for tipping in restaurants.

Taxi drivers do appreciate a tip and in many cases really earn it by helping with bags, taking a smart route, and giving information. Anything from 50p to £1 is usual in short haul trips, and after £10, a tip of 10% to 15% is fine. You won't be abused for giving a lousy tip, and you may be warmly thanked for a good one. Use your best judgment.

In the good hotels, just tip the staff in pounds the same way you would at home in dollars: £1 or £2 a bag for bellhops, a fiver for the maid. Remember that this city is very expensive, and while to you a pound may be $1.65, here it can only buy about the same amount that a dollar can at home.

LONDON'S MEDIA

Newspapers

London has a huge selection of newspapers, from the solemn to the sleazy. Make a point of reading at least a couple of them while you're here.

The Times   Now owned by media king Rupert Murdoch, it aspires to be a great newspaper, but is merely good, with a big Sunday edition that has something for everyone.

The Independent   A decent broadsheet with some good writing and a very good Sunday edition.

The Observer   A Sunday-only paper with all the sections you'd expect; a fine read.

The Guardian   Well-written liberal newspaper.

The Daily Telegraph   Right-wing broadsheet with big Saturday and Sunday editions.

Financial Times   Printed on pink paper, a must for the businessperson.

International Herald Tribune   100% fluff-free paper of choice for American expats—it features the best of the *Washington Post* and the *New York Times* and has no advertising. Great editorial section with weekly contributions from America's favorite columnists, and *Doonesbury,* too.

Evening Standard   Tabloid-sized afternoon newspaper, a little light on news, but featuring good local stories and entertainment listings.

Daily Mail   Usually manages to have a star, a royal, or a socialite on the cover. Fairly good money section. Relatively free of hard news.

Daily Express   Conservative middle-brow newspaper, not unlike the *Mail.*

The Sun   And now, the sleazy tabloids. This is the home of the infamous Page Three Girl, the gratuitous photo of a topless woman placed on the third page. Its content is similarly absurd. Read it and laugh.

There are the other tabloids that you may not want to be caught dead reading: *The Daily Star,* like the *Sun,* full of the important news of women's breasts, murder, and sex scandals, and the ***Sport,*** which doesn't even bother to pretend it's anything but a titillation rag.

Magazines

The Big Issue You must buy this magazine: It provides the homeless with some income (feel free to give the vendor a tip when buying it) and it has some of the most interesting articles on London you can find. It's often guest-edited by some literary or media worthy.

The Economist Very serious and informative conservative money and politics mag.

Harpers and Queen Glossy magazine devoted to the rich, famous, and beautiful, a bit like the *Tatler* in its social diary, but with more beauty articles.

Hello! Weekly rag that makes *People* look like *The New Yorker*. Lots of Hollywood celebs, minor royalty, gossip, puzzling media creations, and a weekly television and radio guide. Seems to be the family photo album for people like Sarah Ferguson and Posh Spice. ***O.K.*** is its closest competitor and it's easy to get them mixed up: The same photos appear in both these weeklies.

The Literary Supplement Like the *New York Times Review of Books,* this is a ripping good intellectual read, with articles and book reviews written by some of the brightest people in the world of letters. After you've read a few pieces you'll wonder how you've lived without it, but it can prove curiously resistant to picking it up and getting started.

Private Eye Funny, political satire—it's the scourge of the establishment, any establishment. Might be a bit obscure for nonresidents, but worth a try.

Punch Now owned by Mohammed Al Fayed, it's sold throughout Harrods and has certainly lost its punch. Don't bother, unless you happen across editions from the nineteenth century.

The Spectator Entertaining with intelligent wit, politically to the right.

Tatler House (or castle) organ of aristocrats, social climbers and wannabes. Features such edifying articles as guides to eligible rich bachelors and bachelorettes. Endless pages of photos of dull social gatherings of marquesses, dukes, and barons. Good info on how to spend all your money in one day.

Time Out The most comprehensive weekly magazine on what's going on in London. A must for the tourist and local alike.

W. H. Smith, the bookstore chain, has an enormous range of magazines and newspapers from all over the world.

Television

TV in England is paid for by subscription to the tune of £91 a year. This means that there are no commercials on BBC 1 and BBC 2, except for their own products. It's a lovely change of pace from American television. BBC 1 is the weakest of the British TV stations, with lots of cheaply produced cooking shows, talk shows, and animal programs. BBC 2 used to be very stuffy, but now regards itself as quite hip. It produces some good drama, imports the occasional good movie, and has some good current affairs shows. The independent station ITV is on channel 3 and currently produces the most expensive dramas seen on British TV. It's funded by commercials, which only appear (mercifully) every 15 minutes. Channel 4 is also a commercial station, but it's definitely the hippest. Conscientiously irreverent, wacky, and envelope-pushing, it has an hour of news nightly at 7 p.m. It has a very successful film division, which produced *Four Weddings and a Funeral* and *Trainspotting*. It also was responsible for the brilliant television comedy *Absolutely Fabulous*. There's a new movie channel on 5.

Cable, which will be found in all the good hotels, provides Sky One (another of Rupert Murdoch's toys), which has CNN, MTV, and plenty of movies and television programs from the United States. Do yourself a favor and watch some of the BBC—there are some truly wonderful shows on it, many of which, like the *Antiques Road Show,* have been copied in the United States, or like *Masterpiece Theatre,* are shown on PBS.

Radio

The radio is mostly BBC, which has five national networks. The radio is in many ways quintessentially British: until the 1950s, BBC radio presenters were required to wear dinner jackets when reading the news. This Britishness is best heard on BBC Radio 3 and 4. Try to catch the shipping forecast at 6 p.m. daily on Radio 4. It is eccentric and incomprehensible to the lay person, and it articulates perfectly the voice of an old island culture.

The local listings in newspapers and magazines will tell you what is on when.

- Radio 1: Pop music at 98.8 FM
- Radio 2: Light entertainment at 89.2 FM
- Radio 3: Classical music and related topics at 91.3 FM
- Radio 4: To my mind, the best thing in British media. Like National Public Radio, but much more, with short stories, serials, dramatizations, interviews, quizzes, comedies, and plays. The hackles of every Radio 4 lover were raised last year when there were rumors of

the Beeb's intention to "dumb down" the unusually intelligent programs to appeal to more people. No word on if this plot has been
launched as of yet. Listen to it, and you decide.

- Capital FM: Top-ten pop music on 95.8 FM and oldies on Capital Gold on 1548 kHz.
- Classic FM: More classical music on 100.9 FM (an English friend
told me that no Brit will ever complain about classical music played
at ear-deafening decibels)
- Jazz FM: Great jazz and blues at 102.2 FM
- Newstalk: All news all the time, with phone-in commentary that
can be quite interesting at 97.3 FM

Telephones

Criminally, some pinheads at British Telecom (BT) decided to remove and
sell off the majority of the red phone boxes that were such a pleasing and
distinctive hallmark of London. They have been kept in many of the tourist
areas, but mostly you'll see soulless and ugly glass boxes with tons of sex
trade advertising (it's the specific job of one person to remove these cards
each week, but they go back up immediately). The public phone booths
here take either coins or BT phone cards. Just to make things more confusing, there's now a competitor, Mercury, which has its own phone booths
and phone cards. Coins are your best bet, and you can make a very quick
call for 10p. Some of the public phones in restaurants have a system in which
you wait for the call to be answered before putting the money in—otherwise
you lose it. Read the directions before using a pay phone.

Like the area codes in the United States, you don't need to dial the 0171
or 0181 prefix if you're calling from that area, but you do have to do so when
you're out of that zone. Many cell phones, however, require that you punch
in the prefix no matter where you are.

The telephone jacks in England will not fit an American modem cord, so if
you have your laptop and want to get online, ask the hotel for an adaptor or
buy one at a department store (Harrods, John Lewis, Peter Jones, and so on
carry them, as does Dixons).

*Note: Please keep in mind that as of October 2000, all 0171 phone prefixes
change to 0207 and all 0181 prefixes become 0208. The remaining seven numbers stay the same.*

Some Important Numbers
▪ 00: International dialing code; that is, if calling the United States States, dial 00 + 1 (the U.S. country code)   ▪ 100: General operator   ▪ 112: Emergency for police, fire, or ambulance   ▪ 153: International directory inquiries   ▪ 155: International operator   ▪ 192: U.K. directory inquiries   ▪ 999: Emergency for police, fire or ambulance

PUBLIC TOILETS

London has earned the admiration of its tourists and the appreciation of its dwellers by its plentiful and clean public conveniences, also called WCs or loos. The secret may be that there's usually a small charge for their use, and people tend to be more respectful when they've invested some money. Twenty pence (hold onto those coins, they're very important) gets you 15 minutes in a free-standing cubicle, which is washed and sterilized automatically after each use. There always seems to be toilet paper in these loos as well as in the free lavatories found in the parks and in some Undergrounds and squares. Although we can't tell you it's okay to walk into a pub or a restaurant and use the toilet if you aren't a customer, it is true that many people here aren't too uptight about that, especially if you look semi-respectable and are relatively discreet.

MAIL

Get your stamps for postcards and letters from a newsagent or a Mail Boxes shop. The post offices tend to be extremely crowded, as lots of people pay their bills there. If you want to get special-edition stamps, you will have to queue up at the post office. An overseas postcard stamp costs 38p, and an overseas letter is 64p. Remember to put the air mail sticker on your mail and don't forget to write "U.S.A." at the bottom of the address. I once had a letter addressed to New York, New York, returned because I didn't write the country on it.

STORE HOURS

This is where you get to really appreciate the American way: Most retail shops here are on a rather old-fashioned schedule of 10 a.m.–6 p.m. and closed on Sundays. However, much to the dismay of the more traditional who deplore the Yankee incursions on their way of life (and to the delight of anyone with a job), stores are starting to open on Sundays. Some supermarkets and convenience stores are opening 24 hours a day, and even the great hold-outs—Harrods, John Lewis, and Peter Jones—are open later on Wednesday and Thursday. Call and check before you take off for any shop, especially on a Saturday, when strange hours may be in effect.

CRIME

There's a perception of London as one of the safest cities in the world, fostered by the fact that the bobbies (policemen) don't carry guns. Also, because of the strict gun laws in England, there just aren't the number of gunshot fatalities that plague the United States. Compared with other European cities, London is among the least violent, with one of the lowest homicide rates (2.1 homicides per 100,000 people in London; 18.1 in Moscow). Compared to New York City, London is practically peace-loving: only 160 murders for the year from April 1997 to March 1998, compared to 462 in New York; 5,371 cases of grievous bodily harm in London, 18,093 in New York. However, women take note: There were 1,838 rapes in London, compared to 1,165 in New York. Robberies are also about the same in both cities. All these numbers have apparently continued to rise in the year since the statistics were taken. Mugging, purse-snatching, and pick-pocketing are common, so try to remember these tips:

- Keep your pocketbook close at all times, sling it across your chest if possible; don't leave it sitting unattended in public places.
- Don't put your wallet in a backpack unless it's in an inside zipped pocket.
- Put your wallet in a front pocket.
- Use a money belt when carrying large sums.
- Don't hang around counting your money after using an ATM.
- Watch your belongings on the Underground and on buses.
- Don't wear flashy jewelry or an expensive wristwatch.
- Avoid night buses after 2 a.m.; use a taxi or minicab instead; women may be happier using one of the women's minicab companies that were formed after a spate of minicab-related rapes (Lady Cabs, phone (0171) 254-3501, or Lady Cars, phone (0181) 655-3959) or calling a black taxi (Dial a Cab, phone (0171) 253-5000 or Radio Taxis, phone (0171) 272-0272).
- Never allow yourself to be picked up by a minicab on the street; always phone for one.
- Leave your passport in a safe at the hotel and carry a photocopy of the information page.

- Ignore any implausible story you might hear on the street; this town is full of talented con artists.
- Stay out of the parks after dark.
- Travel in groups late at night if possible.
- If you buy something at a very expensive store, don't parade around with the bag too long—get it back to your hotel or put the bag in a less ritzy one (there are jewelers on Bond Street who now offer a plain bag to their customers).

The emergency phone number is 999; *don't* use it unless it is truly an emergency, which a robbery isn't unless it's attended with violence. To report a crime, call directory assistance at 192 for the number of the nearest police station.

HOMELESS AND BEGGARS

The best way to help the homeless is to buy *The Big Issue* magazine, which is sold on the street by licensed vendors. Part of the money goes to the vendor, and you would be kind to also give the vendor a tip. They work hard in all weather for very little money. It's also an excellent magazine you'd be interested in reading. There are an estimated 2,500 homeless on the streets of London, not so many compared to New York, but far too many in a society that was, until Margaret Thatcher's famous "return to Victorian values," committed to taking care of its own. I'm happy to give money to the people sitting on sleeping bags asking for spare change, especially when I consider the sums I spend just to get the basics in London, but many people are opposed to giving cash on various grounds. Giving a sandwich or some food is a good alternative.

RELIGION

Here are some phone numbers to help you find a place to worship in your own way. If you're not picky, feel free to drop into any of the wonderful churches all over London for a bit of beauty and peace.

Anglican: St. Paul's Cathedral, (0171) 236-4128, or Westminster Abbey, (0171) 222-7110 or (0171) 222-5897

Baptist: (0181) 980-6818

Buddhist: (0171) 834-5858

Catholic: Brompton Oratory, (0171) 589-4811, or Westminster Cathedral, (0171) 798-9055

Evangelical: (0171) 582-0228

Greek Orthodox: (0171) 222-8010

Jewish: Liberal Jewish Synagogue, (0171) 286-5181, or United Synagogue, (0181) 343-8989

Methodist: (0171) 222-8010

Pentacostal: (0171) 286-9261

Quaker: (0171) 387-3601

GAY LONDON

When Oscar Wilde was arrested at the Cadogan Hotel in the last days of
the nineteenth century on charges of homosexuality, that afternoon's boat
to Calais was so crowded with single gentlemen that it almost sank. The
law banning homosexuality was often enforced more for political reasons
than anything else, but it made being a homosexual in England fraught
with real danger. And it was all the more peculiar because of the tacit
acceptance of gay relationships in the male segregated public (that is to
say, private) school system of the upper classes. Homosexuality was seen
as an adolescent phase that one grew out of. In 1967 the outdated law was
finally changed, and London can now boast the most happening gay scene
in Europe. There are gay hotels, bookshops, health clubs, religious groups,
bars, nightclubs, cafes, travel agencies, publications, and even a taxi company. The best neighborhoods are in Soho (Old Compton Street in particular) and Earl's Court. Clapham Common, Hampstead Heath, and the
Brompton Cemetery are popular green spaces for hanging out and meeting people—and maybe doing a little cruising.

There is an excellent book by Graham Parker called *Gay London* (published by Metro Publications, PO Box 6336, London N1 6PY), which can
be found in most bookstores and tourist centers. It lists and reviews every
possible venue or service for the gay community in London. Unless you
have an updated edition (first edition was in 1997), it might be wise to
check club, pub, and other information against the more current weekly
magazines.

Here are a few numbers that may come in handy:

In the United States, call the International Gay Travel Association in
Florida at (305) 292-0217, or leave a message at (800) 448-8550. They will
have plenty of information about gay-friendly tours and services. Pick up
or call for a copy of *Out and About,* a magazine that offers reviews of the
best hotels, clubs, gyms, and so on in the world; call (800) 929-2215.

London Lesbian and Gay Switchboard: 24 hours a day, 365 days a year;
(0171) 837-7324. They can offer help, information or counsel on any issues
related to being gay in London.

New York Hotel: The most luxurious gay hotel in London, but a bargain at under £100 for a double room. 32 Philbeach Gardens, Earl's Court, SW5, phone (0171) 244-6884.

Russell Lodge: Gay guesthouse near the British Museum and walking distance of Soho. 20 Little Russell St., Bloomsbury, WC1A, phone (0171) 430-2489.

Gay's the Word: The first—and to date the only—specifically gay and lesbian bookshop in the United Kingdom. 66 Marchmont St., Bloomsbury, phone (0171) 278-7654.

The Clone Zone: There are two conveniently located shops, one at 64 Old Compton Street (phone (0171) 287-3530) and one at 266 Old Brompton Road (phone (0171) 373-0598) in Earl's Court. You'll find books, cards, magazines, sex toys, clothes, and—most importantly—people to answer questions you may have about what's up in London.

Covent Garden Health Spa: Luxury health club for men in the heart of Soho. 29 Endell Street, phone (0171) 836-2236.

You can check out the scene in *Time Out* or in any of these free mags distributed in London's clubs and pubs:

Boyz, phone (0171) 296-6110

QX (Queer Extra), phone (0171) 379-8448 or *www.dircon.co.uk/qxmag*

Get It, phone (0171) 240-9154

Freedom, phone (0171) 837-9666

GaytoZ, phone (0171) 793-7450 or *freedom.co.uk/gaytoz*

HEALTH

You may want to take out medical insurance before you leave, since unless you're an EU citizen, you won't be covered by the National Health Service. You may be eligible for free emergency care, but anything else, including follow-up or specialist services, will be paid for out of your pocket. Check your existing policies to see if they cover medical services abroad. If they don't, call Mutual of Omaha at (800) 228-9792 or Healthcare Abroad at (800) 237-6615. Both companies offer good coverage at a good price.

Pharmacies are open 24 hours and on Sundays on a rotating basis. Call your front desk or the local police station for a list. Bliss Chemist, 5 Marble Arch, is open until midnight every day; phone (0171) 723-6116.

Dentist   For dental problems, call the Dental Emergency Care Service 24 hours a day at (0171) 937-3951. They will give you the name of the nearest dental clinic.

Doctors   The better hotels will have their own doctor on call. If not, contact Doctor's Call at (0181) 900-1000, and they will get you help. There's a private clinic in the famous Harley Street (number 117A) where you can seek medical help; call Medical Express at (0171) 499-1991. It's open 9 a.m.–6 p.m., Monday through Friday, 9:30 a.m.–2:30 p.m. on Saturday, and closed Sunday.

In England the emergency room is called the Casualty Department. Call 999 or 112 for an ambulance. You'll be taken to the nearest hospital, or if your symptoms are not life-threatening, you'll be advised which is the closest hospital to you.

We really don't think you'll get sick—London has good water and food. But you had better watch out for the cars. You will automatically look in the wrong direction when crossing the street, which is why you'll see directions ("Look Left") written on the street. Also keep a beady eye out for bicyclists and motorcyclists. They drive like maniacs here.

Chiropractor   Knightsbridge Chiropractic Clinic is right next to Harrods and highly recommended. Dominic Cheetham is a wonderfully gifted cracker (in both the wise and osteopathic sense) and can help you with any airplane pains. Call (0171) 589-8977.

If you're looking for 12-step meetings, there are plenty in London. Call for times and places.

- Alcoholics Anonymous, (0171) 352-3001
- Narcotics Anonymous, (0171) 730-0009
- Overeaters Anonymous, (0142) 698-4674

Part Five

Getting around London

Public Transportation

The most important thing to take out with you in London is a good map and/or the *London A to Z* (called *A to Zed* here) pocket-sized book: The map for the overall big picture, and the *A to Z* for the small streets. You won't regret the extra weight in your bag. Don't load yourself down with too much other stuff; you can always pick up water or snacks along the way. You will— one hopes—end up walking a fair amount, and huge backpacks are not conducive to making this a fun trip. A camera is a must because you never know when you'll run into a horse-drawn carriage or a battery of the queen's guards outfitted as if waiting for the Battle of Waterloo. Strange details on buildings or gates will want recording, and you may never pass that way again. Bring extra film. Also, be sure to carry a few 20p coins for the public toilets.

London is a city that is trying to make its public transportation as attractive as possible in order to keep the cars off the road and reduce the woeful traffic jams. Though they haven't been very successful—there are more cars on the road now than ever before, and the number keeps climbing—they do have some future plans to tax drivers and raise parking fees and improve the public transportation services with the revenue. At present on the Underground there are plenty of delays and interruptions of service, and on the weekends they make repairs, which causes whole lines to be shut down. Buses, when not stuck in traffic, have an infuriating habit of arriving at long last in packs. But seven times out of ten, the Underground will get you wherever you're going quickly and efficiently, and the double-decker buses are a fun way to see London. Just avoid public transport during rush hours, and resign yourself to taking a cab late at night.

For any questions you might have regarding London travel information, call (0171) 222-1234. You can speak to a human to get information on any facet of travel, including how everything is running.

TRAVEL ZONES

London is divided into six travel zones (which have nothing to do with the zones outlined in this book) with Zone 1 in the middle of central London and the rest radiating outward in circles that end at Zone 6 in the suburbs and at Heathrow in the west. Most of what you'll be doing in London will fall within Zones 1 and 2. Bus and tube fares rise with each zone you travel through. The Department of Transport has discussed the possibility of simplifying fares by making one flat fee, but the size of London and the cost of gas unfortunately makes such a master stroke impractical.

TRAVEL CARDS

The best deal for traveling on public transportation is the Travel Card, which gives you unlimited travel on the tube, buses, and most Overland Rail Services in Greater London, including the Docklands Light Railway. The Travel Card will save you time and money. A one-day off-peak travel card for Zones 1 and 2 (bought after 9:30 a.m.) costs only £3.80, whereas a round-trip tube ticket in the same zones costs £3.40. A weekend card is £5.70, and a weekly card costs £17.60—a very good deal if you're planning on being in London for a week. You'll need a passport-sized photo to get the weekly card. Most stations have photo machines for precisely this purpose.

The Family Travel Card is also a great deal: £3 for adults on a one-day card and 60p for children. The family must consist of at least one adult and one child between the ages of 5 and 15; they need not be related. For tourists, alas, there are no senior or student discounts; you have to be a London resident. Travel Cards can be bought at tube stations and also at certain newsagents. Travel cards aren't valid on certain designated night buses or Air Buses.

BUSES

There is no better view in the world than that of London from the top first-row seat of a double-decker bus. Many of the old buildings seem to have been designed expressly for the view from the top of the bus: The statues and gargoyles that decorate some of the fine architecture of the city are at eye level when you're riding up top. There are 17,000 bus stops all over London, so you should be able to get pretty close to whatever your destination may be.

Types of Buses

- Routemaster. This is the old-style double-decker. You get on at the rear, take your seat, and wait for the conductor to come collect your fare.
- Double-decker, front entry. These are the newer buses, used solely by some routes and for all-night buses. You get on in front, pay the driver, and take your seat. Try to have change: The driver may not be able to break a bill, especially a 10 or 20. A Travel Card makes paying much less of a hassle, but remember they don't take them on many night buses.
- Single-decker buses. These tend to be for shorter journeys through London. Same price as the others, less room inside. Pay on entering or use Travel Card.
- Night-buses. Night buses tend to cost more than buses in the day; they follow the same route, but run less often. You can't use a Travel Card on most night buses. It is advised that you not sit alone on the top of a night bus late at night; there are many drunks and more sinister types out then.

Here's how the buses go 'round and 'round:

Get on the Bus   Most bus-stop shelters have a big map of London with the bus routes on it. There is also a list of the stops of each number bus on the route. Be careful that you're standing at the correct bus stop: On Oxford Street or Hyde Park Corner, for example, there are many buses and many stops. If your bus number is not written on the red and white sign, it won't stop there. The bus stop with a red symbol on a white background indicates a compulsory stop, and the signs with a white symbol on a red background are known as request stops. Supposedly, a bus will always stop at a compulsory stop, but don't believe it. When you see your bus, wave your hand to flag it down, or it may just sail sedately by (if it's full, it will definitely sail by, so don't take it personally). When getting out, ring to stop the bus in advance of your stop. Ask for help if you're not sure where your stop is.

Paying Your Way   The fares of the buses are determined by how far you travel, so you should know the name of your destination. The fares go up every year, but at time of publication, the fare for Zone 1 is £1, Zones 2 – 4 £1.20, and it goes up from there to Zone 6. (I remind you: These London transport zones have nothing to do with the zones in this book.) Children under age 5 ride free, children ages 5 to 16 pay a child's fare of 40p in Zones 1 and 2 until 10 p.m. at night, after which they pay full fare. Fourteen- and 15-year-olds must carry child-rate photocards, and if your child looks borderline you may be hassled by some persnickety conductors. Photocards are available in any post office, take a passport-sized photo and proof of age.

THE TUBE

The first tube line ran in 1863 and carried 40,000 people the first day. It now carries millions of passengers a day; at rush hour it feels as if there are millions in your train car alone. Avoid it at peak time if possible.

It is the best possible way to get around London, even with the breakdowns and delays. The streets are just so choked that buses are too iffy if you need to get somewhere quickly. The tube's main failing is that it doesn't run 24 hours a day. The last trains leave central London around midnight and begin again around 5:30 a.m. You pay according to zones, as outlined in the buses section above, with Zone 1 costing £1.40 and going up from there. Your best bet is the Travel Card as described above, or buying a Carnet, in which you get ten Zone 1 tickets for £10 (£5 for kids), a savings of £4. The ten tickets come in a handy holder with a tube map on it. You'll be asked if you need a holder when you get your ten carnet tickets. You do. *Beware:* If you are traveling with an invalid ticket (such as trying to leave a Zone 3 station with a Zone 1 ticket) you are liable to be fined £10 on the spot. You will certainly be asked to pay the difference. Look on one of the big maps they have posted near the vending machines and ticket window—it will show you what stations fall in which zones.

Tickets Please To buy a ticket for your trip, you can stand in line and buy one at the ticket window or use one of two machines. There is a big machine, which has in alphabetical order all the possible stations you might go to. You pick you station and the type of ticket you want (adult single journey, child single, adult return, and so on), and the machine will tell you how much money to put in. Be careful that the No Change Available sign isn't displayed. The other machine is simpler, but assumes you know how much your ticket will cost and what travel zones you'll be in. You will most likely be buying the £1.40 ticket that works in Zones 1 and 2.

Put the ticket in the front of the turnstile with the black stripe down. It will come out the top of the turnstile. Don't lose it; put it in a convenient pocket because you will need to put it into another turnstile as you exit your destination. A lost ticket will cost you £10, so hold on to it.

Reading the Map The tube map is an amazing feat of workmanship. Before it was standardized in 1931 by transport hero Harry Beck, it looked like an explosion in a string factory, with lines snaking all over central London. The map is not an accurate geographical representation of London, and much time and grief will be saved if you look at the *A to Z* first. For example, you don't have to take the tube from Piccadilly Circus to Leicester Square, Covent Garden, Trafalgar Square, Charing Cross, or even Tottenham Court Road and Oxford Circus. All these stations are within a five-to ten-minute walk of one another. Locate your destination and identify the color of the line (black-and-white tube maps will have a different pattern for each line). Look for the key to the lines at the right bottom of the map. There are 11 underground London lines; to change lines, you must find the station that has white circles outlined in black connecting the lines. The conductor may tell you while you're on board which lines you can catch at the next station, but you're better off using your map and your head. If you look at Baron's Court, for example, you will see by the two circles that you can get either the Piccadilly or the District trains there. But look to the left and you'll see that although both lines pass through Ravenscourt Park, you cannot change to the Piccadilly line there. If you get on a train and are totally confused, look at the map above the windows—it's a straight line of the stops on that particular train and is much easier to read than the big map.

Which Way?   Be aware of what direction you're traveling. Trains don't run uptown or downtown as they do in New York City. Depending on the line, they go north, south, east, or west. Each platform has a sign indicating direction, but they may not be opposite each other; they might be in different parts of the station (some London tube stations are vast, so this can be an issue). See where you are on your map and figure out which direction you want to go in and go to the correct platform.

Check the front of the train for its destination! This causes more trouble than anything except strikes (of which there are many). There are a few lines, you will see on the map, that split off into different directions: District west-bound, Piccadilly west-bound, Northern north- and south-bound, Central east-bound, Metropolitan west-bound. Look at the map to see where your line terminates, and make sure you get on the train with that name; for example, if you're taking the Piccadilly line to Heathrow, make sure it says Heathrow and not Uxbridge or Rayners Lane or Acton Town (that's the station at which it splits off, so you can get out and wait for another train in the same direction). If you do get on the wrong train, you can correct your mistake at one of the stations along the way. It's a bit disconcerting to end up in the wrong place entirely, I know from grim experience.

You will notice the red symbol of British Rail at several of the tube stations. This indicates that you can make connections to British Rail services at that station or within an easy walking distance. Note also where, in the outer parts of the map, the lines may become patterned—this means that there is restricted service in that area, or that this line only runs to these stations at peak hours.

Tube Etiquette

Native travelers on the Underground in London are very quiet, especially at rush hour. Tourists who converse in loud voices are looked at with some disapproval, as they are breaking a tacit taboo. Recent years have seen the rise of the weekend train buskers who do a song between stations and pass the hat before they move onto another car. They are tolerated by the day trippers, but would probably be strung up if they tried entertaining the daily commuters.

Another important rule is to always stand to the right of the escalators to allow free passage to people who want to walk. Failure to observe this rule will always be met with an impatient reprimand. As in any big city, rush hour is a nightmare, and it is best to try to avoid the tube at this time.

You must never leave a bag unattended at an Underground station. This is not so much an invitation to thieves (although it is certainly that) as it is an alarm to the commuters who will treat it as a possible explosive device. London has had its share of terrorist bombings, and people tend to be jumpy. You may notice that there are no trash cans on any London tube platform—trash cans are a good place to hide a bomb.

There is no smoking allowed on the Underground platforms or trains.

TAXIS

The famous black taxi cab of London is not always black now: Many are besmirched by advertising painted all over the body, a disturbing sight indeed. This is also becoming common on buses. The taxis in London cruise the streets or line up in queues. If they are available, the yellow light atop the car will be on, and you may wave them down. You can usually get a taxi on the opposite side of the road to stop for you, so don't despair if none are going your way. They are famous for being able to make U-turns on a dime . . . or on a 5p piece.

Seekers of the Knowledge   As much a part of the London scene as their automobile, the taxi drivers are a respected part of the work force. They have remarkable powers of navigation, of which they are justifiably proud. They train for three to five years, memorizing every street and landmark in London. You'll sometimes see people on mopeds, with maps clipped to the handlebars, looking around and making notes. These are student cab drivers. They have to learn, by heart, 60,000 routes across and around London. During their exams they have to recite these "runs" to their examiner, citing traffic lights, one-way systems, roundabouts, and landmarks. During this recital, the examiner will do everything he can to distract the student, often playing a difficult customer, hurling insults, singing, or arguing. Those who pass this stringent test are said to have "the Knowledge."

How to Take a Taxi   It may be because of the respect to which they feel entitled that the preferred etiquette when hailing a cab is that you do not enter the cab until you have told the driver, from the curb through the window, where you want to go. Do *not* ask if he knows the way; he's trained to know and what's more, he will not admit it if he doesn't. (I say "he" because there are few women cab drivers at this time.) Although to be fair, plenty of cabbies will gracefully turn to their oversized *A to Z*. When getting out of the cab, you are likewise expected to pay through the window, standing on the curb. This works to both your and the cabbie's advantage: you can get out and reach easily into your pocket or purse, and the driver doesn't have to turn around and reach through the partition. Smoking is prohibited in taxis, although if you see the driver light up, you can ask him if you might as well. Don't eat or drink in a taxi: Many cabbies own their cars—which cost upward of £26,000—and are fiercely protective of their well-being.

It is my sad duty to report that in recent years, some cab drivers, when hearing a foreign accent, will sometimes take a less than direct route to bump up the fare. These people are definitely the exception rather than the rule, and with the serpentine routes usually taken quite legitimately by a taxi, it's often hard to tell if they are playing games. Personally, American accent and all, I have never been run around like this—at least I don't think so. In his best-selling, hilarious book about England, *Notes from a Small Island,* Bill Bryson observes that although London taxi drivers are absolutely the most excellent in the world, they do have a couple of idiosyncrasies: One is that they are incapable of driving for any distance in a straight line: "no matter where you are or what the driving conditions, every 200 feet a little bell goes off in their heads and they abruptly lunge down a side street." My own experience with London cabbies is that they are absolute geniuses at getting from point A to point B with the least amount of traffic and in the shortest amount of time. They know London better than anyone.

Worth Almost Every Pound   Consequently, I learn more about London and its roads when I take a cab, so much that I can justify the expense, which can be considerable. A short trip will cost about £5; a trip from central London to, say, Hampstead, will be about £18. It's not a good idea to take a taxi in traffic; the tube is always a better bet. But if you don't know where you're going and you're in a hurry, it can be fun to jump in a taxi and watch London go by from the dark comfort of its very civilized interior. Sometimes you can also get a great conversation out of the deal.

Some drivers, on hearing an American voice, will want to tell you about their experiences in the United States or give you a heads up as to what to expect in England. Cabbies are a talkative and opinionated lot, so much so that *Private Eye,* the satirical magazine, often runs op ed pieces by "Lord Justice Cabdriver."

You can call a black taxi if you're staying in a place where they don't cruise regularly or if it's late at night. Some companies charge extra for booking over the phone or using a credit card—ask when you call.

Computer Cabs, phone (0171) 286-0286
Data Cab, phone (0181) 964-2123
Dial a Cab, phone (0171) 253-5000
Radio Taxis, phone (0171) 272-0272

MINICABS

Minicabs are a much less reliable option than the black cabs, but they are cheaper and come in very handy in many instances, such as being far from a tube stop in an outlying area or needing to get back to your hotel very late at night when there's not a black cab in sight. There are plenty of reputable minicab companies, including some that have only women drivers. You can't hail a minicab on the street; in fact, *do not* get into one that stops and offers you a ride. It's not at all kosher; there are a lot of scams and dicey drivers out there. You must call to book a car; in that way you have some recourse should anything go wrong. Minicab drivers are not required to have "the Knowledge," which may be made abundantly clear by how lost they can get, but because there's a flat fee, there's at least no economical downside to this. Make sure you agree on a price when booking the cab, and confirm it with the driver when you get in. Tipping is normally between 10% and 15%. The cars are usually two-door compacts—nowhere near as roomy as the black cabs—so if you have four large or five regular people, get a black cab. Here are some good minicab companies:

A & A Chauffeurs Ltd., phone (0181) 952-6677
College Cars, phone (0181) 863-4148
Greater London Hire Ltd., phone (0181) 444-2468
Pegasus, phone (0171) 622-2222
UK Chauffeur Services, phone (0171) 935-5000

In response to a number of rapes committed by minicab drivers a few years ago, some companies were formed that feature only women drivers:

Lady Cabs, phone (0171) 254-3501
My Fare Lady, phone (0171) 379-9130
Lady Cars, phone (0181) 655-3959

MOTORCYCLE TAXIS

Motorcycle taxis are a new travel twist, currently also enjoying success in Paris, another clogged European city. The bike will get you through the worst possible traffic in a very short time, and the helmets are equipped with microphones so you can tell the driver to slow down. Not for the faint of heart. Call Addison Lee Taxy-Bike (their motto: "Safe, Sedate, and You Won't Be Late") at (0171) 387-8888. Ask for the passenger bike department.

RAIL SERVICES AND DOCKLANDS LIGHT RAIL

Travel Cards can be used on some of the local commuter lines in London. The North London line is a good way to cross greater London as it cuts a swath from west (Richmond) to east (Woolwich) with stops at various tube stations along the way. It's above ground, which is a nice change of pace from the mole tunneling of the tube. Call (0345) 484-950 for all train inquiries.

If you are using British Rail to get out of London, ask about the discounts they offer. There are a number of various discount cards, which you may not think apply to you, as they are good for a year, but the savings can be enormous. Ask at any major rail station or travel agent. You can apply for the discount at the same time you buy your tickets.

The Docklands Light Rail (phone (0171) 363-9700) is a relatively new wrinkle in East End public transportation. It is clean, quiet, has no conductor, and rides above the ground. It services the East End and Canary Wharf area, and is one way to get to Greenwich if you fancy diving beneath the river—you go to Island Gardens and walk through the foot tunnel under the Thames. It is also becoming a tourist option: They offer special tickets that combine rail travel with riverboat trips, plus deals on certain attractions, such as the National Maritime Museum at Greenwich. These special trains leave at Tower Gateway every hour on the hour starting at 10 a.m., and you will hear interesting commentary from a guide as you ride.

Getting around on Your Own

RENTING A CAR AND DRIVING IN LONDON

It's not a good idea to rent a car to drive around London. London is a confusing, frustrating, and dangerous place to drive, even for those who are already used to driving on the left. Although you need only present a valid driving license from any country or state to rent a car, traffic laws and driving customs are quite different from other countries, and in London everything is speeded up so that you won't have a chance to slowly get used to this new style of driving. If you are driving out to the country and must rent a car, it might be best to take the tube out to Heathrow or Gatwick and rent a car from there to avoid the problems of central London's notorious traffic.

If you do find yourself driving in England, here's a tip: The best way to remember which side of the road you're supposed be on is to just keep yourself and your steering wheel (which is on the right side of the car, instead of the left) toward the middle of the road, as you'll be accustomed to doing in the United States. As long as you remember to remain in the middle of the road, you'll be all right. And don't let the way the cars are parked throw you—you can park facing any old direction in England.

In London, the parking regulations are strict—look at lampposts to find signs outlining them. You can't park on a double yellow line ever; your car will be clamped with a Denver boot or towed. If you're clamped, there will be a sticker telling you where to pay for its removal and the additional fine; if you're towed, call (0171) 747-7474 to find out where your car was taken.

There are resident permits for parking in most neighborhoods, and you cannot park in these areas except at night. Read the signs carefully. There are meters and Pay and Display spaces for visitors to use. Pay and Display works like this: Park your car; find the ticket machine; pay the correct amount for the desired time; and display the ticket on your windshield or dashboard. There are a number of National Car Parks (signs say NCP) around central London: call (0171) 499-7050 for locations.

The central numbers for the big rental companies (cars will cost about £60 a day) are as follows:

Avis, phone (0171) 917-6700

Eurodollar, phone (0171) 278-2273

Europecar, phone (0171) 387-2276

Hertz, phone (0171) 278-1588

Expect to pay about £35 to fill up the tank with gas.

BICYCLING

As a way of getting around London, biking is just slightly suicidal. I have a bike, I use it to get to where I need to go, and I find it convenient and economical. However, it's more than the exercise that gets my heart rate up; it's the potent combo of fright and fury at the cavalier behavior of the motorists. It's pretty common for cyclists to get hit by cars while riding around London. This could really ruin your vacation. If you want to take advantage of the great parks and vehicle-free paths in London for fun, fine. Just look mighty sharp as you're riding through the strees, and wear a helmet. Call the London Cycling Campaign at (0171) 928-7220 for information about renting bikes, cycling routes, safety, and security.

MOTORBIKE HIRE

On the off chance that you might want to up the two-wheeling ante, you can rent a motorbike or moped at Scootabout, 1–3 Leeke Street, WC1, phone (0171) 833-4607. All you need is a foreign motorbike or British driving license . . . and nerves of steel.

WALKING

Please do. You'll be surprised at how far you can go by foot—a lot faster at times than on the bus, and certainly more pleasantly than on the tube. You'll get to see small architectural curios, drop into inviting shops and restaurants, and find alleys and mews that you wouldn't see by cab. Keep your *A to Z* handy and get lost. You'll thank yourself for it.

Remember the maniac drivers, and be aware that your instincts when crossing the streets are all wrong. Take it slowly and *don't* try to outrun a walking light—the drivers will scare the devil out of you.

The zebra crossings, however, are where you get your own back—they belong to the pedestrian. When you see a flashing yellow light and a cross path marked with white stripes, you are in the right of way—cars *must* stop for you. There may be one or two foreigners who haven't quite got the hang of this system, so don't stride out without sensible caution.

Around big intersections such as Piccadilly Circus, Marble Arch, and Hyde Park Corner there are "subways," which are walkways beneath the street. They are well indicated with signposts, so you'll be able to know which way to go. Some are actually quite interesting—Hyde Park Corner has painted tiles giving you the goods on the duke of Wellington (whose house is right there) and the parks of London. Some of them use exit numbers and seem to go on forever. Avoid them late at night, some of the subways become little villages of sleeping homeless people.

Walking is the most interesting, healthy, revealing, ecologically sound, and inexpensive way to get around London, so bring the most comfortable shoes you have.

Lost and Found

If you have left something in one of the above public conveyances, which is easily done when you're tired and jet-lagged, take heart: You just might get it back. Here are the numbers for lost property:

Buses, phone (0171) 222-1234

Black taxis, phone (0171) 833-0996

Train stations

    Euston, phone (0171) 922-6477

    King's Cross, phone (0171) 922-9081

    Liverpool Street, phone (0171) 928-9158

    Paddington, phone (0171) 313-1514

    Victoria, phone (0171) 922-9887

    Waterloo, phone (0171) 401-7861

Tube trains, phone (0171) 486-2496

Part Six

Entertainment and Nightlife

The London Scene

When *Newsweek* ran its "London: Coolest City On The Planet" cover story a few years ago, the accolade went straight to London's head. Even now, one can scarcely pick up a British newspaper or magazine without uncovering some allusion to this momentous pronouncement. Even the government is impressionable enough to have adopted "Cool Britannia" as a policy slogan.

Yet London surely need not have waited to be fêted by *Newsweek* before feeling itself to be once again the cultural capital of the world. For no other metropolis can rival London for the overall quality and quantity of its theaters, opera, ballet, concert halls, jazz venues, art galleries, antiques fairs, auctions, exhibitions, cinemas, cabarets, comedy clubs, television, historic buildings, historic walks, private clubs, nightclubs, pubs, shops, restaurants, and publishing houses. Many more books and magazine titles are published in the United Kingdom than in the United States, and Londoners enjoy four quality national newspapers—each on a par with the *New York Times*—and numerous tabloids, many of which are at least as trashy as America's worst.

Although London remains English in character, it has, since World War II, become a microcosm of the defunct British empire with one person in five now hailing from an ethnic minority. The Indian, Oriental and Afro-Caribbean influences have made enormous contributions to the London scene and helped make it as vibrantly international as New York.

As anyone who knows his or her James Bond is aware, gambling is legal in Britain. Along with the high-tone and the seedy casinos, most high streets have an easily recognizable Ladbrokes betting shop—look for long, diagonal red strips—where one might place a wager on the horses, cricket results, snow at Christmas, or when the Martians, led by Elvis, may be expected to land.

Soho in W1 (Zone 7) is the epicenter of London's nightlife: a dazzling conglomeration of practically everything London has to offer. The best way to have an inkling of what is going on is to pick up copies of London's two leading listings magazines: *Time Out* and *Hot Tickets*, which comes with *The Evening Standard* on Thursdays.

Welcome, then, to the capital city of the land that produced William Shakespeare, the world's greatest poet; welcome to "This sceptre's isle / This other Eden, demi-paradise / This precious stone set in the silver sea / This blessed plot, this earth, this realm, this England."

THEATER

London theater comes in three categories: The West End, London's equivalent to Broadway; off–West End, ditto; and fringe, which equals off-Broadway.

West End

Although the term "West End" refers to an area of central London, it also indicates cultural status and therefore encompasses the **Royal National Theatre**, which is located south of the Thames. West End theaters are famous for their musicals and mainstream productions, but drama in the West End is of variable quality, ranging from the sublime to the overtly commercial.

However, the theaters of London's West End enjoy such renown that Hollywood actors able to command millions of dollars per film clamor to appear in them for a relative pittance and, more often that not, to mixed reviews. Nicole Kidman recently sent London's jaded theater critics into a frenzy of appreciation when she tastefully removed her clothes on stage at the Donmar Warehouse.

If you're online, try *www.officiallondontheatre.co.uk* for a listing of current plays, plus reviews, phone numbers, and tips. You can even have a seating plan faxed to you of the theater in which your choice is playing.

When purchasing tickets for the theater, it is helpful to remember to never buy a ticket from a tout (essentially, a scalper type) because he or she will charge an astronomical sum for it. Instead, you should queue up in front of the discount ticket booth, a little house located on the south side of the grassy part of Leicester Square (Leicester Square tube). It is a tan building with a clock on top of it. You can also identify it by the lines forming on either side of it: The west side is for night performances, the east side sells matinee tickets. They charge up to £2 for a service fee and accept cash only. The booth is open Monday through Saturday from noon to 6:30 p.m., Sunday from noon to 3 p.m. Be sure you go to this booth only and not one of the many shop fronts around Leicester Square that call themselves discount, but actually offer no deals at all.

The discount ticket booth doesn't accept telephone inquiries and may not have tickets for every show you wish to see, so you might want to acquire a list of the theaters that use the standby scheme from SOLT, 32 Rose St., London WC2E 9ET (phone (0171) 557-6700)

Many theaters offer half-price tickets on Mondays and for dress rehearsals. Some also grant concessions to students and old age pensioners. Queuing for return tickets before a performance can also sometimes yield a discount.

Free advice and information about access to London arts and entertainment venues for people with disabilities is available from **Artsline**, 54 Chalton St., NW1 (phone (0171) 388-2227).

Tickets for West End musicals are elusive and expensive at £35, although you can obtain advance tickets with your credit card by phoning **Ticketmaster** (phone (0171) 344-4444) and **Firstcall** (phone (0171) 497-9977). However, booking fees add around 10% to the price of a ticket, and many theaters charge a telephone booking fee, which is often not mentioned in the listed price. Therefore, the least expensive way to acquire a ticket is to turn up at the box office in person. West End theaters are, obviously, at the top end of the market. The Royal National Theatre presents plays in repertoire so that, in any given week, at least five can be seen in one of the three theaters contained within its sprawling, neo-brutalist dimensions.

Under the direction of the former Royal Shakespeare Company and West End impresario Trevor Nunn, the National offers the widest possible range of work, encompassing classical as well as new and neglected plays from the whole of world drama. On the lighter side, the National also offers musicals and even works for children, six days a week throughout the year.

Productions leading into the millennium include the recently deceased poet laureate Ted Hughes's new version of *Aeschylus; The Orestia,* directed by Katie Mitchell; and *The Brent Mysteries,* the National Theatre of Brent's take on medieval mystery plays. The **Royal National Theatre** is at South Bank, SE1 (box office phone (0171) 928-2252; info phone (0171) 633-0880, Waterloo tube/rail). The box office is open 10 a.m.–8 p.m. Monday–Saturday.

The Royal Shakespeare Company is the main conduit through which the immortal genius of the Bard is imparted. The RSC, whose home is in Stratford-upon-Avon, is also based in the Barbican's two theaters; the enormous Barbican Theatre itself and a smaller space called the Pit. The RSC also includes works from new and classical writers in its repertoire, as long as they are relevant to Shakespeare. Recent triumphs include *Richard III,* with Robert Lindsay; *A Winters' Tale,* starring Anthony Sher; and a production of C. S. Lewis's *The Lion, The Witch, and the Wardrobe.* The Royal Shakespeare Company is located at the Barbican Centre, Silk Street, EC2 (phone (0171) 638-8891; info, phone (0171) 638-4141, Barbican tube or Moorgate tube/rail). The box office is open 9 a.m.–8 p.m., Monday–Saturday. Tickets are £6–24.

The authentic re-creation of **Shakespeare's Globe Theatre,** close to its original site, is the achievement of American expat actor Sam Wannamaker's long-term dream project. Sadly, Wannamaker died shortly before the completion of the Globe's restoration.

Although its basement remains open throughout the year to provide the world's largest exhibition devoted to the life and work of Shakespeare and the theater of his time, the roofless Globe's theatrical season is limited to May through September. The Globe's indoor theater, however (built to a design by Inigo Jones circa 1616), opens in the new millennium for year-round performances. Shakespeare's Globe is on New Globe Walk, SE1 (phone (0171) 401-9919, Blackfriars tube). The box office is open from 10 a.m.–6 p.m. Tuesday–Saturday. Matinees are at 2 p.m. Saturday and 4 p.m. Sunday. Tickets are £5–25.

Restaurants in the vicinity of the larger theaters often offer preshow menus at reduced prices, as do some of the theaters themselves—the cuisine served up at the National is particularly palatable.

Off–West End

Off–West End theaters often provide the most outstanding productions in terms of creativity because they offer writers, directors, and actors an artistic freedom that can sometimes be lacking in the more commercially motivated organizations. With emphasis firmly on the modern and avant garde, the **Almeida** (Almeida Street, N1 phone (0171) 359-4404, Angel tube) features cerebral drama from top writers and actors. Although tickets can be a bit pricey, the **Donmar Warehouse** (Thomas Neal's, Earlham Street, WC2, phone (0171) 369-1732, Covent Garden tube) under Sam Mendes has garnered raves from critics in recent years. **The King's Head** (115 Upper St., N1, phone (0171) 226-1916, Angel tube) is London's most venerable pub theater, frequently putting on top-quality, small-scale revues and musicals. Then, too, the King's Head also features hour-long luncheon plays that can be consumed along with your fish and chips, and a late (midnight) license with live music in the bar.

Regent's Park Open Air Theatre (Regent's Park, NW1 phone (0171) 486-2431 or (0171) 486-1933, Baker Street tube) provides for those who like their theater al fresco. Set in the middle of the eponymous park and furnished with a bar and snacking facilities, this charming summer theater is an ideal venue in which to see the company's vastly entertaining version of *A Midsummer Night's Dream*. Be prepared, however, for the vagaries of British weather.

Fringe

Fringe theater can be found throughout London, but like British weather, is variable and generally of patchy quality. Still, the following theaters do provide the occasional ray of histrionic sunshine:

The **New End Theatre** (27 New End, NW3, phone (0171) 794-0022, Hampstead tube) is situated in upmarket Hampstead. Those with an ear for a good tune might investigate the musicals staged at **The Bridewell** (Bride Lane, off Fleet Street, EC4, phone (0171) 936-3456, Blackfriars tube). New writing and a thriving bar can be found in plentiful supply at the legendary **Old Red Lion** (St. John Street, EC1, phone (0171) 837-7816, Angel tube).

Although a tuxedo is no longer requisite attire when attending the theater, the British middle classes still appear to dress more elegantly than we do; black tie remains mandatory for any gala charity night where royals may be present. Certainly suits and smart dresses are the norm in West End and off–West End theaters—although you may retain the egalitarian sneakers, baseball cap, jeans, and Hawaiian shirt for some of the fringe theaters; preferably the more avant-garde ones.

LAUGHS IN LONDON

The British frequently congratulate themselves on their ironic sense of humor and justly so: Surely no other country has produced so many comic novelists of the caliber of Henry Fielding, William Makepeace Thackeray, Jane Austen, E. F. Benson, George Meredith, Anthony Trollope, Jerome K. Jerome, Evelyn Waugh, Tom Sharpe, Kingsley Amis, and, of course, the divine P. G. Wodehouse, to name only a few.

British humor extends even to some of their politicians, notably Alan Clarke on the right and Tony Banks on the left, both of whom are given to entertaining quips that would soon see them hounded out of office in overly earnest America. Winston Churchill was undoubtedly the wittiest of leaders and is imminently quotable, although not perhaps here, as many of his jokes were of a decidedly salty nature.

Britain's quality newspapers are also a good source of dry humor; outstanding writers include Matthew Paris of *The Times* and Auberon Waugh, Boris Johnson, and Craig Brown of the *Telegraph*. *The Londoner's Diary* in the *Evening Standard* is also amusing, as are the gossip columns in *The Telegraph* and *The Times*.

Although British sitcoms are currently in the doldrums, the BBC has an unrivaled roster of past triumphs. If you are staying in one evening, try renting videos of *Fawlty Towers, Black Adder, Yes Prime Minister, Jeeves and Wooster,*

Drop the Dead Donkey, Alan Partridge, Rising Damp, Only Fools and Horses, The Comic Strip, and *Absolutely Fabulous*—they are all masterpieces of television comedy.

It is therefore not surprising that London has more comedy outlets than anywhere else on earth. The humor on display varies in quality and includes traditional improvisation and physical, surreal, and observational comedy. Most venues are replete with bars and restaurants, so should the acts occasionally fall short of the mark, you are at least spared the sufferings endured by those trapped in their seats of publicly funded avant-garde theaters.

Comedy Store at Haymarket House, Oxedon Street, SW1 (info phone (0142) 691-4433; bookings, phone TicketMaster at (0171) 344-4444, Piccadilly Circus tube), is the venue from which alternative comedy exploded onto British television screens. Such stars as Jennifer Saunders (of *French and Saunders* and *Absolutely Fabulous)*, Keith Alan, Ben Elton, and Ric Mayall began their careers here. The Comedy Store is open Tuesdays through Sundays.

Comedy Cafe is one of the handful of clubs in London devoted entirely to comedy and takes the generous precaution of granting free admission on Wednesdays—when new acts make their debuts. Comedy Cafe is at 66 Rivington St., EC2 (phone (0171) 739-5706, Old Street tube) and is open Wednesday through Saturday.

The Comedy Spot also offers a degree of largesse in that the £8 admission comes with a free meal if you book before 8 p.m. The Spot also features a mix of veteran and neophyte performers, all of whom are entertaining. The Comedy Spot is at The Spot, Maiden Lane, WC2, phone (0171) 379-5900, Covent Garden tube.

P. G. Wodehouse attended public school in Dulwich, and a residue of the great man's comic genius probably lingers on at the **East Dulwich Cabaret** (East Dulwich Tavern, One Lordship Lane, SE22, phone (0181) 299-4138, East Dulwich rail) where leading lights in the fields of comedy, music, and theater converge to create a delightful ambience.

CLASSICAL MUSIC

London, arguably the premier music capital of the world, is endowed with four highly regarded orchestras, two internationally renowned arts establishments, numerous ensembles, and a correspondingly wide range of concerts.

Although the Barbican's London Symphony Orchestra remains the capital's leading ensemble, with the London Philharmonic only just behind, the South Bank Centre's London Philharmonic Orchestra has been gaining in strength. Then, too, the Royal Philharmonic Orchestra enjoys a distinguished history, despite having to get by without public funding. Many of the world's leading musicians flock to London stages, often for the city' s frequent music festivals, especially the Proms, held each year from July to September at the **Royal Albert Hall** (Kensington Gore, SW7, phone (0171) 589-3203; info, phone (0888) 915-0252; box office, phone (0171) 589-8212, Gloucester Road or South Kensington tube). The Albert Hall is a prodigious Victorian building that sometimes plays host to pop gigs and even wrestling bouts. Yet the Albert recalls the glories of its heyday during the Henry Wood Promenade Concerts, when a splendid array of music is presented. And, tickets for the promenade section (the area in the front of the stage without seating) are on offer for a trifling £3.

If you aspire to observe the English well-to-do at leisure during your stay and wish to hear the beautiful Angela Gheorghui sing, we suggest a visit to the freshly redeveloped **Royal Opera House** (Covent Garden, WC2, phone (0171) 304-4000; info, phone (0171)240-1200, Covent Garden tube) With tickets costing up to £135 you will be made to pay dearly for this rarefied glimpse into the worlds of society and art, but the edifying spectacle shall remain with you always. The ROH is scheduled to reopen in December 1999.

Wigmore Hall (36 Wigmore St., W1 (phone (0171) 935-2141, Bond Street tube) is the best place in town to hear piano recitals and chamber groups. Although the hall was revamped not long ago, Wigmore continues to serve up a largely traditional fare.

If you have enjoyed concert broadcasts by the BBC's World Service while sojourning abroad, you might care to attend one of Radio 3's live Monday Lunchtime Concerts held in the converted church of **St. John's Smith Square** (Smith Square, SW1, phone (0171) 222-1061, Westminster tube). St. John's, located near the Houses of Parliament, nestles in the area of antique civility, and the church itself is possessed of a magical ambience.

It is easy to lose one's way down the labyrinthine corridors of that monster of modernism, the **Barbican Centre** (Silk Street, EC2, phone (0171) 638-8891; info, phone (0171)638-4141, Barbican tube). Still the fact that the Barbican has superb acoustics, is home to the London Symphony Orchestra, and hosts the Great Orchestras of the World Series may grant courage to the intrepid.

The **South Bank Centre** is still another gulag-type of edifice where the Royal Festival Hall (RFH1) is the main auditorium for symphony concerts; the smaller Queen Elizabeth Hall (RFH2) puts on semi-stage operas and chamber groups; and recitals as well as ensembles are performed in the intimate setting of the adjacent Purcell room (RFH3). The

South Bank Centre comes complete with restaurants, cafes, and bars and is equipped with book and record shops. Perched just above the Thames next to Waterloo Bridge, the South Bank Centre can be found at South Bank, Belvedere Road, SE1, box office, phone (0171) 960-4242; recorded info, phone (0171) 633-0932, Waterloo tube.

Finally, we draw your attention to several open-air festivals held over the summer. First, the **Hampton Court Palace Festival** in Hampton Court, East Molsey, Surrey (festival box office, phone (0171) 344-4444), June 10–20. Hampton Court rail/riverboat from Westminster or Richmond to Hampton Court Pier (April –October). The impressive historic palace grounds are a great aid to those romantic and imaginative souls who appreciate classical music. Tickets range from £18–£35.

The Holland Park Theatre stages an array of music, theater, and dance performances in one of London's loveliest parks. You are sheltered from the harmful effects of storm and sun by an enveloping canopy. The Holland Park Theatre is open June 24–August 22 at Holland Park, Kensington High Street, W8 (box office, phone (0171) 602-7856; info, phone (0171) 603-1123, High Street Kensington or Holland Park tube).

BALLET

When one thinks of dance in London, a flood of terpsichorean images come pirouetting to mind: *The Red Shoes,* Fontaine and Nureyev, Fred and Adele Astaire, Sadler's Wells, The Royal Ballet, Covent Garden, and so forth.

Dance has been growing steadily in popularity throughout the 1990s, abetted by such festivals as Dance Umbrella (phone (0181) 741-5881) and those numerous events organized by the Palace (phone (0171) 387-0031). Two of the largest and most active dance venues are the **Barbican Centre** (phone (0171) 638-4141) and **South Bank Centre** (phone (0171) 633-0932). For a full listing for both these venues, look under classical music.

However, until the Royal Ballet's homebase in the Royal Opera House opens again for business in December 1999, that august company must twinkle its toes in other venues. For details, telephone (0171) 240-1066 or (0171) 304-4000 or consult the Web site at *www.royalballet.org.*

The refurbishment of Sadler's Wells has been completed at last, and there are now two branches of the theater: the more intimate and central **Peacock Theatre,** Portugal Street, off Kingsway, WC2 (box office, phone (0171) 314-8800, Holborn tube), which served as its interim house; and the technological marvel of the revamped Sadler's Wells. This theater has extensive bars, state-of-the-art flying and lighting equipment, an ultra-flexible stage—twice its original size—and an 80-seat orchestra pit, among other attractions. Scintillating dance is to be found at **Sadler's Wells,** Rosebury Avenue, EC1 (phone (0171) 863-8000, Chancery Lane tube). Vast in scale, yet graceful in outline, the **London Coliseum in St. Martin's Lane,** WC2 (phone (0171) 632-8300, Charing Cross tube/rail), presents such leading dance companies as the English National Ballet and The Royal Ballet during its Christmas and summer seasons.

LIVE JAZZ, POP, AND ROCK

Yes, London still swings, although the pendulum now lingers longer over cosmopolitan music than it did in the 1960s. London is a matrix of performing talent, and on any given Saturday night there will be well over 100 gigs being played throughout the city at appropriately deafening volume levels. Tickets vary in price from a fiver or less for pop gigs, to more than £30 if you should like to hear Elton John pound the piano in a stadium.

Again, as with the theater, you must never buy tickets from scalpers because the practice is illegal and their merchandise is probably forged. It is always best to purchase tickets from the concert venue itself. You will usually not be charged a booking fee if you pay with cash.

The thriving London jazz scene has, over the years, given the world such international luminaries as John McLauglin, George Shearing, and Dave Holland, which is indicative of the talent found here. Numerous restaurants, bars, pubs and cafes continue to pleasantly enhance their atmosphere with live jazz music—see *Time Out* and the *Evening Standard's Hot Tickets* magazine for details. Among the leading jazz venues for largely local talent (all of which are profiled in the following club section) are Ronnie Scott's, The 606 Club, Vortex, Jazz Café, China Jazz, Pizza Express, Pizza on the Park, and Bull's Head.

The Barbican and South Bank Centre often present top international (inevitably American) stars, and two big jazz festivals are held in the autumn: the Soho Jazz Festival and the Oris London Jazz Festival.

The Notting Hill Carnival held in late August is Europe's largest street festival and features huge sound systems pumping out reggae, rap, and drum bass. Be warned though, this event is not for the agoraphobic or timid—there are entirely too many muggers, pick-pockets, and deranged people pumped full of alcohol for it to suit every sensibility.

Gargantuan rock structures include the 100,000-seat **Wembley Arena, Stadium and Conference Centre** (Empire Way, Wembley, Middlesex phone (0181) 902-8833, Wembley Park tube); the 20,000-seat **Earl's Court Exhibition Centre** (Warwick Road, SW5 phone (0171) 385-1200, Earl's Court tube); and the 12,500-capacity **London Arena** (Limeharbour, Isle of Dogs, E14 phone (0171) 538-1212, Docklands Light rail). Of course, the sheer vastness of these coliseums tends to undermine the sonic and visual aspects of performance, and refreshments are overpriced along a similar scale. Still, if you must see the Rolling Stones or Robbie Williams, then you'll go to these places.

Smaller-scale and hence more civilized venues are preferable in every way. The **Shepherd's Bush Empire** (Shepherd's Bush Green, W12 phone (0181)749-7474, Shepherd's Bush tube) had previously been the BBC Television Theatre before developing into a top popular music spot. The Empire has a three-tiered seating arrangement, but we suggest you acquire an upstairs ticket as the ground floor slants downwards.

The **Brixton Academy** has a 4,300-person capacity with a seated balcony and standing ground level. Many popular bands have selected BA to perform in, and the place has a good atmosphere. However, it does lie within one of London's more dodgy areas, so use common sense and don't go wandering around after the gig. Instead, head straight over to the nearby tube station or, better still, hail a black cab. Beware of unlicensed minicabs, which are often unsound structurally, overpriced, and sometimes driven by criminals. Brixton Academy is at 211 Stockwell Rd., SW9, phone (0171) 924-9999, Brixton tube.

The **Mean Fiddler** is renowned as London's top venue for Irish and country music, but also presents pop and rock acts. The Fiddler is an agreeable place in which to spend an evening, and success has enabled its owner to extend his domain to quite a few venues, including the Jazz Café. Mean Fiddler, 28a High St., NW10 (phone (0181) 961-5490; info line, phone (0181) 963-0940, Willesden Junction tube/rail/N18 bus).

DANCE CLUBS

London has a huge range of nightclubs, offering everything from hard-core techno to smooth jazz to table-top dancers. London's clubs generally provide excellent quality. However, although they compete for your custom, thriving London clubs—and this is true of clubs anywhere—may sometimes refuse to admit you on the basis of a doorman's arbitrary decision.

Therefore, it may be a good idea not to set your heart on one club when there are so many to choose from. Only do make an early start—before 11 p.m.—then, should the doormen prove intractable, you have the option—indeed, satisfaction—of repairing to a rival club.

Many clubs offer reduced admission rates before 10:30 p.m., and then it is easier to gain admittance at that hour: A club that is quiet at 11 p.m. can often be packed to the rafters by midnight.

Some clubs in London start late and carry on until 6 a.m.—with their busiest period being between 11:30 and 2 a.m. If you intend to dine at the club, we recommend you book a table for 10 p.m., after which you will be permitted to stay on for the dancing. Not all clubs serve dinner; call the club and ask for information.

For disco dancing the following clubs (all profiled in the following section) are recommended: Embargo, Hanover Grand, Leopard Lounge, Ministry of Sound, and the Cafe de Paris.

Swing dancing comes in several categories in London. Ballroom dancing is held on Saturday afternoons and evenings and Sunday afternoons in such elegant venues as the legendary **Savoy Hotel** (1 Savoy Hill, WC2, phone (0171) 846-1533, Embankment tube) and the **Palm Court at the Waldorf** (WC2, phone (0171) 836-2400, Aldwych tube) to live music. Incidentally, the tea dances held in the Waldorf's Palm Court are so popular that tables must be booked at least six weeks in advance. Ladies should always be arrayed in gowns and dresses, and gentlemen attired in either black tie or lounge suits.

Jump Jive Nights are altogether more frenetic affairs, which is reflected in the zoot suits, army uniforms, and bobby socks donned by punters for bopping to music of the 1940s. Jitterbugs are held on Wednesday nights at **Notre Dame Hall** (5 Leicester Place, WC2, phone (0171) 437-5571, Leicester Square tube), a top spot for swing dancing, as is the **Dover Street Restaurant and Bar** (8/10 Dover St., W1, phone (0171) 629-9813 or (0171) 491-2958, Green Park tube). In addition to swing bands, Dover Street also books R&B outfits and dinner jazz combos, so you might want to phone ahead to find out which night would be most suitable for your visit. **The 100 Club** (100 Oxford St., W1, phone (0171) 636-0933, Oxford Circus tube) features jump jive dancing and early evening dance lessons on Mondays.

For Latin dancing you might wish to try La Salsa held on Friday nights at the **Loughborough Hotel.** The three packed floors of the chic South American venue feature a Brazilian bar, live bands, and classes beginning at 9:30 p.m. La Salsa entertains an integrated crowd consisting largely of regulars, and the atmosphere is harmonious. The Loughborough Hotel is on Loughborough Road, Brixton (phone (0171) 771-3134 or (0171) 642-5806). Take a black cab to this venue, where, at the close of festivities, the doormen will direct you to a reputable minicab firm only 30 seconds away from the club.

Dancing the tango is a romantic way to spend an evening, and the best place in town to do so is at **Tangomania, The Dome—Boston Arms** on the corner of Junction Road and Dartmouth Park Hill, N19 (phone (0171) 690-5835 or (0171) 281-5869, Tufnell Park tube). Tangos are danced there on Monday, Wednesday, and Sunday to the strains of Los

Mareados. Classes are held at the beginning of the evening and dancers at all levels are welcome. Other Latin hot spots include **Bar Rhumba** (36 Shaftsbury Ave., W1, phone (0171) 287-2751, Leicester Square tube); **Salsa** (Charing Cross Road, WC1, phone (0171) 379-3277, Leicester Square tube); **Cuba** (11 Kensington High St., W8, phone (0171) 938-4137, Kensington High Street tube); and **Havana,** Fulham (490 Fulham Rd., SW6, phone (0171) 381-5005, Fulham Broadway tube).

BARS AND PUBS

The British are, generally speaking, formidable drinkers, with the pub having stood since time immemorial as the central institution in the British experience. And it is that golden rule of pub etiquette—respectful reserve—that has enabled people from all walks of life to mingle successfully.

Keeping pace with the British as they effortlessly knock back pint after pint is not an easy task for the uninitiated. Still, accomplished American boozers, after putting in an appropriate amount of time and practice, should be able to hold up their end of the proceedings, eventually. If, however, you have inadvertently permeated the wall of British reserve to strike up an acquaintance with some friendly natives in a pub, and it is your turn to spring for a round but you haven't finished your pint, it is better to swallow one's pride, rather than keep everyone waiting, and head over to the bar, cash in hand.

Incidentally, though it is not customary to tip bartenders in pubs, those serving expensive drinks in upmarket clubs and bars sprinkled across West London often do expect gratuity. And, although they have a vague understanding of what a Bloody Mary is, you will draw a blank for most British bartenders of you ask them for, say, a Cape Cod, a Sea Breeze, or even a Screwdriver. You will have to instead explain that it is a vodka and cranberry and so on that you require. When your drink arrives you will find to your dismay, that spirits in Britain are, by law, served up in paltry amounts called gills or measures (that is, thimblefuls), so you might want to ask for a double.

It's no surprise that the British lead the world at the sport of drinking pints of beer. Their superb beer comes in a variety of appealing guises, including lager (light continental beer), bitter (rightly named Anglo-Saxon ale), mild (concocted with chocolate malt), cider (fermented apple juice), and shandy (half lager, half lemonade). Best of all are real ales, the boozy equivalent of organic whole-meal bread.

Pub food also can be surprisingly good, depending on the overall quality of the pub itself. Most pubs are strongly historical in ambience, with walls festooned with attractive eighteenth- and nineteenth-century bric-a-brac. In winter, many pubs have a roaring fire, and in summer, a beer garden.

Although bars with a special hours certificate may remain open until 3 a.m., pubs tend to close at 11 p.m. on weekdays and at midnight on weekends. Britain, however, is forging ever closer ties with Europe, and licensing laws are expected to soon be extended until they fall into line with those of other EU member states.

If you wish to include a visit to an archetypal olde worlde inn on your agenda, you could not do better than the **Prospect of Whitby** (57 Wapping Wall, E1, phone (0171) 481-1095, Wapping tube). Whitby dates back to 1520 and is mentioned in Pepys's diary. The pub is renowned for its Elizabethan pewter bar, flagstone floors, cast-iron hearths, and small round windows.

A haven for journalists and scribblers of all types since before 1666, when it was singed by the Great Fire, **Ye Old Cheshire Cheese** (145 Fleet St., EC4, phone (0171) 353-6170, Blackfriars tube) is a storybook tavern replete with blazing fires, nooks and crannies, wooden floors, and sundry bars and dining sections. During your visit to Old Cheesy, you may as well raise a glass to previous regulars Thackeray, Johnson, Voltaire, Pope, and Tennyson.

By contrast, **The Saint** (8 Great Newport St., WC2, phone (0171) 240-1551, Leicester Square tube) is ultramodern with its patronizing door staff; chic, spotlit décor; and attractive cocktails and cuisine.

If Britain's inclement weather causes you to yearn for sunnier climes, you might like to go to **Trader Vic's** for a taste of the tropics. Home of the Mai Tai cocktail and exotic and delicious food, Vic's is something of a mood lagoon. Trader Vic's is in the Park Lane Hilton (22 Park Lane, W1, phone (0171) 208-4113, Green Park tube).

Those of you who enjoy a good cigar along with cocktails and seafood would undoubtedly enjoy **Little Havana** (1 Leicester Place, Leicester Square, WC2, phone (0171) 287-0100, Leicester Square tube). Little Havana stays open late, features live Latin music and cabaret, appropriately exotic settings, discount cocktail jugs served 5–7 p.m., and a cigar lounge.

We now make mention of three exclusive venues that you might not be able to get into but ought to know about. First, the still fashionable **Atlantic Bar & Grill** (20 Glasshouse St., W1, phone (0171) 734-4888, Piccadilly Circus tube); next, **The Metropolitan Bar** (Old Park Lane, W1, phone (0171) 447-1000, Hyde Park Corner tube), which, at press time, is awash with pop and soap stars; and finally, **Pharmacy,** a bar and restaurant decorated and part owned by Damien Hirst, Britain's most notorious conceptual artist. Pharmacy is at 150 Notting Hall Gate (phone (0171) 221-2442, Notting Hill tube).

A SEXY CITY

The oldest profession has long flourished in London, with some of its more accomplished practitioners establishing links with the greatest names in England. Indeed, many noble lines were started by the illegitimate progeny of a royal sire and his concubine—an argument the Labour Party has used in its attempts to abolish the right of hereditary peers to sit in the House of Lords.

Although prostitution is not as endemic as it was during its Victorian heyday, when even Tory Prime Minister Gladstone used to prowl the streets, supposedly in quest of fallen women in need of reforming, one cannot enter a telephone box in the central London of today without noticing the numerous salacious cards deposited within.

Soho is the sex center of London, and the area around Old Compton Street hosts quite a few sex shops and strip clubs. Beware of unlicensed venues, though, for they are, quite literally, tourist traps. A common practice of these establishments is to plant a siren-like hostess at the door who lures her victim inside for a drink and a show. The punter subsequently discovers that the bill for her orange juice and his beer comes to some astronomically unreasonable figure—and there are always a number of belligerent security staff on hand to ensure that customers pay up.

Perhaps the safest sex shows to attend are those held at the following venues. **Stringfellow's,** 16 Upper St. Martin's Lane, Covent Garden, WC2, (phone (0171) 240-5534, Leicester Square tube). Poodle-dressed Peter Stringfellow's club pays host to the mass-market sort of celebrity: soap stars, footballers, and Page Three Girls. The place is rife with 1980s glamour and pleasant enough in its way, particularly since Stringfellow's came into possession of a table-dancing license.

Astral, 5 Brewer St., W1 (phone (0171) 287-7988, Piccadilly tube). Astral offers a sophisticated burlesque atmosphere reminiscent of London in the 1950s and 1960s. The club contains 300 boudoir-styled alcoves, a celebrated chef in Andy Campbell, Casablanca-era cocktails, and an extensive wine list ranging from prize-winning offerings from the new world to the finest Grande Marque Champagne.

Sophisticats at Voltane, 1 Marylebone Lane, W1 (phone (0181) 201-8804 or (0181) 201-8968, Bond Street tube). Presided over by the amiable Catman, David Simones, Sophisticats was recently the subject of a seven-part television documentary and features ballerinas and showgirls from all over the world. Indeed, Sophisticats has a distinctly Parisian decadence about it; in addition to the twice-nightly Catgirl cabaret, the club also provides table dancing, caviar girls, and cocktail waitresses. Recommended, although as a private club, you must call first to see if you can get a reservation.

The Mayfair Club and Restaurant (15 Berkeley St., W1, phone (0171) 629-0010, Bond Street tube) is, like Sophisticats, a private members' club. However, American visitors may be admitted to these august venues provided they phone beforehand to make a reservation. The club hosts a girlie cabaret from Monday to Thursday from 7 p.m. until 2 a.m., while the restaurant features an à la carte Italian menu and serves from 7 p.m. to midnight.

GAMING IN THE UNITED KINGDOM

The gaming industry in Great Britain is one of the most carefully regulated in the world. All casinos across England, Scotland, and Wales are licensed under the Gaming Act of 1968, which stipulates that unless already a member or the guest of a member, a player must register at the casino 24 hours before entering to play. The Gaming Act is designed to protect the public purse from the perils of compulsive gambling. Or, in the language of strictest legalese: It is a legal requirement that the membership application form is signed on the premises of the casino. A passport, driver's license, or suitable identification is required. Authorization of all new memberships takes 24 hours. The casinos of London Clubs International begin with the magnificent **50 St. James** (50 St. James St., SW1, phone (0171) 491-4678, Piccadilly tube), which opened as London's first purpose-built gaming club in 1828 and is, along with the legendary **Les Ambassadeurs Club** (5 Hamilton Place, W1, phone (0171) 495-5555, Hyde Park tube), at the top end of the market. These exclusive and lavishly appointed clubs are frequented by royalty, the aristocracy, and celebrated figures from the world of entertainment.

Midmarket venues include the **Rendezvous Casino** (14 Old Park Lane, W1, phone (0171) 491-8586, Hyde Park tube), with its spacious gaming floor, French-influenced bistro, and relaxed sports bar; and **The Sportsman Casino** (40 Bryanston St., W1, phone (0171) 414-0061, Hyde Park tube), designed in the style of a Mississippi riverboat. As well as offering roulette, blackjack, and baccarat, the Sportsman boasts a dice game that has proven to be particularly popular with American visitors.

The mass-market **Golden Nugget Casino** (22 Shaftesbury Ave., W1, phone (0171) 439-0099, Piccadilly tube) is the largest and busiest casino in the London Clubs group and offers a fast-moving environment and fast food to go with it. The atmosphere of this casino is both friendly and informal. Games include roulette, baccarat, blackjack, and stud poker.

FREELOADER'S FORUM

Visitors to London rapidly discover the disparity in prices between goods and services purchased in America and their English equivalents. British merchandise is far more expensive due to a legalized swindle, the so-called Recommended Retail Price Index, whereby prices are fixed at scandalously high leves by agreement between manufacturers and retail outlets.

But please do not complain about Britain's rip-off prices to those working on the shop floor, because although company bosses are raking it in, the poor worker at the checkout counter makes considerably less than he or she would in America. Yet the British can also be generous, as evidenced by the bonanza of free activities taking place throughout London.

Free Music

Many churches in central London such as **St. John's** (Waterloo Road, Waterloo tube), **St. Martin–in–the–Fields** (St. Martin's Place, Leicester Square or Charing Cross tube), and **St. Pancras Church** (Euston Road, Euston tube) offer free lunchtime classical concerts and recitals, as do music schools such as the **Royal College of Music** (phone (0171) 591-4314) and the **Royal Academy of Music** (phone (0171) 873-7300).

You can also hear some of the capital's best jazz musicians at the aptly named **Freestage at the Barbican** (Silk Street, EC2, phone (0171) 638-8891, Barbican tube) and at the South Bank's **National Theatre** (phone (0171) 452-3000) and **Royal Festival Hall** (phone (0171) 960-4242); both venues can be reached from Waterloo station.

The **100 Club** (100 Oxford St., W1, phone (0171) 636-0933, Oxford Street tube) presents a well-liked series of swing and trad gigs during Friday lunchtimes. Some bookshops are also given to presenting free music: Try **Border's Books** (197 Oxford St., W1, phone (0171) 292-1600, Bond Street tube), **Helter Skelter Music Bookshop** (4 Denmark St., WC2, phone (0171) 836-1151, Tottenham tube), and **Filthy MacNasty's Whiskey Cafe** (68 Amwell St., EC1, phone (0171) 837-6067).

Islington Bar (342 Caledonian Rd., N1, phone (0171) 609-4917, King's Cross tube) presents Conspirators in Dub on Thursdays and Extending Family on Fridays where admission is free before 9:30 p.m. Free Fridays can also be found at the **Cock Tavern** (Phoenix Road, NW1, phone (0171) 387-1884, Euston tube), where the Latin and hard house dance grooves can be absorbed along with pints and alco-pops costing only £1.50, which is as cheap a pint as can be found in London. Numerous bars, restaurants, and pubs also supply the punter with free music. Check *Time Out* and *Hot Tickets* for listings.

Free Comedy

With the practice of adding canned laughter onto television soundtracks having been universally condemned, the BBC now requires a constant supply of jolly spectators willing to be audience members for their comedy productions. For free tickets—just imagine the fun you'll have telling everyone back home that you appeared on British TV—contact the BBC Ticket Unit at Room 30, Design Building, BBC TV Centre, Wood Lane, W12 7RJ, phone (0181) 576-1227.

Free Films

Free documentaries are sometimes shown at the Whitechapel Gallery (phone (0171) 522-7878, Whitechapel tube), whereas art house films are shown periodically on Saturday afternoons at the Clore Gallery inside the Tate Gallery, Millbank, SW1 (phone (0171) 887-8000.

Nightlife Profiles

606

A highly regarded jazz club and restaurant open for over 25 years
Who Goes There: Yuppies, buppies, and bohemians, young and old

90 Lots Rd., SW10
(0171) 352-5953

Zone 11: Chelsea and South Kensington
Cover: There is no cover except for a Music Charge of £4.75 per person on Sunday–Thursday, and £5.45 on Friday and Saturday, which is added onto the bill at the end of the night
Prices: Modest to reasonable
Dress: Casual

Food available: An extensive European-based menu featuring a wide selection of meat, fresh fish, and vegetarian meals. The cuisine at the 606 has been praised by the *Sunday Times* and TV's *The Restaurant Show*, among others
Hours: 8:30 p.m.–2 a.m. Monday–Saturday; Sunday 8:30 p.m.–11:30 a.m.

What goes on: There are two jazz groups on each night from Monday through Wednesday playing from 9:30 p.m. until 2 a.m. One band is featured, playing from around 10 p.m. until 2 a.m. The groups are selected from a variety of up-and-coming players and other more established musicians. The music ranges from traditional to contemporary with an emphasis on the modern.

Setting & atmosphere: A basement club with a relaxed atmosphere, the 606 is a great place to take a date for a late supper and a bottle of wine.

If you go: Don't ask any of the bands to play "Tie a Yellow Ribbon."

BAGLEY'S

A gigantic disco and bar
Who Goes There: Youthful dancers and soaks

Cross Freight Depot, Off York Way, N1
(0171) 278-2777

Zone 15: Regent's Park and Camden Town
Cover: £5.20 on Saturday
Prices: Cheap by club standards

Dress: Variable
Food available: Snacks
Hours: Closes Saturday at 6 a.m.

What goes on: Sweat rises like smoke off the dance floor.

Setting & atmosphere: Bagley's is colossal, with five dance floors, six bars, and something different going on in every room.

If you go: You will be part of a heaving, throbbing mob of young movers.

BROWN'S

Glamorous disco
Who Goes There: Brown's has been an oasis to the stars for the last 12 years and continues to be so. Although ostensibly a private members' club, the public is permitted entrance on Friday and Saturday nights

4 Great Queen St., WC2
(0171) 831-0802

Zone 7: Soho and the West End
Cover: £15
Prices: Expensive, but then so is being a star

Dress: Fashionable
Food available: None
Hours: Closes at 4 a.m.

What goes on: The club has a three-tiered social system with the downstairs dance floor as Midgard, the second floor as the Rainbow Bridge, and the VIP bar on the third floor standing as Asgard—home of the gods.

Setting & atmosphere: Loud, glamorous, and urgent.

If you go: Don't pester the celebs for autographs.

BULL'S HEAD

A lovely pub and jazz club
Who Goes There: The 25–55 age group; actors, musos, film and telly people

373 Lonsdale Rd., SW13
(0181) 876-5241

Zone 12: West London: Hammersmith, Chiswick, Richmond, Kew
Cover: Anywhere from £3–8 depending on the celebrity of the band
Prices: Modest
Dress: In the words of the immortal Cole Porter, anything goes

Food available: Home-cooked European and English fare with pastries and puddings
Hours: Relaxed pub hours (i.e., the place is supposed to close at 11 p.m.)

What goes on: Most of the modern greats have played here.

Setting & atmosphere: The Bull's Head is a beautiful pub facing the Thames that was built in 1684 with the stables—now the bistro—added on in 1700. The mood is convivial.

If you go: Offer to buy the musicians a pint.

CAFE DE PARIS

London's most renowned club
Who Goes There: Everyone who is anyone in London

3–4 Coventry St., W1
(0171) 734-7700

Zone 7: Soho and the West End
Cover: £10
Prices: Somewhat pricey
Dress: Elegant

Food available: French cuisine presided over by an ex–Anton Mosimann chef
Hours: Closes at 3 a.m.

What goes on: Live jazz music accompanies dinner, after which a DJ spins records for the more athletically inclined. The cafe is furnished with numerous bars.

Setting & atmosphere: Since its launch in the 1920s, the Cafe de Paris has been synonymous with high society—even the queen has given a party there. Such luminous performers as Marlene Dietrich, Maurice Chevalier, Fred Astaire, Noël Coward, Frank Sinatra, Edith Piaf, and your humble correspondent have graced its stage. Plush, opulent, and elegant, the Cafe's art deco design was influenced by the operas *Don Giovanni* and *La Bohème*. A 50-foot bar encompasses the oval ballroom, and the restaurant is highly regarded.

If you go: You will be dining, drinking, and dancing in style. You may, however, need to know the right people to get in. Therefore we suggest that you circumvent all of the nonsense at the door by booking a table for dinner. Please do not turn up in your baseball cap and sneakers.

CAMDEN PALACE

A labyrinthine disco
Who Goes There: 21- to 30-year-olds

1a Camden High St., NW1
(0171) 387-0428

Zone 15: Regent's Park and Camden Town
Cover: £10–15
Prices: Average
Dress: Club clothes—almost anything goes
Food available: Burgers and fish and chips, and so on
Hours: Closes on Saturday at 8 a.m.

What goes on: Drinking, dancing, and flirting through the dawn.

Setting & atmosphere: Camden Palace was opened in 1981 by that deservedly famous club entrepreneur Rusty Egan, and his then partner, Steve Strange, as London's answer to Studio 54. And though the club may not be as happening as it was in those halcyon days, it is still ticking over nicely. Formally a theater, the club's interior also offers a striking display of tech noir sculptures along with its balconies, bars, alcoves, and dance floor.

If you go: You will boogie through to breakfast.

CHINA JAZZ

An elegant art deco–styled jazz club, restaurant, and bar
Who Goes There: The well-to-do, film stars, celebrities, politicians, and aristocrats

12 Berkeley Square, W1
(0171) 499-9933

Zone 8: Mayfair and Piccadilly
Cover: No cover charge
Prices: Upmarket
Dress: Ladies should be in dresses, and men must wear a tie
Specials: Live jazz every evening
Food available: Chef Cheung Hong is the first Chinese chef to be awarded a coveted Michelin star in Britain; his mastery in the art of Cantonese cooking—that most sophisticated of Chinese cuisines—is displayed to its best advantage in such exquisite dishes as scallops stir-fried with wild mushroom sauce and breast of duck barbecued with lychees
Hours: Monday–Friday noon to 3 p.m., 6 p.m. to 1 a.m. (last orders at midnight). Saturday: 6 p.m. to 1 a.m. Sunday: 3 p.m. to midnight (last orders at 10 p.m.)

What goes on: You may dine in the restaurant or take in the live jazz while relaxing in the cocktail lounge.

Setting & atmosphere: Inspired by the art-deco elegance of the 1930s, China Jazz features both original artwork and specially commissioned reproductions. Set in the legendary site of Berkeley Square, this venue retains the aura of an exclusive members club.

If you go: Dress very well and remain cool in the presence of celebrities.

CRAZY LARRY'S

Caters to a Hooray Henry set out to get drunk and find girls
Who Goes There: Young twentysomethings

533 King's Rd., Chelsea, SW6
(0171) 376-5555

Zone 11: Chelsea and South Kensington
Cover: £10
Prices: Not too bad, for London
Dress: Smart, casual
Food available: Snacks
Hours: Closes at 2:30 a.m.

What goes on: A place for fledgling clubbers just out of university to have a sweaty bop. It's a bit sporty as well, with its satellite video screen hookup. And Crazy Larry's is well known for its '70s, '80s, and '90s nights.

Setting & atmosphere: The decor is functional, as is the music. The object is to get the sporty young grads away from the bar and out onto the dance floor.

If you go: Remember to say "yah" rather than "yo."

DOVER STREET RESTAURANT & BAR

A large and justly popular jazz restaurant and bar
Who Goes There: Numerous personalities from the worlds of stage, film, television, and sport mingle with white-collar workers

8–10 Dover St., W1
(0171) 491-7509

Zone 8: Mayfair and Piccadilly
Cover: Free before 10 p.m. Monday–Thursday, £7 pounds after 10 p.m. Free before 9 p.m. and £10 pounds after 10 p.m. Fridays & Saturdays see a basic £3 reduced music cover charge for diners with a charge of £10 after 10 p.m.
Prices: Reasonable
Dress: Smart, casual; jeans and sneakers are not permitted
Specials: The Dover Street

Restaurant Gourmet Menu available for £45 per person (including music cover, service, and VAT) offers a glass of champagne on arrival followed by a tempting selection of French and English cuisine
Food available: French, Italian, English, and even vegetarian fine dining
Hours: Monday–Friday 5:30 p.m.–3 a.m., Saturday 7 p.m.–3 a.m.

What goes on: Fine dining, live music, dancing, and DJs.

Setting & atmosphere: Dover Street has been established as one of London's most atmospheric restaurants and jazz venues for over 20 years and has recently been refurbished to become the largest venue of its kind in the capital. This place swings.

If you go: Remember to adhere to the dress code.

EMBARGO

Chelsea's always-in-vogue designer dance club
Who Goes There: The young Chelsea set

533b King's Rd., SW10
(0171) 351-5038

Zone 11: Chelsea and South
Kensington
Cover: £10
Prices: Slightly pricey

Dress: Stylish
Food available: A modern European restaurant serves dinner
Hours: 9 p.m.–2:30 a.m.

What goes on: Along with Circa in Mayfair, Embargo was also opened by Rusty Egan and was therefore the vogue place to be during Rusty's tenure. Embargo still draws a classy celebrity crowd who dance the night away to thunderous house DJs.

Setting & atmosphere: A modern designer club with clean, hard surfaces and mirrors, Embargo is often attended by beautiful young women.

If you go: Don't disturb the beautiful young people.

EMPORIUM

Most discos would love to have the design and sound of this place
Who Goes There: Sports stars and soap stars

62 Kingly St., W1
(0171) 734-3190

Zone 7: Soho and the West End
Cover: £15
Prices: Expensive

Dress: Smart—no sneakers
Specials: You must be kidding
Food available: An expensive

What goes on: The pop celebrities discuss show biz and football over deafening DJs while waiters dance attendance on them.

Setting & atmosphere: A high-tech and ultramodern club glistening with the sheen of success.

If you go: Browse through a few tabloids beforehand so that you'll be able to recognize the subjects of the latest scandals.

THE END

Great place for pumping house with a restaurant called A.K.A. adjoined
Who Goes There: The young and energetic

16a West Central St., WC1
(0171) 379-4770

Zone 7: Soho and the West End
Cover: £12
Prices: Average
Dress: Aggressively

Food available: Snacks
Hours: Open until 7 a.m. on a
Saturday morning

What goes on: Dancing, drinking, and flirting.

Setting & atmosphere: The designer furniture lends the place an element of class, while the water fountains, which have refreshed many a parched dancer, are an unusually generous touch.

If you go: Don't stray too far from the water fountains.

THE FRIDGE

Brixton's most celebrated disco
Who Goes There: The clientele varies according to what is on during any given night, but the Fridge has been playing host to the gay and lesbian market for some time now

Town Hall Parade, Brixton Hill, SW2
(0171) 326-5100

Zone 5: South London
Cover: £12
Prices: Average
Dress: Casual

Food Available: Fast
Hours: Closes at 6 a.m. on
Saturdays

What goes on: Dancing and trancing out to techno.

Setting & atmosphere: A vast dance floor, a huge bar, capacious balconies, and the liberality of head honchos Andy and Sue have combined to make the Fridge a place to really let it all hang out. Highly recommended for the open-minded.

If you go: Call a respectable minicab company to get home.

HEAVEN

Gay paradise
Who Goes There: Straights and gays

Villiers Street, WC2
(0171) 930-2020

Zone 7: Soho and the West End
Cover: £8
Prices: Average
Dress: Flamboyant

Food Available: Dinner
Hours: Closes on Saturdays at
4 a.m.

What goes on: A gay old time is had by all, even by the heteros, who are also dying to get into Heaven.

Setting & atmosphere: The crowded rooms pulsate to techno music.

If you go: Arrive early. Heaven is notorious for the length of its queues.

HIPPODROME

Tourist trap
Who Goes There: Unwary tourists

Leicester Square, W1
(0171) 437-4311

Zone 7: Soho and the West End
Cover: £10
Prices: Slightly pricey

Dress: Smart
Food Available: Restaurant
Hours: Closes at 3:30 a.m.

What goes on: Drinking, dancing, and flirting.

Setting & atmosphere: A gigantic lighting rig, black mirrors, a large neon sign over the entrance, and a superb sound system playing chart toppers.

If you go: Don't admit it.

HANOVER GRAND

A popular discotheque
Who Goes There: Fashionistas on Thursday, while the house set
attends on Friday and Saturday

6 Hanover St., W1
(0171) 499-7977

Zone 7: Soho and the West End
Cover: £12
Prices: Uppish
Dress: Smart/casual

Food available: No
Hours: Closes Saturday at 4:30 a.m.

What goes on: Roger Michael, one of London's top club promoters, welcomes the models and fashionable on Thursday nights for his Next Big Thing evenings, while Fresh 'n' Funky on Wednesday draws the dance crowd.

Setting & atmosphere: The club has a capacity for 800 people, making it fairly large. And the venue has three floors with the dancing taking place on ground level.

If you go: Go on a Thursday.

JAZZ CAFE

Modern club geared toward rap, soul, funk, and jazz
Who Goes There: 20–55-year-olds, depending on whether jazz or rap
is featured

5 Parkway, N1
(0171) 916-6060

Zone 15: Regent's Park and
Camden Town
Cover: £6–22 according to the
popularity of the act
Prices: Average
Dress: Anything goes

Food Available: Dinner is offered
via a modern European menu
Hours: The Jazz Cafe remains open
until 2 a.m. on Saturday

What goes on: This club's name is something of a misnomer, as is the radio station Jazz FM's. Both entities attempt to confer the superior artistic status of jazz on lesser forms of music. Thus the Jazz Cafe, on any given night, may have rap, soul, or funk bands performing rather than jazz groups. I therefore suggest that you consult the listings pages of *Time Out* or *Hot Tickets* magazine before going.

Setting & atmosphere:　The bar leads onto the dance floor, where there are some seats available. The restaurant is situated on the balcony overlooking the stage and projectors transmit arty neon images onto the awnings.

If you go:　Tell the soul band that is performing that you thought you were coming to a jazz club and then ask them to attempt a rendition of John Coltrane's "Giant Steps."

LEGENDS

A stylish disco located in Mayfair
Who Goes There: The fashionable

29 Old Burlington St., W1
(0171) 437-9933

Zone 8: Mayfair and Piccadilly
Cover: £15 on Saturdays
Prices: Average
Dress:: Stylish, of course

Food available: À la carte
Hours: Legends closes at 4 a.m. on Saturday

What goes on:　Drinking, dancing, and flirting.

Setting & atmosphere:　Legends is a beautiful ground-floor bar in Mayfair with a pumping sound system on the dance floor. The place positively shimmers with elegance and has been the venue for memorable parties.

If you go:　Remember that you are in the vicinity of Savile Row and behave accordingly.

LEOPARD LOUNGE

A fashionable disco where '70s kitsch meets '80s New York
Who Goes There: The young Chelsea/Fulham set comprised of the attractive daughters and sons of the rich and famous

The Broadway, Fulham Rd., SW6
(0171) 385-0834

Zone 11: Chelsea and South Kensington
Cover: £10–20 is average
Prices: Slightly cheaper than average

Dress: Smart/casual
Food available: Sushi and snacks
Hours: Closes at 3 a.m.

What goes on: Caged go-go dancers perform on the stage, as does the occasional live band, making the amenities here largely those of a traditional disco. The Leopard Lounge draws one of the best crowds in London.

Setting & atmosphere: LL is made up of three different areas: The main dance floor is overlooked by a balcony; behind that is the VIP Room.

If you go: Say hello to your host, Mr. H, who is reputed to be something of a dude.

MADAME JO JO'S

A camp cabaret club
Who Goes There: Increasing numbers of London's fashionable, smart, young set appreciate the art of cabaret, as do the usual drag queens, tourists, and clubbers

8 Brewer St., W1
(0171) 734-2473

Zone 7: Soho and the West End
Covers: £15 on Saturday night
Prices: Slightly on the expensive side
Dress: Flamboyant, if you wish to be acknowledged by the performers
and regulars; otherwise, the code is for smart/casual attire
Food available: Snacks
Hours: Open until 3 a.m. on Saturday

What goes on: Lenny Beige's Club Indigo on Tuesdays is a well-publicized extravaganza of kitsch entertainment, and other nights feature amusing drag queen–led frivolities.

Setting & atmosphere: A bordello-styled cabaret, Madame Jo Jo's is appropriately situated in the midst of the Soho porn district it satirizes so effectively. Plus, the lounge-core music is wonderful.

If you go: You'll find that Madame Jo Jo's offers up surprisingly sophisticated entertainment.

MINISTRY OF SOUND

The United Kingdom's most famous disco
Who Goes There: Regulars who've been coming for over five years, as well as newcomers

103 Gaunt St., SE1
(0171) 378-6562

Zone 6: Greenwich and the Docklands
Cover: £15 on Saturdays
Prices: Slightly expensive

Dress: Glamorous
Food available: Snacks
Hours: Closes on Saturday at 9 a.m.

What goes on: Young to youngish clubbers bopping to monotonously loud and repetitious drum 'n' bass grooves.

Setting & atmosphere: Ministry of Sound is a vast converted warehouse located in the not exactly salubrious boondocks of Elephant and Castle, so you must be sure to take a cab both there and back. You will need plenty of energy because this place will blow your head off. Check the listings pages of the press for the nights on which American DJs are imported to show the locals how it is done.

If you go: Wear your dancing shoes.

NOISE BAR

Its name is appropriate
Who Goes There: Gorgeous party people

10 Wardour St., W1
(0171) 437-3671

Zone 7: Soho and the West End
Cover: No cover
Prices: Average

Dress: Gorgeous
Food available: Snacks
Hours: 6 p.m.– 4 a.m.

What goes on: Punters attempt to converse while well-known DJs and their accomplices blast out drum 'n' bass records over the mixing desk.

Setting & atmosphere: Situated at street level, Noise boasts a modern industrial interior. The bar's facade consists of curved Privalite glass windows, which, after an electrical current has been passed through them, can be either clear or opaque. The purple and copper bar dispenses a comprehensive list of premium-brand spirits, bottled beers, wines and champagnes, and an extensive cocktail list.

If you go: Try either the Hurricane—a mixture of Bacardi, Myer's Dark, and tropical juices; or the Typhoon, made up of Amaretto Di Saronno, Archers Peach Schnapps, Blue Curaçao, grenadine, peach puree, and orange juice.

PIZZA EXPRESS

An intimate jazz club and restaurant recently dubbed "London's best live music venue" by *Time Out* magazine
Who Goes There: Pizza and jazz lovers of both the tourist and local variety.

10 Dean St., W1
(0171) 439-8722

Zone 7: Soho and the West End
Cover: £10–20, depending on the status of the band
Prices: Average
Dress: Smart/casual

Food available: Italian: pizza, pasta, lasagne, salad Niçoise, and so on
Hours: Opens at 8 p.m. with shows beginning at 9 p.m. Closes at midnight

What goes on: Eighty percent of the bands booked are celebrated Americans of the status of Tal Farlow, Art Farmer, Kenny Garret, and Roy Haynes. Pizza Express also books top British talent such as Martin Taylor and Guy Barker.

Setting & atmosphere: Pizza Express is an intimate basement club equipped with modern stage lighting and sound. The environment is friendly, sophisticated, and relaxed. The food and wine are excellent, and the music is superb. A memorable night out.

If you go: You will enjoy yourself.

PIZZA ON THE PARK

An upmarket jazz/cabaret club/restaurant
Who Goes There: Generally an older crowd of the 45+ category

11–13 Knightsbridge, SW1
(0171) 235-5273

Zone 10: Knightsbridge and Belgravia
Cover: £16–18 if you book in advance, £20 if you turn up at the door
Prices: Fairly average, which is somewhat surprising considering the venue's posh location
Dress: Smart/casual
Food available: Italian
Hours: Opens at 7:30 p.m., closes at midnight

What goes on: Jazz and cabaret shows begin at 9:15 and end at 11:15 p.m.

Setting & atmosphere: The club is located on the site of a Victorian tea shop, which was saved from demolition in 1986 by Peter Boizot. Boizot then commissioned Enzu Apicella to transform the place into a modern jazz/cabaret club. POTP is clubby, intimate, dimly lit, and freshly flowered.

If you go: Try the wild Scottish smoked salmon, reputed to be the best in town.

RONNIE SCOTT'S

London's premier jazz club
Who Goes There: Yuppies, buppies, musicians, and arty types come to hear the world's best jazz musicians in the downstairs club, while the younger set tends to congregate around the upstairs dance floor

47 Frith St., W1
(0121) 643-4525

Zone 7: Soho and the West End
Cover: Varies. Free if you belong to the Musician's Union. £14 is normal for a Saturday
Prices: A little lower than average
Dress: Smart
Food available: A full menu of modern European cuisine
Hours: The club closes as 3 a.m. on Saturday

What goes on: Affluent diners and drinkers are serenaded by famous musicians downstairs while others choose to attend the upstairs disco.

Setting & atmosphere: Ronnie's is pushing 40 now and is as close as London will ever get to the classic sort of jazz club you have seen in countless films.

If you go: Prepare for an enjoyable evening.

SOPHISTICATS AT VOLANTE

The only private members' club in Europe to offer a nude cabaret show along with table dancing, dining, and drinking
Who Goes There: A surprising number of women; office workers, and businessmen

Volante, 1 Marylebone Lane, W1
(0171) 486-7135

Zone 14: Bayswater, Marlyebone, Little Venice, St. John's Wood
Cover: £20
Prices: Reasonable

Dress: Smart/casual
Food available: Dinner
Hours: Monday–Thursday 7:30 p.m.–3:30 a.m.

What goes on: Beautiful catgirls disport themselves in an engagingly athletic manner, both on and off the stage, under the genial stewardship of the Catman, David Simones.

Setting & atmosphere: The ambience is distinctly Parisian and not at all sleazy. Indeed, Sophisticats has been lauded in a number of upmarket publications including *Arena,* the *Sunday Telegraph,* and *Sunday Times.* Quite a few of the Sophisticats showgirls have experience from the ballet and from West End shows, and the cabaret they present is as artfully choreographed as it is erotic.

If you go: Behave yourself.

TURNMILLS

The disco where all-night clubbers end up
Who Goes There: Hard-core club hoppers; Turnmills also hosts Trade, Britain's top gay night

63b Clerkenwell Rd., EC1
(0171) 250-3409

Zone 3: The City, Clerkenwell, and Barbican
Cover: £10, Saturday
Prices: Lowish

Dress: Casual
Food available: Dinner
Hours: 10:30 p.m.–7 a.m.

What goes on: In addition to the mandatory drinking and dancing, this club provides a few pinball machines.

Setting & atmosphere: Candlelit tables and an Electronica bar area provide a refreshing contrast to the throbbing chaos of the dance floor.

If you go: Take a taxi both there and back—if you last until 7 a.m. you will be in no condition to find your way home.

THE WAG CLUB

One of London's most enduringly popular dance clubs
Who Goes There: A combination of young regulars, visitors, and the occasional pop star

Wardour Street, W1
(0171) 437-5534

Zone 7: Soho and the West End
Cover: £8
Prices: Lowish

Dress: Smart/casual
Food available: Snacks
Hours: Closes Saturday at 5 a.m.

What goes on: Drinking, dancing, and flirting.

Setting & atmosphere: Presided over by the multitalented Chris Sullivan, the Wag features a large downstairs bar and dance floor along with a few tables, while upstairs is the restaurant, bar, and another, smaller, dance area.

If you go: Try out both floors.

THE VORTEX JAZZ BAR

A highly regarded jazz club–cum–cafe, bar, and restaurant
Who Goes There: Arty types

139–141 Stoke Newington Church St., N16
(0171) 254-6156

Zone: Northeast London, out of zones
Cover: £2–6
Prices: Reasonable
Dress: Informal
Food available: The cafe serves coffee, cappuccino, teas, cakes, and mainly vegetarian hot meals, soups, and salads
Hours: Monday–Thursday 10 a.m. to 11:30 p.m. Friday and Saturday 10 a.m. until midnight. Sunday 11 a.m. to 11 p.m.

What goes on: The Vortex is so civilized that even its audience has been lauded by *The Times* for its educated and enthusiastic response to the mainstream to avant-garde jazz music presented there. The Vortex also plays host to special guest club nights devoted to international music, cabaret, women musicians, and young contemporary artists. The club also welcomes visiting musicians from America and mainland Europe.

Setting & atmosphere: The Vortex is a first-floor venue in the heart of Stoke Newington. Intimate, shadowy, and seedy with no nonsmoking areas.

If you go: Carry a prominently displayed copy of Camus's *No Exit* with you.

Part Seven

Exercise and Recreation

Spectator Sports

FOOTBALL

Soccer, or football as the English call it, is more than a national obsession—
it is a religion with devotees and acolytes. The days when rival fans would
do bloody battle in the streets are mostly gone due to CCTV, hi-tech detec-
tive work, and well-organized policing at games, as well as reconstruction
of the grounds themselves. However, the fever burns as strong as ever. There
is huge money in football these days and the top teams, who belong to the
Premiership, are all locked into cable TV deals that have the exclusives on
their matches. Consequently, tickets for these games are expensive,
(£12–50), whereas tickets for the teams further down the league are cheaper,
(£8–15). It is well worth a visit to a Premiership game, as the class (and
price) of players these days is phenomenal. The spectators themselves are
also worthy of close attention: Listen to the songs and chants of appreciation of their own teams or, more often, venomous and cruel derision of the
visitors.

The football season runs from August 16 to May 17. Games are 90 minutes long, with injury time and extra time if it is important that there be a
winner (as in for a cup final). Most of the clubs will take credit card bookings over the phone, which is crucial for Premiership games. They take place
on Saturday afternoons and in the evenings on weekdays. Wrap up warm,
and if the conclusion of the game is obvious ten minutes before the final
whistle, leave early to avoid the crush and possible trouble. Avoid the standing seats at the clubs further down the league, as this is where trouble, if it
breaks out, is more likely to occur.

Premiership Teams in London

Arsenal   Arsenal Stadium, Avenall Road, N5. Phone (0171) 704-4000. Arsenal tube, Piccadilly line. Tickets £14–35.

Chelsea   Stamford Bridge, Fulham Road, SW6. Phone (0171) 385-5545. Fulham Broadway tube, District line. Tickets £16–50.

Charlton Athletic   The Valley, Floyd Road, SE7. Phone (0181) 333-4010. Charlton rail. Tickets £18–22.

Tottenham Hotspurs   Whitehart Lane, High Road, N17. Phone (0181) 365-5000. White Hart Lane rail. Tickets £18–36.

West Ham United   Boleyn Ground, Green Street, E13. Phone (0181) 548-2748. Upton Park tube, District line. Tickets £18–31.

Wimbledon   Selhurst Park, Whitehorse Lane, SE25. Phone (0181) 771-8841. Norwood Junction, Selhurst, or Thornton Heath Rail. Tickets £12–20.

National League Teams

Barnet (Division 3)   Underhill Stadium Barnet Lane, Barnet, Herts. Phone (0181) 441-6932. High Barnet tube, Northern line. Tickets £8–14.

Brentford (Division 2)   Griffin Park, Braemar Road, Brentford, Middlesex. Phone (0181) 847-2511. Brentford rail. Tickets £8–15

Fulham (Division 1)   Craven Cottage, Stevenage Road, SW6. Phone (0171) 736-6561. Putney Bridge tube, District line. Tickets £10-14.

Leyton Orient (Division 3)   Matchroom Stadium, Brisbane Road. Leyton tube, Central line. Phone (0181) 926-1111. Tickets £10–13.

Millwall (Division 2)   The Den, Zampa Road, SE16. Phone (0171) 232-1222. South Bermondsey rail. Tickets £11-£15.

Queens Park Rangers (Division 1)   Loftus Road Stadium, South Africa Road, W12. Phone (0181) 740-0503. White City tube, Central line. Tickets £10–20.

Watford (Division 1)   Vicarage Road, Watford. Phone (0192) 349-6010. Watford High Street rail. Tickets £14–20. Sir Elton John is chairman.

CRICKET

Despite the fact that it is a truly international sport (at which the Brits have not excelled for years), there is something quintessentially English about the game of cricket. It is sedate, difficult to understand, and full of quaint language. For example, a "maiden over" is a series of six balls, bowled in a swinging overarm motion, during which no runs are scored. The games sometimes last for days, interrupted frequently by rain and tea. It is considered vulgar to thrash one's opponent by too many runs; when it is clear the losing team cannot win, the winning side "declares" and gives the other team a chance to recover some of their dignity. You can see this game played on many a village green during the season, which runs from mid-April to early September, but there are two main venues in London, Lords and the Oval. Tickets for international games need to be booked well in advance, but the league games, played between counties, are much easier to see.

Where to See It

Lords   St. John's Wood Road, NW8. Phone (0171) 289-1611. St. John's Wood tube, Jubilee line. Home of the MCC (Marylebone Cricket Club, governors of the sport long associated with British elitism), this is often considered the home of cricket. Tickets from £10.

The Oval   Kennington Oval, SE11. Phone (0171) 582-6660. Oval tube, Northern line. International cricket is often played here, tickets for which range from £20 to £40. Tickets for county matches are £7 and £3 for children under age 16.

RUGBY

This is a brutal and violent game similar to American football, but without the padding. Again, the rules are characteristically British: The ball, shaped like an American football, is passed backward or sideways, never forward; during the scrum, the players crouch with their faces or shoulders between the thighs and against the buttocks of the player in front and push against a similarly tightly packed huddle of the opposition. The ball is thrown into this mass of steaming, muddy flesh, from which it is booted out. Whoever catches it then dashes along the field to score a try (touchdown), which is then converted by kicking it over the goal posts for extra points. Like cricket, it is a quintessentially British sport at which the natives no longer truly excel. The New Zealanders, French, South

Africans, and Fijians are marvelous rugby players, but also like cricket, tickets for international games are hard to get. The season runs from September to May, and it is enjoying something of a resurgence in popularity due to the amount of money it now attracts. Top teams are The Harlequins, The London Irish, Saracens, and The Wasps. Wrap up warmly if you go.

Where to See It

Richmond   Athletic Ground, Kew Foot Road, Richmond, Surrey. Phone (0181) 410-6002. Richmond tube, District line. Tickets £8–15.

Rosslyn Park   Upper Richmond Road, Priory Lane, Roehampton, SW15. Phone (0181) 876-1879. Barnes rail. Tickets £5.

Twickenham Rugby House   Rugby Road, Twickenham Middlesex. Phone (0181) 892-2000. Tickets vary in price depending on the game. Tickets for the Five Nations series are almost impossible to get and are distributed to the faithful via the various clubs. You can see cup finals for the leagues for which tickets range between £14 and £30.

Clubs

Blackheath   Rectory Field, Charlton Road, SE3. Phone (0181) 293-0853. Blackheath rail. Tickets £10–14.

N.E.C.Harlequins   Stoop Memorial Ground, Langhorn Road, Twickenham, Middlesex. Phone (0181) 410-6000. Twickenham rail. Tickets £12–17. Under age 16, £1.

London Irish   The Avenue, Sudbury On Thames, Surrey. Phone (0193) 278-3034. Sudbury rail. Tickets £15 for nonmembers. Under age 16, £6.

London Scottish   Athletic Ground, Kew Foot Road, Richmond Surrey. Richmond tube. Phone (0181) 410-6002. Tickets £8–15.

London Welsh   Old Deer Park, Kew Road, Richmond, Surrey. Phone (0181) 940-8155. Richmond tube, District line. Tickets £10–15.

Saracens   Vicarage Road, Watford. Phone (0192) 349-6010. Watford High Street rail. Tickets £10–24.

Wasps   Loftus Road Stadium, South Africa Road, W12. Phone (0181) 743-0262. White City tube, Central line. Tickets £10–16.

BOXING

Big fights happen in big venues, like Wembley Arena. Publicity will be large scale, and tickets are always expensive. There are smaller venues for amateur or semiprofessional fights, and these will be advertised in local papers, *Time Out,* or on posters. You can catch a good pro or amateur fight at York Hall, Old Ford Road, E2 (phone (0181) 980-4171). This place has a serious East End vibe and has hosted amateur matches since 1929. Tickets are £10. Tickets for pro fights are priced by the promoters. Call for details.

TENNIS

Wimbledon fortnight starts the last week in June, and demand for tickets always far exceeds the supply. For years, a ballot system has been operated. To get tickets for Centre Court or Number One Court you have to write, enclosing a self-addressed envelope, for an application form between September 1 and December 31: The All England Tennis Club, P.O. Box 98, Church Road, London SW19. Tickets range from between £24 and £60 for Centre Court and £15 to £42 for Number One Court. Take the tube to Wimbledon (District line). Bring a hat or umbrella and plenty of sunblock. There will be lots of queuing, so be prepared. The strawberries and cream are expensive (£1.85 for a punnet of no fewer than ten strawberries), but the museum is worth a visit.

RACING

Horse racing is very popular in Britain. You can see it almost every day on television, and every high street has at least one betting shop, or "turf accountant," as the Brits like to call them. Gambling is legal in Britain, and bookies will give odds on almost anything, from the gender of the next royal birth to whether it will snow on Christmas Day. A day at the races is as popular with the upper classes (who own the horses and can be seen at Ascot wearing ridiculous hats that are never worn anywhere else), as it is with the working classes.

The flat season runs from April to September, and the jumps or steeplechase runs from October to April. As well as branches of the major corporate bookies like William Hill and Coral, there are many trackside bookies with whom it is much more fun to bet. They usually take win-only bets, with a minimum stake of £5. Watch the extraordinary ballet of arm swinging and hand signaling as they establish the odds. More complicated bets (exactas, trifectas, accumulators, and so on) can be made at the corporate bookies, or tote, as mentioned before.

All the tracks are just outside London and are well serviced by rail. Take a coat and umbrella just in case. There are bars and restaurants, which serve notoriously bad food, so be warned. A day at the races is exactly that, so be prepared for a longish haul.

Where to See It

Ascot Race Course   High Street, Ascot, Berks. Phone (0134) 462-2211. Ascot rail. Admission is £5–15, depending on whether you sit in the grandstand or the silver ring. (The royal enclosure is closed to commoners!) You can catch Her Majesty in June having a punt. Good competitive racing can always be seen here.

Epsom   Epsom Downs, Epsom, Surrey. Phone (0137) 247-0047. Epsom Downs rail. Admission is £5–16. This is where the Derby (pronounced Darby) is held in June. Derby Day is a big betting day in England and is something of a national mood lifter. The winner is always part of the headline news, and most people have a bet.

Kempton   Park Staines Road East. Phone (0137) 247-0047. Sunbury on Thames. Kempton Park rail. Admission is £10–27. This course hosts the King George VI stakes on Boxing Day. There is a new restaurant, but earlier warnings about the food hold true.

Sandown Park   The Racecourse, Portsmouth Road, Esher, Surrey. Phone (0173) 247-0047. Esher rail. Admission is £10–26. For serious punters, this track is supposed to be the best equipped in the London area. It hosts the Whitbread Gold cup in April.

Windsor   Maidenhead Road, Windsor, Berks. Phone (0175) 386-5234. Windsor and Eton Riverside rail. Admission £4–14. This is a pretty part of England and worth a visit in its own right. The castle (still very much in use by Her Majesty) is worth a visit and overlooks the course. The Thames is green and beautiful out here, and you can take a boat to and from the race track from the town, making a grand day out.

GREYHOUND RACING

These sleek animals tear round the track after a wooden hare on a rail. They run amazingly fast, and the race is over in a minute or less. The same deal with the corporate and trackside bookies applies, as do the warnings about food. There is a lot of beer drinking at the dog races, and it is a very entertaining evening out. Lots of characters and florid language. Again, all tracks are well serviced by public transport but are far from the center of London.

Where to See It

Catford Stadium   Adenmore Road, SE6. Phone (0181) 690-8000. Catford or Catford Bridge rail. Admission is £4. Races start at 7:30 p.m. on Mondays, Thursdays, and Saturdays.

Romford Stadium   London Road, Romford, Essex. Phone (0170) 876-3345. Romford rail. Admission £4 and free on the popular side of the stadium on Mondays and Wednesdays. All races start at 7:30 p.m. and are held Mondays, Wednesdays, Fridays, and Saturdays.

Walthamstow Stadium   Chingford Road, E4. Phone (0181) 498-3300. Walthamstow Central tube (and then a minicab from there). Admission is £4 and races are held at 7:30 p.m. on Tuesdays, Thursdays, and Saturdays.

Wembley Stadium   Stadium Way, Wembley, Middlesex. Phone (0181) 902-8833. Wembley Park tube. Admission £4. Races start at 7:30 p.m. on Fridays and Saturdays.

Wimbledon Stadium   Plough Lane, SW17. Phone (0181) 946-8000. Wimbledon tube. Admission is £4 and races start at 7:30 p.m. on Tuesdays, Fridays, and Saturdays.

Participation Sports

GYMS AND LEISURE CENTERS

Working out and staying in shape is as popular in Britain as it is in the United States, and gym culture flourishes. There are plenty of expensive and trendy gyms to work out or go posing at, but unless you have membership they can be expensive for a daily visit (£15–25). There are far too many to list here, so look in the Yellow Pages under Leisure Centres, or call Sportsline at (0171) 222-8000. Among the most popular is a chain of gyms called Holmes Place. These boast the usual extras like juice bars, saunas and steam rooms, Jacuzzis, and so on. Many hotels have their own facilities. What follows is a small list of sport and leisure in central London.

Chelsea Sports Center   Chelsea Manor Street, SW3. Phone (0171) 352-6985. Sloane Square or South Kensington tube. Has a good pool and the usual weights, aerobics classes, and so on.

Jubilee Hall Leisure Center   30 The Piazza, Covent Garden, WC2. Phone (0171) 836-4835. Covent Garden tube. Very good location, fully equipped. Many classes.

London Central YMCA　112 Great Russell St., WC1. Phone (0171) 637-8131. Tottenham Court Road tube. Also very central, and totally comprehensive. Lots of classes.

Queen Mother Sports Center　223 Vauxhall Bridge Rd., SW1. Phone (0171) 630-5522. Victoria tube. Very central, this center has been modernized to the tune of over £1 million and has a complete range of facilities, equipment, and classes.

Seymour Leisure Center　Seymour Place, W1. Phone (0171) 723-8019. Marble Arch tube. This center has an Olympic-size pool, steam rooms, cardiovascular machines, and a snooker room (snooker is more complicated than pool and good fun).

BICYCLING

You take your life into your hands bicycling around the streets of London, but there are parks to bike in that are wonderful. You can rent bikes by the golf driving range in Richmond Park; call (0181) 948-3209 for information. The London Bicycle Tour Company runs guided tours and also rents out bikes; call (0171) 928-6838.

INLINE SKATING

Hyde Park by the Albert Memorial is where you'll see the really good skaters—there is a cone course there, as well as the hockey players. There are tracks all around Hyde Park that are excellent for skating.

HORSEBACK RIDING

Though not exactly the sport of choice of the masses, there are beautiful places to ride in London. Hyde Park is an old favorite, with well-trodden riding paths like Rotten Row. Do not assume that riding in Hyde Park is without danger: You have to traverse a few streets and cross a busy main road to get into the park. The beasts are mostly of the warhorse variety, but you can occasionally get a bolter, and there's one place where they all want to canter.

Hyde Park Stables　63 Bathurst Mews, W2. Phone (0171) 723-2813. Lancaster Gate or Paddington tube. Closed Mondays. A ride around the park costs £30 for experienced riders. If you are a novice, they will insist you take a lesson, which will set you back £30 if you are part of a group, or £60 for individual lessons. The owners have recently opened another stable across the park, in South Kensington, where lessons are also available.

Ross Nye Stables   8 Bathurst Mews, W2. Phone (0171) 262-3791. £25 per hour, lessons at the same price. They won't take anyone under age six or anyone who weighs over 200 pounds. The stables are closed for a couple of months in the summer. Beginners and experienced riders are allowed, and children are encouraged.

Wimbledon Village Stables   24 High St., Wimbledon, SW19. Phone (0181) 946-8579. Wimbledon tube. £20 per hour during the week, £25 on weekends. This is outside London, but worth a trip if you want to avoid automobile traffic. They have small classes for beginners, and you will be taken on a rugged ride through Wimbledon Common, Putney Heath, and Richmond Park, all of which are semiwild expanses of parkland. Look out for deer. A much more beautiful experience than Hyde Park, though less convenient.

ICE SKATING

Considering the fact that it never really gets cold enough for any of the natural bodies of water to freeze over, there is a surprising number of proficient skaters in London, some of whom can be seen whizzing around at breakneck speeds on London's many ice rinks. Admission and skate rental is cheap, and it can be a fun night out.

Broadgate Ice Rink   Broadgate Circus, Eldon Street, EC2. Phone (0171) 505-4068. Liverpool Street tube. Admission is £5, skate rental £2. This is a tiny outdoor rink in the middle of London, among the glass castles of the financial district. Plenty of room to watch if you don't skate.

Queens Ice Bowl   17 Queensway, W2. Phone (0171) 229-0172. Bayswater or Queensway tube. Admission is £5 and skate rental is £1.50. A trendy joint, Friday and Saturday nights are disco nights. Good Chinese and Indian restaurants in the immediate neighborhood for après skate. For those that find falling over again and again too painful, there is bowling at the same venue.

SWIMMING

Most of the leisure centers listed earlier have pools, but it is worth noting that almost every borough of London has at least one municipally run pool, some of which are more salubrious than others. To find your nearest pool, consult the Yellow Pages or call Sportsline on (0171) 222-8000. Following is a list of some of the better ones.

The Lido at Hampstead Heath   Mansfield Road, NW3. Phone (0181) 458-4548. Gospel Oak rail. Admission £2.90. This is London's biggest outdoor pool and is only really worth going to on a hot day.

The Oasis   32 Endell St., WC2. Phone (0171) 831-1804. Covent Garden or Holborn tube. Admission £2.45, free for children under age 5. There is also an outdoor pool.

Putney Leisure Center   Dryburgh Road, SW15. Phone (0181) 785-0388. Putney tube. Admission £2.50. This is an L-shaped pool with a wave-making machine. There is also a fully equipped gym with classes.

Richmond Swimming Baths   Old Deer Park, Twickenham Road, Richmond, Surrey. Phone (0181) 940-0561. Richmond tube or rail. Admission £2.90.

KARTING

A very popular form of high-thrills entertainment, go-karting is catching on among laddish groups of young men. Not cheap, but definitely exhilarating. The karts don't go all that fast, but it feels like they do.

Daytona Raceway   54 Wood Lane, W12. Phone (0181) 749-2297. White City tube. You can race for £35 or have a practice session of 20 minutes for £15.

Playscape Pro Racing Battersea Kart Raceway   Hester Road, SW11. Phone (0171) 801-0110. Sloane Square tube, the Number 19 bus over the bridge. £37.50 for two hours.

For those with an appetite for more adrenalin, Silverstone Circuits in Northampton is an exciting day out. You can race carts or sign up for a day at the driving center where you can learn to drive Formula 4 and even Formula 1 cars. Call the Silverstone Driving Center at-(0132) 785-7271 for details.

BUNGEE JUMPING

If you just can't get enough thrills with any of the above sports, you can jump off a crane by the Thames.

Adrenalin Village   Chelsea Bridge Tower, Queenstown Road, SW8. Phone (0171) 720-9496. Sloane Square tube then 137 bus. £35 plus £15 membership fee to jump 200 feet then bounce back up. It's fun to just watch, too; maybe even more fun.

YOGA, ETC.

The Life Centre   15 Edge St., W8. Phone (0171) 221-4602. Notting Hill Gate tube. 60-minute class £7.50, 90-minute £9.50. The Life Centre offers a huge selection of classes in yoga (Sivananda, Ashtanga, and Iyengar) as well as in t'ai chi and Pilates. You can also get massages and a number of other alternative therapies here.

Sivananda Yoga Vedanta Centre   51 Felsham Rd., SW15. Phone (0181) 780-0160. Putney Bridge or East Putney, #14 bus. Daily yoga classes for all levels, some classes are free of charge, open classes £7 or less. Satsang and lectures as well.

WATER SPORTS

For those who enjoy messing about on the river, there is plenty to do on the Thames and in the surrounding reservoirs and docklands.

Royal Docks Water-Ski Club   Gate 16, King George V Dock, Woolwich Manor Way, E16. Phone (0171) 511-2000. Gallions Reach, Docklands Light railway, or North Woolwich rail. Beginners welcome; there are also courses and stunts for experienced skiers. Also speedboat driving and water-boarding. Phone for details.

Docklands Watersports Club   Gate 14, King George V Dock, Woolwich Manor Way, E16. Phone (0171) 511-2000. Gallions Reach, Docklands Light railway, or North Woolwich Rail. For jet-skiing enthusiasts, this facility offers rental of craft, wetsuits, and use of the club. Prices start at £25 for 30 minutes.

Capital Rowing Center   Polytechnic Boathouse, Ibis Lane, W4. Phone (0181) 742-1997. Chiswick rail. For those who enjoy playing galley slave, £30 will buy you five hours of tortuous tuition.

GOLF

As you would expect, there are no golf courses in the capital itself. The English Golf Union is an excellent resource for all golf information and can be reached at (0152) 635-4500. However, the Regents Park Golf School (Outer Circle, Regent's Park, NW1, phone (0171) 724-0643, Baker Street tube) is open daily. Membership starts at £60. There is a driving range, and you can have lessons from professionals. Call for details.

Golf Courses in Outer London

Brent Valley   Church Road Cuckoo Lane, W7. Phone (0181) 567-1287. Hanwell rail. 18 holes. £9.25 per round, £14 on weekends.

Chingford Golf Course   Bury Road, E4. Phone (0181) 529-5708. Chingford rail. 18 holes. £10 weekdays and £14 on weekends.

Richmond Park   Roehampton Gate, Richmond Park, SW15. Phone (0181) 876-3205. Barnes rail. There are two 18-hole courses, priced at £13 mornings, and £10 from 1 p.m. to dusk. On weekends, the morning price is £16 and £13 in the afternoons and evenings.

TENNIS

Almost all London parks have tennis courts, which cost very little to play on. Bring your own racket and balls. There is usually a grass court or two and a few asphalt ones. It's very informal, just turn up on any weekday and you will almost certainly be able to play. For the serious player call the Lawn Tennis Association Trust at the Queens Club in West Kensington, phone (0171) 381-7000. They will provide you with a booklet called "Where to Play Tennis in London."

Part Eight

Shopping in London

It's safe to say that everything is cheaper in the United States than in London. It's common that any Londoner going to America, from taxi drivers to investment bankers, brings an empty suitcase to fill with the incredibly low-priced clothing and household goods found in Anytown, U.S.A. I would venture to say that goods and services in London tend to cost in pounds what they cost in dollars in the United States, meaning that the average price of anything in London is about 60% more than in the U.S., which is about the exchange rate. According to a survey done by the *London Times* in late 1998, Britons spend as much as 52% more for their cars than the least expensive EU equivalent; a shopping basket of groceries costs 36% more than the same goods in France, 54% more than in Germany, and 45% more than in America. Caveat emptor (buyer beware), however, may come to be seller beware, as the government starts to crack down on what the *Evening Standard* calls "rip-off Britain." The exceptions, according to a neighbor who's lived here for many years, are lettuce and school fees. I would add to that list Marmite and lavender. Not much help for the tourist, but see the list below for shopping suggestions.

So as not to completely dash your shopping dreams, let me hasten to emphasize that London has a vibrant shopping scene, with stores, stalls, and shops as far as the eye can see and some goods that are difficult to find elsewhere. Some of these things, like the hundreds of items with the Harrods name and logo plastered on them, you wouldn't necessarily want to find anywhere else, but others, like Liberty scarves, bespoke shirts from Harvie & Hudson, and Crown Perfumery scents, are a must for the worldly shopper. If you come during the big sales, the best being during the month of January (there's also one in August) you just might be able to pay North American prices for stuff you can't readily get in the States.

Wise Buys in London

The following items are worth buying in London because of their high quality or their unavailablity in the United States. See our "Where To Find..." section later on in this chapter for information on where to find these items.

Antiques

If you're smart and go to the early morning Bermonsey Market, or check out the Camden Passage on Wednesdays, you'll find a huge selection in London at decent prices. You used to not have to pay VAT on antiques, but alas, those days are over.

Aromatic Body Stuff

Bath oils, salts, soaps, and so on are everywhere here and in many cases cost less than in the United States, notably at the Body Shop. Culpepper the Herbalist, Neal's Yard Remedies, Floris, and Penhaligon also are cheaper here than in the few places they are sold in the States, and Boots the Chemist has their own line of reasonable quality goods of this ilk.

Bone China

Look in the stalls on Portobello Road in Notting Hill on Saturday Market day, or at the Reject China Shops (phone (0171) 434-2502) for patterns you can't find in America. Even Harrods can provide some deals at sales times, and their stock is enormous. Crystal goods, too, can be cheaper than in the States.

Books

London is a city of readers, and there are thousands of bookstores, for every interest and from every age since Gutenberg. You can get books here that are only published in England, antiquarian volumes in gorgeous sets, and secondhand books by the crateful. The old books are really worth your while—I once saw a book from the 1600s with real bookworm bore-holes in it for £500. Problem was that it was in Latin.

Children's Clothing

Some children's clothing may be, if not cheaper, then of better quality and value than in the States. English smock dresses and French baby clothes are beautiful, and you don't have to pay VAT.

Designer Clothing

Secondhand, that is. There are tons of resale shops in which you can get "preowned" Chanel, Gucci, Westwood, or whatever for good prices. A lot of ladies seem to have worn these clothes twice and then moved on to the next big thing. There are outlets in which you might find semi-good deals on brand new English and French designer clothes, but it's an iffy business, dependent on exchange rates and the size of the VAT refund.

Fabrics

England has long been known for its gorgeous fabrics; try John Lewis or Peter Jones for the best deals on locally made material and things like trim and curtain swags. Amazing selection.

Handmade Lampshades

I know a craftsperson who can make the most elegant lamp for low prices unheard of in the United States and ship it to you; she also has a great selection of fabrics for very competitive prices. Call Sally Harclerode at (0171) 581-2681.

Souvenirs of London

Yes, cheaper here than anywhere, but avoid the airport and museum shops. The best buys are on the street in stalls—Oxford Street, Leicester Square, Soho (Tottenham Court Road), and Piccadilly Circus are the places to look.

Stationery

Filofaxes, the personal organizer so well-loved by well-heeled professionals in the States, are an indigenous English product and much cheaper here than anywhere else, especially at sale time.

Time to Shop

Stores in central London open late and close early: The usual times are 10 a.m. to 6 p.m., with a few heartier souls opening at 9 a.m. (but closing at 5 p.m.), and a very few, like Waterstone's Bookstores, staying open until the ungodly hour of 9:30 p.m. Some places, such as those in Covent Garden and some fashionable stores, don't open until 10:30 or 11 a.m. If you simply must buy something in the morning, call the store first, or save the shopping for after lunch.

There is a "late" night for shopping: Stores stay open till 7 or 8 p.m. on Thursdays on Oxford Street and most of the Regent Street and West End area. Just to keep you on your toes, Knightsbridge and Chelsea's late night is Wednesday. Sunday is still relatively sacrosanct as a day of rest for shopkeepers, although more stores in the major shopping streets are starting to open for a half-day, from noon to 5 or 6 p.m. Shockingly, Harrods recently started breaking with tradition to open on Sundays during the weeks leading up to Christmas (can't imagine why). Street markets follow their own muse as far as opening hours and days go, as you'll see on page 247.

Paying Up

All the major credit cards are taken at most shops, with the rather puzzling exceptions of the major department stores of John Lewis, its partner store in Sloane Square, Peter Jones, and the Marks and Spencer chain. Some stores are willing to take traveler's checks in British sterling, but they don't even want to hear about U.S. dollar checks. If they are kind enough to cash them, you can bet it won't be at a rate favorable to you. (Bring a passport to cash traveler's checks.)

The credit card is a good way to go, as you'll have a record of your purchases and the exchange rate will be fair. The rate used will be that on the day the credit purchase clears the credit card company or bank. So don't think that just because the pound is down one day, you should run out and charge up a storm—it could go up again and cost you a pretty penny. But please, don't make yourself crazy over these things that you can't control.

As for VAT

Value Added Tax is the mind-boggling 17.5% they put on all goods and services except for books, food, and children's clothing. Most of what you buy will have the VAT already figured into the price on the tags, but others, especially fancy knick-knack stores and other places whose prices are already out of this world, try to prevent total sticker shock by putting a discreet "+VAT" after all those zeros. If you have your goods shipped directly from the store, the VAT will be deducted from the price, but you'd have to be paying a lot of money to have the cost of shipping balance out. Which brings in the important subject of paying duty on your imported goods when you arrive in your home country. You are allowed $400 per person of goods duty-free, and families may combine this allowance. The next $1,000 worth of goods gets charged a flat 10%—after that it will vary according to what type of import you're bringing.

Yes, you may be able to get some the VAT you've paid back, but it requires a little footwork. I'll let Her Majesty's Customs and Excise Department explain it all, but first, let me get this off my chest: I admit it, VAT is expensive, and if you're buying a £1,000 watch or £600 silver salt and pepper shakers, go ahead, fill out the form, stand in the line, and get the refund. However, I see so many visitors spending around £50 or £100 in a museum shop or a clothing store (very easily done, by the way) only to invest so much of their vacation into struggling to get a portion of this tax back. They are visiting this country, using the public transport, walking on the sidewalks, enjoying all the fruits of the National Trust's hard work to make an England worth visiting, walking through the magnificent parks, taking pictures of the changing of the guard, and so on, and they think they are such very savvy travelers for getting back less than £10 on every £100 they spend, at some cost to the ease and happiness of their holiday. I don't get it. It seems so much more sensible to spend time in London looking at the amazing sights, eating at great restaurants, taking a day trip to Stonehenge, and breathing in the culture, rather than running around with VAT refund forms trying to get a bargain in a city where such a thing is pretty much hopeless. Okay, I feel better. Here's how VAT refund goes.

VALUE ADDED TAX REFUNDS—THE OFFICIAL STORY

Here are the highlights from a pamphlet produced by HM Customs and Excise and published here by their kind permission, entitled "Guide to Tax Free Shopping—the VAT Refund Scheme" (VAT/704/3/93).

What is the retail export scheme?   When you visit the U.K., you pay Value Added Tax (VAT) on most things you buy. The retail export scheme allows you to obtain a refund of the tax on certain goods you intend to export from the European Community (EC).

Can I buy goods under this scheme?   Yes, if you are an overseas visitor who:

- has not been in the EC for more than 365 days in the 2 years before the date you buy the goods; and
- you intend to leave the EC with all the goods in your personal luggage, within 3 months of the date you bought them.

How do I know which shops operate the scheme?   The shops that operate the scheme usually have a sign in the window advertising the scheme as "Tax-free shopping." If in doubt, ask for the "Tax-free" sales assistant.

What must I do to obtain a VAT refund?

- ask the shop to complete a VAT or Tax-free shopping form;
- obtain an EC certification stamp when you leave the EC;
- post or hand in your stamped forms to obtain your VAT refund.

Do I get all the tax back?   Most shops charge a small administrative fee which will be deducted from the tax refunded to you.

What export documents will I be given? The shop will give you one of the following VAT refund documents:

- the Customs Form VAT 407(1993); or
- a shop or refund company's tax-free shopping form; or
- a retail export scheme sales invoice.

These documents are available only from shops operating the scheme.

When must I export the goods? You must permanently export the goods from the EC within 3 months of purchase.

Do I have to carry all the goods bought under the scheme in my hand baggage? You must always carry items of high value and jewelry, furs, cameras, watches, silverware, and small antiques in your hand baggage— but if the goods are too large to carry on board an aircraft you may pack them in your hold baggage. If you do this, you must contact the Customs export officer before you check in. The airline will tell you how to do this.

Do I get the VAT refund document back? You must give the document and show the goods to Customs at the port or airport when you finally leave the EC. The Customs export officer will certify the document and return it to you so that you can get a refund. These procedures may take some time so please arrive at least two hours before you are due to depart. (Author's note: I would make that three and a half hours in summer.)

What if I leave the EC on a through (transit) flight via another Member State? There are special rules for goods being carried on through flights which leave the EC via another Member State.

- Hand baggage: goods carried on as hand baggage and VAT refund documents must be produced to Customs in the Member State of final transfer before leaving the EC.
- Hold baggage: if you are leaving the U.K. on such a flight and intend carrying large or heavy goods in hold baggage, you should ask the shopkeeper for a separate VAT refund document for those goods. The goods and VAT refund document must be produced to UK Customs before departure from the UK.

How do I get a refund? There are several methods to try for getting a refund. You may:

- post the certified document back to the shopkeeper; or
- post the certified document to a VAT refunding company; or

- hand the certified document to a cash refund booth at the point of departure, if the shopkeeper has authorized you to do so (a charge may be made for this service).

Which countries are in the European Community?   You cannot buy goods under this scheme if your final destination is one of the EC Member-States or other territories listed below:

Belgium, Denmark, France, Germany, Greece, Holland, Ireland, Italy, Luxembourg, Monaco, Portugal, Azores and Madeira, Spain and Balearic Islands, United Kingdom, and the Isle of Man.

Important Reminder

If you do not produce the goods and VAT refund document to the Customs export officer when you finally leave the EC you will not get a refund of VAT.

The Unofficial Version

Only non-British subjects and non-EU members qualify for VAT refund, and they have to leave the country with their goods within six months.

You will not get the entire 17.5% back—it's more like 10% to 15%, plus an additional fee, and can actually be as little as 4% with some refund companies.

Ask what is the minimum you must spend in a given shop to qualify for the papers being filled out—it can vary, although the law puts the minimum at £50. Some shops will refuse outright, some will charge at least £5 for issuing the papers.

You must have the refund form filled out at the place of purchase! You cannot get it done anywhere else by anyone else. Bring your passport to the store.

There are refund companies that handle the VAT refund, and they have set the refund at different rates. The clerk can tell you which company the shop uses and help you decide whether it's worth your while or not.

You have to show your VAT refund purchases at the airport Customs, usually (and most easily) in carry-on luggage. Factor the size of the item against the amount of the refund times the degree of hassle you're willing to go through.

Go to the Customs official to get the VAT papers before you check in your luggage.

Allow time for all the forms to be filled out—about five minutes for each one.

After you go through passport control, line up at the VAT desk to show them what you've bought and the papers that go with them.

You then get the papers back, mail them to the shop, or take them to the Tax-Free Europe desk. Tax-Free Europe is a tax refund company that many stores are starting to use to expedite the VAT returns. They give you a cash refund at the airport, but a lot of your money stays in their hands. There's also VatBack, which will do a credit card refund by mail, which takes about three months, but you'll get a bigger percentage back. They also give immediate cash back, at £18.50 for over £500 of goods, or £8.60 for £100.

If your VAT refund items are too big for carry-on, budget an extra hour at the airport, as you will need to have a security guard watch you go through passport control and then return the items to your airline for checking.

In the summer and after sales, there are outrageously long lines at the VAT refund desk at Heathrow, and this is getting worse all the time as people have started working the VAT refund scheme in earnest.

There is also the possibility of getting back the VAT from a hotel or holiday apartment, as well as from car rental—ask the concierge or the person you book with for the forms and the information.

Salespeople's Attitudes and Behavior

Salespeople in London are (although one hates to make a generalization about such things) among the most laid-back in the world. It's not that they don't want to make a sale, it's just that they don't want to be perceived as pushing anyone to buy something. Except in a few upscale stores, where the staff is rigorously trained to look like they give a damn, the salespeople in London will surprise and perhaps bewilder you with their laissez-faire attitudes. Personally, I find it a relief from the kind of sales style in which you are forced to engage in banter (read: pressure to buy) with salespeople when all you want to do is have a look, but if you are in need of assistance, you will have to get used to approaching them. There's nothing malicious or lackadaisical about them, it's just that this is not a culture in which overeager striving is admired. Even the famous funny East End sales patter at the markets is more a tradition of being quick and clever than it is of making a sale. The correct response is to be equally laid-back and not get demanding and rude—London salespeople are masters of the cold dismissal, and you won't win.

The Big Shopping Neighborhoods

Beauchamp Place and Walton Street   Beauchamp Place (Beauchamp is pronounced "Beecham," don't ask why) is a swiftly changing street these days, due to skyrocketing rents and the fact that two buildings on it collapsed in the fall of 1998 after heavy rains. Who knows what will replace them, but I have no doubt that they will be expensive boutiques. The Reject China Shop dominates the entrance to Beauchamp Place at Brompton Road, with two floors of china plates and accessories. As you make your way up the street, you'll find jewelry (Dower & Hall, Ciro, Foli Follie, The Watch Department, Annabel Jones), shoes and purses (Sergio Rossi, Franchetti Bond, Anello & Davide), hats (John Boyd), secondhand and clearance designer clothes (Bertie Golightly, Designer Sale Shop), deluxe underwear (Janet Reger), and, of course, designers (Bruce Oldfield, Isabel Kristiansen, Pamela Stevens, Caroline Charles, Ronit Zilkha, Paddy Campbell, and others). This is also the street to see fashionable women push food around on their plates at the restaurants Floriana's and San Lorenzo.

At the end of Beauchamp, make a right into Walton Street and get ready to ready spend some money. Baker and Spice is a fantastic bakery that supplies many of London's finest restaurants; get something to bring back to the hotel, like the garlic bread. There are a slew of interior decorators whose shops have some wonderful curiosities, trendy jewelers, and a couple of decent restaurants. Try Patrizia Wigan Designs for children's clothing: There are always sale items that are so beautiful you'll buy something even if you don't have kids. There's Stephanie Hopper, who features old portraits whose faces have been erased and dog faces painted in — very strange, very popular with Americans apparently; Chelsea Textile Design has fearsomely expensive and awesomely beautiful hand-embroidered reproductions of seventeenth- and eighteenth-century linens; Tappisserie for wealthy craftspeople has hand-painted needlepoint designs that are stunning; reasonably priced monogrammed linen and unreasonably expensive Porthault sheets are at the Monogrammed Linen Shop on Walton Street; and an extraordinary display of glass and crystal work by contemporary British artists at The Room. Don't miss the slice of Italy at the Farmacia Santa Maria Novella (expertly hidden at 117) for creams, candles, and soaps. Scent and cosmetic making maven Jo Malone's shop has become such a popular place that at Christmas, there are lines going down the street of people waiting to get into the tiny store, which is why, by the time you read this, they may have moved (call (0171) 581-1101 to find out). Everyone on the street is happy to ship their products to America, so if you want to buy new or antique children's furniture at Dragons, some wonderful lamps at the store of the same name, or fine Aubusson reproduction carpets at the Orientalist, it's no problem to send them directly home.

Fulham Road   Before you get to the trendy Joseph Boutique at Brompton Cross, where Fulham Road actually starts, you'll pass some very haut monde stores of fashion: Tokio, The Library, Issey Miyake, and NK Space (two designer boutiques, a designer and a cosmetics place). From the Bromptom Cross to Edith Grove, Fulham Road is a stretch of shops that range from the heights of fashion, antiques, and housewares to the best Notting Hill Charity Shop in London. It encompasses the so-called "Beach," a block or so of pubs and restaurants that are popular with the twentysomethings. The Michelin Building houses the upscale housewares of The Conran Shop, as well as the restaurant Bibendum, named after the Michelin tire man, whom you can see immortalized in tile there. From there you can stroll along and look in windows containing housewares, tiles, and watches. Voyage, famous for its £1,200 trimmed cardigans and its locked-door policy that once turned away Madonna, has two stores here, one for women and one for men. Butler & Wilson is an antique clothes and jewelry store that has a ton of tiaras, including a huge one on the top of the building. The jeweler Theo Fanell, a delightful Wedding Shop with secondhand dresses, and the upscale stationery store Papyus all precede the block devoted to expensive antiques. There's a good bookstore, Pan Books, past the Virgin Cinema, that stays open to 9:30 p.m., as does the best Italian deli in the world, Luigi's. Don't miss Wok Wok, with excellent Asian food served fast and easy. After the store A Touch of Brass, which sells guess what, the shopping scene peters out and you're on your way toward Fulham and the antiques stores in that area.

New and Old Bond Street   Wow, what a stretch of real estate these streets are! Starting from Oxford Street, New Bond Street starts off with a battery of designer shops and clothing boutiques such as Warehouse, Cecil Gee, Next, Guess, Emma Somerset, Armani, Cerruti 1881, Versace, Herbie Frogg (it's the so-called Sale Shop—the really expensive one is down the way on Old Bond), Calvin Klein, Tommy Hilfiger, Miu Miu (Prada), Lanvin, Guy LaRouch, Thierry Mugler, Donna Karan, Yves Saint Laurent, Ermenegildo Zegna, Chanel, Ralph Lauren, Valentino, Nicole Farhi—the list goes on and on; suffice it to say they're all here. Not to mention designer shoes, fine art, jewelry (Tiffany and Cartier, natch), Hermès scarves, and so on. Smythson of Bond Street is a stationery store that begs your jaw to drop with its £23 pigskin mini-post-it-note holder, or the blank writing book for £59. There's a bench on the great divide (a pedestrian walkway) between New and Old Bond streets, on which you will see two very realistic statues of

Winston Churchill and Franklin Roosevelt. Old Bond is more of the same: exactly the same, in fact, in the cases of Donna Karan, Ralph Lauren, Armani, Versace, and others. In case you forgot to spend £260 on a T-shirt on New Bond, you'll get a second chance on Old Bond.

Kensington Church Street   This is the street of antiques, with shops stretching from Kensington High Street all the way to Notting Hill Gate. It's a great place to window shop and cruise in and out of the stores whose displays strike your fancy. As with all antiques stores, their inventory is always changing, but there are a few places that specialize in certain periods and styles. The Pruskin Gallery is known for its art nouveau, art deco, and 1940s objets d'art and furniture; Patrick Sandberg has eighteenth- and early nineteenth-century furniture and decorations; Meissen porcelain can be found at Davies Antiques and Staffordshire figurines at Oliver Sutton; Hampson & Lewis features arts and crafts silverware and jewelry; there's Berwald Oriental Art; and antique clocks and scientific instruments are sold at both Raffety and Roderick Antique Clocks. There are also wonderful mirror stores and a great crystal chandelier place. The prices can be quite high on this street, but it's fun to look, and you never know when you'll find something you really love. Kensington Place Restaurant is a popular eating spot on this street.

King's Road   This was the place to be in the 1960s and 1970s, when Mary Quant set up shop to sell her revolutionary miniskirts, and Vivienne Westwood kept changing the name of her and Malcolm McLaren's punk chic boutique. The Mary Quant place is now a Hampstead Bazaare store, selling flowy skirts and blouses, but the Vivienne Westwood store still has the fast-moving backward clock outside, and the floor still slants dangerously inside. King's Road is long and full of quickly changing boutiques and trendy stores, but there are some places that will, one can only hope, always be there. Starting at the Vivienne Westwood end (the western part near World's End) and heading to Sloane Square, you'll find thrift shops: Oxfam, Trinity Hospice, and Imperial Cancer Fund will have the occasional great buys. Some fabric stores along the way include Anna French, Thomas Dave, Osbourn & Little, and the Designer's Guild. Wilde Ones will take care of all your New Age needs, but at a steep cost. Lello Bracio, Johnny Moke, and the Natural Shoe Store offer the latest in shoes, both comfortable and stylish. Old Church Galleries has wonderful old and rare prints, and there are some good antiques and reproduction places along the way, including Antiquarius, an umbrella housing many stalls with lots of goods. Check out Steinberg and Tolkien and be sure to go downstairs—they have the most amazing selection of vintage clothes in London, it's more like a museum than a store, with prices to match. Other stores include Marks and Spencer, Lush, Conran's Habitat, lots of boutiques for clothes, and at the end, Peter Jones, the stolid department store. Plenty of good restaurants and a Starbucks, too.

Sloane Street   There are two blocks of stores on this street between Brompton Road in Knightsbridge and Sloane Square that are shockingly chock-full of every hot designer you can think of. It's like a mini–Bond Street: Chanel, Dior, Dolce & Gabbana, Valentino, Prada, Lacroix, Tomasz Starzewski, Max Mara, Katharine Hamnett, Gianfranco Ferre, Armani, Ally Capellini, Alberta Ferretti, Iceberg, Hermès, and Gucci. If you don't find the designer store you need, there's always Harvey Nichols right at the end of the street. The street smells of money and lots of perfume.

Oxford and Regent Streets   The word that jumps to mind when I think of Oxford Street, to be brutally honest, is "boring." It has lots of chain stores, too many people, and a couple of flower and fruit stalls that are the only good reason to go here—although I must say that the department store John Lewis is usually my reason for being in the neighborhood. Selfridges, Marks and Spencer, Dixons Electronics, Debenhams, The Body Shop, The Gap, Virgin Megastores—these are not places that a tourist needs to go. However, turn the corner at Oxford Circus down Regent Street, and you will probably enjoy stopping in at Liberty, the Tudor-style department store that has a fascinating architecture and some interesting goods. Hamley's, the big toy store is down the street; there's also a Pastimes, in which you can find really good gifts that exploit to the max our affection for a vanished Olde England. Avoid the Disney Store, but drop by the British Air Travel Store—they have a wonderful selection of travel goods and London books. Burberry's, Jaeger, and Aquascutum offer some high-class and high-priced clothing.

Markets

Bermondsey Market   (also known as the New Caledonian Market) Bermonsey Square, SE1 (tube: London Bridge, Borough). Open Friday only, 5 a.m. to 2 p.m. The early bird definitely gets the worm here, and that means arriving in pitch darkness to vie with the dealers buying antiques of every description, including clothing and jewelry. It's a serious place, and supposedly the "really good" stuff is gone before 9 a.m., but if you're not a dealer that shouldn't bother you.

Camden Market   Camden Town, NW1(tube: Camden Town). Open Thursday and Friday 9 a.m. to 5 p.m. and weekends from 10 a.m. to 6 p.m. An absolute must for teens and twentysomethings, this market has very hip clothing, jewelry, records, and lots of curious-looking young people to watch. The whole of Camden has the most appealing vibration, it's almost like a latter-day Haight-Ashbury, complete with head shops, local crafts, incense, and Indian fabrics. There are plenty of good food stalls and cafes in the area and lots of outdoor seating in warm weather. Be sure to stop in at the Victorian Market Hall, which is open daily and has three floors of shops and stalls of everything from London souvenirs to antiques to books— something for everyone.

Follow Chalk Farm Road to The Stables, a weekend market of antiques and second-hand goods.

Camden Passage   Camden Passage, N1 (tube: Angel). Open Wednesday from 10 a.m. to 2 p.m. and Saturday from 10 a.m. to 5 p.m. Not to be confused with the above Camden, this is an interesting antiques and collectibles market open on Wednesdays, but the Passage itself has permanent antiques stores open all week.

Columbia Flower   Columbia Road (east of Ravenswood Street), E2 (tube: Old Street). Lots of beautiful flowers. For tourists, the point is to check out the scene.

Covent Garden   The Apple Market, W2 (tube: Covent Garden). Open daily 10 a.m. to 7 p.m. A must-see, especially on the weekends when the buskers (street entertainers) are around and throngs are milling. The market is set up in stalls and includes everything from crafts to woolens, with a juice bar and other food stalls thrown in. The stationary market that used to house the fruit, vegetable, and flower sellers is now given over to more upscale clothing, decoration, and body care purveyors. On Monday, there is an antiques market that features lots of jewelry, silver, and knickknacks at relatively reasonable prices.

Greenwich Markets   Greenwich, SW10 (take BritRail from Charing Cross). Open Saturday and Sunday, 9 a.m. to 6 p.m. There are a number of markets in Greenwich and you should have no trouble finding because the town is small and you just can't miss them. There's the Crafts Market in the center of town; the Bosun's Yard Market, which also sells crafts and such; the Canopy Antiques Market, which is really a flea market with plenty of interesting junk; and the Greenwich Antiques Market, which is on the high street, and has many stalls of vintage clothes, as well as a variety of collectibles and antiques.

Leather Lane Market   Leather Lane, EC1 (tube: Chancery Lane). On this site has been a market for more than 300 years. As you may guess, it does have leather goods, and not too expensive either. Besides the indifferent clothing, the other stuff probably won't get your attention, mostly electrical, household, CDs, and so on, but it's got good atmosphere.

Petticoat Lane   Middlesex Street and environs (tube: Liverpool Street). Open Sunday only, 9 a.m. to 2 p.m. Petticoat Lane used to be located on a street of that name until the Victorian sensibilities became too delicate to handle the reference to ladies' unmentionables. Tons of stalls line a number of streets in the area, selling clothing, shoes, household goods, crafts, you name it.

Portobello Market   Portobello Road from Notting Hill end to the Ladbroke Grove end (tube: Notting Hill Gate). Antiques: 7 a.m. to 6 p.m. Saturday; General Market: 9 a.m. to 5 p.m. Monday through Wednesday; Organic Market: 11 a.m. to 6 p.m. Thursday; Clothing and knickknacks: 7 a.m. to 4 p.m. Friday, 8 a.m. to 5 p.m. Saturday, and 9 a.m. to 4 p.m. Sunday. As you can see, Portobello Road isn't just about antiques. On Saturday, at the Notting Hill end, there are stalls galore of antiques as well as the stores along the road that are often closed on weekdays. There are a few multiple-dealer buildings that are worth a look around, and do stop in at Neil Phillips for a gander at some great stained glass windows (they're open during the week, too). It's a major scene, so come early. As you head toward Ladbroke Grove, clothing takes over, and at the end of the street, you turn left on Westbourne Grove Road and walk through a densely packed stall site of secondhand clothes, head shop–type paraphernalia, vintage shoes, food, and loud music. The teenagers adore it.

St. Martin–in-the-Fields Market   St. Martin's Lane, WC2 (tube: Charing Cross). Have a look around when you're in the Trafalgar Square area. It's mostly clothing and teenage items, although one might find some nice and inexpensive secondhand velvet jackets from the 1970s. Lots of neo-hippie gear. While you're at it, go see the gift shop in the crypt of St. Martin–in-the-Fields Church.

Spitalfields Market   Commercial Street between Lamb and Brushfield Streets, E1 (tube: Liverpool Street). The general market is open Monday through Friday, from 11 a.m. to 3 p.m., and opens at 9 a.m. on Sunday. The Organic Market is open from 11 a.m. to 3 p.m. on Friday; and from 9 a.m. to 3 p.m. on Sunday. Sunday is the best time for Spitalfields— combine it with a trip to Petticoat Lane. It has the most extensive offering of delicious organic foods, as well as lots of fast Indian and other international meals. You can look at the crafts while you eat your vegetables in tofu skin dumpling.

Walthamstow   Walthamstow High Street, E17 (tube: Walthamstow Central). Open from 8 a.m. to 6 p.m., Monday through Saturday. Billed as Europe's longest daily street market, there are 450 stalls and 300 shops at this market in the northeast of London. It's mostly ordinary consumer goods for a bargain—food, clothes, electrical equipment, and the like, but it is fun to see, and in the summer there is live entertainment.

Department Stores

These are most like the American stores we know so well, although they're more expensive. John Lewis and Peter Jones (same store, different names) have everything you might need in life, and at a lower cost than most anywhere else, but beware: They don't take credit cards. Harrods pretends to have everything under the sun, but really doesn't and charges at least a few quid more than John Lewis. Marks and Spencer have clothes and food and a very limited selection of grocery items. Selfridges, Debenhams and Harvey Nichols are somewhat similar to each other: lots of fashions, cosmetics, and a cafe or two.

Debenhams   334–338 Oxford St., W1, phone (0171) 580-3000. Many branches. Not much to come for, except a few designers.

Fortnum & Mason   181 Piccadilly, W1, phone (0171) 734-8040. You might not think of this as other than a food emporium, but in fact F & M has floors other than the ground floor of jellies and jams that carry clothing, clocks, and gifts. The interior is beautiful, and the cream tea is classic.

Harrods   87–135 Brompton Rd., SW1, phone (0171) 730-1234. An annoying place that has the nerve to charge a quid for use of a ridiculously fancy bathroom. High prices and bad taste abound, but the food halls are wonderful—look up at the ceilings.

Harvey Nichols   109–125 Knightsbridge, SW1, phone (0171) 235-5000. Beloved by rich fashionistas, there are floors of designer clothes here, plus a good restaurant on the fifth floor flood hall.

John Lewis   278–306 Oxford St., W1, phone (0171) 629-7711 and **Peter Jones**   Sloane Square, SW1, phone (0171) 730-3434. These stores' motto is "Never Knowingly Undersold." There's nothing fancy or trendy here, but they are good, solid department stores that actually do carry everything, from picture hooks to computers, at good prices. They only take debit cards, Delta, Switch, or Solar. Bring cash.

Liberty   210–220 Regent St., W1, phone (0171) 734-1234. A wonderful store, in the Tudor style that perks up the Georgian cool of Regent Street. Full of interesting items and home to the famous Liberty fabrics. Good antiques.

Marks and Spencer   458 Oxford St., W1, phone (0171) 935-7954. Branches everywhere. M&S, or Marks and Sparks as it's known, isn't really a department store, but it does carry a lot of good stuff. With its own St. Michel name brand, it provides food and fashion. Apparently, their underwear is worn by 70% of all Londoners, and I can vouch for its comfort and design. I know of a few Americans who stock up whenever they're in town. Solid if unimaginative clothing is offered in every possible size.

Selfridges   400 Oxford St., W1, phone (0171) 629-1234. This may be the home of Europe's largest perfume department, but it is somewhat confused in other ways. It's not a place that people go to specifically to get things other than delicacies from their wonderful food halls, which excel in the Middle Eastern varieties.

Where to Find ...

ANTIQUES

There are so many antiques stores in London, from White Chapel to Hammersmith, that an entire book could be devoted to listing them. What I will point you toward are the antiques arcades that are plentiful here, and let you wander through the great variety of antiques to be had among the stalls: jewelry, books, clothing, furniture, clocks, silver, decorative arts, knickknacks, and more. See page 247 for the Bermonsey, Camden Passage, Camden Lock, and Portobello Antiques Markets. **Alfie's Antique Market,** 13-5 Church St., NW8, phone (0171) 723-6066 (tube: Edgeware Road), is open Tuesday–Saturday 10 a.m.–6 p.m. **Antiquarius,** 131–141 King's Rd., SW3, phone (0171) 351-5353 (tube: Sloane Square), is open Monday–Saturday 10 a.m.–6 p.m. **Bourbon-Hanby Antiques Centre,** 151 Sydney St., SW3 (on corner of King's Road), phone (0171) 352-2106 (tube: Sloane Square), is open Monday–Saturday 10 a.m.–6 p.m.; Sunday 11 a.m.–5 p.m. **Gray's Antiques Market and Gray's Mews Market,** 58 Davies St., W1 (off Oxford Street) (tube: Bond Street), is open Monday–Friday 10 a.m.–6 p.m. Portobello Road has a huge number of arcades with multiple stalls open on Saturday, often from 5 a.m. Try the **Portobello Antiques Arcade** at 139, **Admiral Vernon** at 141–149, **Geoffrey Van** at 105, or **Chelsea Galleries** at 67.

AUCTION HOUSES

These can be a lot of fun, and you can also get some amazing items, as the treasures of the empire continue to pass through hands. Bargains are not to be had by the likes of common folk, as the dealers know what they're doing and how to do it, but you can give it a go. Call to find out what is being sold and when, and go take a look at the catalogs to familiarize yourself with the prices. These are the four most prestigious auction houses in London, not to mention in the world: **Bonhams,** Montpelier Street, SW7, phone (0171) 393-3900, Branch: 65–69 Lots Rd., SW10, phone (0171) 393-3900; **Christie's,** 8 King St., SW1, phone (0171) 839-9060, Branch: 85 Old Brompton Rd., SW7, phone 0171) 581-7611; **Phillips,** 101 New Bond St., W1, phone (0171) 629-6602, Branch: 10 Salem Rd., W2, phone (0171) 229-9090; and **Sotheby's,** 34–35 New Bond St., W1, phone (0171) 493-8080.

BEAUTY AND BATH STORES

Culpeper the Herbalists, 8 The Market, Covent Garden Piazza, WC2, phone (0171) 379-6698 (tube: Covent Garden), sells bath salts, oils, teas, spices, essential oils—they've got it all here. A branch is located at 21 Bruton St., W1, phone (0171) 629-4559. **Lush,** 7 & 11 The Market, Covent Garden Piazza, WC, phone (0171) 379-5423 (tube: Covent Garden), is a wonderful place for chocolate massage bars, soaps by the hunk, fizzy bath bombs, and homemade oatmeal masks. Made to look like a delicatessen, it has very good gifts A branch is at 123 King's Rd., SW3, phone (0171) 376-8348. **M.A.C Cosmetics,** 109 King's Rd., SW3, phone (0171) 349-0601 (tube: Sloane Square), is a Canadian company that offers the new trendy makeup, yet doesn't cost the world. A branch is located at 28 Foubert's Place, W1, phone (0171) 439-0501. **Neal's Yard Remedies,** 15 Neal's Yard, WC2, phone (0171) 379-7222 (tube: Covent Garden), is a great place for homeopathic remedies, fresh herbs, essential oils, soaps, and hair care products, all in beautiful blue glass bottles. Branches too numerous to mention, call for information. **Space NK Apothecary,** 37 Earlham St., WC2, phone (0171) 379-7030 (tube: Covent Garden), offers the latest and greatest in cosmetics and beauty products at its popular store, which seems to be taking over the London high streets. Branches too numerous to mention, call for information.

BOOKSTORES

There are many chain bookstores in London, which have branches everywhere. Call to find the one nearest to you: **Books Etc.,** phone (0171) 379-

6838; **Dillions,** phone (0171) 434-9617; **WH Smith,** phone (0171) 261-1708; and **Waterstones,** phone (0171) 434-4291.

Then there are the more unusual stores.

Atlantis Bookshop, 49a Museum St., WC1, phone (0171) 405-2120 (tube: Tottenham Court Road), caters to a very particular audience with psychic research, witchcraft, and supernatural phenomena. Incredible deals are to be had in the remainder book shop, **Book Thrift,** 22 Thurloe St., SW7, phone (0171) 589-2916 (tube: South Kensington), whose emphasis is on fine arts books for a fraction of the original cost. Buy immediately, since when the stock is gone, it's gone for good. **European Bookshop,** 5 Warwick St., W1, phone (0171) 734-5259 (tube: Piccadilly Circus), sells books and mags in most European languages.

The Folio Society Gallery, at Henry Southeran, 2 Sackville St., W1 (tube: Green Park), has a catch, but it won't bother a die-hard fine-book lover: You have to join the society with the responsibility of buying four books as the price of membership (the difficulty is limiting yourself to only four). These books are magnificent, well bound and illustrated as in the old days, and the titles available are classics of every kind. If you're interested in real antiquarian books, Henry Southeran, on the ground floor, is the place to look.

Forbidden Planet, 71–75 New Oxford St., WC1, phone (0171) 836-4179 (tube: Tottenham Court Road), billed as "The Science Fiction Entertainment Store," has got it all, from toys to videos and every kind of printed matter you can imagine. **French's Theatre Bookshop,** 52 Fitzroy St., W1, phone (0171) 387-9373 (tube: Warren Street), has play scripts beyond compare. A must for the theater student or aficionado.

Hatchard's, 187 Piccadilly, W1, phone (0171) 439-9921 (tube: Piccadilly Circus), is London's oldest bookstore, with a very fine selection and a great atmosphere. **Helter Skelter,** 4 Denmark St., WC2, phone (0171) 836-1151 (tube: Tottenham Court Road), is a music bookshop with sheet music, mags, music-related art, and all possible fiction and nonfiction about the subject. **Librairie La Page French Booksellers,** 7 Harrington Rd., SW 7 (tube: South Kensington), has everything for the French student, young and old. **Pan Bookstore,** 158 Fulham Rd., SW10, phone (0171) 373-4997 (tube: South Kensington, then 14 bus toward Fulham), has lots of signed editions of recently published books.

Politico's, 8 Artillery Row, SW1, phone (0171) 828-0010 (tube: St. James's Park), has great political paraphernalia, plus a fine selection of books of biography, reference, and history. **Stanford's,** 12–14 Long Acre, WC2, phone (0171) 836-1915 (tube: Leicester Square), has the biggest collection of maps, globes, and travel books you will ever see. **Talking Bookshop,** 11 Wigmore St., W1, phone (0171) 491-4117 (tube: Bond Street), has the best selection ever seen of books on tape: a huge wall of unabridged fiction from classics to this year's bestsellers. They also have books on CD. Not cheaper than the United States necessarily, but an extraordinary range.

Antiquarian and Secondhand Books

Let us not forget the antiquarian and secondhand books. It would behoove anyone interested in browsing to take a walk down Charing Cross Road or around Soho to look in at the many secondhand bookstores they have there. The prices are very low, and you could get your hands on some very fine antique books for a couple of quid. Many of the secondhand bookstores listed below also have antiquarian books locked behind glass cabinets. Antiques neighborhoods, markets, and arcades, as listed in this book, will also have many shops and stalls featuring old and beautiful books. Visit: **Any Amount of Books,** 62 Charing Cross Rd., WC2, phone (0171) 240-8140 (tube: Leicester Square); **Books Bought Bookshop,** 357 King's Rd., SW3, phone (0171) 352-9376 (tube: Sloane Square); **Gloucester Road Bookshop,** 123 Gloucester Rd., SW7, phone (0171) 370-3503. (tube: Gloucester Road); **Skoob Books,** 15 Sicilian Ave., WC1, phone (0171) 404-3063 (tube: Holborn); and **Unsworths Booksellers,** 15 Bloomsbury St., WC1, phone (0171) 436-9836 (tube: Tottenham Court Road).

DECORATIVE HOME ACCESSORIES

Architectural Components, 8 Exhibition Rd., SW7, phone (0171) 581-2401 (tube: South Kensington), has brass fittings for every possible household use. **The Conran Shop,** Michelin House, 81 Fulham Rd., SW3, phone (0171) 589-7401 (tube: South Kensington), has a lot of interesting, though expensive, things for bed, bath, kitchen, and nursery in a modern style. Very traditionally English in style, **General Trading Company,** 144 Sloane St., SW1, phone (0171) 730-0411 (tube: Sloane Square), has everything you can imagine wanting for the home or tabletop. **India Jane,** 140 Sloane St., SW1, phone (0171) 730-1070 (tube: Sloane Square), has some good buys in the way of Indian silver and picture frames.

The **London Silver Vaults,** 53–64 Chancery Lane, WC2, (tube: Chancery Lane), is actually thirty-five shops selling silver, old and new, and for every budget. **Past Times,** 146 Brompton Rd., SW3, phone (0171) 581-7616 (tube: Knightsbridge), is a store I love and always find something to buy in. Full of faux Olde English stuff from every period, it is a great place to buy gifts, from garden goods to desk accessories to books. Numerous branches; call for information.

The **Reject China Shop,** 134 Regent St., W1, phone (0171) 434-2502 (tube: Oxford Circus), is a great place to replace missing Spode or Wedgwood plates, or pick up a cow creamer. Branch: 1 Beauchamp Place, SW3, phone (0171) 225-1696 (tube: Knightsbridge). **Sally Harclerode,** by appointment, phone (0171) 581-2681, is a woman who makes the most incredible lampshades imaginable, and has been doing so for the rich and famous for some time. She also can get you the best fabrics and silks around for a lot less than you'd pay in the United States and ship it all to you. **Thomas Goode,** 19 S. Audley St., W1, phone (0171) 499-2823 (tube: Green Park), is a don't-miss-it English shopping experience with major china, silver, and crystal as well as knickknacks. Have a spot of tea there, too.

DESIGNER CLOTHES

Below is a list of some of London's homegrown designers. They are certainly London's best-known designers, and not all sell their clothes in the United States. Some have their own boutiques, but unless you just want to see what they have on offer, you're better off buying in the department stores and boutiques that carry their clothes. If it's an internationally known designer, you're better off sticking to buying in the States, if possible.

Hussein Chalayan, Caroline Charles, English Eccentrics, John Galliano, Ghost, Joseph, Katherine Hamnett, Nicole Farhi, Bella Freud, Alexander McQueen, Bruce Oldfield, Red or Dead, Paul Smith, Pierce Fionda, Lainey Keogh, Zandra Rhodes, Tomasz Starzewski, Phillip Treacy (hats only), Catherine Walker, Amanda Wakeley, Vivienne Westwood, Matthew Williamson all have stores here. Check the phone book for locations and phone numbers.

Designer Boutiques

Harvey Nichols, Harrods, Selfridges, and Liberty will likely carry some or all of the above designers' clothes. Here are a few boutiques that carry many of England's designers:

Browns, 23–27 South Moulton St., W1 phone (0171) 491-7833 (tube: Bond Street), has a huge selection of all the big names. **Joanna's Tent,** 289B King's Rd., SW3 phone (0171) 352-1151 (tube: Sloane Square), and **Koh Samui,** 50 Monmouth St., WC2, phone (0171) 240-4280, are others to try.

Designer Resale Shops

Such a good idea, these shops. It's hit or miss, but you can get your hands on some very expensive designer threads and shoes for a fraction of what they'd cost new. Unfortunately, there tend to be more size 4s than 14s, but shoes and purses will work for anyone. Some good places to try are: **Bertie Golightly,** 48 Beauchamp Place, SW3, phone (0171) 584-7270 (tube: Knightsbridge); **Catwalk,** 52 Blandford St., W1, phone (0171) 935-1052 (tube: Baker Street); **The Dresser,** 10 Porchester Place, W2, phone (0171) 724-7212 (tube: Marble Arch); **L'Homme Designer Exchange,** 50 Blandford St., W1, phone (0171) 224-3266 (tube: Baker Street), for men; **The Loft,** 35 Monmouth St.; WC2, phone (0171) 240-3807; and **Sign of the Times,** 17 Elystan St., SW3, phone (0171) 589-4774 (tube: Sloane Square). When visitng **Pandora,** 16–22 Cheval Place, SW7, phone (0171) 589-5289, see also, along this same street, **The Dress Box** (#8), **Renate** (#4), **Salou** (#6), and **Strelios** (#10).

FABRICS

Anna French, 343 King's Rd., SW3, phone (0171) 351-1126 (tube: Sloane Square, then 11 or 22 bus), sells children's room fabrics, as well as sheer, lacy, and flowery patterns. **Beaumont & Fletcher,** 261 Fulham Rd., SW3, phone (0171) 352-5594 (tube: South Kensington, then 14 bus), offers period (eighteenth- and nineteenth-century) and reproduction fabrics of a very high standard. **The Decorative Fabrics Gallery,** 278–280 Brompton Rd., SW3, phone (0171) 589-4778 (tube: South Kensington), has a wide range of traditional and upscale fabrics, with good export service. **Osbourne & Little,** 304–308 King's Rd., SW3, phone (0171) 352-1456 (tube: Sloane Square), sells traditional and modern designs, all of high quality. **VV Rouleaux,** 54 Sloan Sq. (Cliveden Place), SW1 phone (0171) 730-3125 (tube: Sloane Square), has the best collection of ribbons, trimmings, and braids in London.

LINENS

Irish Linen Company, 35–36 Burlington Arcade, W1, phone (0171) 493-8949 (tube: Piccadilly Circus), sells Irish linen and Egyptian cotton sheets and table clothes. **Monogrammed Linen Shop,** 168 Walton St., SW3, phone (0171) 589-4033 (tube: South Kensington), has a good stock of expensive, beautiful linen that can be monogrammed to order. **The White House,** 40–41 Conduit St., W1, phone (0171) 629-3521 (tube: Bond Street), sells unbelievably lovely bedclothes at unthinkably extravagant prices.

MUSEUM SHOPS

My favorite stores in London are the gift shops at museums and other attractions, and I'm not alone: There's a shop called the **Museum Store** with a selection of goods from museums all over the world (37 The Market, Covent Garden, WC2, phone (0171) 815-1343, tube: Covent Garden). It's well worth a visit. The following gift shops are also highly recommended: The **British Museum's** shop offers the best gifts for old and young—reproductions of museum treasures such as the Lewis chess pieces, and Roman coins or jewelry. **Hampton Palace's** shop has the best all-around selection of housewares, books, food, and decorative arts. **Museum of London's** shop has the best books on London. The **National Gallery** and **National Portrait Gallery** shops have the best postcards, calendars, and art books. The **Natural History Museum** shop has the best nature selection for kids; tons of plastic and stuffed animals. The **Queen's Gallery** shop has the best royal-related items. The **Royal Academy** has art books and cool T-shirts. The **Science Museum** has great gifts for children (look for glow-in-the-dark skeleton pajamas). The **Tate Gallery** ties with the National Gallery for best selection of art books and postcards. The **Victoria and Albert Museum** has the best reproduction jewelry, decorative arts, and books on design and interior decoration.

PERFUMERIES

One of the great things about London is its proximity to France, home of a thousand scents. The interest in aromas has wafted across the English Channel, and you can find some of the best perfumes in the world at the following stores. **L'Artisan Parfumeur,** 17 Cale St., SW3, phone (0171) 352-4196 (tube: South Kensington), has scents for men, women, and children(!). Candles too. **Crown Perfumery,** 51 Burlington Arcade, W1, phone (0171) 408-0088 (tube: Green Park), is a must-go place, where scents made specially for the likes of Queen Victoria, the duke and duchess of Windsor, Oscar Wilde, and Isadora Duncan can be sniffed. They can't be bought anywhere else, and you will love them. **Floris,** 89 Jermyn St., SW1, phone (0171) 930-2885 (tube: Piccadilly Circus), is the classic English fragrance and soap maker, in business since 1730. Potpourri and candles. **Jo Malone,** 154 Walton St., SW3, phone (0171) 581-1101 (tube: South Kensington), is a wildly popular store with remarkable, imaginative scents and creams. Call to check on their address—they plan to move to bigger quarters soon. **Penhaligons,** 41 Wellington St., WC2, phone (0171) 836-2150 (tube: Covent Garden), has been a lovely place with lovely smells since 1870. It's a great place for gifts, and has numerous branches. **Les Senteurs,** 227 Ebury St., SW1, phone (0171) 730-2322 (tube: Sloane Square), has very unusual fragrances, straight from France.

SHOES

Birkenstock, 37 Neal St., W2, phone (0171) 240-2783 (tube: Covent Garden), the hippy shoe from the 1960s has never been so popular or mainstream. The real thing costs a bundle in the United States, but here you can get such styles as the Vegan, which contains no animal parts, or the Classic, which does, for slightly, and in some cases much, less. **Dr Marten's Department Store,** 1–4 King St., WC2, phone (0171) 497-1460 (tube: Covent Garden), is five floors of Doc Marten shoes at prices that may be competitive with those in the States. Sale time is really the only time to find a bargain. **Emma Hope,** 53 Sloane Square, SW1, phone (0171) 259-9566 (tube: Sloane Square), offers amazingly elegant and quite expensive shoes. **Jimmy Choo,** 20 Motcomb St., SW1, phone (0171) 235-6008 (tube: Knightsbridge), is a very au courant shoemaker, beloved of the stylish young women of London and, increasingly, the world. **John Lobb,** 9 St. James St., SW1, phone (0171) 930-3664 (tube: Green Park), is the oldest, grandest, and most expensive of the bespoke shoemakers—one of these classic pairs of English leather shoes will set you back about £1,500, and it will take months to get them, but they say it's well worth it. **Natural Shoe Store,** 325 King's Rd., SW3, phone (0171) 351-3721 (tube: Sloane Square), has the best in comfort shoes: Ecco, Birkenstock, Arche, Krone Clogs, and American brands such as Bass, Dexter, and Rockport. Don't even think of getting the American brands, but check the prices on the Europeans.

STAINED GLASS

Neil Phillips Stained Glass, 99 Portobello Rd., W11, phone (0171) 229-2113 (tube: Notting Hill Gate), has the most fabulous selection of stained glass that can be seen here or at their Birmingham warehouse. The prices, styles, and antiquity of the stained glass vary wildly from week to week, so make a point of visiting a few times. You may find something small and wonderful that you can take home on the plane.

VINTAGE CLOTHING

Steinberg and Tolkien, 193 King's Road, SW3, phone (0171) 376-3660 (tube: Sloane Square), has an astonishing, wonderful range of vintage clothing, from Victorian to the 1970s, from Worth to Balmain to Schiaparelli to Biba to Halston. It's the place where costume designers from films come to dress their actors, where actors come to play, and where designers come for inspiration. Go for the fun of seeing the largest vintage clothing collection in London, and be sure to go downstairs.

WOOL AND CASHMERE

Wool and cashmere in London is from Scotland or Ireland and is more expensive and of better quality than the Chinese kind. Still, the best time to buy is during sale times, and many of the wool stores will have sales during the summer to move the goods and take advantage of the influx of tourists—many of whom aren't prepared for the chilly London summer and will have need of some woolens. Liberty, Harrods, Marks and Spencer, Debehams, and other big stores have good wool departments.

Scotch House, 191 Regent St., W1, phone (0171) 734-4816 (tube: Oxford Circus), has scarves, kilts, jackets, capes, gloves, and everything else that can be made from wool and cashmere. Call for information on branches. **Shirin Cashmere,** 12 Beauchamp Place, SW3, phone (0171) 581-1936 (tube: Knightsbridge), has a much more elegant selection than the Scotch House, with prices to match. **Westaway & Westaway,** 64–65 Great Russell St., WC1, phone (0171) 405-4479 (and 92–93 Great Russell Street, phone (0171) 636-1718) (tube: Holborn), is two shops overflowing with sweaters in every color and size possible, at the best prices possible.

Part Nine

Sight-Seeing and Tours

An Embarrassment of Riches

A trip to London surely must be on every dedicated traveler's wish list. For the indefatigable sight-seer, there is an endless itinerary to follow. For one in need of a little R and R, there are theaters to enjoy and parks to kick back in. For the scholar, there is so much to learn, so much to swoon over. For more contemporary types there are clubs and shops that rival New York and Paris. There's so much to see and do in London that you must try to restrict yourself to only that which you find fascinating, or you'll find yourself very, very tired. There are the obvious tourist attractions — the Tower of London, the British Museum, Trafalgar Square — and then there are the other bits that make London so wonderful: the parks, the themed walking tours, the obscure collections, and the marketplaces. Only you can determine what is most interesting to you and your companions, but we can help you to make your decisions.

DISSENSION IN THE RANKS

In a place like London, with so many varied attractions, you can easily disagree with your traveling companions as to what are the most important sights. You may think that visiting the Globe Theatre without seeing a play is a yawn, and your spouse may be bored silly by the very idea of a tea and coffee museum. There are two ways to go about solving these fundamental problems of taste, time, and touring. One is to compromise: You see one of mine, and I'll see one of yours. This at least addresses honestly the issue of not being keen on the attraction, instead of going along grudgingly and being clearly uninterested. The other is to split up and go your own way. This has the great advantage of making it less likely that you will grow tired of each other's company, and ensures a ready store of dinner conversation as you each recount your experiences.

KNOW THY LIMITS

Everyone has a threshold at which sight-seeing moves from being a joy to a torture. Your feet hurt, the lines are too long, the weather is appalling, you're hungry. These thresholds vary from person to person, but to the disabled, the elderly, and the very young, the passage over it can be not just uncomfortable but risky. There are a number of attractions in London in which you'll find no wheelchair access, or there are incredibly steep stairs, or all the exhibits are too high for the young or a wheelchair-user to see. You do not want to put yourself (or your companions if they are any of the above) in the position of finding out too late that the attraction just won't work. Although we try to tell you whether a place is disabled- or child-friendly in our listings, it is always a good idea to call first and find out for sure. There are improvements being made all the time in the interests of easier access at most attractions, museums, churches, and stately homes, so check ahead. Also, there are some places that call themselves disabled-friendly, but which in reality have a limit on the number of wheelchairs allowed in at a time. For children, you might want to find out of the museum you're visiting has any activities for kids—the Victoria and Albert and the British Museum are just two of the "grown-up" museums that are trying to keep the children entertained, but they only do so on weekends or school holidays.

Tourist Information Centers

The **London Tourist Board** has a number of extremely well-stocked tourist centers, as befits a city so supported by visitors. You can pick up an armful of pamphlets, brochures, maps, and fliers, as well as reserve tickets, tours, and hotel rooms.

Heathrow Airport Terminals 1, 2, 3. Open daily from 8:30 a.m. to 6 p.m.

Liverpool Street Underground Station Open Tuesday–Saturday 8:15 a.m. to 6 p.m.; Sunday from 8:30 a.m. to 5 p.m.; and Monday 8:15 a.m. to 7 p.m.

Selfridges, 400 Oxford St., in Basement Services Arcade, W1 (tube: Bond Street). Open Monday through Wednesday, Friday and Saturday from 9:30 a.m. to 7 p.m.; Saturday 9:30 a.m., to 8 p.m.

Victoria Station, SW1, in the forecourt of the station. Open from 8 a.m. to 7 p.m. (fewer hours in the winter).

Visitorcall will provide recorded details of events; phone (0183) 912-3456.

Touring

JUMP ON THE BUS

The best thing to do on the first day in a city is to take a hop-on, hop-off bus tour and just stay on throughout the tour. This gives you the lay of the land, and if the day is bright, the open top of a double-decker bus is the best place to get the sunlight that helps you get over jet-lag. London has a number of these buses, with stops at all the major attractions. It is crucial that you get on the bus as early as possible to avoid the crushing traffic jams that can make the tour a carbon monoxide–scented bummer. If you see traffic building up and just can't stand sitting in it anymore, hop off and continue your tour the next day or later that afternoon. The tickets are good for 24 hours, which is great—you can break up the tour nicely. But if you intend to take the two-day option, remember to get on the bus on day one around 2 or 3 p.m. so that you'll get the early morning the next day. The tour companies do pretty much the same tours at the same prices, and offer commentary throughout. Check the bus stop to make sure your particular tour bus stops there. You can pick up the bus at anyone of the major attraction and intersections, such as the Tower of London, Madame Tussaud's, Green Park, Hyde Park Corner, Harrods, in front of the Victoria and Albert Museum, and so on. Ask at your hotel where the closest stop is for you.

Big Bus Company, (phone (0181) 944-7810), has a Green Route (90 minutes) and a Blue Route (60 minutes) with live commentary. Buses run every 15 minutes or so. They have 60 different stops, at all the big attractions. Adult £12, children £6. Tickets are good for 24 hours.

London Pride, (phone (0170) 863-1122) has six different tours and routes, and you will have to change buses to get the full city tour. Buses run approximately every 10–30 minutes. They offer a very good Fast Track deal, by which you can buy your entry tickets (often at a small discount) to a number of attractions on the bus and go straight to the ticket-holders' entrances, which in some cases can mean jumping a pretty long queue. The Grand Tour and the Blue Tour offer eight language options, and 100 hop-on, hop-off stops. For the Grand Tour: Adults £12, children £6. Tickets are good for 24 hours.

The Original London Sightseeing Tour, (phone (0181) 877-1722), also offers eight foreign-language tours, Fast Entry Tickets, and four different touring options. It makes 80 stops. Adults, £12, children under age 16, £6. Tickets are good for 24 hours.

Harrods (phone (0171) 730-1234, ask for Coach Tours) has a city tour that costs £18, and is more deluxe than the hop-on, hop-off buses. The luxury consists of a smooth double-decker bus on which there is a toilet, tea and cookies, and headphones with recorded commentary in different languages. You can't leave the bus to see the sights, and the 1 p.m. tour is guaranteed to be stuck in all kinds of horrendous traffic (take the morning one if possible). This is particularly abhorrent to children, who will fall asleep or get cranky. This tour is best for cold or rainy days, or people who just want to sit and have a comfortable look at London. When you book your seats, try to get the top front row for the best view. Harrods also has a number of other tours—Stratford, Windsor, and so on—which change by season and year. Harrods charges more than the other Coach Tours operators, but the advantage is that the bus leaves directly from Harrods and doesn't drive all over the city picking up people before starting off.

ON YOUR OWN

You don't have to spend all that much to get a decent double-decker bus ride. There is the famous **number 11** bus that takes you past many of the same sights the tourist buses do for a mere fraction of the cost. Pick it up on the King's Road at World's End or the Chelsea Town Hall, and you'll have a good look at that famous mod street, go through Victoria, past Westminster Abbey, Whitehall, Trafalgar Square, up the Strand to St. Paul's Cathedral, and finish in the East End at Liverpool Street. All for under £2.

The **number 15** is also wonderful: I met a couple of elderly Londoner ladies on it once, and they told me they often get on it to take in the sights and visit with one another without having to spend money (British seniors, or old age pensioners, as they're called, ride free). Pick up the 15 at Paddington and ride to Marble Arch, up Oxford Street, down Regent to Piccadilly Circus, down Haymarket to Trafalgar Square, up the Strand (which turns into Fleet Street), St. Paul's Cathedral, the Tower of London, and end up at Petticoat Lane (Middlesex Street), which has a market on Sunday mornings, as well as some stalls during the week.

The **number 14** goes from Tottenham Court Road (by the British Museum) over the Thames and west to Putney Heath, passing Piccadilly, Knightsbridge, the museums of South Kensington, and the antiques stores of Fulham.

Bus **route 24** will take you north, from Victoria Station all the way to Hampstead Heath and Highgate, from which you can get an amazing view of London.

To get a look at some of South London, take the **number 2** bus from either Marylebone Station, Marble Arch, or Hyde Park Corner and ride across the Thames through Brixton, up Tulse Hill to Crystal Palace Park, where you can get out and look at the prehistoric creatures imagined and modeled by the Victorians.

Get a bus map at any tourist center or hotel lobby and check out these routes, and any others that look interesting to you. If, as you're traveling, you feel you are going too far afield, just get off and jump on a bus going in the opposite direction. All roads lead back to London.

PRIVATE TOURS

The **Classic Coach Company** offers a small bus in a classic design with room for 11 passengers, who are given a 3-hour guided tour for £17 per seat, or you can hire the entire vehicle for £80 and up. The advantage to this coach tour is that because it's smaller than the double-deckers, you can get into small streets and squares that you couldn't see on the other tours. And it's very cool looking, with plenty of windows to gape from. Tours go daily at 8:30 a.m., 10 a.m., and 1 p.m. Call (0181) 390-0888, 24 hours a day, or ask your hotel to book you a spot.

You can also hire a black cab to take you around London, creating your own tour, seeing only those sights that interest you most. Call **Black Taxi Tours of London** at (0171) 289-4371, fax (0171) 224-2833. A two-hour tour, day or night, will cost about £65, and you can have a maximum of five people. The great thing is that you can avoid traffic jams and get into the squares, mews, and back streets that no tour bus can take you to.

SEEING THE HIGHLIGHTS

The double-decker big bus tours are designed for seeing the sights of London in a general way. They don't take into account how long you might want to linger at any museum or attraction, but they do give you the basics. You can see where everything is in relation to everything else, perhaps find out how long the lines are for certain attractions, figure out what can be done in a day or a week, and which area seems most intriguing. By doing a general tour first thing, you can then make plans for the days ahead more efficiently and specifically. You'll learn that you won't be able to do the Tower of London on the same day you take a walk in Hampstead Heath, which is so far away that it's off any standard London tour itinerary. Or that a trip to the National Gallery can be combined with a visit to the adjacent National Portrait Galley, a look in at St. Martin–in-the-Fields, feeding pigeons in Trafalgar Square, and you will still have time left over for taking pictures at the Eros statue in Piccadilly Circus and a visit to Madame Tussaud's Rock Circus.

You can customize your days in London in many ways—going to museums, visiting attractions, shopping in the markets, strolling in the park, attending a matinee, going on guided walks, and riding along self-guided bus trips—that it's unlikely you could have a down day unless you really wanted one.

SIGHT-SEEING COMPANIES

There are a lot of tour companies in London doing very similar tours for roughly the same amount of money. You can find their brochures in any hotel lobby. A word of caution: They have many courtesy hotel pick-up points in London, which sounds very convenient—who doesn't want to fall out of their hotel room into a waiting coach at 8 a.m.? But yours may just be the first stop of 15, and if you get stuck in the normal London traffic, you can be on the bus for an hour before you actually get started on the tour. You'll probably find it less annoying to meet your bus at the final departure point. When you reserve your seat, find out where the bus will actually leave for the tour, then take the tube or a taxi to get there. The downside to this evasive action is that you may not get the seat you want on the bus, but as every seat does have a window, it shouldn't be the end of the world. (The best seat, however, is clearly the top floor front row.)

The tour companies offer London tours of half-day, morning, night, or full-day, as well as two days, plus tours to such places as Windsor and Leeds Castles, Eton, Hampton Court, Stonehenge, Bath, Stratford-upon-Avon, Oxford, Cambridge, Salisbury, Brighton, Dover, Canterbury, York, Chester, Warwick Castle, the Lake District, Scotland, and even Paris and Amsterdam. The price of the tour almost always includes entrance fees for the attractions and meals, and in the case of the overnight trips, accommodations.

The companies are:

Astral Travels, phone (0700) 078-1016 or (0870) 902-0908, fax (0707) 071-2035, email info@astraltravels.co.uk, Web *www.AstralTravels.co.uk* (mini-coach day tours)

Evan Evans, phone (0181) 332-2222, fax (0181) 784-2835, email: reservations@evanevans.co.uk, Web *www.evanevans.co.uk*

Frames Rickards Sightseeing, phone (0171) 837-3111 or (0171) 637-4171

Golden Tours Deluxe Sightseeing, phone (800) 456-6303 in U.S.; (0171) 233-7030; email goldentours@aol.com; Web *www.goldentours.co.uk*

Visitors Sightseeing, phone (0171) 636-7175, fax (0171) 636-3310

For tours along the river, call **The Royal River Thames Passenger Boat Services** at (0171) 930-4097, fax (0171) 930-1616.

For boat rides along the canals of Little Venice and Camden Lock, call **London Waterbus Company** at (0171) 482-2550 or (0171) 482-2660.

Outside London

Although just getting a taste of London's richness can take all of even a long vacation, it may be a great change of pace to get out into the famous English countryside. There are so many wonderful medieval towns and inspiring cathedrals to see in this country. The above tour companies do such trips conveniently and trouble-free, and you will also be able to double up on many neighboring sights.

You may want to rent a car to do your sight-seeing, but sometimes it's just easier to let others do the driving. Astral Tours, especially, is a good option if you're not fond of big buses with lots of people. Taking a train will work for going to Bath, Oxford, Cambridge, or Stratford-upon Avon, where you can get a hotel room and walk around town, but for trips to Stonehenge, or small medieval towns such as Laycock or Warwick Castle, you are better off going with a tour, in my opinion. Get any of the above companies' brochures and decide where you want to go. Ask how many people have already booked—perhaps you can find a day when it will only be a handful of people. Arrange to meet the tour bus at its last stop so you don't have to tack on too much sitting time while the bus picks people up.

SOME GOOD SIDE TRIPS

Bath   One-and-a-half hours from Paddington station (170 miles). Gorgeous Georgian town with Roman relics and famous for its Sally Lunn cakes. Jane Austen once lived here.

Brighton   One hour from Victoria station (53 miles). A jolly outing for seaside and amusement-park fun. Little shopping streets and alleys, and the Brighton Pavilion, the Oriental fantasy of George IV.

Cambridge   One hour from King's Cross station (85 miles). A quiet university town, with beautiful river views and significant buildings.

Canterbury   Eighty minutes from Victoria station (50 miles). The old pilgrimages used to come to the cathedral, in which St. Augustine converted King Ethelbert in 597, and Thomas à Becket was murdered.

Hatfield House   Twenty minutes from King's Cross station (20 miles). The place where Queen Elizabeth I spent her childhood.

Oxford   One hour from Paddington station (56 miles). University city of "dreaming spires," it's a good jumping-off place for the Cotswolds.

St. Albans   Thirty minutes from King's Cross station (25 miles). An old Roman stronghold, St. Albans has ruins and rose gardens.

Salisbury   One-and-a-half hours from Waterloo station (84 miles). Salisbury has a wonderful old cathedral and many crooked little streets; Stonehenge is a short drive away.

Stratford-upon-Avon   Oddly, there are no direct trains from London. Paddington to Leamington Spa and on to Stratford takes about 3 hours (91 miles). Shakespeare's town—born, married, and buried there—is devoted to him, but has other attractions as well.

Windsor   Thirty minutes from Waterloo station (20 miles). Storybook castle by the Thames, and a fine old town with good pubs. Playing fields of Eton are nearby.

Not to Be Missed in London: A Highly Subjective List

- The British Museum
- St James's Park
- The Victoria and Albert Museum
- The Tower of London
- Museum of London
- St. Paul's Cathedral
- The Wallace Collection
- The Globe
- Hampton Court Palace
- Westminster Abbey
- Holland Park
- The Science Museum
- The National Gallery
- A street market on the weekend
- Hyde Park on Sunday

Romantic London

One really doesn't associate London with romance in the way one might Paris or Venice, but that's not to say there aren't some romantic places to go with your beloved. Judging by the snogging (kissing) that goes on in Hyde Park, I'd have to say that taking a blanket, a jug of wine, and your special someone to the park for a lie around in the sun is one of London's favorite pastimes for couples, and it's free. If you need exercise, get in a paddle-boat built for two and tool around the Serpentine. Take a night cruise along the Thames, or sit on a bench at sunset on the Thames at the end of Oakley Street, watch the birds circling overhead, and wait for the lights to illuminate the spectacular Albert Bridge. Avoid pubs: The bright lights and smells of grease, beer, and cigs just don't spell romance.

A romantic restaurant would be **Momo** (25 Heddon St., off Regent Street, W1, phone (0171) 434-4040), a middle eastern restaurant that's done up in *Arabian Nights* fantasy style. The quite expensive **Pont de la Tour** (Butler's Wharf, 36D Shad Thames, SE1 phone (0171) 403-8403) has gorgeous views of Tower Bridge, which can be pretty romantic, unless you truly only have eyes for each other.

The most romantic hotels are **The Portobello** (ask for the room with the round bed) and **The Gore** (The Venus, the Tudor, or the Miss Ada Suite). And, of course, you can't go wrong at the **Ritz** for romance—check out the weekend break prices, and tell them you want a honeymoon-type room or, better still, a suite (see "Part Three, Hotels" for more information).

Agent Provocateur (16 Pont St., SW1, phone (0171) 235-0229) sells *very* sexy underwear—erotic and sophisticated at the same time. And for chocolate massage oil bars and bath salts–for-two go to **Lush** at Covent Garden (phone (0171) 240-4570) or in Chelsea (123 King's Rd., SW3, phone (0171) 376-8348).

Oh, Such a Perfect Day

What constitutes a perfect day in London will naturally depend on who's in your party and what your keenest interests are. One person's poison is another one's mead, as they say. But if I were to try to conjure up a day that would hit as many of my personal favorite high notes as possible, it would go something like this:

Breakfast at Patisserie Valerie—the croissants are unlike any other, and the cappuccino is perfect. Although there are other branches in London (Soho and Marylebone), the one at which to start the perfect day is in Knightsbridge at 215 Brompton Rd. (phone (0171) 823-9971). Buy your morning papers from the Press Bureau next door, and check out the huge selection of magazines.

After breakfast, make a left out the door and go down to look at the Brompton Oratory Church across the road. It's an amazing edifice, with small chapels lining the enormous hall, and a rotunda to rival St. Paul's. Go through the church yard and out to Ennismore Gardens, which you'll take up to Hyde Park—a couple of blocks. Amble around the park, go to the riding ring and see if any of the queen's guards are exercising their horses or rehearsing any ceremonies. Go feed a duck or two at the Serpentine.

Exit the park at Exhibition Road and head for the Victoria and Albert Museum down the street (opens at 10 a.m., noon on Monday). Wander around the stained glass windows upstairs, sit in the Fakes and Forgeries Statue Court, and go admire the William Morris tea room. If the weather's good, sit in the Pirelli Courtyard for a spell, then walk or take a taxi up Sydney Street to the Chelsea Town Hall. Across from the hall is an Antiques Center that you can browse around in briefly, and then, if the weather's warm, have lunch outside at the Chelsea Marketplace.

Stroll down the King's Road toward Sloane Square, maybe do a little window shopping, and catch the 11 bus wherever possible. Take the 11 past all the great sights: Westminster Abbey, Big Ben, Whitehall, Trafalgar Square, up Fleet Street, to St. Paul's. If you have the energy, climb up to the top of St. Paul's and enjoy the view. If not, just have a seat in the church and admire the craftsmanship that went into this magnificent building, or perhaps rest in the courtyard of the church and watch the tourists. Catch a bus towards Trafalgar Square and go to Leicester Square to buy a half-price theater ticket at the kiosk there for that evening. There's no saying what plays will be available, but it's always great to see an Oscar Wilde play, or maybe go for *The Mousetrap,* the Agatha Christie whodunit that's been playing for half a century—who knows, it could close next month and then how would you feel, having put it off for 50 years? (I would definitely not see an American import or an Andrew Lloyd Weber musical.)

Then, depending on the time, it would be a toss-up between having tea at the Ritz or Fortnam and Masons, or doing some brass-rubbing at St. Martin–in-the-Fields' in the crypt. Take your time with the rubbing, enjoying the atmosphere and the pastime. Buy some gifts in the wonderful shop (there's two—at the Brass Rubbing area and in the other part of the crypt). Then walk over to Covent Garden and watch the buskers (street entertainers) at work. Dinner at last. For the atmosphere and the Yorkshire pudding, try Rules, the oldest surviving restaurant in London (35 Maiden Lane, WC2, phone (0171) 836-5314). Yes, it's a tourist trap, but it is also redolent of a long-gone era, with the photos and cartoons on the wall charting its history since it opened in 1798. And where else can you get grouse, woodcock, and partridge?

You will love the play, especially because you will have paid half-price for some perfectly decent seats. You will love how they sell delicious ice cream right in the theater at the intermission, and you will be proud of yourself for already ordering your refreshments before the play started and finding them waiting for you at the bar at intermission. When the play gets out at 10:30 or 11 p.m., walk over to Ronnie Scott's (47 Frith St., W1, phone (0171) 439-0747) and listen to jazz until it's time to call a minicab and go back to your fabulous hotel (The Gore, Hazlitt's, or Blakes) to go to sleep.

Walking in and around London

Walking is by far the best way to experience London. Grab a map and your camera, select a starting point, and just begin to explore. You never know what you may find once you move off of London's bustling main thoroughfares—a cobbled alleyway with a quaint cafe, a medieval church, or even a dreamy view across the river. Below are a number of suggested walks covering a diverse range of areas. Many cross the paths of some great London attractions and can create an entire day's worth of wandering if you decide to stop off and visit some of the sights along the way.

You might also want to try out London Walks, which features scores of themed walks, built around Jack the Ripper, ghosts of London, lost palaces, The Beatles, rock and roll, literary London, the swinging sixties, Princess Diana, Charles Dickens, and so many more. You can pick up a leaflet at most hotels, check for daily events in *Time Out,* or call:

The Original London Walks, phone (0171) 624-3978, or (0171) 794-1764; fax (0171) 625-1932; email london.walks@mail.bogo.co.uk; Web *www.london.walks.com*

Stepping Out, phone (0181) 881-2933, fax (0171) 405-6036, Web *www.walklon.ndirect.co.uk*

Both companies have excellent guides and a huge selection of walks, both day and night.

THEME WALKS

City of London: Through the Centuries

Time to Allow: 3–4 hours depending on indoor visits

Distance: Approx. 1.5 miles

Sights: Museum of London; St. Botolph, Aldersgate; Postman's Park; St. Bartholomew-the-Great Church; National Postal Museum; Christ Church, Greyfriars; St. Paul's Cathedral; Guildhall; Guildhall Clock Museum and Art Gallery; St. Lawrence Jewry

This walk gives just a glimpse of the vast array of architecture that has evolved in London over the centuries, from the ancient Roman wall that once enclosed the fourth-century city of Londinium, to the skyscrapers of the modern financial district. Begin your wanderings at the Museum of London. Looking out from the museum's terrace, you are surrounded by concrete and glass. This is twentieth-century London, with heavy traffic and office buildings. This is a London that would make a Londoner from the last century (or even just before the Blitz) weep with confusion and sorrow. However, if you know where to look, bits of Old London rise to the surface—the London of medieval peasants, Renaissance grandeur, and Victorian sentimentality. A stop at the museum is great for getting your bearings on London's diverse historical time periods.

After enjoying an engaging few hours of history, head across the traffic circle to Aldersgate. Locate Little Britain Street on the right, on whose corner sits St. Botolph Church. The church's classical Georgian interior is a glorious contrast to its bland and unassuming exterior. Turn right as you exit the church and enter Postman's Park. This hidden churchyard was dedicated by the Victorians in 1900 as a memorial to "heroes of everyday life" who died in acts of bravery. In the center of the intimate park, you will find the protected wall of memorials. One epitaph reads, "Saved a lunatic woman from suicide at Woolwich Arsenal, but was himself run over by the train." Exiting the park on the opposite side, turn right onto King Edward Street, then follow Little Britain around to the left to where it deposits you in Smithfield Square.

In medieval times, the marketplace of Smithfield Green was thriving with merchants, peddlers, peasants, and livestock. Jousts, tournaments, horse fairs, and hangings have all been held here. To your left is St. Bartholomew's Hospital. Begun in 1123 as a priory and hospice, it is London's oldest hospital. Out front is a memorial to Sir William Wallace, known to many as Braveheart. If you venture inside the hospital's main entrance, you will find the small hospital church of St. Bartholomew-the-Less and an eighteenth-century courtyard. Back out on the square and to your right you will see a half-timbered, tudor gatehouse. Through here is a gem of medieval London, the Priory Church of St. Bartholomew-the-Great, also dating back to 1123. Don't miss the opportunity to take a peak at this breathtaking example of original twelfth-century Norman architecture.

Making your way back to Little Britain, turn right onto King Edward Street, using the dome of St. Paul's Cathedral before you as a guide. Past Postman's Park and the National Postal Museum, at the end of Little Britain, are the remains of Christopher Wren's Christ Church, Greyfriars. Originally built in 1691, it was destroyed during air raids in World War II. Today, the tower and walls enclose a lovely garden whose trellises mark the original location of the church columns and center aisle. Cross Newgate Street and turn left. Beyond the tube station entrance is the churchyard of St. Paul's Cathedral. Vastly different from medieval St. Bart's, Christopher Wren's Renaissance masterpiece is the second largest cathedral in the world. Stop here to see the glorious interior or perhaps climb the dome for unparalleled city views.

Wandering back through the churchyard, turn right and head east on Cheapside. Cross over and make a left on Wood Street and then follow Milk Street as it bears to the right. This area was another of London's medieval marketplaces, although the only remnants are the street names—Bread Street, Milk Street, Honey Lane—to remind you of its past. Just ahead is the entrance to Guildhall, the headquarters for the Corporation of London. Behind the bleak twentieth-century facade lies the impressive Great Hall, open 10 a.m.–4:30 p.m. Monday through Friday. Next door, the Guildhall Library houses a Clock Museum (open 9:30 a.m.–4:30 p.m. Monday through Friday) and a remarkable art collection. Also, if you can catch it open, be sure to stop in and see the spectacular interior of the church of St. Lawrence Jewry located on the main road, whose name is derived from its location on the site of London's early Jewish ghetto. Finally, follow King Street south to Victoria Street. Turn right and end your walk at Mansion House tube station.

Old Hampstead Village

Time to Allow: 2 hours

Distance: Approx. 1.5–2 miles

Sights: Church Row, St. John's-at-Hampstead, Fenton House, Admiral's House, Burgh House, Flask Walk and Well Walk, Downshire Hill, Keats House, Hampstead Heath, Hampstead High Street

Also Nearby: Freud Museum, Kenwood House

The history of Hampstead has always been tied closely to its hill, its heath, and its healthy environment, and in the early 1700s Hampstead became a booming spa town. The area's iron-rich water was said to cure all manner of ailments and you could purchase flasks of the vile tasting stuff for 3p a bottle or bathe in it at one of the local bathhouses. Today, narrow streets lined with lovingly restored eighteenth-century homes help the village retain much of its charming Victorian atmosphere.

Arriving in Hampstead via the Underground, you come up London's deepest (and creakiest) elevator shaft near the top of Hampstead Hill in the village center. Heath Street and Hampstead High Street stretch before you, lined with shops, cafes, and restaurants—definitely a great place to stop for tea at the end of your walk. Exiting the tube station, cross over and turn left on Heath Street, then right on Church Row, one of the best-preserved streets in London. Notice the grand wrought-iron work, the remains of early eighteenth-century oil lampstands, and the intricately detailed windows over many of the homes' main entrances. These fan lights, illuminated from behind by candles, helped identify one's home after dark in the days before street lighting. Famous residents here included George du Maurier, Gracie Fields, and H. G. Wells. At the end of the line of trees sits St. John–at–Hampstead, consecrated in 1747. Take some time to wander the graveyard and church then head up Holly Walk.

At the top of the hill on the right, St. Mary's Church is nestled among a row of homes. One of London's oldest Roman Catholic churches, its discreet location was due to its existence before religious tolerance was granted in 1829. Make a right and follow Mt. Vernon down to where it meets up with Hampstead Grove. Turn left. Another worthwhile stop is Fenton House on the right. This wonderfully preserved seventeenth-century home today houses an exquisite collection of Oriental, European, and English china, needlework, and furniture, but its finest attraction is its unique collection of early musical instruments, including Handel's harpsichord. Beyond Fenton House, turn left onto Admiral's Walk. Look carefully at the house and you will see the nautical alterations made by Lieutenant Fountain North in 1775. North adapted the roof to resemble the deck of a ship, complete with flagstaff and cannon, which were fired to celebrate naval victories. Walt Disney fans should find this all vaguely familiar: The character and home of Admiral Boom in *Mary Poppins* was based on this eccentric individual.

At the end of Hampstead Grove, where it runs into the main thoroughfare of Heath Street, you will find a small reservoir on your left. Whitstone Pond, built in 1856, allowed Londoners who had successfully navigated the steep muddy roads to the hilltop to clean their carriages by walking their horses down the ramps and through the pond. Crossing Heath Street, begin your journey down the hill and alongside Hampstead Heath, turning right at Squire's Mount and passing some lovely cottages, which date to 1704. Continue on Cannon Lane, turning left on Well Road, so named for the spring that gave the town its reputation for health. Famous residents here included D. H. Lawrence, J. B. Priestly, and John Constable. Turning left on New End Square brings you past Burgh House, the 1703 home of Hampstead Spa's physician, William Gibbons. Today the building is a lovely local museum, meeting place, and exhibition space. There is a small tea room downstairs if you are needing a snack or rest. To your left is Well Walk and to your right, Flask Walk. Just up Flask Walk on your right, this batthouse was actually in use by some locals until the late 1960s. Cross Well Walk and enjoy a downhill stroll on Willow Road. At the bottom, turn right on Downshire Hill.

Another picturesque street lined with nineteenth-century homes and gardens, its centerpiece is St. John's Church, opened in 1823. If open, it is worth taking a quick peek inside. Turning left on Keats Grove brings you to our last stop. John Keats lived in Hampstead from 1818 to 1820, and it is here that he produced many of his most famous works. The home is carefully restored and decorated as Keats would have known it, and the intimate museum is a wonderful tribute to his short, tragic life. Upon leaving Keats House, turn left and head back up Keats Grove, then left again on Downshire Hill. Make a right on Rosslyn Hill and enjoy some window shopping or stop in one of the many cafes on your way back toward the Hampstead Tube station, just a five-minute walk up the road.

Royal London: From Palace to Parliament

Time to Allow: 3–4 hours

Distance: Approx. 2.5 miles

Sights: Royal Mews, Queen's Picture Gallery, Buckingham Palace, St. James's Park, Cabinet War Rooms, Admiralty Arch, Trafalgar Square, National Gallery, National Portrait Gallery, St. Martin–in-the-Fields Church, Royal Horse Guards, Banqueting House, 10 Downing Street, Cenotaph, Houses of Parliament, St. Margaret's Church, Westminster Abbey

This walk takes you past many of London's most popular sights. London's history, royalty, and fabulous architecture are thoroughly represented as we travel throughout Westminster, the home to London's monarchy and Parliament. The walk affords plenty of opportunities to stop along the way, so the length of the walk depends entirely on your stamina.

Begin your walk at Victoria tube station. Turn right on Buckingham Palace Road, following signs for the palace. Just beyond Lower Grosvenor Place you will find the entrance for the Royal Mews on the left. Housed here in the palace stables is an impressive display of royal carriages; the oldest, made in 1762 for George III, is still used for coronations. Just past the Royal Mews is the Queen's Picture Gallery, a changing exhibition space for the royal monarch's incredible collection of privately owned works of art. Continuing on, you will soon arrive in the palace forecourt, much of which is today a busy traffic circle.

Buckingham Palace has been the official London residence of the sovereign since George III bought the place in 1762. The palace is home and office for Her Majesty, and its elaborately decorated rooms are in continuous use for state affairs, official receptions, ceremonial occasions, and Parliamentary meetings. See the attractions listing for opening times, and be sure to fit a visit into your schedule if possible. North of the palace is Green Park, but you need to locate St. James's Park, to the right of The Mall, as that is our next area to explore.

Enter the park by Birdcage Walk, and wander east along the pond's edge. St. James's is the oldest of London's parks. It started life as part of the private grounds of St. James's Palace, but was opened to the public during the reign of the Stuart monarchs. Cross over the bridge, stopping to take in the stunning views of the palace to the west and the Horse Guards Parade to the east. As you continue to walk along the path beside the lake, quick flashes of Westminster Abbey and St. Stephen's Clock Tower can be seen through the trees, wildlife skitter past or glide by on the water, and if you're lucky, the sun will shine a few rays through the clouds above. Charles II, Samuel Pepys, and John Milton have all enjoyed such views. However, by far the most famous residents of the park are the pelicans, who have delighted visitors to the park since the seventeenth-century. Every afternoon they parade across the lawn on Duck Island to receive their daily fish dinner, and they thoroughly enjoy the sanctuary provided here, along with the 20 or more other species of duck and goose that call St. James's home.

As you reach the other side of the park, continue on, crossing Horse Guards Road. Just in front of you, King Charles Street ends in a pedestrianized stairway, and to the right of this is the entrance to the Cabinet War Rooms. Winston Churchill and his cabinet carried out operations here during World War II. From the War Rooms, turn right on Horse Guards Road, passing the Horse Guards Parade, where the Changing of the Guard occurs daily at 11 a.m. (Sunday at 10 a.m.). Turn right on The Mall and walk under Admiralty Arch and into Trafalgar Square. In the center stands Nelson's Column, the memorial to Britain's best-loved national hero, Admiral Lord Horatio Nelson, who defeated Napoleon at the Battle of Trafalgar in 1806. The square is the location for frequent political demonstrations, London's annual Christmas Tree lighting, and New Year's countdowns. Behind is the National Gallery, where you could spend hours enjoying one of the world's greatest art collections. To the right is the eighteenth-century church of St. Martin–in-the-Fields, definitely worth a stop as its simple but elegant interior offers free lunchtime concerts. Downstairs, the church's Cafe-in-the-Crypt provides wonderfully fresh soups and sandwiches.

Leaving Trafalgar Square, walk down Whitehall (the street directly opposite the National Gallery). You will pass the front of the Horse Guards Building, with its guards at attention, and almost directly opposite is the Banqueting House, all that remains of the great palace at Whitehall, which burned to the ground in 1698. Prior to this loss, the palace was the site of numerous historical events, such as the marriage of Henry VIII to Anne Boleyn and the execution of Charles I during the English Civil War. Others to have lived here included Cardinal Wolsey, Oliver Cromwell, Charles II, and

William III and Mary II. Further along on the right is 10 Downing Street, home of Britain's prime minister, although you are not likely to see much because the street is guarded and gated. The Cenotaph, in the middle of Whitehall, is Britain's memorial to those who died in World War I. It is the focal point of the country's Remembrance Day ceremonies, which include two minutes of silence throughout the entire country on the eleventh minute of the eleventh hour of the eleventh day of the eleventh month each year.

Not far ahead, you will begin to see the towers of the Palace of Westminster coming into view. Once you have arrived in Parliament Square, you have a a number of choices before you. You can wander out onto Westminster Bridge for the best views of Westminster Palace and St. Stephen's Tower. You can sit in on debates in the Houses of Parliament; explore the sixteenth-century St. Margaret's Church, within whose walls Sir Walter Raleigh is laid to rest; or enjoy inspiring hymns sung by the Westminster Boys Choir at Westminster Abbey's daily choral evensong. Possibly the most visited tourist sight in London, this walk leaves you here, by Westminster Abbey, allowing you to spend some time in one of the most picturesque squares, beside one of the most beautiful churches in London.

For Museum Lovers

If you love going to museums, you already have a lot in common with typical Londoners. London is crammed with wonderful museums, many of which are free of charge, many more of which were free until the mid-1970s, but that's another story. There's a remarkable Web site that details current and upcoming exhibitions at 2,000 museums in London and across the country, as well as offers virtual tours of the permanent collections. It's a great way to see some of the smaller, less easy-to-visit museums without leaving your desk. The 24-hour Museum's goal is to represent Britain's entire cultural history—no small undertaking. Visit it on the Web at *www.24hourmuseum.org.uk.*

Saving Money on Museum Admissions

There are ways to save on the admission fee, one of which is to go after 4:30 p.m. at many of the charging museums, when they let people in free for the remaining 80 minutes or so. Or you can purchase the **LondonWhiteCard,** which will save you money if you and your family intend to visit some of the participating museums a lot. Some museums, like the Victoria and Albert in South Kensington, are even more enjoyable when you go for two short visits rather than overdoing it in one long stretch, and this way you don't have to pay twice. You can purchase an individual or family card at Heathrow Airport, British Tourist Authority offices, London Transport Travel Information centers, London Tourist Board centers, or any of the participating museums. In the United States, you can call Marketing Challenges International at (800) 869-8184 to buy one ahead of time, but be sure your plans include multiple visits to the following museums (they promise the list will continue to grow):

- Apsley House and The Wellington Museum
- Barbican Art Gallery
- BBC Experience
- Design Museum
- Hayward Gallery
- Imperial War Museum
- London Transport Museum
- Museum of London
- Museum of the Moving Image (closed until 2002)
- National Maritime Museum, Royal Greenwich Observatory, and Queen's House (all in Greenwich)
- The Natural History Museum
- Royal Academy of Arts
- Science Museum
- Theatre Museum
- Tower Bridge Experience
- Victoria and Albert Museum

The prices are as follows:

- Individual adult, three-day card: £16
- Individual adult, seven-day card: £32
- Family (two adults and four children age 16 and under), three-day card: £32
- Family seven-day card: £50

Given that the average entry fee for the above venues is £5.50 for adults and £3 for children age 5 to 16 years, you can see that the individual adult would need to go to a museum at least four times in three days and six times in seven days to make it worthwhile. As I say, this option is for the dedicated and energetic museum-goer. The Family seven-day card is a better deal if you have more than one kid; however, it may be impractical to bring the children to enough museums enough times to make it worthwhile. Only you can determine if the London WhiteCard is more economical than paying a straight entry fee or, in the case of many of the venues, a reduced family entry fee. Check the entry fees of the attractions below to help you make your decision.

Museums and Attractions

Important Note: Please be sure to call the following places before you go: Opening times—and indeed, their very existence—can be subject to change without notice.

For a look into London's parks and green spaces, see Green and Pleasant Lands: Parks of London on page 354. Also, at the end of this chapter is a profile of Greenwich.

Albert Memorial

Type of Attraction: Outdoor memorial to a beloved prince consort

Location: Kensington Gardens, west of Exhibition Road, SW7 (tube: High Street Kensington Tube)

Admission: Free

Hours: Daily dawn to dusk

When to Go: A sunny day, or at night when the floodlights are switched on

Special Comments: Bring binoculars so you can see the amazing detail of the high parts of the memorial. One detail you won't be able to see is that in the statue of Prudence, which is usually depicted with a young girl's face on front and an old woman's face on the back, has the face of Michelangelo instead of the old woman. His beard forms part of the young girl's hair. This was a private homage to the great artist, who is also immortalized in the frieze running round the base.

Overall Appeal by Age Group:

Pre-school	Grade School	Teens	Young Adults	Over 30	Senior Citizens
★★	★★	★★	★★	★★	★★

Author's Rating: ★★

How Much Time to Allow: 30 minutes, plus time to hang around on the steps. It's a good people-watching place, with talented inline skaters there on weekends.

Description and Comments   This memorial is no small thrill to see, as it had been covered in plastic and scaffolding for the last decade while being restored. It had been stripped of its gold in 1915, so we are in the privileged position of being the first generation in almost a century to see it in all its exuberant neogothic gilded glory. There are some Londoners who find the entire thing hideous and are appalled at the millions of pounds spent in its conservation. But whatever one might think of its artistry or fiscal responsibility, the fact remains that it is a visual knockout. Check it out at night with the floodlights on it to appreciate a view the Victorians were denied.

Built by a grieving Queen Victoria after her husband's death from typhoid at the age of 42, it cost three times as much as one of the finest churches built in Kensington at the same time and caused an uproar in Parliament. It is fittingly placed in "Albertopolis," the once far-flung environs of South Kensington that were transformed by Prince Albert's creation of a center for arts, sciences, and learning. He paid for all this with the proceeds of the Great Exhibition of 1851, another of his brainstorms. Look at his statue: He's fondly cradling the catalog for the exhibition.

The memorial can be seen from many angles in Hyde Park and Kensington Gardens, but don't imagine you have experienced its full flavor until you have looked the buffalo square in the eye.

Touring Tips Make this part of your Kensington Palace/Gardens and Hyde Park day.

Apsley House (The Wellington Museum)

Type of Attraction: Former home of the duke of Wellington filled with fine paintings

Location: 149 Piccadilly, W1, Zone 8 (tube: Hyde Park Corner)

Admission: £4.50 adults, £3 concessions, children under age 12 free

Hours: Tuesday–Sunday 11 a.m.–5 p.m.; last entry 4:30 p.m.

Phone: (0171) 499-5676

When to Go: Any time

Special Comments: There is no wheelchair access: There are steps into house and steep steps to the next floor. If you walk along the pedestrian subway below Hyde Park Corner, you can see the story of Apsley House and the duke of Wellington rendered on the tiles on the wall, a good way to prepare for the visit to the house, which lacks descriptive commentary.

Overall Appeal by Age Group:

Pre-school	Grade School	Teens	Young Adults	Over 30	Senior Citizens
★	★★	★★	★★★	★★★	★★★

Author's Rating: ★★★

How Much Time to Allow: 45 minutes to an hour, more if you really love old masters

Description and Comments This grand house used to be known as 149 Piccadilly until it was given to the duke of Wellington as a splendid reward for his military successes in the Napoleonic Wars. He, true to form, grandiously renamed it Number One London. Apsley House has the fascinating ability to seem like a country estate while sitting on one of the most well-traveled patches of road in the entire world. While the Mad Hatter's tea party of cars, trucks, and buses whirls around the Hyde Park Corner traffic circle in front of the house, the windows in the back look out onto a serene vista of Hyde Park, the rose gardens, and the occasional horseback riders transporting the viewer to a fantasy London of a gentler vintage. It is of interest to art lovers for the works of such old masters as Velázquez, Goya, and Rubens, along with some lesser luminaries; and also for the dining table with a centerpiece of silver that will knock your eyes out. The basement has a collection of political cartoons that will teach you about the duke of Wellington and his times quite entertainingly.

Touring Tips   This is a very small, quick-hit kind of place, and it fits in well with a walk through Hyde Park, moving on through Green and St. James's Parks.

Bank of England Museum

Type of Attraction: Historical displays tracing the rise of banking

Location: Threadneedle Street, museum entrance on Bartholomew Street, EC2, Zone 3 (tube: Bank)

Admission: Free

Hours: Monday–Friday, 10 a.m.–5 p.m.; closed weekends and bank holidays

Phone: (0171) 601-5545

When to Go: Any time

Special Comments: Disabled-friendly; portable ramps available on request, which are necessary as so many of the displays are waist-high and must be looked at from a height

Overall Appeal by Age Group:

Pre-school	Grade School	Teens	Young Adults	Over 30	Senior Citizens
★★	★★	★★	★★	★★	★★

Author's Rating: ★★

How Much Time to Allow: 60 minutes

Description and Comments   This is the only part of the massive fortress that is the Bank of England—known as "The Old Lady of Threadneedle Street"—that mere mortals can go into. I like the fact that you don't have to show any of your own cash to get in to see theirs. And what masses of it are shown: gold bars, hand-written notes, farthings, shillings, all strangely inert for such potent symbols of worldly power and possibilities. The Bank of England was formed in 1694 as a scheme to lend money to the government to pay for King James II's war against France. The bank evolved from using gold and notes of credit to striking coins and printing banknotes, all the while taking admirable care of the nation's finances. The bank was attacked once during the Gordon Riots of 1780, when the nearby Newgate Gaol was emptied of marauding prisoners, but successfully repulsed all on-comers, earning its own simile "as safe as the Bank of England."

The displays require quite a bit of reading, as well as a particular inter-est in money and banking. There is a display of an old bank, modeled after the first Bank of England designed by Sir John Soanes in the late eighteenth century, with mannequins of wigged clerks and a huge fireplace behind mahogany counters. A video shows real footage from the building of the present bank in the 1930s, and there are interactive computer screens that cover a lot of information. A display shows the evolution of the banknote from 1694 to the present; you can see what happens to cash when it gets old and tired.

Bethnal Museum of Childhood

Type of Attraction: Largest museum of toys in the world

Location: Cambridge Heath Road, E2, Zone 4 (tube: Bethnal Green)

Admission: Free

Hours: Monday–Thursday and Saturday, 10 a.m.–5:50 p.m.; Sunday 2:30 p.m.–5:50 p.m. (closed Friday)

Phone: (0181) 980-2415 (recording), (0181) 983-5200 (duty officer)

When to Go: Any time

Special Comments: Wheelchair access, but call ahead to arrange it (phone (0181) 983-5205). Art workshops available for children over age three on Saturdays

Overall Appeal by Age Group:

Pre-school	Grade School	Teens	Young Adults	Over 30	Senior Citizens
★★★	★★★	★★★	★★★	★★★	★★★

Author's Rating: ★★★

How Much Time to Allow: 90 minutes

Description and Comments   Housed in a building directly across the street from the Bethnal Green tube Station (a big plus when dragging children along), the Museum of Childhood is part of the Victoria and Albert Museum, and is, unlike the V&A, still free. It has an unparalleled collec-tion of children's toys and accessories: doll-houses from as far back as the seventeenth century, model trains, hobby horses, old mechanical games and toys (you must pay 20p to use them), dolls of every possible kind, teddy bears, and even old-fashioned prams and nursery furniture. The children seem to prefer pumping the mechanical toys full of coins to admiring the antiquities behind glass, which is a proper childlike response—they want to play, not look. Try the weekends, when there are workshops for the kids.

British Library

Type of Attraction: New and controversial replacement for the beloved old reading rooms at the British Museum

Location: 96 Euston Road, NW1, Zone 5 (tube: King's Cross)

Admission: Free

Hours: Monday–Saturday 10 a.m.–5 p.m., Sunday 2:30–6 p.m.

Phone: (0171) 412-7000

When to Go: Any time

Special Comments: Full wheelchair/disabled access

Overall Appeal by Age Group:

Pre-school	Grade School	Teens	Young Adults	Over 30	Senior Citizens
★★	★★	★★★	★★★	★★★★	

Author's Rating: ★★★★

How Much Time to Allow: 1 hour

Description and Comments   The embattled (and expensive: £500 million!) project to move the reading rooms from their beautiful, longtime niche at the British Library was one of those necessary concessions to age that no one really wants to make. However, since the opening visitors and readers have been grudgingly admitting that it is a vast improvement over the cramped old quarters. Even Prince Charles, who scorned the exterior as "a collection of brick sheds groping for significance" (among other choice insults), was duly impressed with the interior. The fact is that, however lacking in aesthetics the place may be, it's still a veritable Aladdin's cave of treasures, and an improved one at that. Manuscripts such as the Lindisfarne Gospels from the tenth century, James Joyce's first draft of *Finnegan's Wake*, a copy of the Magna Carta from 1215, the Gutenberg Bible, and plenty of documents related to the greatest English writer of all, Shakespeare, are only some of the magnificent material on view here.

The library offers to the public a fine bookstore, a cafe, and three exhibition galleries. There's the John Riblat Gallery, in which are displayed some of the library's most ancient and valuable manuscripts and maps. There's a wonderous room called "Turning the Page" in which a computer allows you to virtually flip through four texts: the Lindisfarne Gospels, the Diamond Sutra, DaVinci's notebooks, and the Sforza Hours. Whatever enmity you may feel for the brutal modern dimensions of the new library is melted away by the awestruck feeling of joy that we live in an age where one can see such things. And hear such things: James Joyce and other authors reading from their work, and music of all types, too. In the Pearson Gallery of Living Words are educational exhibits, one of which explores the history of writing, another is a reading area, and a good display of children's literature. There are a few interactive fun things to do, such as design a book or check out the evolution of recorded music. The third gallery houses the Philatelic Collections, with 8 million items. This is a bit too arcane for me, but pure heaven for stamp collectors. This is not a tourist attraction really: It is for people who love and respect books, so take care who you take along with you.

Touring Tips   Sign up for a guided tour to see the parts of the library not open to the public.

British Museum

Type of Attraction: One of the greatest museums of the world, with treasures and booty from the British empire

Location: Great Russell Street, WC1, Zone 2 (tube: Tottenham Court Road)

Admission: Free

Hours: Monday–Saturday 10 a.m.–6 p.m., Sunday 2:30–6 p.m.

Phone: (0171) 636-1555; *www.british-museum.ac.uk*

When to Go: Early morning, weekdays

Special Comments: Wheelchair-accessible, get leaflet from information desk with details. There is a major overhaul in progress for 2002, in which a huge covered courtyard will unify the various parts of the building, with the famous domed Reading Room of the erstwhile British Library in the center.

Overall Appeal by Age Group:

Pre-school	Grade School	Teens	Young Adults	Over 30	Senior Citizens
★★★★	★★★★	★★★★★	★★★★★	★★★★★	★★★★★

Author's Rating: ★★★★★

How Much Time to Allow: 2–4 hours

Description and Comments   This is the granddaddy of all museums, founded in 1753 with Sir Hans Sloane's collections and added to over the years of England's greatest booty-looting power. The Elgin Marbles, found apparently abandoned in the dust around the Parthenon by Lord Elgin in 1800, have come to be an ongoing and defining controversy over who owns what and why in the museum trade. The marbles are proof to nationalists (Greek especially) of the Empire's arrogance and even thievery in the appropriation of other nations' treasures; conversely, they are used as an example of how without the intervention of interested parties like the British, such treasures might have been lost forever. Putting such debates aside, you can only marvel at the far-reaching grasp of the British Museum, the number-one tourist attraction in London, with over 7 million visitors a year. It's not even so much that there are artifacts from practically every civilization throughout time, it's that what artifacts they have are so important. The Rosetta Stone, the Lindow Man, the Egyptian mummies, and prehistoric pieces are finds that have literally changed history.

After Sir Hans Sloane bequeathed his remarkable collection of art and artifacts to the state, the earl of Oxford's rare manuscripts were added to the mix, and thus began the marriage of museum and library that was dissolved in 1997, when the British Library moved to more spacious housing. During the years following Sloane's donation, the collection grew rapidly, as it became the scholarly and patriotic thing to do to leave one's finest possessions to the museum. The Napoleonic Wars provided a major transfer of treasure when the British defeated the French at Alexandria, and the stolen goods of Napoleon's empire-building campaigns were seized by the victorious British. A new building was needed to accommodate the collection, and the Greek-revival building you see today was built over the course of 20 years, finished in 1854. Still, it was crowded—a veritable Victorian parlor of clutter—and the spillover soon benefited the Victoria and Albert Museum; further rearrangements are yet to be anticipated. The best of these plans is the restoration and opening to the public of the British Library Reading Room, the famous domed cathedral of the intellect where Karl Marx wrote *Das Capital,* and countless other important writers and scholars have labored for over two centuries. While the restorations and rearrangements are in progress, the museum will seem to be in a bit of a mess, but be patient and give the place all the benefit of the doubt—these plans are definitely a necessary measure, and the British Museum will be even more magnificent than ever when completed.

There is no doing the British Museum justice in a guide book. It really must be experienced, multiple times if possible. Here you can travel to the ends of the four directions of the globe, throughout centuries of humankind's time on earth, and see just about every little thing that we've thought up along the way: mummies, pottery, clocks, painting, tools for war and peace, sculpture, personal decoration, household goods, treasures of gold and precious stones, and far more. It's far too big to try to cover in one visit, so consult the map and the interests of your group before heading to the galleries. There's a good guide book sold in the bookstore (an *excellent* bookstore!) that's worth getting.

Touring Tips As with most museums, getting there before the school buses arrive is key. It is hard to gaze with the proper wonder at the Rosetta Stone when you're being jostled by an army of uniformed schoolchildren. There are gallery tours given that can help you make the most of the visit. It is a large museum, so make full use of the map. The main gift shop is wonderful, with fine reproductions of jewelry and sculpture; be sure to also check out the children's gift shop for inexpensive gifts for all ages.

Buckingham Palace, Summer Opening

Type of Attraction: Stately home of the queen

Location: Buckingham Palace Road, SW1, Zone 9 (tube: Green Park)

Admission: £10 for adults; £5 for children ages 5–16, under age 5 free

Hours: August to September, daily 9:30 a.m.–4:30 p.m.

Phone: Information (recorded) (0171) 799-2331; credit card ticket purchase (0171) 321-2233; general inquiries/group booking (0171) 839-1377

When to Go: If you purchase tickets from the ticket office in Green Park, go at 9 a.m.–3 p.m. The lines are murder otherwise

Special Comments: Wheelchair users are required to prebook. The Queen's Gallery is not wheelchair-accessible, but the Royal Mews are (see page 331). I personally wouldn't inflict this tour on a preschooler, although they assure me that the young'uns seem to love it.

Overall Appeal by Age Group:

Pre- school	Grade School	Teens	Young Adults	Over 30	Senior Citizens
★	★★	★★	★★★	★★★	★★★

Author's Rating: ★★½

Description and Comments Buckingham House was purchased by King George III in 1761 from the duke of Buckingham. Like most real estate, the three most attractive points were location, location, location. Situated between St. James's and Hyde parks, with a tree-lined avenue affording views of Westminster and even St. Paul's dome, it was like a country estate in the city (or rather, near the city, as west of Buck House was still country). It was a private residence, the official court remaining—as it does to this day, if only in name—that of St. James's. When George IV ascended the throne,

he had his favorite architect, John Nash, remodel it in the grandiose style
you see today.

There are only two months in which you can view the state rooms at
Buckingham Palace, so plan accordingly. In 1996, Queen Elizabeth II
decided to open some of the palace to the public to pay for the restoration
of Windor Castle, which was severely damaged by a fire in 1992. I suspect
that they may have paid for the work several times over by now: There are
7,000 visitors a day, seven days a week for eight weeks paying £10 a head—
well, you do the math.

It's an amazing spectacle, even more so when you ponder that for all the
years of the palace's existence, loyal subjects of the Crown never had a
prayer of setting foot in these august precincts, and now they're letting the
likes of you and me in to eyeball the queen's goods. And what goods they
are: treasures of painting, sculpture, furniture, and decoration beyond
description, so I won't even try. (Neither do they: you have to buy the official guidebook to know what you are looking at; there are no signs anywhere.) I will say that after a while, I felt rather unsettled, if not revolutionary, by the endless, priceless display. And there were hundreds of other
rooms you're not allowed to see. The view through the numerous French
doors along the rooms is magnificent, looking out along the back garden
rolling regally along, a piece of ye olde English countryside within earshot
of the roar of Hyde Park Corner.

Warning   This is not an attraction for everyone, not least because of the
ridiculous lines you have to wait in. It's a lot of money and a lot of effort
for what is essentially an inert stately home. You could feel equally, if not
more satisfied with a good book on the palace.

Touring Tips   Don't bring in any bags, so you can avoid the baggage security check. Before your tour time, do go buy the official guide from the gift
shop next to the palace at the Queen's Gallery—you'll save yourself a wait
on the way into the palace. I repeat: It's important to get this book if you
want to know what is what, because just as in your own home, there are no
labels on the goods. The guides are there to answer questions, and they're
very knowledgeable. There's no guided tour per se, you just go in and follow the group. The way they arrange the tours is that you are given a tour
time on your ticket, and they will call it when it's your time. (If you are a
real early bird, you will glide in quite easily.) Don't bother lining up until
you're about 15 minutes away from your time. You might wander around
the gift shop or St. James's Park in the meantime.

Burgh House

Type of Attraction: Lovely period home/arts center providing exhibitions, concerts, and lectures

Location: New End Square, Hampstead, Zone 1 (tube: Hampstead)

Admission: Free

Hours: Wednesday–Sunday noon–5 p.m., bank holidays, 2–5 p.m.

Phone: (0171) 431-0144

When to Go: Any time

Overall Appeal by Age Group:

Pre-school	Grade School	Teens	Young Adults	Over 30	Senior Citizens
★	★	★	★★	★★★	★★★

Author's Rating: ★★

How Much Time to Allow: 1 hour to see Hampstead Museum exhibit; other times depend on lecture or concert lengths

Description and Comments   The meandering streets of Flask Walk and Well Walk are picturesque reminders of when Hampstead was a thriving spa village. To step out of the sometimes brisk Hampstead breeze, you might stop at this well-maintained Queen Anne home in the heart of quiet Hampstead village. Today, Burgh House contains a modest museum of local history along with other traveling exhibitions, but it is much more well known among the locals for its ongoing series of concerts, including opera, chamber music, and jazz. (Call for a current schedule.) There is also a charming tea room downstairs.

Touring Tips   To continue your Hampstead wanderings, be sure to include a walk down Church Row to the eighteenth-century St. John's Church and cemetery, as well as finding your way over to Keats House.

Carlyle's Museum

Type of Attraction: Victorian home of the sage of Chelsea

Location: 24 Cheyne Row, SW3, Chelsea, Zone 11 (tube: Sloane Square)

Admission: Adults £3, children £1.50

Hours: March 29 through November 2, Wednesday–Sunday and bank holidays 11 a.m.–5 p.m.

Phone: (0171) 352-7087

When to Go: Any time it's open

Special Comments: It's an old house with steep stairs; no wheelchair access

Overall Appeal by Age Group:

Pre-school	Grade School	Teens	Young Adults	Over 30	Senior Citizens
★	★★	★★	★★★	★★★	★★

Author's Rating: ★★★

How Much Time to Allow: 60–90 minutes

Description and Comments   It's likely that Thomas Carlyle may not mean anything to most people these days; he was a great essayist and historian in his own time (1795–1881), known and admired by all the Victorian literati. His house was a salon of luminaries such as Charles Dickens, George Eliot, Alfred Lord Tennyson, and Frederic Chopin, drawn as much by the sage of Chelsea's wisdom as by the famous wit of his wife, Jane. What is marvelous about the house, in the absence of any great feeling for its former owner, is that it was made a museum only 15 years after Carlyle's death, and so has an abundance of authentic minutiae—a hat hung on a hook, clothing in a drawer—that is lacking in most literary shrines of this sort. All the furnishings are authentic, and the atmosphere is beyond the wildest dreams of a Victoriana-phile.

Touring Tips   Be sure to look at all the blue plaques around here to see the kind of neighbors Carlyle enjoyed.

Chiswick House

Type of Attraction: Stately home with major gardens in west London

Location: Burlington Lane, W4, Zone 12 (tube: Turnham Green, or Chiswick by rail)

Admission: Adults: £3, children £1.50

Hours: April to September, daily 10 a.m.–6 p.m.; October to March, daily 10 a.m.–4 p.m.

Phone: (0181) 995-0508

When to Go: In good weather: the garden is splendid

Special Comments: Limited disabled access; call for details

Overall Appeal by Age Group:

Pre-school	Grade School	Teens	Young Adults	Over 30	Senior Citizens
★	★★	★★	★★	★★	★★

Author's Rating: ★★★

How Much Time to Allow: 1 hour

Description and Comments   It's a bit of a hike from either the train station in Chiswick or the tube at Turnham Green, but for anyone interested in

Palladian design and eighteenth-century over-the-top splendor, this is the place. Built in 1725 by Lord Burlington and William Kent, it has at its heart an octagonal room with a dome that is classically symmetrical. Its original purpose was more to show off Burlington's extensive art collection than to live in, but alas, most of those treasures have long since been retired to museums. However, the decoration, carvings, and statuary that remain are magnificent, and the William Kent ceilings are as sumptuous as those he did at Kensington Palace. In summer, the gardens are spectacular, filled with wonderful follies—mock ruins that were all the rage in the eighteenth and nineteenth centuries—ponds, statues, benches, and formal gardens.

Touring Tips   This can be combined with a trip to Hogarth's House and a visit to Chiswick High Street. Have lunch at Mackintosh's Brasserie (142 Chiswick High St., W4, phone (0181) 994-2628), an excellent bistro that combines high-quality cuisine with good prices and a child-friendly atmosphere (crayons for doodling on the table).

Clink Exhibition

Type of Attraction: Re-creation and exhibition of a medieval prison

Location: 1 Clink St., SE1, Zone 5 (tube: London Bridge)

Admission: £4 adults, £3 seniors, students, and children

Hours: Daily 10 a.m.–6 p.m.

Phone: (0171) 403-6515

When to Go: Any time

Special Comments: This attraction is not accessible to wheelchairs or baby strollers as the entrance to the basement site is down a rather dark flight of stairs and the exhibit itself includes a number of narrow doorways that must be stepped over

Overall Appeal by Age Group:

Pre-school	Grade School	Teens	Young Adults	Over 30	Senior Citizens
†	★	★	★	★	★

† Too creepy for preschoolers

Author's Rating: ★

How Much Time to Allow: 30 minutes

Description and Comments   Be warned, this place is a rip-off. The Clink began as a dungeon for disobedient clerics, debtors, and prostitutes. Charles Dickens's parents spent time here when he was a child, forcing the young Dickens to acquire his first job in a tanning factory in an attempt to repay some of his parents' debt. The prison was under the jurisdiction of the bishop of Winchester who "policed" this red-light district and collected revenues from the prostitutes, who were known as the Winchester Geese (they dressed in flowing white gowns and from the other side of the Thames looked like geese as they promenaded). The remains of the bishop's former home, Winchester Palace, can be seen just down the road.

The exhibition presents itself as a re-created medieval dungeon. Its exhibits include some dismal cell re-creations, diagrams of medieval torture devices, and fact boards on some of the prison's prior inhabitants. Though one might think that the ghoulish subject matter of high interest to grade-school kids and teens, most of the information must be read from the mounted displays, something kids seem to grow weary of too quickly.

Touring Tips   If you do decide to explore this area, be sure to include a stop at Southwark Cathedral and Shakespeare's Globe Theatre, both within only a few minutes walk of the Clink Exhibition.

Courtauld Institute Gallery

Type of Attraction: Lovely and impressive collection of Impressionist and post-Impressionist paintings

Location: Somerset House, Strand, Zone 2 (tube: Covent Garden or Holborn)

Admission: £4 adults, £2 seniors, free for children and students under age 18. There is free admission for all on Monday between 10 a.m. and 2 p.m.

Hours: Monday–Saturday 10 a.m.–6 p.m., Sunday and bank holidays noon–6 p.m.

Phone: (0171) 848-2526

When to Go: Any time

Special Comments: The gallery is fully accessible for visitors with disabilities. There is a ramp entrance and lifts to all floors. Special sign-language interpreted talks are also run occasionally. Call for details at (0171) 848-2549

Overall Appeal by Age Group:

Pre-school	Grade School	Teens	Young Adults	Over 30	Senior Citizens
★	★★★	★★★	★★★	★★★	★★★

Author's Rating: ★★★

How Much Time to Allow: 2–3 hours

Description and Comments   The Courtauld Gallery is an integral part of the Courtauld Institute of Art. The gallery originated out of textile magnate Samuel Courtauld's private collection from the 1930s, but has grown considerably since that time. It is most famous for its priceless Impressionist works, which include Van Gogh's *Self Portrait with Bandaged Ear*, Degas's *Two Dancers*, Renior's *La Loge*, and Manet's *Déjeuner sur l'herbe*. It is worth noting however, that the medieval and early Renaissance works in galleries 1 and 2 are also quite impressive, with paintings by Brueghel, Bellini, and Rubens, which were subsequent additions to the collection.

Someset House itself is quite impressive, with its grand facade that used to include a path right down to the river. It was built in 1770 and has the distinction of having been the first big office building in London.

Touring Tips   The gallery has a fantastic educational booklet called "Courtauld Gallery Trail," available at the admissions desk. It includes children (aged 5–12) in the study of the gallery's fine art collection by asking practical questions that teach children how to look at and learn from its paintings. A great way to encourage a child's respect for and enjoyment of fine art.

Cutty Sark

Type of Attraction: Last of the great sailing clipper ships restored
Location: Greenwich Pier, Zone 6 (tube: Greenwich, on Docklands Light Railway)
Admission: £3.50 for adults; £2.50 for children, students, and seniors; £8.50 for family
Hours: Daily 10 a.m.–5 p.m.; last admission at 4:30 p.m.
Phone: (0181) 858-3445
When to Go: Early in day
Special Comments: Access for the disabled limited to entrance level of ship. Seniors may also find a few of the stairways difficult to maneuver, although most have been well adapted for visitors' use

Overall Appeal by Age Group:

Pre-school	Grade School	Teens	Young Adults	Over 30	Senior Citizens
★★	★★★★	★★★★	★★★	★★★	★★★

Author's Rating: ★★★
How Much Time to Allow: 45–90 minutes

Description and Comments   First launched in 1869, the *Cutty Sark* spent seven years in the China Tea trade, but actually became famous as a wool merchant ship in the years that followed, able to sail from England to Australia in only 72 days. The ship's main hold contains a history of this well-known tea clipper (there's a small gift shop there, too), but it is the lower

hold that most impresses with the largest collection of merchant ship fig-
ureheads in Britain. The colorful display was amassed by Captain John Cum-
bers of Gravesend, better known as Long John Silver. Tours of the ship can
be arranged at no additional charge simply by asking. Children love to
explore the restored ships' cabins, which give an alarming indication of the
difference in class between captain and crew.

Touring Tips   From the *Cutty Sark's* bow you can also see the much smaller
Gipsy Moth IV, in which Francis Chichester first sailed solo around the
world.

Design Museum

Type of Attraction: History of design of everyday items, with four floors of
    exhibits

Location: 28 Shad Thames, SE1, Zone 5 (tube: Tower Hill)

Admission: Adults £5.50, children £4, family ticket £12 (2 adults and
    2 children)

Hours: Daily 11:30 a.m.–6 p.m.

Phone: (0171) 378-6055

When to Go: Any time

Special Comments: Completely wheelchair- and disabled-accessible

Overall Appeal by Age Group:

Pre-school	Grade School	Teens	Young Adults	Over 30	Senior Citizens
★	★	★	★★	★★	★★

Author's Rating: ★★

How Much Time to Allow: 60–90 minutes

Description and Comments   This is, in my opinion, a specialist museum.
Many might argue with me on that, saying that all people must have some
interest in seeing a variety of interestingly designed chairs or a collection of
well-made appliances, but I know many people who would snort at such an
assertion.

Be that as it may, the museum is well attended and appreciated by Londoners and tourists, who flock here to look at the mass-produced designs
of the twentieth century that we've lived with, perhaps without even noticing what they really looked like. One need only look at the collection of
evolving TV sets to see that our household items have their own history,
which are inextricably linked to our domestic memories. Cars, office furniture, radios, and household utensils are all part of a permanent collection,

which is added to regularly and shares the modern bright space with a rota of exhibits such as the modern movement in Britain, or 40 years of the mini-automobile. New ideas and design breakthroughs are highlighted here. The Design Museum was created by restaurant and furniture king Terence Conran, on the south bank of the Thames by Tower Bridge, and the cafe and restaurant have splendid views.

Touring Tips   If you have the London WhiteCard, you can tack this onto your day at the Tower of London—it's right across the bridge. Unless you are quite specifically interested in design, I wouldn't spend the money on this museum.

Dickens House Museum

Type of Attraction: Literary shrine to the great Charles Dickens

Location: 48 Doughty St., WC1, Zone 3 (tube: Russell Square)

Admission: Adults £3.50, children £1.50, family £7

Hours: Monday–Saturday 10 a.m.–5 p.m.

Phone: (0171) 405-2127

When to Go: Any time

Special Comments: Many steps in this Victorian house; no wheelchair access

Overall Appeal by Age Group:

Pre-school	Grade School	Teens	Young Adults	Over 30	Senior Citizens
★	★	★	★	★	★

Author's Rating: ★

How Much Time to Allow: 40 minutes

Description and Comments   I am a big Dickens fan, and I was so hoping for more from this museum; it is sad that London, the city that Dickens made real for so many readers, doesn't have a better temple to him. Dickens actually only lived in this house for two years, so his spirit certainly does not walk these (linoleum) floors the way you sense Carlyle's does in his house. There are manuscript pages that are exciting to see, lots of wonderful illustrations from his books, as well as portraits of the writer—which make it worth the trip. The gift shop sells some fine old editions as well as new ones of Dickens and some of his contemporaries.

Touring Tips   Watch the video in the basement first; it's very good.

Freud Museum

Type of Attraction: English home of famous psychoanalyst Sigmund Freud

*Location:*20 Maresfield Gardens, South Hampstead, NW1, Zone 1 (tube: Finchley Road)

Admission: Adults £4, children under age 12 free

Hours: Wednesday–Sunday noon–5 p.m.

Phone: (0171) 435-2002

When to Go: Any time

Special Comments: Limited access for disabled. No lift to upper floor

Overall Appeal by Age Group:

Pre-school	Grade School	Teens	Young Adults	Over 30	Senior Citizens
★	★	★★	★★	★★	★★

Author's Rating: ★★★

How Much Time to Allow: 2 hours

Description and Comments   Founder of the basic concepts behind current psychoanalysis, Sigmund Freud brought terms like "free association," "id," and "ego" into general use. The house at 20 Maresfield Gardens, Hampstead, was Freud's home for the last year of his life, after he fled the Nazis in Vienna in 1938. It continued to be home to his daughter, Anna, until her death in 1982, and on her request, it now celebrates the life and work of her father. Inside, each room is carefully decorated as it had been in 1938, and the museum contains all of the possessions from Freud's former home in Vienna in which he had lived for over 47 years. The exhibition's center-piece is Freud's library and study, including his famous analytic couch and numerous antiquities.

Touring Tips   A wonderfully informative video is available for viewing upstairs. The 45-minute film, partially narrated by Anna Freud, contains silent black-and-white footage of Freud at home in Vienna as well as a description of the family's harrowing escape in 1938.

The Globe Theatre

Type of Attraction: Magnificently reconstructed Shakespearean theater

Location: New Globe Walk, Bankside, SE1, Zone 3 (tube: Mansion House)

Admission: Globe Exhibition and guided tour £5 adults, £4 seniors and students, and £3 children. Prices for performances run from £5 (standing room), to £25 (tiered seating)

Hours: Daily 10 a.m.–5 p.m.; check with the box office for performance times and dates

Phone: (0171) 902-1500

When to Go: Any time

Special Comments: The exhibition is easily accessible for wheelchairs, and seating for performances include theater boxes (£15 per person) to space in the yard (£5 per person)

Overall Appeal by Age Group:

Pre-school	Grade School	Teens	Young Adults	Over 30	Senior Citizens
★	★★	★★	★★★	★★★★	★★★★

Author's Rating: ★★★★

How Much Time to Allow: 1–2 hours for museum and tour

Description and Comments   Brilliantly reconstructed as an almost exact replica of its former self (and founded by the late American actor and director Sam Wanamaker), The Globe officially opened in 1998 and is a delightful place to learn about the world's greatest playwright. In his day, Shakespeare's plays were also performed at The Rose and occasionally The Swan, but it was at The Globe that Shakespeare made his literary name. The exhibit contains a fact-filled museum on the life and times of the Bard, including some amazing tools used to make the building. In their strict adherence to creating a theater made exactly as it would have been constructed in Shakespeare's time, they even used a pedal-operated lathe made out of leather and wood, a machine you can see here, to make the 500 banisters around the theater. The tour of the theater, often led by actors and very well done, describes marvelous details about Elizabethan theater and the notorious Bankside area of brothels, the Clink prison, and the corrupt bishop of Winchester. Performances run in the summer months, allowing you the full experience of the Bard's plays outdoors, under natural light, as it used to be. The box office says that the best seats are not seats at all but the standing area in front of the stage, where the "groundlings" stand, the actors may mingle, and the rain may pour (the show must go on through wind or sleet or rain, but don't worry, they sell rain ponchos). The more adventurous may want to check out the standing area. Contact the box office (phone (0171) 401-9919) for current show times and dates.

Touring Tips   The complex also contains a cafe, as well as a more upscale restaurant with a view of the river and the City across it.

Guards Museum

Type of Attraction: Small museum of limited appeal to any but military enthusiasts

Location: Wellington Barracks, Birdcage Walk, SW1, Zone 9 (tube: St. James's Park

Admission: Adults £2, children £1, family £4

Hours: Daily 10 a.m.–4 p.m.

Phone: (0171) 414-3271

When to Go: Any time

Special Comments: Phone ahead to use lift to bypass steps

Overall Appeal by Age Group:

Pre- school	Grade School	Teens	Young Adults	Over 30	Senior Citizens
★	★	★	★	★	★

Author's Rating: ★★

How Much Time to Allow: 30–40 minutes

Description and Comments   This museum is sure to warm the hearts of young people interested in the army, or military personnel interested in history. The guards, whom you can see every other day at 11:30 a.m. (every day from April to August) performing their ceremonial duties in scarlet coats and the distinctive bearskin hats in front of Buckingham Palace, have been around for about 300 years, since the days of King Charles II. The museum is small, but the shop is great for toy soldiers.

Guildhall

Type of Attraction: Corporate headquarters for the City of London

Location: Gresham Street, Zone 7 (tube: St. Paul's or Mansion House)

Admission: Free

Hours: Guildhall: Monday–Friday 10 a.m.–5 p.m. Guildhall Clock Museum and Library Bookshop: Monday–Friday 9:30 a.m.–4:45 p.m.

Phone: (0171) 606-3030 ext. 1460

When to Go: Any time

Special Comments: Plenty of access for disabled with ramps or stairlifts available

Overall Appeal by Age Group:

Pre- school	Grade School	Teens	Young Adults	Over 30	Senior Citizens
★	★★	★★	★★	★★	★★

Author's Rating: ★★

How Much Time to Allow: 1–1½ hours

Description and Comments "Guildhall has witnessed traitors' trials and heroes' welcomes, freedom ceremonies and glittering state occasions." The seat of London's municipal government for over 800 years, it is still used for official ceremonies, state banquets, and the annual installation of the lord mayor of London. Although surrounded by twentieth-century government offices and largely reconstructed after a World War II bombing, the Great Hall still impresses. Its walls are original and date to the fifteenth century. An array of monuments line the hall in honor of national figures from the past 3 centuries, and banners of the 12 Great Livery Companies hang from above. The complex itself also houses over 700 examples of timekeeping in its rather small Clock Museum; its Art Gallery, due to open in summer 1999, will house the Corporation of London's impressive collection of works depicting London life from the fifteenth century to the present. (The Corporation of London has a Web site for its extensive Art Gallery collection entitled "Collage" [The Corporation of London Library and Art Gallery Electronic], which can be accessed on the Web at: *collage.nhil.com.*) Before you leave, be sure to stop and see the splendid interior of St. Lawrence Jewry, the official church of the Corporation of London, located just across the courtyard from the Guildhall.

Touring Tips The fifteenth-century crypt and nineteenth-century Old Library are generally off-limits to the public, but it is well worth asking if it might be possible to see them. Guided tours include these spots and can be arranged by calling (0171) 606-3030 ext. 1460.

HMS *Belfast*

Type of Attraction: Perfectly preserved Royal Navy battle ship from World War II permanently moored in the Thames

Location: Morgans Lane, Tooley Street, SE1, Zone 5 (tube: London Bridge)

Admission: Adults £4.70, children £2.40

Hours: March to October, daily 10 a.m.–6 p.m.; November to February, daily 10 a.m.–5 p.m.

Phone: (0171) 940-6328

When to Go: Avoid weekends; call to see if any class trips are scheduled

Special Comments: They've made every effort to make most of the ship accessible to disabled, but there are many areas impossible for wheelchairs to pass

Overall Appeal by Age Group:

Pre-school	Grade School	Teens	Young Adults	Over 30	Senior Citizens
★★	★★★	★★★	★★	★★	★★

Author's Rating: ★★

How Much Time to Allow: 90 minutes

Description and Comments A bit of floating history, the HMS *Belfast* was built in 1938 and pressed into service at the D Day landings. Decommissioned in the 1960s, the HMS *Belfast* is run by the Imperial War Museum. It's a popular tourist attraction, although its appeal is not universal. You can explore all seven levels of this huge battleship and check out the boiler room, the cabins, and the gun turrets, as well as exhibitions and videos about life on board in 1943 and the history of the Royal Navy. Boys of all ages tend to love this ship, and those very interested in World War II may find it an enlightening experience.

Hampton Court Palace

Type of Attraction: London's most impressive royal palace

Location: East Molesey, Surrey, approximately 12 miles outside of central London; Zone 12 (tube/train: Hampton Court Station (British Rail), accessible directly from Waterloo)

Admission: Adults £10, children ages 5–15 £6.60; this includes admission to the gardens and maze

Hours: March to October, Monday 10:15 a.m.–6 p.m., Tuesday–Sunday 9:30 a.m.–6 p.m. In October to March the palace closes on Monday at 4:15 p.m. and at 4:30 p.m. all other days

Phone: (0181) 781-9500

When to Go: Any time

Special Comments: Good disabled access including ramps to the Tudor Kitchens and in some areas of the gardens as well as lifts to the first floor of palace and handicap toilets

Overall Appeal by Age Group:

Pre-school	Grade School	Teens	Young Adults	Over 30	Senior Citizens
★★	★★★	★★★★★	★★★★★	★★★★★	★★★★★

Author's Rating: ★★★★★

How Much Time to Allow: Head out early, giving yourself the full day to enjoy Hampton Court and arriving back in London in time for dinner or perhaps a trip to the theater

Description and Comments   One of the nicest things about Hampton Court Palace is its location. If you have been running all over the city of London, deciphering bus schedules and tube maps, a trip outside this fast-paced metropolis is a relaxing treat. Hampton Court is easily reached by train from Waterloo or Wimbledon stations, but if you have time, the best way to approach the palace is by water. Boat tours up the Thames run in the summer months from Richmond (for a half-hour ride) or Westminster (for a full hour-long excursion). Approaching the palace in this manner affords an unequaled view of the majestic King's Apartments, the magnificently cultivated Privy gardens, and the vast parklands that once served as Henry's private hunting grounds. For river tour schedules and pricing information call (0171) 930-4721.

The powerful and influential lord chancellor to Henry VIII, Cardinal Wolsey built Hampton Court Palace in 1516 and proceeded to live there quite lavishly. In 1528, after Henry inquired about such an extravagant home for a member of the clergy, Cardinal Wolsey offered it to the king. After Wolsey failed to secure from the pope Henry's much-desired annulment from Catherine of Aragon in 1529, Henry accepted his offer, no doubt with a malicious glee. Enhancements to the palace continued under Henry, who created the enormous Tudor kitchens, and beautifully redesigned the chapel. Alterations were also made by the famous architect, Christopher Wren, under the direction of William and Mary, and further changes were instigated by Queen Anne. Wren had intended to demolish the palace and redesign it in the new neoclassical styles, but, luckily, interest was lost when Mary died. The resulting conglomerate is a palace of distinctly different architectural appearances, which allows visitors to clearly distinguish some of the most important design styles in England's history.

As you enter the palace through the Great Gatehouse, you come into the Base Court and beyond that the Clock Court. Looking around, you will discover Henry's medieval Great Hall on your left, contrasted with William and Mary's Renaissance colonnade on your right. Behind you is Anne Boleyn's Gateway and the entrance to Henry VIII's State Apartments, and above the gateway is the court's namesake, the astronomical clock installed by Henry in 1540.

The palace is organized into six walking tours, and then there are still the gardens and maze in which to wander. With all this to see, your best bet is to decide whether you want to start inside or out. I usually find that after an hour or two inside the vast halls I need get outside for a bit and can then return to more fully enjoy the rest of the palace. Costumed guides offer tours of Henry VIII's Apartments, the King's and (in summer) Queen's Apartments at no additional charge; this is always a good way to start your visit, as the fascinating story of Hampton Court is immediately brought to life by these experienced historians.

If you prefer to head out on your own, audio guides of Henry's apartments and the Tudor kitchens are also available at no additional cost. Of significant interest in Henry's Great Hall are the hammer-beam ceiling and stunning medieval tapestries. The rather plain hallway leading to the king's chapel is the Haunted Gallery and claims to be the wandering ground for the ghost of Henry's fifth wife, Catherine Howard. Just before her arrest for adultery (and, therefore, high treason) she is said to have run to the chapel to plead for mercy from the king, who was inside but did not acknowledge her cries. Instead, armed guards dragged her, kicking and screaming, back to her chambers to contain her. She died on the block, as had Anne Boleyn before her.

The King's Apartments give one a glimpse into the court life of William III with all its pomp and ceremony: the intimidating King's Guard Chamber, and the king's *two* bedchambers, the magnificent State Bedchamber, alongside the much simpler private one in which he actually slept are evidence of a very peculiar sense of self-importance. Also worth a look are the smaller but no less impressive Georgian Rooms, completed for Queen Caroline in 1728, and the recently reopened Wolsey Rooms with the Renaissance Picture Gallery, full of treasures from the private collection of Queen Elizabeth II.

Outside, you have a wide choice of garden styles to match the rooms they surround. The grandest of these is William III's Fountain Garden, which stretches before the palace's east front in a semicircle. On the southside is the Privy Garden, currently restored as William III would have seen it. Beyond this are the sunken Pond Gardens and Tudor-style Knot and Herb Gardens, while on the opposite side of the palace you will venture into the less manicured Wilderness, with its garden of evergreens and the ever popular maze, originally laid out in 1714.

Touring Tips   A sunny day makes Hampton Court's ornate gardens a fantastic picnic spot for families. Alternately, you might head to the Tiltyard Tearoom for an enjoyable light meal, or wander beyond the Lion Gates for a number of cozy pubs, all serving some wonderfully traditional lunchtime fare.

Hogarth's House

Type of Attraction: Summer house of the brilliant satirist and painter, filled with his engravings

Location: Hogarth Lane, Great West Road, W4, Zone 12 (tube: Turnham Green or Chiswick rail)

Admission: Free

Hours: April to October, Tuesday–Friday 1–5 p.m., Saturday and Sunday 1–6 p.m.; November to March, Tuesday–Friday 1–5 p.m. Closed Monday and month of January

Phone: (0181) 994-6757

When to Go: As part of a day in Chiswick (Chiswick House is a short walk away)

Special Comments: Disabled access; tours by appointment

Overall Appeal by Age Group:

Pre-school	Grade School	Teens	Young Adults	Over 30	Senior Citizens
★	★	★★	★★	★★	★★

Author's Rating: ★★

How Much Time to Allow: 1 hour

Description and Comments   If you go to Chiswick House in the morning, you might want to come here in the afternoon. It used to be a quiet, country retreat for the great painter and satirist William Hogarth, but is now located on a particularly busy section of the A4. For the Hogarth fan, a visit here is a must: More than 200 of his most famous prints are here: *Marriage a la Mode, A Rake's Progress, A Harlot's Progress,* and more, and it's quite delightful to take your time over them in this setting that the master called home for 15 years, until his death in 1764.

Touring Tips   Make this visit part of your trip to Chiswick, and see Chiswick House as well. Have lunch or dinner at Mackintosh's Brasserie (142 Chiswick High St., phone (0181) 994-2628), the best restaurant in the area, and great for kids.

Houses of Parliament: House of Lords and House of Commons

Type of Attraction: Britain's working chambers of government

Location: Parliament Square, SW1, Zone 9 (tube: Westminster)

Admission: Free

Hours: Debates in both houses begin daily from 2:30 p.m. Public admission to the "Strangers' Gallery" is from 4:30 p.m. until at least 10:30 p.m., Monday–Thursday; and 9:30 a.m. to 3 p.m. on Friday. Question time (accessible only by special prebooked tickets) is Tuesday and Thursday 2:30–3:30 p.m., with the prime minister's Question Time running from 3:15–3:30 p.m.

Phone: (0171) 219-3000

When to Go: For the Stranger's Gallery, it's a good idea to arrive after 6 p.m., when the waiting line has diminished. Both houses are in recess at Christmas, Easter, and from August to the middle of October

Special Comments: Security is very tight. Allow plenty of time to clear security checks. Do not bring food, drinks, mobile phones, or pagers. They will allow you in with a camera as long as it stays in your bag as absolutely no photography is permitted

Overall Appeal by Age Group:

Pre-school	Grade School	Teens	Young Adults	Over 30	Senior Citizens
†	†	★★	★★	★★★	★★★

† Not appropriate for young children.

Author's Rating: ★★

How Much Time to Allow: 1–2 hours depending on how long you'd like to observe the debates (giving at least 30 minutes to clear security)

Description and Comments   The first Parliament was convened in 1254 and consisted of lords, bishops, abbots, knights, and local citizens. Today's Parliament, closely based on its predecessors, includes the sovereign, the House of Lords—which used to be made up of hereditary peerage members, but now must be elected or appointed to their positions—and the House of Commons—members elected from their respective English, Welsh, Scottish, and Northern Irish communities. The current buildings in which they meet, built between 1840 and 1860, have become the most recognized trademarks of London. Unfortunately, public access to their grand interior is generally limited to observing either house during their daily debate sessions. If you are interested in viewing Parliament in action, simply join the queue at St. Stephen's Gate, withstand the tight security procedures (don't be surprised if it takes you up to an hour to be cleared), and then watch MPs (ministers of Parliament) argue political issues for their constituents.

Touring Tips   For a more intimate look at the Palace of Westminster and the opportunity to tour the areas generally off-limits to the public special permits are required, but it is well worth the effort provided you have ample time to conduct the necessary correspondence and settle the arrangements. Write a few months in advance to: Public Information Office, House of Commons, London SW1A 2PW. Be sure to include the exact dates for your visit to London, the total number in your party (not to exceed 16 people), your home address, and your London address and telephone. Permits will be mailed, so be sure to allow enough time to finalize your plans. For information only you may call (0171) 219-4272.

Permits allow you unchaperoned access as you follow a printed guide through splendidly decorated lobbies and corridors and the grand Westminster Hall as well as the two houses. If the house is in recess (see above), tours will be granted two to five days a week. When the house is in session tours will only be scheduled for Friday. Information that will enable you to hire guides to take you through will be sent along with the permits, but these must be arranged separately and cost approximately £25, whether your group includes 2 or 16 members.

If you can't get into the Houses of Parliament for any reason, visit Jewel Tower (Abingdon Street, SW1, by Westminster Abbey, phone (0171) 222-2219, 10 a.m. to 4 p.m. in winter, to 6 p.m. in summer; small fee), where you can see an interactive virtual reality tour of both houses.

Imperial War Museum

Type of Attraction: British military experience from 1914 to the present

Location: Lambeth Road, SE1, Zone 5 (tube: Elephant and Castle)

Admission: Adults £5, children age 5–17 £2.50, family ticket £13

Hours: Daily 10 a.m.–6 p.m.

Phone: (0171) 416-5320; *www.iwm.org.uk*

When to Go: Any time

Special Comments: Discounted entry fee for disabled; for disabled parking call (0171) 416-5262

Overall Appeal by Age Group:

Pre-school	Grade School	Teens	Young Adults	Over 30	Senior Citizens
★	★	★★	★★	★★	★★

Author's Rating: ★★

How Much Time to Allow: 1 hour

Description and Comments Housed in the famous former lunatic asylum known as Bedlam, the Imperial War Museum is an oddly appropriate present tenant, dedicated to the madness that is twentieth-century war. It is a sobering museum, especially the section on the liberation of Belsen, which will be expanded into a permanent exhibit on the Holocaust to be completed in 2000. It was hard not to be offended by the blithe displays of the awful hardware of destruction: guns, tanks, zeppelins, V2 rockets, bombers. You are given an insight into the horror of war by the recreation of the sights and sounds and smells of the Blitz, a clock counting down the numbers of war deaths in this century, and the nightmare of life in a World War I trench, but then it seems you are invited to appreciate the machinery of it. Perhaps by way of making some definite statement on the side of pacifism, the Imperial War Museum has created a beautiful Peace Garden on its grounds, which was dedicated by the Dalai Lama in May 1999.

Dr. Johnson's House

Type of Attraction: Literary attraction in historical house

Location: 17 Gough Square, EC4, Zone 2 (tube: Blackfriars)

Admission: Adults £3, children £1, under age 10, free

Hours: Monday–Saturday 11 a.m.–5 p.m.; October to April, 11 a.m.–5 p.m.

Phone: (0171) 353-3745

When to Go: Any time

Special Comments: No wheelchair access, steep stairs

Overall Appeal by Age Group:

Pre-school	Grade School	Teens	Young Adults	Over 30	Senior Citizens
★	★	★	★	★	★

Author's Rating: ★

How Much Time to Allow: 27 minutes for video, 10–15 minutes for the house

Description and Comments   I like Samuel Johnson more than the average bloke on the block, but even I wasn't overly impressed by this house, the only surviving domicile of the 17 he lived in. I might have felt differently had the admission been free; however, I do respect and support the fact that this house on prime property has managed to avoid the wrecking ball for 250 years. This alone makes it worth the visit and the price. Dr. Johnson spent 11 years in this house working on his famous dictionary, but it falls short of providing the kind of atmosphere that makes a literary museum come alive. There aren't a whole lot of artifacts or furniture, although the collection of mezzotints and books on Johnson are impressive. You must watch the video, very well done and interesting, which does make the remarkable Johnson and his biographer, Boswell, come to life.

Kensington Palace State Rooms

Type of Attraction: Stately home in the middle of Kensington Gardens

Location: Kensington Gardens, Broad Walk, Zone 13 (tube: Kensington High Street)

Admission: Adults £8.50; children £6.10, under age 5 free, family ticket £26.10

Hours: April to October, daily 10 a.m.–5 p.m; October through March, daily 10 a.m.–4 p.m.

Phone: (0171) 937-9561

When to Go: Morning in summer; any time in winter

Special Comments: Nearby parking for disabled may be arranged in advance; phone to ask permission. Wheelchair access toilets, and ramp to Orangery, but many steps inside the palace

Overall Appeal by Age Group:

Pre-school	Grade School	Teens	Young Adults	Over 30	Senior Citizens
★★	★★★	★★★★	★★★★	★★★★	★★★★

Author's Rating: ★★★★

How Much Time to Allow: 1½ hours

Description and Comments Kensington Palace is the former home of Princess Diana, and the place where Princess Victoria was told that she had become queen. It's not a grandiose palace like Buckingham or Windsor, which makes it in some ways more interesting. It was built in 1605 and sold to King William and Queen Mary in 1689 as a country escape from the noxious fumes of Whitehall, which were aggravating the king's asthma. The monarchs immediately hired Christopher Wren and Nicholas Hawksmoor to improve the house. Queen Anne later added more improvements, such as the Orangery, which was her "Summer Supper House," and acres of gardens. George I turned what was essentially a country estate into a palace, and it's fascinating to note the different between the homey oak-paneled dining room of William and Mary and the over-the-top decor of William Kent's innovations. George II was the last monarch to make Kensington Palace a primary residence, as Buckingham Palace became the townhouse of choice to succeeding kings and queens. King George II and Queen Caroline made extensive additions to the gardens that can be enjoyed today, such as Broad Walk, the Round Pond, and the Serpentine. In 1841, the gardens were opened to the public, when the palace became a source of "grace and favour" apartments for offshoots of the royal family, as it remains.

You can see the bedroom in which Princess Victoria lived with her mother, the duchess of Kent, until she was 18 and made queen. This is quite a claustrophobic setup, and quite impossible to picture any modern mother-daughter pair living in such proximity, especially with the scores of rooms all around. There are some fine examples of furniture, and brilliant trompe l'oeil ceiling paintings and murals by William Kent. Two oddities that must be seen are the wind dial by which King William III could tell how fast his ships might be approaching, and the massive clock in the Cupola Room that used to play tunes by Handel, Corelli, and Geminiani, and which, even minus this feature, represents a marvelous marriage of sixteenth-century technology and art.

There is a court dress exhibition which takes the viewer through the sartorial styles and often bizarre traditions of being presented at court. On a modern note, there are some dresses of the present queen that highlight just how distant the glamorous royal past of Kensington Palace is.

Touring Tips   Make this part of a day in the park. Early birds get the worm here, but it's also nice to come later in the day and follow up your visit with tea at the Orangery next door. Be sure to take advantage of the audio tour, it's very thorough and interesting.

Kenwood House (The Iveagh Bequest)

Type of Attraction: World-class art gallery within an elegant neoclassical Georgian villa

Location: Hampstead Lane, Hampstead Heath, NW3, Zone 1 (tube: Highgate, then 210 bus)

Admission: Free

Hours: April to September, daily 10 a.m.–6 p.m.; October to March, daily 10 a.m.–4 p.m.

Phone: (0181) 348-1286

When to Go: Any time, but preferably on weekdays and in good weather so you can enjoy the Heath

Special Comments: Call to arrange limited wheelchair access

Overall Appeal by Age Group:

Pre- school	Grade School	Teens	Young Adults	Over 30	Senior Citizens
★	★★★	★★★	★★★	★★★	★★★

Author's Rating: ★★★★

How Much Time to Allow: 2 hours in the house, plus time for tea or a walk around the grounds and on the Heath. It's a good day out.

Description and Comments   Kenwood is the most elegant exponent of architects Robert and James Adams's early Georgian design. It is gorgeous, with Adams and Chippendale furniture and decoration, which, combined with the stunning masterpieces hanging on the walls and the exceptional views, make Kenwood House an attraction for all seasons.

Built in 1700, the house belonged to the earls of Mansfield until 1925. The family auctioned off the contents of the house in 1922, and then leased the house first to a Russian grand duke; then to a social-climbing American millionairess. Kenwood was threatened with suburban development, until it was saved by brewery magnate Edward Guinness, earl of Iveagh, who purchased it to house his extensive collection of seventeenth-century Dutch and Flemish and late eighteenth-century British paintings. Some of the original furniture has been tracked down and replaced in Kenwood, and although the display is unimpressive on the whole, there are a few examples of Adams-designed pieces to be seen, and more furniture being added all the time. You'll find the library (also known as the "Great Room" with good reason) as magnificent a re-creation of early-Georgian neoclassical living style as can be seen anywhere in the world.

Lord Iveagh's bequest of paintings includes works by Sir Joshua Reynolds, George Romney, J. M. W. Turner, Gainsborough, and Raeburn. There are a number of absolutely unmissable old masters here, such as Rembrandt's *Self Portrait* and Vermeer's *The Guitar Player*. As an art gallery, it is right up there in the top ten of London.

A number of somewhat quirky displays of miniature portraits, jewelry, ceramics, and 1,300 Georgian shoe buckles are the result of Kenwood attracting legacies from a variety of collectors.

Touring Tips   Combine this visit with a trip to Hampstead Village and the Heath. If you're visiting in the summer, combine it with the weekend concerts.

Lambeth Palace

Type of Attraction: Private thirteenth-century home of the archbishop of Canterbury

Location: Lambeth Palace Road, Zone 5 (tube: Lambeth North)

Admission: £2.50 each

Hours: Usually midafternoons on Wednesday and Thursday only

Phone: (0171) 928-8282

When to Go: By prearranged tour only (see details below)

Special Comments: Requests for permission to see the palace must be made in writing to: Social Secretary, Lambeth Palace, London SE1 7JU. Allow at least 1 month to allow for correspondence to settle arrangements.

Overall Appeal by Age Group:

Pre-school	Grade School	Teens	Young Adults	Over 30	Senior Citizens
†	★	★	★★★	★★★	★★★★

† Not appropriate for preschoolers

Author's Rating: ★★★

How Much Time to Allow: 1½ hours

Description and Comments   A medieval gem on the south side of the Thames, Lambeth Palace has been the home to the archbishop of Canterbury for seven centuries. The palace is well off the beaten path of most tourist routes due to the fact that it is not open to the public as a tourist site. However, if you are of a mind to see something that even most of the locals haven't, you can get yourself beyond its hulking gatehouse door. The palace allows visits at select times to prearranged groups only. You can request permission to join a group already booked for a tour, assuming that the group has not reached its limit of 30 people. Requests should be made in writing at least a month in advance (to allow for reply correspondence). Indicate the dates you will be in London and to ensure a speedy reply, enclose a self-addressed envelope (airmail-stamped if necessary). Tours are given by residents of the palace, often the social secretary herself or one of the palace's religious members, and last about 70 minutes.

The buildings date back to the thirteenth century and its halls have echoed the footsteps of many notable Britons. Among them are Thomas More, who lived in the gate tower while serving as a page boy from the age of 12, and Oliver Cromwell, who dined with his men in the thirteenth-century chapel. The palace's most impressive building is the early seventeenth-century library with its exceptional hammer-beam roof, where you are surrounded by shelf after shelf of ancient books and illuminated manuscripts, some of which date back to the ninth century. Also worth seeing are the ancient chapel and crypt, although the chapel's new ceiling frescoes are definitely of a twentieth-century style.

Touring Tips   Bus number 3 or number 159, both via Whitehall and Westminster, would drop you just near the palace. Lambeth North tube station is a bit of a walk.

Leighton House Museum and Art Gallery

Type of Attraction: Unusual house of pre-Raphaelite painter Lord Frederick Leighton

Location: 12 Holland Park Rd., Zone 13 (tube: High Street Kensington, then bus 9, 10, 27, 33, or 49 to Odeon Cinema)

Admission: Free, £2 for audio tour

Hours: Monday–Saturday 11 a.m.–5:30 p.m.

Phone: (0171) 602-3316

When to Go: Any time

Special Comments: Not wheelchair accessible—many steps to top floor

Overall Appeal by Age Group:

Pre-school	Grade School	Teens	Young Adults	Over 30	Senior Citizens
★	★	★★	★★	★★	★★

Author's Rating: ★★★★★

How Much Time to Allow: 30 minutes

Description and Comments   If you are a true lover of the pre-Raphaelites —Edward Burne-Jones, John Millais, of course Frederick Leighton, and others —this is a must-see. Lord Leighton, whose magnificent painted hallway can be seen in the Victoria and Albert Museum, dedicated his home as "a private palace devoted to art." The main attraction is the Arab Hall, which is a Victorian fantasy of the Middle East, with Isniuk tiles, elaborately carved and gilded woodwork, and the mosaic frieze. There is a wonderful sunken fountain in the middle of the room, which furthers the impression of a courtyard straight out of the pages of *The Arabian Nights.* The top floor is Leighton's old studio, and the huge windows, skylights, and the dome are clearly the heart's desire of any nineteenth-century painter. There's a good collection of Victorian paintings on the lower floor, including Leighton's *Roman Mother;* upstairs you can see temporary exhibits of a widely varied nature. The house is sadly lacking in furniture and knick-knacks, and despite the stuffed peacock in the hall, one wishes for more of the decorative exuberance that must have been obtained when Lord Leighton lived here.

Touring Tips   Combine this with a trip to Holland Park and the Linley Sambourne House.

Linley Sambourne House

Type of Attraction: Perfectly preserved house of wealthy Victorian punch cartoonist

Location: 18 Stafford Terrace, Kensington, W8, Zone 14 (tube: High Street Kensington)

Admission: Adults £3, children £1.50

Hours: Open March 1 through October 31, Wednesday 10 a.m.–4 p.m., Sunday 2 p.m.–5 p.m. Closed from November 1 to February 28

Phone: (0181) 994-1019

When to Go: When it's open, which is only Wednesday and Sunday

Special Comments: Lots of stairs and no wheelchair access

Overall Appeal by Age Group:

Pre-school	Grade School	Teens	Young Adults	Over 30	Senior Citizens
★	★★	★★	★★★	★★★	★★★

Author's Rating: ★★★

How Much Time to Allow: 1 hour

Description and Comments   This place is a veritable time machine, plunking one smack down in the middle of the late Victorian–early Edwardian era, with the sumptuous clutter that caused the backlash of modernism. William Morris designs adorn both wall and floor, and there are a few stained-glass windows to love. A predominant thought on seeing the vast collection of clocks, vases, gim-cracks, and knick-knacks was of pity for the poor servant in charge of dusting. The immense aesthetic weight of all the pretty possessions can be a bit tiring, but it is an amazing piece of preservation.

Touring Tips   Combine with a trip to Holland Park and/or the Frederick Leighton House.

London Aquarium

Type of Attraction: Wonderland of fish on the bank of the Thames

Location: County Hall, Riverside Building, Westminster Bridge Road, SE1, Zone 5 (tube: Westminster or Waterloo)

Admission: Adult £7, children £5, under age 3, free

Hours: Daily 10 a.m.–6 p.m., last entry, 5 p.m.; bank holidays 10 a.m.–6:30 p.m.

Phone: (0171) 967-8000

When to Go: Avoid weekends and school holidays if possible; go early

Special Comments: Fully accessible for disabled persons. To avoid steps, go around building to Belvedere Road to reach entrance. Picnic area available for packed lunches.

Overall Appeal by Age Group:

Pre-school	Grade School	Teens	Young Adults	Over 30	Senior Citizens
★★★★	★★★★	★★★	★★★	★★★	★★★

Author's Rating: ★★★★

How Much Time to Allow: 2 hours

Description and Comments   In Southbank's County Hall and the former home of the Greater London Council is the most unlikely conversion in London: three dimly lit and atmospheric floors of enormous tanks filled with sea life and freshwater fish of every kind. The Atlantic tank holds 800,000 liters of water and tons of sharks, eels, and stingrays. It's most impressive, although I felt badly for the magnificent sharks whose snouts have been damaged by hitting the glass walls. There's a petting pool for kids to stroke manta rays, who actually seem to invite these caresses. In the Pacific tank, even bigger than the Atlantic, reside more sharks, rays, groupers, and smaller fish. The piranha tank is interesting, especially at dinner time, when you get to see what a real-life feeding frenzy looks like (call ahead to find out when the feeding times for various fish are).

This is not the most amazing aquarium in the world by a long shot, and if you have access to a good one where you live, you might as well leave this off your list, but it has been proven to me time and again that when it comes to taming small children, fish take the cake.

Touring Tips   There's a McDonald's next to the aquarium, which has its own entrance to the aquarium. There's also a wonderful gift shop with models of sea life for every budget.

London Dungeon

Type of Attraction: Dummy-driven yuck-fest with historical pretenses

Location: 28–34 Tooley St., SE1, Zone 5 (tube: London Bridge)

Admission: Adults £8.50, children £6.50

Hours: April to September, daily 10 a.m.–6:30 p.m.; October to March, daily 10 a.m.—5:30 p.m.

Phone: (0171) 403-0606

When to Go: Weekdays when it opens—it gets pretty crowded midday

Special Comments: Wheelchair access; don't bring small children

Overall Appeal by Age Group:

Pre-school	Grade School	Teens	Young Adults	Over 30	Senior Citizens
†	★	★★★★	★★	★★	★

† Too scary for preschoolers.

Author's Rating: ★

How Much Time to Allow: 90 minutes

Description and Comments   I am the first one to line up for the weird and horrible—the only thing I didn't yawn over at Madame Tussaud's was the Chamber of Horrors—but this place hit me the wrong way. The relentlessness of the gore without much context was disturbing, and the "Jack the Ripper Experience" was just plain offensive. There are a number of different sections, such as medieval, justice, ecclesiastical, and torture, but the huge emphasis on Jack the Ripper just goes to show you how much "history" they're really pushing here. The hordes of French teenage boys who were there during my visit seemed to find it hilarious. They cheered wildly when we saw a dummy guillotined. There's a little boat ride that takes you on a trip to Traitor's Gate, which at least gets you off your feet for a bit. The best part was the gift shop, where I picked up a life-size skull candle and some fun Halloween stuff.

Touring Tips   Drop off the teens here and go wait for them in the Bella Pasta across the street, or take a look at nearby Southwark Cathedral while the youngsters do their thing.

The London International Gallery of Children's Art

Type of Attraction: Museum of local and international children's artwork
Location: O$_2$ Centre on Finchley Road, Hampstead, Zone 1 (tube: Finchley Road, Jubilee line)
Admission: Suggested donations of £2 for adults and £1 for children
Hours: Saturday 11 a.m.–5 p.m., Sunday noon–6 p.m., weekdays 2–6 p.m., although hours may vary, so call before setting out
Phone: (0171) 435-0903
When to Go: Any time
Special Comments: Very good handicap access, with lifts throughout the O$_2$ Centre and a disabled lift that leads directly into the children's gallery
Overall Appeal by Age Group:

Pre-school	Grade School	Teens	Young Adults	Over 30	Senior Citizens
★★	★★★	★★	★★	★★★	★★★

Author's Rating: ★★★
How Much Time to Allow: 30 minutes to view gallery; call for workshop times

Description and Comments   The London International Gallery of Children's Art was created to celebrate the work of children from all over the world. This small but impressive gallery produces exhibitions which teach as well as inspire and provides a window through which to view the diversity of children's experiences. In addition, children's activities and workshops often run concurrently with particular exhibitions. Although a brief stop, it is refreshing and can easily be incorporated into an afternoon spent wandering in Hampstead. Call ahead for current exhibition and activities information.

Touring Tips If you are lucky enough to be visiting when gallery activities or workshops are scheduled, it is a great idea to have the kids attend one while you go off and explore the treasures of Hampstead for a while. From Finchley Road, bus number 268 will drop you right in the center of Hampstead village.

London Transport Museum

Type of Attraction: A fun, interactive museum of trams, buses, and trains of old and new London

Location: 39 Wellington St., off Covent Garden Piazza, WC2, Zone 7 (tube: Covent Garden)

Admission: Adults: £4.95; Children: £2.95

Hours: Daily 10 a.m.–6pm (Friday open at 11 a.m.)

Phone: (0171) 565-7299

When to Go: Any time

Special Comments: Wheelchair and stroller access; cafe and gift shop

Overall Appeal by Age Group:

Pre-school	Grade School	Teens	Young Adults	Over 30	Senior Citizens
★★★★	★★★★	★★★	★★★	★★★	★★★

Author's Rating: ★★★★

How Much Time to Allow: 1 hour

Description and Comments This is one of the best venues for kids in London, and adults love it, too. Although many might yawn at the idea of a museum dedicated to that most prosaic feature of urban life, public transportation, this museum is so cleverly and earnestly organized that it's impossible not to get swept up in the fun of it. From horse-drawn stagecoaches and omnibuses that you can climb on, to buses that you can pretend to drive and underground switches you can pretend to throw, this is an interactive museum that most kids are gonna love. You're given a ticket that you go around to numbered sites and stamp, until you've filled up your card and seen all there is to see. There are videos of old-time trams and buses and a wonderful short film on the touching last trip of the last tram in London, with everyone singing "Auld Lang Syne." There's so much for grown-ups to learn here, too, such as why the fares on buses and trains in London have to be so complicated and that 40,000 people took the first Metropolitan Underground Line on its first day. Alas, we don't find out why you can wait forever for your bus and then three will come all at once, or why it's taking so long for the Jubilee line to be finished.

The gift shop has a huge selection of great postcards and Underground posters, and a wealth of books about London's transport. You can get just about anything here with the Underground map on it, even slippers.

Touring Tips   Buy the museum guide if you have children under age 12— there's a fun pull-out section with games and educational pursuits in it. Combine this trip with a visit to Covent Garden, also fun for the kids, especially on weekends. Call or visit their Web site (*www.ltmuseum.co.uk*) to check for lectures, tours, films, and family activities.

London Zoo

Type of Attraction: Modernized old zoo set at the edge of Regent's Park

Location: Regent's Park, Zone 15 (tube: Camden Town)

Admission: Adults £9, children age 4–14 £7, family ticket £28

Hours: Monday–Saturday 10 a.m.–5 p.m.; 10 a.m.–6 p.m. on Sunday and bank holidays

Phone: (0171) 722-3333

When to Go: When it's warm and not raining

Special Comments: Wheelchair access

Overall Appeal by Age Group:

Pre-school	Grade School	Teens	Young Adults	Over 30	Senior Citizens
★★★★	★★★★	★★★	★★★	★★★	★★★

Author's Rating: ★★★

How Much Time to Allow: 2 hours

Description and Comments   The London Zoo is supposedly in some financial trouble, as there are no significant subsidies from the government to help it operate. It is trying its best, and the education that it provides on endangered species is invaluable, as is the experience of seeing Asian lions, lemurs, and rhinos in the flesh—it makes the possible loss of these animals to extinction all the more horrific. The zoo has tried hard to be the best it can be and has created a small but full environment of hooved, winged, and four-legged friends, but it may have already seen its day. Of course this might just be true for all zoos that have been unable to completely conform to the new ideas of keeping animals in captivity in a humane way—a concept that could be considered a contradiction in terms.

Opened in 1828, the zoo has clearly evolved from the old animals in cages standard, but it can't be all things to all animals, as is clear from the Bactrian camel, used to the torrid aridity of the Gobi Desert, standing listlessly in the chilly, damp air of London. Or the gorilla rocking back and forth, giving his viewers reproachful looks. On a brighter note, the reptile house is magnificent, with cobras, pythons, and even alligators in nicely designed environments, plus a teaching center with snake skins and things made from the hides of unfortunate animals. The aquarium is also quite comprehensive and well housed. There are a lot of monkeys and a petting zoo for children. The shop is fantastic and will fulfill all your animal paraphernalia needs, with books, stuffed animals, knick-knacks, gim-cracks, and geegaws.

Madame Tussaud's Waxworks

Type of Attraction: World-famous display of wax dummies, chosen most arbitrarily

Location: Marylebone Road, NW1, Zone 14 (tube: Baker Street)

Admission: Adult £9.50, children under age 16 £6.25, seniors £7.15, children age 4 and under free. Combined tickets to London Planetarium: Adult £11.75, children under age 16 £7.75, seniors £8.95

Hours: Daily 10 a.m.–5:30 p.m.. Opens at 9:30 a.m. on weekends, bank holidays, and summer

Phone: (0171) 935-6168

When to Go: They advise that you go in the afternoon to avoid the queue, but there always seems to be a line there, no matter what the time, even a half hour before it opens. Go a day before or book over the phone and get a ticket so you can get on the prepaid line. Forget the weekends.

Special Comments: Limited wheelchair access

Overall Appeal by Age Group:

Pre-school	Grade School	Teens	Young Adults	Over 30	Senior Citizens
★★	★★★	★★★	★★★	★★★	★★★

Author's Rating: ★★

How Much Time to Allow: 1 hour

Description and Comments I am not the one to talk to about Madame Tussaud's because I found it ridiculous—I might have been more pleased with it if it were not for the lines, the price, and the milling hordes inside. I also think that it may have been more interesting in the days before film, when you really didn't know what the personages of the day looked like. However, I have many friends who loved it, so I decided to try to give it the benefit of the doubt. It's certainly one of London's most visited attractions. As you walk in there's a "Garden Party" presided over by mostly British celebs, and not the big ones. I defy any American to tell me who Chris Evans or Lenny Henry are (and they're the A-list celebs here). However, there was also Arnold Schwarzenegger, Dudley Moore, and some sports figures that may ring a bell. I liked the section on the history of the wax works, where you got to see the unfortunates who'd been decommissioned and decapitated and ended up with their heads on the shelf: Liza Minelli, Nikita Krushchev, Sammy Davis Jr., and W. C. Fields were but a few. The making of these wax works is fascinating. We got to see how Jerry Hall came to be formed, with video and all; Interestingly, there's no sign of her ex anywhere—how gratifying that must be for her. It seemed to me that the 1970s were a particularly bad time for making dummies (see the movie stars and American presidents) but the 1990s are proving to be something of a golden age. Some of the newer dummies are frighteningly real, down to the gleam in the eye. One can't say for sure about the verisimilitude of the old ones, like Voltaire, but I must say that Princess Diana was a pretty good imitation. I loved the surreal display of the duke of Wellington staring down at the wax effigy of his old nemesis, Napoleon, an event that actually transpired.

There is a pretty silly ride in a miniature black taxi that rushes you through the history of London (from Elizabeth I till now) at a breakneck pace. All you can do is giggle as you fly along. Things improved (for me anyway) in the Chamber of Horrors, over which is the Dante inscription, "All Hope Abandon, Ye Who Enter Here!"—a sentiment perhaps more fitting for the end of the queue outside. It is a sobering and disturbing exhibit, which manages to even approximate the smell of unwashed bodies and despair (also reminiscent of the queue outside) in the prison section. But of all the horrors, murderers, and bloodiness, there is surely nothing more chilling than the display of Madame Tussaud herself, lantern held aloft, searching a mountain of decapitated bodies for the head of her former employer, Marie Antoinette. I think they should dump the celebrities and make the museum all about the madame: the young Marie Grosholtz Tussaud started out in the late 1700s assisting a doctor who specialized in making wax anatomy forms. Her talent for portraiture was so extraordinary that she was hired to teach art to the children of the doomed king and queen of France. When the French Revolution came, she was imprisoned (rooming with the future Josephine Bonaparte) and marked for the guillotine. Marie was saved by those who thought to have her make death masks of the aristocrats, many of whom she had known. She spent many a night poking through the bloody corpses for the heads she was commissioned to work on. What a way to make a living.

In an interesting juxtaposition, you are moved from the stomach-turning Chamber of Horrors straight into the cafe. The gift shop is big, but there's not much to buy, even for a gift shop aficionado like myself.

Touring Tips   As I said, book a ticket in advance by phone or in person, so that you can avoid the lines, or at least minimize waiting time.

Millennium Dome

As of press time, the expensive and controversial Millennium Dome was still under construction on the Isle of Dogs in Zone 6. The intent is to make it a kind of Great Exhibition of the twentieth century to rival that of 1851. It will be huge, that much we know, and it will include a specially produced half-hour film of the famous BBC comedy Blackadder, in which Blackadder and his sidekick Baldrick time travel through British history. There will be exhibits of all sorts, and supposedly a couple of huge statues representing man- and womankind. The big question on everyone's lips, after "Why?" is "Will it be done on time?" We shall see.

The Monument

Type of Attraction: Tower commemorating the Great Fire of 1666

Location: Monument Street, EC3, Zone 3 (tube: Monument)

Admission: Adults £1.50, children 50p

Hours: Daily 10 a.m.–6 p.m. (last admission 5:40 p.m.)

Phone: (0171) 626-2717

When to Go: In summer, come between 10 and 11:30 a.m., or between 4 and 5 p.m. Any time during winter

Special Comments: Pass on this if you are: a preschooler, out of shape, infirm in any way, elderly, already tired, or afraid of heights and close quarters

Overall Appeal by Age Group:

Pre-school	Grade School	Teens	Young Adults	Over 30	Senior Citizens
★★	★★★	★★★★	★★★		Depends

Author's Rating: ★★★★

How Much Time to Allow: 20 minutes

Description and Comments   The Monument, at 202 feet high, was once as visible as St. Paul's Dome, which was certainly no coincidence, as Christopher Wren designed both. The monument was to commemorate the Great Fire of 1666 that was actually responsible for making Wren, King Charles II's chief surveyor, one of London's most prolific architects. If laid down on its side, the monument would reach directly to the spot on Pudding Lane where the fire started. It also has a precise linear relationship to St. Paul's, no doubt a touch that Wren relished.

The 311 steps to the top take about 5 minutes to walk, though it seems much longer. The stairs are pie-shaped, which makes passing on them a little delicate. There is no stated etiquette for who takes which part of the steps as the climbers and descendants squeeze by each other, but the guard assured me that good manners and awareness are all that's necessary to negotiate the pass. I went on a rainy day when only a few hardy souls were to be seen, and I had no problem with passing the few that I did. There are three or four window seats on which to take a little breather while ascending. The view is quite fine—spectacular in fact—and the best possible place to see Tower Bridge. Sadly, the views of the Tower of London and the whole of St. Paul's have been severely compromised by the new buildings. I was assured by a taxi driver that the view used to be much more amazing. He also told me that his four-year-old son was completely freaked out by the height. Look down the stairwell when you get to the top—it's like an Escher drawing or something out of Alfred Hitchcock's *Vertigo*.

Touring Tips   Bring a camera, and don't forget to pick up your certificate as you leave, commending you on your climb.

Museum of London

Type of Attraction: Museum of 2,000 years of London history

Location: London Wall and Aldersgate, Zone 3 (tube: St. Paul's or Barbican)

Admission: £4 adults; £3 children, students, and seniors; those with disabilities and children under age 5 free. A family ticket (5 people, including up to 2 adults) is £12. Tickets are valid for readmission for 1 year

Hours: 10 a.m.–5:50 p.m., Sunday noon–5:50 p.m.

Phone: (0171) 600-3699

When to Go: Any time, although you may be navigating around large groups of schoolchildren if you go to early on weekdays while school is in session—after 2:30 p.m., they're gone

Special Comments: Good handicap accessibility with a number of ramps and lifts for all floors

Overall Appeal by Age Group:

Pre-school	Grade School	Teens	Young Adults	Over 30	Senior Citizens
★★	★★★★	★★★★	★★★★	★★★★	★★★★

Author's Rating: ★★★★

How Much Time to Allow: 2–3 hours

Description and Comments   The Museum of London tells the story of London from its first settlers back in 400,000 B.C. to the present, using a variety of eye-catching displays and fascinating reconstructions. Its chronologically themed tour route allows visitors to travel through London's history, diverging to explore more closely the time periods each finds most intriguing. Attention is given to each major time period, from prehistoric and Roman London to the London of World War II and on to the present. This museum is kid-friendly, with some interactive or tactile displays. A few not-to-be-missed exhibits include a large section of London's fourth-century town wall, located outside but incorporated into the museum's Roman London exhibition through a window overlook, the 1757 gilded Lord Mayor's Coach, and re-created nineteenth-century street scenes and shops.

There are exhibits here that can be quite fascinating—a recent one had to do with Londoners' bodies over the centuries and displayed skeletons, corsets, and bones ravaged by such diseases as rickets and syphilis. It is a very well-presented museum, and it manages to make London's history feel quite intimate. There's a real cell from Newgate Prison that is perfectly chilling, and the Victorian shops give one the strangest sense of déjà-vu. The displays about the years of the Blitz are riveting, making you realize just how appalling it was living under the constant bombardment. There's an Anderson shelter that people used to live in at night in their backyard, and it's all set up with books and lamps, just the way it must have been. Seeing it must be quite a disturbing experience for those who actually went through the war—it's real enough for those who didn't. If you are even slightly interested in London's history, this museum is a must-see; if you're not, you will be after a visit. The gift shop has a huge assortment of books on London and English history for all ages. There's a good cafe there, too.

Touring Tips   For an introduction to many of the exhibitions and information on current temporary exhibits check out the museum's Web site at *www.museumoflondon.org.uk.* Also, call ahead to find out how many schools are booked to visit that day—if it's a lot, come after 2:30 p.m.

Museum of the Moving Image (MOMI)

MOMI closed at the end of August 1998 as the first stage of the redevelopment of the British Film Institute's south bank complex. MOMI will be re-created in a planned BFI film center that will also include the National Film Theatre and Library. Renovations are not due to start until 2002. Meanwhile, part of the MOMI collection will go on a national tour, while other elements are expected to move to the Science Museum.

National Gallery

Type of Attraction: Splendid art gallery of 700 years of European painting

Location: Trafalgar Square, WC2, Zone 7 (tube: Leicester Square)

Admission: Free, charge for special exhibits

Hours: Monday, Tuesday, Thursday–Saturday 10 a.m.–6 p.m.; Wednesday 10 a.m.–8 p.m.; Sunday noon–6 p.m.

Phone: (0171) 839-3321

When to Go: Any time, but avoid major exhibits on weekends

Special Comments: Wheelchair accessible

Overall Appeal by Age Group:

Pre-school	Grade School	Teens	Young Adults	Over 30	Senior Citizens
★	★★★	★★★★	★★★★★	★★★★★	★★★★★

Author's Rating: ★★★★★

How Much Time to Allow: As long as you can physically handle

Description and Comments   This is one of those few and far between amazing art museums in which every time you turn around you see the original of some utterly familiar image—Holbein's *The Ambassadors,* Van Gogh's *Sunflowers,* or Monet's *Water Lily Pond.* It is the repository of about 2,300 paintings from the past 700 years of European art culture; you can spend hours gazing slack-jawed at paintings by Titian, Rembrandt, Carravagio, Vermeer, Velazquez, Michelangelo, Da Vinci, Van Eyck, and other old masters too numerous to mention. As if that weren't enough, the East Wing is filled with Impressionists, featuring some 50 paintings on a sort of permanent loan from the Tate Gallery. You'll see Seurat, Pissarro, Gauguin, Degas, Corot, and others. The collection is laid out quite methodically and has excellent inscriptions next to each painting. The special exhibits are always worth paying for, and do get yourself a headset to listen to the tour.

The National Gallery was founded in 1824 under King George IV, when the government purchased 38 important paintings—from artists such as Raphael, Van Dyck, and Rembrandt—from the estate of John Julius Angerstein. The collection was housed in Angerstein's house in Pall Mall until the permanent edifice was completed between 1832 and 1838. The building was commissioned with a few strange requirements, such as the cupola crowning the front portico, initially ridiculed as a mustard pot, with the two bell towers on either side looking like pepper shakers. The architect, William Wilkens, was also asked to use a portion of a former royal palace in his design, so the slightly ungainly appearance may be due to these requests. Built on the site of the old King's Mews, the National Gallery looms over Trafalgar Square somewhat glumly, but inside it is a feast for the eyes—and it's still free!

The new Sainsbury's Wing houses the oldest paintings, from between 1260 to 1510. Don't miss Jan Van Eyck's *Arnolfini Marriage* in Room 56, and look for the artist reflected in the mirror. The West Wing has paintings from 1510 to 1600, including Tintoretto's *St. George and the Dragon*. The North Wing (1600–1700) has dedicated Room 27 to Rembrandt, and includes other seventeenth-century geniuses whose paintings have an almost supernatural power that no reproduction can capture. The East Wing takes us from 1700 up to 1920, with Canaletto and Turner's land- and seascapes giving way to the English portraits and social scenes of Gainsborough, Reynolds, and the prodigious Hogarth, whose series *Marriage a la Mode* can be seen here. Rooms 43–45 are always crowded with Impressionism fans looking at Rousseau's *Tropical Storm with Tiger,* Renoir's *Umbrellas,* Van Gogh's *Chair,* and so many more. Picasso is represented in Room 46, though there are no really major items here, except for *Minotauromachia.* You may wonder where many of the English painters of this period are: They're in the Tate Gallery (see page 340), which takes the National Collection through the twentieth century.

There's a Pret a Manger in the basement for excellent sandwiches and salads, and in the Sainsbury Wing is a more upscale restaurant serving decent food. The gift shops, one big and one little, are filled with the most wonderful collection of books, postcards, and calendars, and must be visted.

Touring Tips   Take advantage of the lectures and recorded tours available here; they are a great aid to your visit. There is also a computer in the Micro Gallery, where you can look up and print out information of the art and artists.

National Maritime Museum and Queen's House

Type of Attraction: Largest maritime museum in the world

Location: Romney Road, Greenwich (tube: Greenwich on the Docklands Light Railway)

Admission: Prices quoted include entrance to Maritime Museum, Queen's House, and Royal Observatory. £5 for adults, £4 seniors and students, £2.50 for children age 5–16, £15 for family ticket (2 adults and 3 children). Discount tickets to the *Cutty Sark* are available on display of a NMM ticket

Hours: Daily 10 a.m.–5 p.m.

Phone: (0181) 312-6565

When to Go: Any time on weekdays; early in the day on weekends

Special Comments: Fully accessible with lifts for disabled, touch talks for visually impaired, and sign-interpreted talks. Call for details.

Overall Appeal by Age Group:

Pre- school	Grade School	Teens	Young Adults	Over 30	Senior Citizens
★★★	★★★★	★★★	★★★★	★★★★	★★★★

Author's Rating: ★★★★

How Much Time to Allow: 2–3 hours for the museum and 1–2 hours for Queen's House Millennium exhibition

Description and Comments Reopening fully in April 1999, the National Maritime Museum has been restructured and revitalized just in time for the millions of Millennium Dome visitors expected to arrive in the coming year. Its new galleries will include lots of interactive displays exploring the impact of the oceans on our daily lives, as well as our destructive impact on the seas. Exhibitions will include the re-creations of steerage and first-class cabins and deck sections from an oceanliner, thousands of ship models, hundreds of navigational instruments, and galleries devoted to the history of British naval conquests and accomplishment. Of particular interest to adults will be the elaborate Horatio Nelson exhibition which pays homage to the famous admiral who defeated Napoleon at the Battle of Trafalgar. Kids however, will have to be dragged out of the All Hands Gallery, a fascinating interactive collection of exhibits, tools, and experiments of nautical principles. The fun includes raising and lowering signal flags, working a crane to load a ship's cargo, or attempting some deep-sea engineering. It is fully expected that the new galleries will continue to hold tight to this tradition of intellectually stimulating and highly interactive displays.

The Queen's House, adjacent to the museum, is also undergoing major refurbishment, but will reopen in December 1999 with an international exhibition entitled "The Story of Time." Included will be 300 objects that demonstrate our perception of time, ranging from astronomical instruments, manuscripts, costumes, and fossils. The interior of the house has been restored to the days of Charles II, and the Royal Apartments on the upper floor are especially dazzling.

Touring Tips The museum offers a wide range of children's educational workshops and activities, many free of charge. There are Pirate Workshops, the Crowsnest Club for those under age six, and Shipmates for those age seven and older. For details and a full schedule of planned events call (0181) 312-6608, or write the National Maritime Museum, Greenwich, London SE10 9NF. You can also gather information by checking out the museum's Web site at *www.nmm.ac.uk.*

National Portrait Gallery

Type of Attraction: Collection of the most famous faces in British history
Location: St. Martin's Place; adjacent to National Gallery (tube: Leicester Square or Charing Cross)
Admission: Free (except for special exhibitions)
Hours: Monday–Saturday 10 a.m.–6 p.m. and Sunday noon–6 p.m.
Phone: (0171) 306-0055
When to Go: Any time
Special Comments: Very good handicap accessibility with lifts to every floor
Overall Appeal by Age Group:

Pre-school	Grade School	Teens	Young Adults	Over 30	Senior Citizens
★	★★	★★★★	★★★★	★★★★	★★★★

Author's Rating: ★★★★★
How Much Time to Allow: 2–3 hours

Description and Comments   Of all the museums that London has to offer, the National Portrait Gallery holds particular appeal. First of all, it's free and in the middle of a very interesting area. It's across the street from St. Martin–in-the-Fields Church, and sitting at the right-hand side of the National Gallery, just off Trafalgar Square. It's quite manageable in a few hours, unlike the eight miles of the Victoria and Albert or the grand halls of the National Gallery. Its modest size allows for relaxed browsing without the feeling that you must rush or you won't see everything. The NPG gives the casual student of England a direct line to its history through the faces of its most interesting and important people.

You start at the top (you can take an elevator) with the lean faces of the early medieval kings, through the Tudors, with Holbein's imagery of Henry VIII (and his many wives), on to the Stuarts in the seventeenth century, to the nineteenth-century Victorians and through to portraits and photos of the current royal family. Andy Warhol's 4x4 image of Queen Elizabeth II is a bit of a lark; while the famous portraits and photos of Diana, princess of Wales, with a death date below them are really quite poignant.

As you take this visual voyage through the ages, notice the changing styles of portraiture and what kinds of people each age deems worthy of being painted or photographed. You will see people from various disciplines—science, literature, politics, art, and entertainment—whose contributions to English life reached far beyond this small island. With the help of the NPG sound guides, the amount of history you absorb will change how you perceive London's most famous sights. Back on the ground floor are the most recent portraits, as well as the acclaimed photographic gallery and a few smaller but very impressive small exhibition galleries for which a small fee is usually charged.

Touring Tips   The basement contains the newly refurbished Portrait Cafe. The Cafe-in-the-Crypt of nearby St. Martin–in-the-Fields offers good lunch fare in a delightfully creepy setting (gravestones under your feet really get your appetite going).

Natural History Museum

Type of Attraction: Collection of old and modern exhibits on everything to do with the natural world, housed in a wonderful Victorian edifice

Location: Cromwell Road, South Kensington, SW7, Zone 11 (tube: South Kensington)

Admission: Adults £6.50, children free up to 17 years of age; free to all 4:30 p.m. –5:50 p.m. Monday–Friday, after 5 p.m. on weekends

Hours: Monday–Saturday 10 a.m.–5:50 p.m., Sunday 11 a.m.–5:50 p.m.

Phone: (0171) 938-9123

When to Go: Any time during the weekdays, although watch out for lines of buses along Cromwell Road, which indicate hordes of schoolkids; weekends can be quite crowded, so go early

Special Comments: Complete disabled access

Overall Appeal by Age Group:

Pre-school	Grade School	Teens	Young Adults	Over 30	Senior Citizens
★★★	★★★★	★★★	★★★	★★★	★★★

Author's Rating: ★★★

How Much Time to Allow: 2 hours or more

Description and Comments   Part of the South Kensington cultural revolution of the nineteenth century, the Natural History Museum was formed by the British Library's collections of Sir Hans Sloane, which were divvied up and sent to South Ken in the 1860s. It's a grand old institution, housed in a majestic building that is worth a visit on its own. Notice the animal statues on the outside, and the terra-cotta monkeys and other beasts climbing on stone vines in the lobby. It has all the hallmarks of a gothic cathedral, an impression that architect Alfred Waterhouse intended to inspire the proper reverence for nature. It is a huge place, full of many surprises and some really fine examples of educational curating, such as the Ecology Gallery, in which you walk through a rain forest. It has plenty of interactive permanent displays and temporary exhibits, some of which have been very good, such as the one on human biology. The newly remodeled Earth Galleries (entrance on Exhibition Road) are entered via a long escalator that goes through a model of the earth and features a re-creation of a convenience store in the Kobe earthquake. The Earth Galleries are full of see-and-touch educational exhibits, which is fine with kids, but perhaps not so wondrous for grown-ups. As a grown-up myself, I am much more impressed with some of the old displays: dioramas of exotic animals, including the extinct dodo bird, and cabinets full of butterflies, all the bounty brought back from the far-flung reaches of the empire, much of which is utterly irreplaceable and of great scientific importance. But the dinosaur exhibit is quite good, and of interest to old and young alike. It is set out in such a way that one follows along paths and climbs up stairs, which keeps the kids active and happy, while the parents can take the time to read the information posted there. The gift shops are excellent for children's educational toys and books, as well as geological booty.

Touring Tips   Be sure to look at the entire front of the building on Cromwell Road: In a witty reflection of the statues of artists that adorn the front of the neighboring Victoria and Albert Museum, the Natural History Museum has statues of animals on its facade. If the line at the Cromwell Road entrance is long, enter at the Earth Galleries on Exhibition Road.

Old Bailey

Type of Attraction: London's Central Criminal Courts

Location: Old Bailey Street, EC4, Zone 3 (tube: St. Paul's)

Admission: Free

Hours: Monday–Friday 10:15 a.m. and 1:45 p.m.

Phone: (0171) 248-3277; ask for List Office

When to Go: Arrive for the times given. The public gallery in each courtroom has a limited number of seats, and bailiffs may not allow access once court is in session

Special Comments: Do not bring backpacks, cameras, food, mobile phones, or pagers. They will not permit these items and there is no cloak room for storing them

Overall Appeal by Age Group:

Pre-school	Grade School	Teens	Young Adults	Over 30	Senior Citizens
†	†	★★	★★	★★★	★★

† Not appropriate for children.

Author's Rating: ★★

How Much Time to Allow: As much time as your interest in the court proceedings allows

Description and Comments   Although most interesting to those with a background in law, the cases held in London's Old Bailey are criminal cases, and just about anyone will find both the content of the cases and the etiquette of the British courtroom intriguing for some length of time. Wigged and traditionally robed barristers address each other as "friend" and the judge as "milord," and politely assert their case while the defendant sits at the rear of the courtroom, visibly separated from the "gentlemen's proceedings" going on in front of him.

The Old Bailey was built on the site of Newgate Prison, the noxious and notorious prison that held criminals (of the innocent and guilty variety) and public executions from the twelfth century until it was destroyed in 1902. Not the best feng shui for a court, one might say, with God only knows how many desperate ghosts hanging around. This court saw the spectacle of Oscar Wilde's trial—"the butterfly broken on a wheel"—as well as those of the Yorkshire Ripper and the wife-killer Dr. Crippen.

Touring Tips   The entrance to the Public Galleries is off of Newgate Street and down Old Bailey, past the original courts building as well as its contemporary addition, to Warwick Passage on the left. Call ahead to find out what cases are currently on the docket and at what point in the proceedings they are. Dial the number above and then ask for the List Office.

Old Operating Theatre, Museum, and Herb Garret

Type of Attraction: Haunting museum of old medical equipment and an early Victorian operating theater

Location: 9A St. Thomas's St., SE1, Zone 5 (tube: London Bridge)

Admission: Adults £2.90, children £1.50, family £7.25

Hours: Daily 10 a.m.– 4 p.m.

Phone: (0171) 955-4791

When to Go: Any time

Special Comments: The stairs in this old house are very, very steep. There is no wheelchair access

Overall Appeal by Age Group:

Pre-school	Grade School	Teens	Young Adults	Over 30	Senior Citizens
†	★	★★	★★★	★★★	★★★

† Not appropriate for preschoolers.

Author's Rating: ★★★★

How Much Time to Allow: 1 hour

Description and Comments In a tiny old house in a street by London Bridge is one of the most fascinating medical museums in London. You must climb up some rather treacherous steps to reach the musty old attic, in which you'll find displayed many of the gruesome medical instruments used before the days of anesthesia—quite sickening to see. I'm sure that the actual design of medical instruments hasn't changed all that much—a bone saw is a bone saw after all—but the understanding that the patient need not feel them actually piercing the flesh renders them much less horrifying. Old-style display cabinets hold forceps, blood-letting and cupping instruments, amputation and trepanning sets, an organ or two in formaldehyde, and other such oddities. Around the room are sheaths of herbs—comfrey for healing bones, penny royal for nausea, willow bark from which aspirin was derived, and elderflowers for what ails you. They soften the otherwise rough interior, and represent the less invasive side of the old healing arts.

The centerpiece of the museum is the operating theater from the early nineteenth century, a case study for postoperative septicity from the days before Dr. Lister figured out the germ theory. The table is made of wood, and under it is a box of sawdust, which the surgeon would kick where necessary to catch the blood; there's a small washbasin in which hands were washed *after* the operation; the room is ringed by semicircular levels of observation areas into which medical students would be crammed like sardines to stand and watch. This is not a place for the faint of heart. The gift shop is packed with interesting books on herbal remedies.

Touring Tips Include this museum with a trip to Southwark.

Pollock's Toy Museum

Type of Attraction: Two cute, creaky Victorian houses joined to make a climbing castle–like adventure into toys past

Location: 1 Scala St., W1P, Zone 14 (tube: Goodge Street)

Admission: Adult £2.50, children £1

Hours: Monday–Saturday 10 a.m.–5 p.m.

Phone: (0171) 636-3452

When to Go: Any time, but call and check to see if a school group is planned

Special Comments: This museum is six rooms on three floors connected by very steep stairs; not wheelchair-accessible or disabled-friendly

Overall Appeal by Age Group:

Pre-school	Grade School	Teens	Young Adults	Over 30	Senior Citizens
★★	★★★★	★★★	★★★	★★★★	★★★★

Author's Rating: ★★★★

How Much Time to Allow: 1 hour

Description and Comments   I can't say it better than Robert Louis Stevenson: "If you love art, folly, or the bright eyes of children, speed to Pollock's." Okay, so he was actually referring to Benjamin Pollock's famous toy theaters of the nineteenth century, but he probably would have been even more hearty in his approval of the Toy Museum. It contains not only Mr. Pollock's cunning toy theaters but five further rooms of toys of every description, as well as displays along the steep staircases. In fact there is probably not one square foot in the place that doesn't display some charming toy, poster, or board game. You'll see rocking horses, American automatic money boxes, Magic Lanterns, ancient jack-in-the-boxes, toy soldiers, folk dolls from around the world, doll-house rooms, puppets, teddy bears, even space toys, and much more. There is something terribly poignant in the sight of toys played with by children long since grown and gone. There are no interactive displays, but it's small and delightful enough to keep children reasonably well entertained for the time it takes to look through, though grownups may want to linger longer. There's a shop on the ground floor with books, toy reproductions, and other fun stuff. Buy generously and support this priceless collection.

Touring Tips   Combine this with a trip to the nearby British Museum

Queen's Gallery, Buckingham Palace

Type of Attraction: Art gallery of rotating treatures from the queen's collection, with new wing planned to house bigger, possibly permanent exhibits

Location: Buckingham Palace, SW1, Zone 9 (tube: Victoria, Green Park, or St. James Park)

Admission: Adults £4, children £2

Hours: Daily 9:30 a.m.– 4:30 p.m.; closed between exhibitions, so call ahead

Phone: (0171) 839-1377

When to Go: Any time, but it can be crowded in summer with the overspill from Buckingham Palace when it's open

Special Comments: At present it is small and not wheelchair-accessible, but when the new wing opens in 2002, it will presumably be completely disabled-friendly

Overall Appeal by Age Group:

Pre-school	Grade School	Teens	Young Adults	Over 30	Senior Citizens
★	★	★★	★★★	★★★	★★★

Author's Rating: ★★★

How Much Time to Allow: Presently 40–60 minutes

Description and Comments   It is difficult to discuss the Queen's Gallery, as the planned expansion will make it a horse of a different color entirely. Currently, it is a small gallery space with a constantly changing collection from the queen's treasure chest of world-class paintings, and your enjoyment of it depends on your appreciation of whatever is on view. In the past, they have shown watercolors by British artists, the art of Albion, and drawings of Michelangelo and Da Vinci. When the new wing is opened, it could show a selection from some of the queen's collection, which includes 20,000 old masters' drawings by Holbein, Canaletto, Da Vinci, Michelangelo, Carracci, and more; 10,000 old masters' paintings, including such artists as Rembrandt, Vermeer, Holbein, Brueghel, Van Dyck, and Rubens; royal portraits by Gainsborough, Reynolds, and Wilkie, as well as George Stubb's magnificent equine portraits; 30,000 English watercolors, a possible half a million prints, and countless sculptures, glass, porcelain, books, and Fabergé trinkets. So keep your fingers crossed that it opens as planned, and prepare to be dazzled.

Touring Tips   The gallery is a great way to pass the time while waiting for the Buckingham Palace tour.

Royal Academy of Arts

Type of Attraction: The venue for the world-famous Summer Exhibition of contemporary artists, record-breaking exhibitions of major artists and art themes, and a small but fine permanent collection of past academicians

Location: Burlington House, Piccadilly, W1, Zone 8 (tube: Piccadilly Circus, Green Park)

Admission: Adults £5.50, children age 12–18 £2.50, children age 8–11 £1

Hours: Daily 10 a.m.–6 p.m.; late-night opening Friday until 8:30 p.m., November and December only

Phone: (0171) 300-8000, recorded information: (0171) 300-5760 or (0171) 300-5761

When to Go: Biggest crowds will be when there's a very popular exhibition; weekends are normally crowded. Get there in the morning if possible

Special Comments: Wheelchair access

Overall Appeal by Age Group:

Pre-school	Grade School	Teens	Young Adults	Over 30	Senior Citizens
★	★	★★★	★★★★	★★★★	★★★★

Author's Rating: ★★★★

How Much Time to Allow: Depends on the exhibit, but 2 hours is a good estimate

Description and Comments   The academy is housed in the beautiful old Burlington House off Piccadilly. The courtyard usually features some exhibit of sculptures, often marvelously at odds with the Palladian grandeur of this last few of the surviving eighteenth-century palazzos. This was England's first art school, founded by Gainsborough and Reynolds, among others, in 1768. To be counted among the academicians was the highest mark of success. Today, it continues its tradition as a venue for new artists by hosting the 200-year-old Summer Exhibition, in which painters and sculptors compete for the honor of displaying their work to an appreciative audience, many of whom come to buy. It's a bit of a hodge-podge and scorned by many of the chattering classes (critics and journalists) and most of the artists who don't get in the exhibit. But everyone keeps trying to win a place on the wall.

The exhibits are usually excellent: A recent record-breaking exhibit was the Monet show in which people had to be let in on a timed basis, and for the last couple of days they had to keep the academy open for 24 hours. A less popular but no less interesting show was of the whimsical Victorian paintings of faeries. A permanent collection includes work from past academicians, as well as its most significant treasure, Michelangelo's marble frieze of Madonna and child.

Touring Tips   For £25, you can become a Friend of the Royal Academy, which allows you use of the very pleasant Friends' Room, free admission plus a guest, and, most important, you can jump the queue for the blockbuster exhibitions. You also get to feel quite virtuous as a much-needed patron of the arts. Call the academy ahead of time, or just come to the Friends' Desk and sign up.

Royal Greenwich Observatory (formerly known as the Old Royal Observatory)

Type of Attraction: Location of the world's Prime Meridian (0 degrees longitude)

Location: Blackheath Avenue, hilltop of Greenwich Park, Zone 6 (tube: Greenwich, on the Docklands Light Railway)

Admission: Prices quoted include entrance to the Royal Greenwich Observatory, Maritime Museum, and Queen's House. £5 for adults, £4 seniors and students, £2.50 for children age 5–16. £15 for family ticket (2 adults and 3 children). Discount tickets to the *Cutty Sark* are available on display of a NMM/Observatory ticket

Hours: Daily 10 a.m.–5 p.m.

Phone: (0181) 312-6565

When to Go: Any time

Special Comments: Not all observatory buildings are fully accessible. Special access days are arranged with BSL signed tours and touch sessions. For details call (0181) 312-6522.

Overall Appeal by Age Group:

Pre-school	Grade School	Teens	Young Adults	Over 30	Senior Citizens
★	★	★★★	★★★	★★★	★★★

Author's Rating: ★★★

How Much Time to Allow: 1–2 hours

Description and Comments   In 1675, Charles II appointed John Flamsteed his Astronomer Royal, with the specific mandate to create better navigational maps for the British empire. Christopher Wren then designed and built an observatory for him on the highest point of the king's royal hunting grounds in Greenwich. Today, this small complex of buildings is a popular museum. You can watch the Accurist Millennium Countdown Clock rapidly counting down to the year 2000 to the hundredth of a second, or place yourself in two hemispheres at the same time as you straddle the Prime Meridian. The museum's oldest part, Flamsteed House, is the restored home of the first Astronomer Royal. Its main galleries tell a variety of the bizarre methods once used to help ships' captains determine their location at sea and the increasingly important race to discover longitude. The remaining buildings contain a number of astronomical tools and telescopes, including Britain's largest, in the impressive Telescope Dome.

Touring Tips   Planetarium shows are given at 2:30 p.m. on weekdays. Entry fee is £2 for adults, and £1.50 for children and seniors.

Royal Mews, Buckingham Palace

Type of Attraction: Where the royal carriages and queen's horses are kept

Location: Buckingham Palace Road, SW1, Zone 9 (tube: St. James's Park or Victoria)

Admission: Adults £4, children £2, disabled free

Hours: October to December, Wednesday noon– 4 p.m.; April to October, Tuesday–Thursday noon– 4 p.m. Subject to sudden closures, so be sure to call first

Phone: (0171) 930-4832

When to Go: See hours above

Special Comments: Disabled are free, and there is good wheelchair access. Call disabled info at (0171) 839-1377

Overall Appeal by Age Group:

Pre-school	Grade School	Teens	Young Adults	Over 30	Senior Citizens
★★	★★	★★	★★	★★	★★

Author's Rating: ★★★

How Much Time to Allow: 40 minutes

Description and Comments   It's a small attraction and only open a few hours a week, but I urge any horse and carriage fancier to go take a look, if only to see the most elegant, cleanest stables in the entire world. Designed by John Nash, the stables retain a Georgian perfection, with freshly painted stalls of a pale yellow and lovely wrought-iron lamps. The horses are just as magnificent as you would expect: strong, perfect, and glossy. How they handle the oddly narrow riding ring is anyone's guess, but what the ring lacks in practicality, it makes up for in beauty. The royal coaches and automobiles are just mind-boggling, especially the gold state coach built for George II in 1761, which is still in use. There's a room with some of the most admirable tack and saddles ever made, which also displays sketches and photos of royal public occasions.

Touring Tips   Try to make this part of your trip to Buckingham Palace, as you can get a combined ticket at a reduced rate.

Royal Naval College

Type of Attraction: Extraordinary example of Renaissance architecture and interiors

Location: King William Walk, SE10, Zone 6 (tube: Greenwich, on the Docklands Light Railway)

Admission: Free

Hours: Daily 2:30 – 4:45 p.m. except Thursday (closed)

Phone: (0181) 858-2154

When to Go: Any time

Special Comments: Since the RNC is still owned by the Royal Navy, be prepared to have your bags searched on entry as part of security procedures

Overall Appeal by Age Group:

Pre-school	Grade School	Teens	Young Adults	Over 30	Senior Citizens
★	★	★★	★★★	★★★	★★★

Author's Rating: ★★★

How Much Time to Allow: Approximately 30 minutes

Description and Comments The Royal Naval College sits majestically on the banks of the Thames and is well worth exploring. Most of the property is off-limits to the public, but the college's spectacular Painted Hall and Royal Chapel are hidden treasures that should definitely be sought out. The buildings of the RNC were begun by Christopher Wren as a new palace for Charles II, but endured numerous revisions before their eventual development as a naval hospital for disabled seamen. It was with these altered plans that the riverfront view of the Queen's House behind it was preserved. The magnificent Painted Hall in the west wing was decorated by Sir James Thornhill and contains a glorious ceiling painting and walls covered in artwork that has a remarkable three-dimensional quality. In the east wing is the Royal Naval Chapel with equally exquisite interiors.

Touring Tips Locate the college's main entrance on William Walk as you get your bearings in Greenwich, and plan your day so that you can return during the RNC's limited opening visitor hours.

St. Bartholomew–the-Great

Type of Attraction: London's oldest monastic church

Location: Little Britain Street, off West Smithfield, EC1, Zone 3 (tube: St. Paul's or Barbican)

Admission: Free; donations gratefully accepted

Hours: Monday–Friday 8:30 a.m.–4 p.m., Saturday 10 a.m.–3 p.m., Sunday 2–6 p.m.

Regular Sunday services are at 9 a.m. and 11 a.m. (choral), with beautifully sung choral evensong at 6:30 p.m.

Phone: (0171) 606-5171

When to Go: Any time

Special Comments: It is best to approach the church from Little Britain Street. If coming from the direction of St. Paul's, you will pass St. Bart's Hospital on your left, and the church will be on your right just as you come into the square at Smithfield. Look for the rustic Tudor gatehouse on your right

Overall Appeal by Age Group:

Pre-school	Grade School	Teens	Young Adults	Over 30	Senior Citizens
★	★	★★	★★★	★★★	★★★

Author's Rating: ★★★★

How Much Time to Allow: 30–45 minutes; twice that if you are staying for a service

Description and Comments   After spending the morning at St. Paul's Cathedral, a great way to continue exploring London is to wander around to a few other nearby churches. It was in this manner that I first found what still remains my favorite London church. The Priory Church of St. Bartholomew–the-Great is *the* oldest remaining church in London's square mile. This exquisite medieval church was founded in 1123 by Rahere, Henry I's court jester. Upon being cured of malaria while on a pilgrimage to Rome, Rahere had a vision of St. Bartholomew and vowed to build a monastery in his honor. St. Bartholomew's is older than any other church in London, and that's saying something. Its ancient Romanesque architecture transports you back to an earlier time. Standing in the doorway, as you look in toward the magnificent medieval stonework, you can almost hear the cattle being herded out on Smithfield Green, or excited peasants gathering for the public executions, jousts, and tournaments that were commonly held there. Moving forward into the church chancel, you are spellbound by images of early monastic life, from the thick Norman pillars to the medieval baptismal font. Looking up you can glimpse "William Bolton's Window," just to the right of the altar. A former prior, Bolton created a private room here so that he could observe parishioners' weekly donations to the alms box.

Touring Tips   St. Bartholomew's is renowned for having an exceptional choir. Try to schedule your arrival to coincide with Sunday evensong— there's no better way to capture the ancient essence of this once great church.

Science Museum

Type of Attraction: Super-abundant collection of scientific and technological odds and ends that add up to a fascinating experience

Location: Exhibition Road, SW7, Zone 11 (tube: South Kensington)

Admission: Adults £6.50, children age 5–17 £3.50, under age 5 free

Hours: Daily 10 a.m.–6 p.m.

Phone: (0171) 938-8008, (0171) 938-8080, or (0171) 938-8000

When to Go: Avoid school holidays and weekends, unless you're there at 10 a.m. It's one of London's most popular museums, so go early or on weekdays

Special Comments: Good wheelchair and disabled access, call Disabled Persons Enquiry Line (0171) 938-9788

Overall Appeal by Age Group:

Pre-school	Grade School	Teens	Young Adults	Over 30	Senior Citizens
★★★★	★★★★	★★★★	★★★★	★★★★	★★★★

Author's Rating: ★★★★★

How Much Time to Allow: As much as you can spare—you could easily spend all day here, there's so much to see. If you're there with children who want to play in the interactive areas, plan to spend at least 3 hours.

Description and Comments   You don't need any particular interest in things scientific to love this most comprehensive collection displaying the progress of technology and science from the dawn of time to today. It is dauntingly large and there is a lot to read, but it allows you to travel where you will from an early hour glass in the Time gallery to the Apollo 10 Command Module in Exploration of Space. Moving exhibits include a miniaturized field with examples of plowing carried out by a number of small tractors, and a stupendously huge mill engine in the middle of the East Hall. You can watch Foucault's pendulum swinging away in the staircase by the East Hall, or check out a replica of a turn-of-the-century pharmacy in the Science and Art of Medicine on the fifth floor. The supermarket Sainsbury's has contributed a "Food for Thought" exhibit that examines every aspect of nutrition, the strangest being the mannequins of a young man and a young woman, showing what food they consumed in a month, how much sweat, feces, and urine they excreted, and how much their hair and nails grew.

Downstairs in the basement is a wonderful place to bring the young children: There's a hands-on gallery where children between ages three and six can build things with giant Legos and play with trucks and trolleys. You'll never get them out of there, which may be why the museum suggests starting at the top and moving downward.

Touring Tips   If you arrive and find a line, go across the street to the Victoria and Albert Museum or the Natural History Museum, and come back late in the afternoon (it's free after 4:30 p.m.), when the families have taken their tired kids home.

St. Paul's Cathedral

Type of Attraction: London's most prominent cathedral

Location: Ludgate Hill, EC4, Zone 3 (tube: St. Paul's or Mansion House)

Admission: Cathedral entry: £4 adults, £3.50 seniors and students, £2 children. Admission to dome and galleries an additional charge of: £3.50 adults, £3 seniors and students, £1.50 children. Family tickets, self-guided tours (with cassette), and guided tours are also available. Call to check prices

Hours: Visitors to cathedral, Monday–Saturday 8:30 a.m.–4 p.m. (Galleries open at 9:30 a.m.). Choral evensong occurs weekdays at 5 p.m. and Sunday at 3:15 p.m. Call the cathedral for other mass times

Phone: (0171) 236-4128

When to Go: Weekdays. Go early in the day to avoid the crowds and catch the best chances for clear sky views from the dome

Special Comments: Good disabled access to cathedral's nave and crypt, but there is no lift access to the galleries

Overall Appeal by Age Group:

Pre-school	Grade School	Teens	Young Adults	Over 30	Senior Citizens
★	★★	★★	★★★★	★★★★	★★★★

Author's Rating: ★★★

How Much Time to Allow: 30 minutes to 1 hour, depending on if you plan to climb to the top of the dome

Description and Comments   There was once a Roman temple to Diana on the site of the present St. Paul's, but even such ancient sanctity did not put the succeeding buildings out of harm's way: The first church was destroyed by fire in around 660. The second was demolished by Vikings. The huge wooden cross was struck by lightning in 1382, and in 1561 a spire was also toppled by lightning. During Henry VIII's reformation, the church turned into a kind of public marketplace. A bishop described the nave in 1560: "The south side for Popery and Usury; the north for Simony [buying and selling pardons]; and the horse-fair in the middle for all kinds of bargains, meetings, brawlings, murders, conspiracies; and the font for ordinary payments of money." The Great Fire of 1666 destroyed the third incarnation of St. Paul's Cathedral, along with four-fifths of the city. As King Charles II's surveyor-general, Christopher Wren became responsible for designing its replacement, which became his masterpiece. The cathedral was finished in a mere 35 years (the first cathedral to be completed by a single architect), and its stone English baroque style, despite being dwarfed by the encroachments of skyscrapers, still dominates the neighborhood. The dome is one of the highest in the world, at 360 feet, and second in size only to St. Peter's Basilica in Rome. Its lantern weighs a massive 850 tons.

Inside the cathedral, there are mosaics and frescoes, the *Light of the World* by Holman Hunt, Jean Tijou's grand sanctuary gates, and the intricate choir stall carvings designed by the most skilled wood craftsman of the day, Grinling Gibbons. The crypt is the resting place of—among other notables—Lord Admiral Horatio Nelson, the duke of Wellington, and Wren himself, whose son composed the Latin inscription on his tomb: "Reader, if you seek his monument, look around." Also in the crypt is the cathedral shop and a small cafe.

The 530 steps that take you to the top of St. Paul's are worth the effort, especially if you are lucky enough to have a clear, or even sunny, day. It is an easy walk to the Whispering Gallery, the first of the three levels, where words whispered on one side of the gallery can be clearly heard on the other. On the second level, the external Stone Gallery provides telescopes and benches, but it is the uppermost Golden Gallery that offers the most spectacular views of London. To see them however, you must submit to considerably more nerve-racking climbing.

Touring Tips   If your interest in Christopher Wren is inspired by St. Paul's, there are a number of other charming examples of his seventeenth-century work, many of which are just around the corner. Some of those closest to the cathedral include: St. Mary-le-Bow (Cheapside), St. Bride's (Fleet Street), and Christ Church (Newgate Street), whose tower is all that remains. A lovely garden now fills what was once the nave.

Sherlock Holmes Museum

Type of Attraction: Small but well-done recreation of a fascinating, if fictional, Victorian bachelor's house

Location: 221B Baker St., NW1, Zone 14 (tube: Baker Street)

Admission: Adults £5, children under age 16 £3, children under age 8 free

Hours: Daily 10 a.m.–6 p.m.

Phone: (0171) 935-8866

When to Go: Any time, especially if you're waiting for Madame Tussaud's to open or are on your way to the London Zoo

Special Comments: No wheelchair access, very steep stairs and plenty of them

Overall Appeal by Age Group:

Pre-school	Grade School	Teens	Young Adults	Over 30	Senior Citizens
★	★★	★★★	★★★	★★★	★★★

Author's Rating: ★★★★

How Much Time to Allow: 30–40 minutes

Description and Comments   I am a Sherlock Holmes fan, and I am also a sucker for anything from the nineteenth century. But even if you are none of the above, I think you'll find this a charming, if expensive, little stop. The self-guided (and short) tour through the little house is like stepping back in time: There are fires laid in all the rooms, which are bursting with curios and furniture, much in the way described in the stories by Sir Arthur Conan Doyle. It is a funny experience, so perfect a re-creation of a fictional place; by the time you leave you may think there really *was* a Sherlock Holmes. The decor is wonderful: There's the violin he so famously played close at hand in the study; leg irons on the bed by a valise half-packed; a medical corner for Dr. Watson; a remarkable early typewriter and a turn-of-the-century telephone. Even the attic is perfect: stuffed with leather goods, hat boxes, and other items we're all too young to remember. Items from the stories are displayed with appropriate quotes from the books, and there's an extraordinary chess set in gold and silver with characters from the books as the pieces. The pawns are bobbies and Baker Street Irregulars, the queens are the housekeeper Mrs. Hudson and Irene Adler, and so forth. You can buy a similar set (though not in metal) in the gift shop, which is full of mugs, tea towels, games, pipes, and deerstalker caps. There are a few valuable books—early editions and the like—but if you don't see what you want, go across the street to the Sherlock Holmes Memorabilia Company shop across the street, where they have some impressive first editions.

Touring Tips   Time your visit so you can have a traditional tea in the charming Hudson's Victorian Dining Room, which is attached to the museum.

Sir John Soane's Museum

Type of Attraction: Fascinating, eccentric collection of sculpture, art, and antiquities belonging to eighteenth-century neoclassical architect Sir John Soane

Location: 13 Lincoln's Inn Fields, WC2, Zone 2 (tube: Holborn, Central Line)

Admission: Free

Hours: Tuesday–Saturday 10 a.m.–5 p.m.

Phone: (0171) 405-2107

When to Go: Any time, although there is an excellent free tour of the museum on Saturday at 2:30 p.m., which is limited to 20 people. It is advised that you arrive early to secure a spot.

Special Comments: The museum is not handicapped-accessible, as it was formerly the private home of Sir John Soane and was directed to be left as he had it. You will even be asked to leave backpacks at the front desk so there is less chance of knocking over any of the hundreds of items that can be seen in each room. Not recommended for very young children with the tendency to touch everything

Overall Appeal by Age Group:

Pre-school	Grade School	Teens	Young Adults	Over 30	Senior Citizens
†	★	★★★	★★★★★	★★★★	★★★★★

† Not appropriate for young children

Author's Rating: ★★★★★

How Much Time to Allow: 1½–2½ hours

Description and Comments Many in London consider this their favorite museum. As small as it is, you can visit this nondescript residence numerous times, with treasures in every conceivable cranny, and discover new things to love about this collection each time. Situated just a stone's throw from one of the early Inns of Court, Sir John Soane bought and reconstructed the Georgian homes at 12, 13, and 14 Lincoln's Inn Fields and began filling them with a rather eccentric collection of art and antiquities. His architectural talent is seen in much of the unique floor plan of number 13, including a glass domed roof and central atrium that allow light over three floors; and the Soanes' dining room and breakfast parlor, both of which incorporate an unusual display of mirrors that reflect light and add illusions of space.

Other remarkable aspects of the collection include the series of paintings by William Hogarth entitled the *Rake's Progress* and *Election,* in an impressive picture gallery of false and hidden walls, a mock medieval monk's parlor containing gloomy casts and gargoyles, and the sarcophagus of Seti I surrounded by rows of antique statuary. Saturday's hour-long tour takes you through all of this and into number 12 as well, where you can see Soane's enormous research library, complete with architectural plans for the Bank of England, Whitehall, and parts of the treasury, along with numerous models of Pompeiian temples.

Touring Tips If you can't manage the Saturday tour, definitely strike up a conversation with any of the museum curators. They are very friendly and love to talk about the plethora of items acquired by Sir John Soane. It is the only way to really appreciate the amount and variety of items you see housed in this very small townhouse.

Southwark Cathedral

Type of Attraction: Small medieval cathedral with famous literary ties

Location: Montague Close, Southwark, SE1, Zone 5 (tube: London Bridge)

Admission: Donations encouraged

Hours: Daily 8 a.m.–6 p.m.

Phone: (0171) 407-2939

When to Go: Any time

Special Comments: Ramps allow access to nave of the cathedral

Overall Appeal by Age Group:

Pre-school	Grade School	Teens	Young Adults	Over 30	Senior Citizens
★	★	★	★★★	★★★	★★★

Author's Rating: ★★★

How Much Time to Allow: 15–45 minutes

Description and Comments   Although it has only been a cathedral since 1905, parts of this building date back to the twelfth century, when it was the Augustinian priory church of St. Mary Overie. In the time span between, the cathedral has been frequented by many notables of the day. William Shakespeare attended mass here regularly, and you will find the gravestone of his brother, Edward, who is interred in the choir aisle. A chapel is dedicated to the founder of Harvard University, John Harvard, who was born in Southwark and baptized in the church in 1607. In addition, there is the tomb of poet John Gower, a contemporary of Chaucer, and a memorial to Shakespeare that includes a glorious twentieth-century stained-glass window depicting almost two dozen of Shakespeare's most famous characters.

Touring Tips   Southwark Cathedral makes a nice pit stop if you are wandering around the Southwark area; especially if you have already been to Shakespeare's Globe Theatre. Also, the Pizza Express located in the chapter house is great for a fast and reasonably priced break.

Tate Gallery, Milbank

Type of Attraction: Museum of English painters, including huge Turner collection

Location: Millbank, on Thames, SW1, Zone 9 (tube: Pimlico)

Admission: Free, donations eagerly accepted

Hours: Daily 10 a.m.–5:50 p.m.

Phone: (0171) 887-8000, recorded info (0171) 887-8008

When to Go: Any time, but avoid midday if there's a big exhibition on

Special Comments: Access for disabled leaflet is available at Information Desks. Six parking spaces and four wheelchairs are available on request: call (0171) 887-8725

Overall Appeal by Age Group:

Pre-school	Grade School	Teens	Young Adults	Over 30	Senior Citizens
★	★★	★★★	★★★★	★★★★★	★★★★★

Author's Rating: ★★★★★

How Much Time to Allow: 2 hours or more

Description and Comments   The Tate Gallery will be changing in the spring of 2000, when the international, twentieth-century modern art will be moved across the river to the new Tate Gallery of Modern Art at the Bankside Power Station. This will leave a completely marvelous collection of English painters and sculptors from the sixteenth to the early twentieth century. The building itself is quite impressive, with Poseidon situated between a lion and unicorn on the top of the building, stately columns adorning the entrance, and halls of beautiful marble and design. The rooms follow a historical sequence that you need not follow, but which is quite revealing. There are plenty of benches from which to enjoy the paintings and the ambience. All the great British artists are here: Hogarth, Stubbs, Reynolds, Blake, Burne-Jones, Constable, and even an honorary Englishman, the American expat James Whistler. The pride of the collection is J. M. W. Turner, whose paintings and memorabilia fill the Clore Gallery. The gift shop has an excellent selection of books, gifts, and postcards, and the cafe is top-notch—remember that spending money in either helps support this excellent, free art gallery.

Tower Bridge

Type of Attraction: History of the bridge and a walk across the top of it

Location: Tower Bridge, SE1, Zone 3 (tube: Tower Hill)

Admission: Adults £5.95, children £3.95, family ticket £14.95

Hours: April to October, daily 10 a.m.–6:30 p.m.; November to March, daily 9:30 a.m.–6 p.m. (last admission is 75 minutes before closing)

Phone: (0171) 378-1928; fax (0171) 357-7935; *www.towerbridge.org.uk*

When to Go: Early morning or around 4 p.m.

Special Comments: Disabled access; call for details and to make plans

Overall Appeal by Age Group:

Pre-school	Grade School	Teens	Young Adults	Over 30	Senior Citizens
★	★★	★★	★★	★★	★★

Author's Rating: ★★

How Much Time to Allow: 90 minutes

Description and Comments   This is the bridge that everyone thinks is London Bridge, and what the American investors thought they were getting when they bought London Bridge in the 1970s to put up in the Arizona desert. Were they ever disappointed to get the real, boring London Bridge. Tower Bridge was built in 1894 and remains a beautiful piece of architecture, as well as a marvel of engineering. It is adequately appreciated from the ground, and I don't really think all that much is gained by waiting in the interminable lines to go in it, but if you can get in without waiting for more than half an hour, it's worth a look. They seem to be straining to provide a tour of some length, with a kind of corny multimedia trip through time to the bridge's inception, but the old films are fun to watch, and the history of how they ended up using this design is interesting, but probably not to small children. However, once you get let out on the walkway high above the Thames, with views everywhere, you can't help but be glad you visited.

Touring Tips   If there's a huge line—one that reaches out onto the bridge go enjoy the south riverside cafes and stores or go to the Tower of London and return when the line has reached inside the ticket area, according to the staff, usually around 4:15 p.m.

Tower of London

Type of Attraction: Ancient, history-rich fortress on the banks of the Thames

Location: Tower Hill, EC3, Zone 3 (tube: Tower Hill)

Admission: Adults £10. 50, children £6.90, children under age 5 free, family £31

Hours: March to October, Monday–Saturday 9 a.m.–5 p.m., Sunday 10 a.m.–5 p.m.; November to February, Sunday and Monday 10 a.m.–4 p.m., Tuesday–Saturday 9 a.m.–4 p.m.

Phone: (0171) 709-0765; *www.hrp.org.uk*

When to Go: The lines get pretty ferocious in the summer; line up early or go later in the day

Special Comments: Lots of difficult stairs and passageways. A limited number of wheelchairs are available, ask at the Group Ticket Office.

Overall Appeal by Age Group:

Pre-school	Grade School	Teens	Young Adults	Over 30	Senior Citizens
★	★★★	★★★	★★★★	★★★★	★★★★

Author's Rating: ★★★★★

How Much Time to Allow: 3 hours or more

Description and Comments   The first time I entered the Tower of London through the Middle Tower, I literally went weak in the knees. To an American with more than a passing interest in English history, a trip to the tower is a transcendent experience. There has been much written about how tourist-ridden it is, but I never found that to be a mitigating factor in my awe and appreciation of it. Yes, it is usually packed with howling schoolchildren and tourists; yes, there are gift shops and snack bars all over the place; and yes, some of the attempts at historical verisimilitude are corny. But this is still one of the most important sites in all of England and was the scene of dramas beyond counting. Numerous guidebooks will tell you that it's hard to feel the essential grimness of the place with all the happy sight-seers around, but I say that with a little imagination and focus, you can sense the ghosts that plague this place of imprisonment, torture, and death.

As anyone who lives there after dark can tell you, the place is lousy with ghosts, and not the happy kind. Macaulay, the nineteenth-century historian, wrote of the small burial ground by the Chapel of St. Peter Ad Vincula: "In truth, there is no sadder spot on earth as this little cemetery. Death is there associated, not, as in Westminster Abbey and St Paul's, with genius and virtue . . . but with whatever is darkest in human nature and in human destiny, with the savage triumph of implacable enemies, with the inconstancy, the ingratitude, the cowardice of friends, with all the miseries of fallen greatness and of blighted fame." It does make you shiver when you hear the roll call of the imprisoned and beheaded: Thomas More, Anne Boleyn, Lady Jane Grey and her husband, Queen Catherine Howard, a host of lords and ladies whose only crime was to end up on the wrong side of the monarch. There were also kings of Scotland and France, William Wallace (alias Braveheart), King Henry VI, the two little princes murdered in their sleep (presumably by their uncle, Richard III), Sir Walter Raleigh, and countless victims of religious persecutions. It is, for all its present serenity and beauty, a place soaked in centuries of blood.

The tower was started as a simple fortification on the Thames in 1066 by William the Conqueror, and grew over the years to include 13 different towers, numerous houses, walks, armories, barracks, and greens, all surrounded by a moat. The moat was drained in 1843 due to the mephitic stink of it, but there are plans afoot to fill it in again, which would be quite pleasing to the eye. The Yeoman Warders, also known as Beefeaters, have been at the tower since the 1300s and are now an invaluable source of information about the tower. They are happy to answer questions, and you may attach yourself to any group that is being entertained and enlightened by a Beefeater. There are Yeoman Warder talks and free tours every day—the Lanthorn Tower and the Middle Tower have information boards outlining the day's talks, tours and events. You will see ravens there: They are a very important part of the tower, and have been kept here with wings clipped for over 600 years. The legend goes that if the ravens should ever leave, the tower will fall and England will be in great danger. There is one there at present, named Thor, who has somehow been trained to imitate human speech, so any disembodied "Hellos" you hear will not always be the work of the ghosts.

One of the most famous sights at the tower is the Crown Jewels. I was not all that interested in them—the line can be awfully long, and while the crowns and scepters are interesting as historical emblems, they are strangely lifeless. Seeing them was not nearly as gratifying as reading the scratched graffiti—in English and Latin—of the unfortunate prisoners in Beauchamp Tower, or sitting under a tree in one of the greens absorbing the atmosphere. It's a good place to hang around, so take your time. The audio tours are great and can be done at your own pace, and the guide book is an excellent investment.

Touring Tips   There is a security check that slows down the entrance—if possible, leave your knapsack or bag at home when you visit.

Victoria and Albert Museum

Type of Attraction: 8 miles of a wide-ranging and breathtaking collection of decorative arts and design

Location: Cromwell Road (second entrance on Exhibition Road), South Kensington, SW7, Zone 11 (tube: South Kensington)

Admission: Adults £5, children under age 18 free, free between 4:30 p.m. and 5:50 p.m.

Hours: Monday noon– 5:50 p.m., Tuesday–Sunday 10 a.m.–5:50 p.m.

Phone: (0171) 938-8500 or (0171) 938-8441

When to Go: Any time, especially on a Late View Wednesday (open seasonally, call to check)

Special Comments: Wheelchair access is from the Exhibition Road entrance; there are ramps over most of the many small sets of steps

Overall Appeal by Age Group:

Pre-school	Grade School	Teens	Young Adults	Over 30	Senior Citizens
★★★	★★★★	★★★★	★★★★★	★★★★★	★★★★★

Author's Rating: ★★★★★

How Much Time to Allow: As much as possible

Description and Comments   The Victoria and Albert Museum is the jewel in the South Kensington Museumland's crown. It houses the most engaging assortment of treasures, and although it has been criticized for not having a strict enough focus, that is precisely its charm. It could be the enormous attic of some mad uncle, wealthy beyond all measure, indiscriminately collecting anything and everything of interest that might make his home more beautiful. The original V&A was part of Prince Albert's grand scheme to make South Kensington a center for arts, science, and learning. When it opened in 1852, funded by the Great Exhibition of 1851, Prince Albert envisioned the South Kensington Museum, as it was known then, to be a repository of applied arts—items that happily married beauty and utility. Such restrictions were hopeless from the start, as treasures started arriving from all over the empire and thousands of legacies. As you wander around the museum—and I believe that's the best way to go, although many would guide you toward the introductory tours that occur daily—you might bear in mind the fact that there are *millions* more objets d'art, paintings, photographs, clothing, textiles, and so on stored away in the basement. The mind boggles.

By 1899, the old housing for the collection was clearly unfit, and work was begun on the present building, named by Queen Victoria, who never passed up an opportunity to honor her long-departed husband. She didn't live to see it completed ten years later, but she presides over its Cromwell Road entrance like a secular version of the Virgin Mary, who tops the Brompton Oratory Church next door. There has been talk about finding a more appropriately descriptive name for this wonderful museum, but I think that evoking the quintessential couple of that inquisitive, acquisitive nineteenth-century British empire is perfect. The building is a real beauty, inside and out, and any visit to the museum should always include a few moments to appreciate the grace of the main entrance dome, the Fakes and Forgeries' immense halls and skylights, the Pirelli Courtyard, and especially the area that in a less populated age served as the museum's eateries: the Poynter, Gamble, and Morris rooms. These rooms are simply magnificent. There's the blue tiled Poynter room with its decorations of the seasons of the year, originally used as a grill room. The Gamble room has been restored to a cafe of less than its former glory, but never mind, it's still a delight to sit in, with its glorious stained-glass windows and neo-Renaissance beauty. The room done by William Morris and Company is especially fine with stained-glass windows by Edward Burne-Jones. It has some nice resonance, too, as William Morris once declared that there could be no one in the world who spent more time in the South Kensington museum than he, lucky man.

You have an endless choice of things to see in the V&A: armor, religious artifacts, stained glass, sculptures, wood carvings, jewelry, musical instruments, iron work, furniture, glass work, clothing, paintings, photographs, and whatever special exhibit is being held at the time, always very well mounted. The clothing exhibit has a dress from Tudor times that they managed to put together with a portrait of a woman wearing it—a rarity indeed. The stained-glass windows upstairs and in the medieval hall are world famous. The forgeries and fakes, copies of famous pieces of art and architecture, are impressive, even if they aren't real, and the room is a peaceful place to rest your feet. The British galleries will be closed until 2002, but when they reopen, do go see the famous Bed of Ware, a Tudor confection that was mentioned by Shakespeare. When you go to see the jewelry gallery, take a look at Frederick Leighton's frescos, and peek into the Art Library. Don't miss the Constables and Rodins in the Henry Cole Wing.

Touring Tips   If you're staying in South Kensington, get a WhiteCard pass or a season pass so that you can go in and out of the museum as much as possible. Or else, go in again after 4:30 p.m. for free. This museum has far too much to see in only one or two visits.

On Wednesday, there's a Late View, with a limited number of galleries open, a lecture in the beautiful old lecture hall past the Silver Galleries, and a gallery talk. The restaurant is open and has candles on the table, and live music is played there as well as in the front hall. It's a wonderful way to pass a Wednesday evening.

The weekends feature a Family Cart, with activities for children. It's extremely entertaining and educational for kids of every age.

Wallace Collection

Type of Attraction: One of the greatest private collections of nineteenth-century Anglo-French art

Location: Hertford House, Manchester Square, W1, Zone 14 (tube: Bond Street)

Admission: Free

Hours: Monday–Saturday 10 a.m.–5 p.m., Sunday 2 p.m.–5 p.m.

Phone: (0171) 935-0687

When to Go: Any time

Special Comments: Good disabled access including an outdoor ramp, lifts to the upper floors, and mostly uncluttered rooms in which it is easy to maneuver

Overall Appeal by Age Group:

Pre-school	Grade School	Teens	Young Adults	Over 30	Senior Citizens
★	★	★★	★★★	★★★★★	★★★★

Author's Rating: ★★★★

How Much Time to Allow: 1–3 hours

Description and Comments   The Wallace Collection is tucked away in a lovely Georgian square between Regent's and Hyde parks. The second marquess of Hertford leased the home, now Hertford House, in 1797, for the good duck shooting available in the area. Today, Hertford House holds the combined acquisitions of five generations of marquesses of Hertford. Between 1750 and 1880, this family formed what has become one of the most impressive collections to display quintessential aristocratic lifestyle and artistic taste in the nineteenth century.

The collection is displayed over this French chateau's two main floors, and some areas are worthy of special note. Galleries 2, 3, and 4 contain some fabulous pieces of Louis XIV furniture and art. A remarkable European Renaissance armory is housed in Galleries 8, 9, and 10, with Gallery 11 devoted to Oriental arms, armor, and art. Hertford House's largest room, Gallery 22, offers one of the finest displays of European paintings to be seen anywhere in the world. This impressive gallery, formerly called "The Long Picture Gallery," houses works by such masters as Titian, Poussin, Rembrandt, Rubens, Van Dyck, and Velázquez. Even if the house were empty of treasures, it would still be worth going to see the carved mantlepieces and elegant design of this architectural paragon of a bygone era.

Touring Tips   Free public lectures and tours on various aspects of the collection are given on weekdays and weekends. Tours usually last about 45 minutes and give good insight into the styles and history of the artists and their times. If you are on a tight schedule, call for touring times, or just arrive and wander on your own until a tour begins.

Westminster Abbey

Type of Attraction: England's most historically important church

Location: Broad Sanctuary, just off of Parliament Square, Zone 9 (tube: St. James Park and Westminster both on the District and Circle lines) are equidistant from the Abbey, although approach from St. James Park and up Tothill Street affords marvelous view of West Front)

Admission: Free admission for services or to visit the nave and cloisters; royal chapels and tombs: £5 for adults, £3 for students and seniors, £2 for children; Chapter House, Pyx Chamber, and Museum: £1 with royal chapels admission or £2.50 for adults, £1.90 for students and seniors, and £1.30 for children

Hours: Royal capels are open Monday–Friday 9:30 a.m.–3:45 p.m., Saturday 9:30 a.m.–1:45 p.m. (Closing times given are for last admission.)

Chapter House, Pyx Chamber, and Museum hours are Monday–Saturday 10 a.m.–3:30 p.m. The Abbey is closed before special services, on Sundays (except for services), December 24–28, Good Friday, and on Commonwealth Observance Day

Phone: (0171) 222-5152

When to Go: Early mornings on weekdays, especially during the busy summer months. If you really hate crowds in close spaces, make a quick call to be sure you aren't arriving the same time as 3 tour groups.

Special Comments: The best way to see Westminster Abbey is to join a verger's tour. These one-hour tours are given by Abbey vergers (custodians) and although they cost an additional £3, they're well worth the money. You learn so much more about the history contained within Westminster Abbey and even jump some of the queues with your guide. In summer the tours run Monday to Thursday at 10 a.m., 10:30 a.m., 11 a.m., 2 p.m., 2:30 p.m., and 3 p.m. (Friday is the same, but there is no 3 p.m. tour.) On Saturday, tours are 10 a.m., 11 a.m., and 12:30 p.m. Winter hours exclude the tours on the half hour. If you are interested, it is a good idea to call ahead just to be sure that a tour group isn't already booked for the tour you were planning to arrive for. Audio guides costing £2 are available in seven languages Monday–Friday 9:30 a.m.–3 p.m. and Saturday 9:30 a.m.–1 p.m.

Overall Appeal by Age Group:

Pre-school	Grade School	Teens	Young Adults	Over 30	Senior Citizens
★	★★★	★★★★	★★★★	★★★★	★★★★

Author's Rating: ★★★★

Additional Tips: My favorite way to experience Westminster Abbey is to arrive for the 3 p.m. verger's tour and then wander the cloisters (especially the lovely Little Cloister) before returning to the nave to wait for the 5 p.m. evensong. It is worth waiting at the head of the line (which starts to form at about 4:15 p.m.), as the first evensong attendees are seated in the stately choir stalls where the atmosphere and view of the Westminster Boys Choir is the best.

How Much Time to Allow: 1½–2 hours for audio guides or verger's tour; evensong is about 45 minutes

Description and Comments   As one of the most popular tourist sights in London, the key here is to avoid touring the Abbey when it is mobbed. You lose sight of the beauty of the interiors (displaying at least four different eras of architecture), the sheer numbers of people buried here (over 3,000), and the incredible amount of history that this building has seen (over 900 years) when you are moving in a sluggish single file line through the chapels. Instead, try to start off your day with a visit or as I mentioned above, end your day with one.

Before you enter the Abbey, take the time to enjoy the lesser-known neighbor. Many people head straight for the entrance and fail to even notice St. Margaret's Church, which shares the churchyard. Built in 1523, this tiny church's simple and uncluttered interior will contrast sharply with the Abbey's appearance as an overflowing mausoleum.

Since 1998, the primary entrance to the Abbey has been through the North Transept, which gives a rather disjointed image of the Abbey on first glance. I suggest that you immediately head back toward the West Front entrance so that you can see the Abbey as it was meant to be viewed. From this perspective you can clearly see the majesty of the tallest nave in England (at 102 feet). In front of you is the Tomb of the Unknown Soldier and to your right is a fourteenth-century portrait of Richard II, the oldest known image of a monarch painted from life. As you head back toward the North Transept, also called Statesmen's Aisle, you pass through Musician's Aisle and end up back near the admissions and information desks. From here you move in a mostly single file line through the smaller chapels of Elizabeth I and Innocents Corner and head toward the fantastic display of English perpendicular architecture that makes up the Henry VII Chapel. The elaborately carved choir stalls here are dedicated to the Knights of the Order of the Bath, whose banners and helmets decorate the stalls. Among the notable names buried in this chapel alone are Henry VII and his wife; King George II and Queen Caroline; Henry VIII's only son, Edward VI; and James I and his lover, George Villiers, the first nonroyal to be buried in this part of the Abbey.

As you head along the south aisle of Henry VII's chapel, you can see the tombs of Mary Queen of Scots; Lady Margaret Beaufort, Henry VII's mother; as well as William and Mary, Queen Anne, and Charles II. Walking back toward the nave, you pass the oak throne dating back to 1300 called the Coronation Chair, which has been used in every royal coronation since then. Just beyond this point, tombs and gatework hide much of the Abbey's most famous tomb, the shrine of St. Edward the Confessor. Unfortunately, this tomb, although recently restored, remains closed to the public. The South Transept of Poet's Corner, however, continues to be a favorite of visitors and contains the grave slabs of, among many others, Geoffrey Chaucer, Robert Browning, Alfred Lord Tennyson, Charles Dickens, Rudyard Kipling, and Thomas Hardy, as well as impressive memorials to William Shakespeare and George Frideric Handel. The last person to have been buried here was Sir Laurence Olivier, who died in 1989.

After exploring the Abbey's interior, be sure you find your way out to the cloisters, where the monks worked, studied, and lived. Visiting on a cold day gives you insight into the hearty constitution these early scholars must have had. Today, the cloisters contain a small shop and cafe. English Heritage also runs a small area just off the east cloisters. This includes the Chapter House, which was the original meeting place of the House of Commons until the time of Henry VIII, and the Pyx Chamber, which served as the sacristy and royal treasury of the earliest church. As you head past the Pyx Chamber toward the Little Cloister and College Garden, glance inside to see the two large chests that date from the thirteenth and fifteenth centuries. These contained the coronation regalia, as well as new coin plates and samples and were evidently constructed inside the chamber. If you look at the Pyx Chamber door, you will notice its security consists of enormous locks and a stone sill that still prevents the door from fully opening and thus removing the chests.

Touring Tips   Photography is not permitted in any part of the Abbey at any of the times mentioned above. If you are a camera buff and will not settle for putting postcards in your albums, plan your visit for Wednesday between 6 and 7 p.m. At this special time, admission is half price and amateur photography is permitted, although no tours or audio guides will be available.

Windsor Castle

Type of Attraction: The queen's country house and a mighty fine old castle at that

Location: Windsor, Hertsfordshire, outside London (tube: British Rail to Windsor)

Admission: Adults £10, children age 5–16 £5, under age 5 free; reduced fee on Sunday when St. George's Chapel is closed

Hours: March to October, daily 10 a.m.–5:30 p.m., last admission at 4 p.m.; November to February daily 10 a.m.–4 p.m., last admission at 3 p.m. St. George's Chapel closed Sunday all year

Phone: (0175) 386-8286; *www.royal.gov.uk*

When to Go: Always call first! Windsor Castle is subject to regular, annual, and sudden closures due to various royal ceremonies and events. The month of June is particularly susceptible to this sort of thing. Otherwise, go any time, but show up early before the tour groups.

Special Comments: Limited wheelchair access, lots of walking

Overall Appeal by Age Group:

Pre-school	Grade School	Teens	Young Adults	Over 30	Senior Citizens
★	★★	★★★	★★★★	★★★★	★★★★

Author's Rating: ★★★★

How Much Time to Allow: Half a day, plus time to wander in Windsor

Description and Comments In November 1992, the world saw film footage of Windsor Castle with smoke and flames pouring out from behind its distinctive crenelated keep and foremen running to and fro with priceless paintings and furniture. The fire destroyed over 100 rooms, and it took 5 years to repair and restore the terrible damage done to the ancient castle. Even if you don't normally like gaping at castles, you might make an exception of Windsor, for the restoration of the gutted and devastated castle—burnt to its medieval stone walls, with roofs collapsed—is a marvel in itself, and the exhibition that describes the process is remarkable.

William the Conqueror, who also built the Tower of London, chose the site in Windsor for a fortress to protect London from western invaders. The castle has been continually inhabited for the past 900 years, and many additions—and deletions, too, through other fires—have been made over those years.

It is presently a place of overwhelming splendor and tremendous riches, which might be best summed up by the awesome Queen Mary's Dolls' House. This is big luxury on a small scale: Sir Edward Luytens designed the multistory doll house in the 1920s, and it took three years and a thousand craftsmen and artists to complete it. It has running water, electric lights, a working elevator, actual miniature books, fine art, gorgeous furniture, and even two tiny thrones with crowns on them. It's a miraculous piece of work; you must see it, and do buy the booklet about it to appreciate touches you might not see, such as the embroidered linen or the wine cellar with one-inch bottles of real spirits.

Another, less frivolous attraction at Windsor is St. George's Chapel, started in 1475 and a stunning example of great medieval architecture, with stained-glass windows of unparalleled beauty. Ten monarchs are buried within its precincts, and there are some stupendously crafted sarcophagi. The crests and banners of the Knights of the Order of the Garter are all there, and you get a feel for the ritual and pageantry that have propped up the ruling classes of England for centuries.

Touring Tips Be sure to make time to wander around Windsor; it's a pleasant little town.

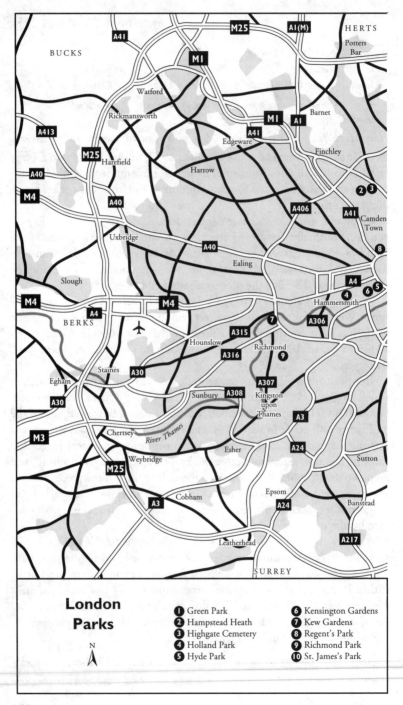

BUCKS

A41

M25

A1(M)

HERTS

Potters
Bar

M1

Watford

Rickmansworth

Barnet

M1

A41

A1

A413

Edgeware

M25 Harefield

Finchley

Harrow

A40

A406

M4

A41

Camden
Town

Uxbridge

A40

2 **3**

8

Ealing

Slough

A4

M4

M4

6 5

A4

Hammersmith

4

BERKS

A4

7

A306

Hounslow

A315

Richmond

Staines

A316

9

Egham

A30

A307

A30

Sunbury A308

Kingston
upon
Thames

M3

Chertsey *River Thames*

A3

Esher

A24

Weybridge

Sutton

M25

Epsom

Banstead

A3

Cobham

A24

Leatherhead

A217

SURREY

London
Parks

N

1 Green Park	**6** Kensington Gardens
2 Hampstead Heath	**7** Kew Gardens
3 Highgate Cemetery	**8** Regent's Park
4 Holland Park	**9** Richmond Park
5 Hyde Park	**10** St. James's Park

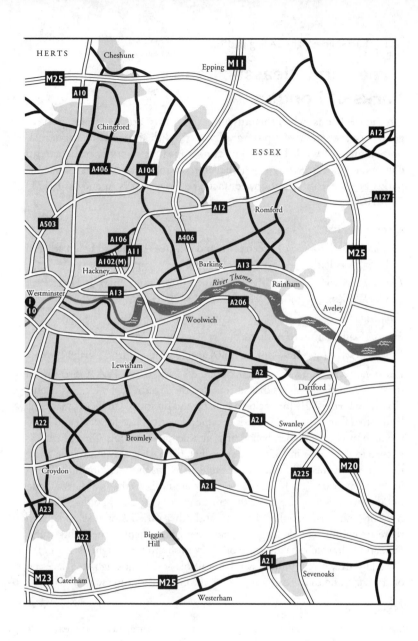

Green and Pleasant Lands: Parks of London

On the weekends, when the museums and tourist attractions are packed, go to the parks and soak up the gratifying English appreciation for nature, both tame and wild. Part of London's appeal as a city is in its careful conservation of greenery—whether in its many squares or its enormous parks. For more information, contact The Royal Parks Agency at (0171) 298-2100.

Green Park

Type of Park: Expanse of green lawn and old trees between Hyde Park and St. James's Park

Location: Between Piccadilly and Constitution Hill, enter at Hyde Park Corner, Zone 9 (tube: Green Park)

Admission: Free

Hours: Daily 5 a.m. to midnight

When to Go: Any time—spring bulbs and blazing autumn foliage

Description and Comments: As in St. James's Park, Green Park was reclaimed from the marshy meadows that surrounded the Tyburn River. Originally purchased by Henry VIII for enclosed grazing and hunting, Charles II made the land into a formal park in 1667. It became a favorite place for duels and highwaymen, military parades, ballooning, and people-watching. Green Park was opened to the public in 1826, and since then people have loved strolling along the east end of the park, admiring the fine mansions there, ending up at Buckingham Palace and St. James's Park. There are no flowerbeds in Green Park, but the crocuses in spring more than make up for that lack, and the 950 magnificent plane, oak, poplar, chestnut, and other varieties of trees to be seen there are completely pleasing. You may rent chairs there in the spring, summer, and fall, which makes a nice break from shopping or sight-seeing in the Piccadilly area. A refreshment stand is available at the Buckingham Palace end of the park, and toilets can be found by the Green Park tube station.

Hampstead Heath

Type of Park: Enormous expanse of country in Greater London area

Location: Hampstead, Zone 1 (tube: Highgate, then take 210 bus to West Gate)

Admission: Free

Hours: Daily 8 a.m. to dusk

When to Go: Any time—spring blossoms and autumn colors

Description and Comments   Though Hampstead Heath is not actually a park per se, it is a most remarkable place, covering a staggering 1,600 acres of country land and offering stunning views over London. There are hills, lakes, wild woods, and landscaped gardens. Hampstead Heath has so much to offer, not the least of which is Kenwood House, a stately home and art museum at the northernmost top of the heath. There are outdoor concerts in the summer on Saturday nights, which are followed by a display of fireworks. People bring blankets and picnic hampers and sit on a hill outside, while those who pay for tickets hunker down a little closer to the music. The Men's and Ladies' Ponds for swimming in the summer are part of a set of lakes along the Highgate border of the heath. There's also a pond for model boats and one for bird-watching. Parliament Hill, across the bicycle track that cuts through the Heath, is the best place in London for viewing the Guy Fawkes' Day fireworks, and in all seasons has spectacular views of London. You can hardly believe you are even near an urban area in many parts of the heath, where mansions on hills look like castles and conspire to make you feel you are in a storybook. You can get a good lunch at the Kenwood outdoor cafe in the summer.

Highgate Cemetery

Type of Park: Wildly overgrown Victorian graveyard

Location: Located on either side of Swains Lane in Highgate; adjacent to Waterlow Park, Zone 1 (tube: Archway, Northern line)

Admission: West Cemetery (access is as part of guided tours only) £3; East Cemetery £1

Hours: West Cemetery: April to September, tours are given Monday–Friday at noon, 2 p.m., 3 p.m., and 4 p.m., Saturday and Sunday from 10 a.m.–4 p.m; October to March, tours are given on weekends only, hourly 11 a.m.–3 p.m. East Cemetery: April to September, daily 10 a.m.–5 p.m., October to March, daily 10 a.m.–4 p.m.

Phone: (0181) 340-1834

When to Go: Any time, although they only allow 20 people on each weekend hourly tour, so if you arrive late you may find yourself wandering the East Cemetery for an hour. Also, the cemetery will close for funerals, so call to check before setting out.

Description and Comments   Opened in 1839, Highgate Cemetery became "the" place to be buried among London's wealthy Victorian families, intellectuals, and artists. One of seven cemeteries designed and opened during this time of continued population explosion, it remains one of the most elaborate and stirring examples of Victorian statuary excess. Overgrown and badly vandalized, the West Cemetery was closed in 1975 and is now diligently cared for by the Friends of Highgate Cemetery. Lush vegetation fills what was once an open, rolling hillside, and volunteers continue to clear overgrown pathways and graves. This extensive foliage creates eerie shadows; this, combined with the cracked and toppled grave markers everywhere, give the cemetery its fabulously gothic atmosphere. Tour guides are well versed on the many famous residents of the cemetery as well as having a number of fascinating anecdotes that explain the elaborate and symbolic Victorian statuary. The cemetery's creepiest section includes the Egyptian Avenue and the Terrace Catacombs.

The East Cemetery allows you to wander on your own, but holds a less eerie charm. Still, it is nice to be able linger where you will and get up close to the graves, some of which contain the most interesting epitaphs. There is a £2 "camera permit fee" for those interested in capturing the morose views. It's best to go early in the day, hopefully on a day containing some sun, as the shadowy effects can create fantastic photographic images.

Holland Park

Type of Park: A 54-acre landscaped marvel with Japanese garden and white peacocks

Location: Holland Park, between Kensington and Shepherd's Bush, Zone 13 (tube: Holland Park Avenue (10-minute walk to park) or Kensington High Street and take westbound buses 9, 10, 27, 28, 31, or 49)

Admission: Free

Hours: Daily 7:30 a.m. to dusk

When to Go: Any time—camellias, roses, irises, and blossoms in spring; dahlias in summer; autumn leaves

Description and Comments   Holland Park once housed the magnificent Holland House, more castle than mansion, where the literati of the early nineteenth century used to flock to mix with the politicians and aristocrats of the day. The house was bombed during World War II, but what remains are fascinating monuments to the past: the surviving wings of Holland House, one now a youth hostel, the wrought-iron gates that formed the entrance to the estate, the Orangery, the ice house from the 1770s, the old stables, and the many walks and enclosures that make up Holland Park.

There is a wonderful variety of flora and fauna here, thanks to Lord Holland—a venerable Victorian gentleman—and his great interest in planting and wildlife. He can be seen as styled by sculptor G. F. Watts, surveying his land, occasionally providing a roosting place for some of the 60 wild bird species that have been spotted in the park. One feature he never saw, which was created in 1991, is the Kyoto Garden, a perfect Japanese garden. The white peacocks gather in the Yucca Lawn, along with numerous rabbits. There is an adventure playground in the park that is a must-do for families with young children.

Hyde Park

Type of Park: Former hunting ground of Henry VIII, now a 350-acre people's park with expansive lawns, sporting activities, concerts, and rallies

Location: Bordered by Park Lane, Knightsbridge, and Bayswater Road, Zone 10 (tube: Hyde Park Corner)

Admission: Free

Hours: Daily dawn to dusk

When to Go: Any time—roses in summer, crocuses and daffodils in spring, fall foliage in autumn, atmospheric bare trees in winter

Description and Comments   During the dissolution of the monasteries in 1536, Henry VIII grabbed a hunk of land from the manor of Hyde and enclosed it for his hunting pleasure. James I opened the park to aristocrats, who took the air daily, a habit that persisted into the early twentieth century, with Rotten Row—originally Route du Roi, king's road—resounding with the beating of hooves and the chatter of the idle classes. Once, Kensington Gardens was part of Hyde Park—and is still separated only by a roadway—but in the mid-1700s, Queen Caroline appropriated 200 acres to make suitable gardens for Kensington Palace.

Hyde Park today is a wonderful escape from the high-decibel traffic noise of Park Lane, Knightsbridge, and Bayswater. One enters the park from any one of those streets, and within minutes of walking toward the Serpentine, the watery heart of the park, a delightful quiet descends. There's so much to do in Hyde Park: There are biking and inline skating paths through and around the edge of the park (do not bicycle on any paths not marked with the outline of a bike); there are cricket and soccer pitches, there are tennis courts, paddle- and rowboats, and one can even ride through Rotten Row on horseback. During the warm months, there are numerous places to rent lawn chairs, and you can get a bite to eat at the Lido or the cafeteria at the east end of the Serpentine. The Rose Walk by Hyde Park Corner is magnificent in June, and the Italian Piazza, with fountains and statues by the Bayswater side, is wonderful at all times. Speaker's Corner, at the northeast of the park, is hopping on Sunday, often featuring born-again Christians yelling at us to repent, no longer on soapboxes, but on little stepladders or overturned buckets. The queen's guards exercise their horses and rehearse their ceremonies in Hyde Park, on the south by Prince's Gate. It's an astonishing thing to be walking through the park and suddenly be set upon by a regiment of sword-waving, plume-hatted horsemen. Hyde Park in sunlight is the best place to be in London.

If you want to get from South Kensington to Piccadilly, or from Knightsbridge to Marble Arch, do yourself a favor and walk through Hyde Park.

Kensington Gardens

Type of Park: Gardens and walkways, fountains, and statues, with a palace as well

Location: Kensington Gore, Zone 13 (tube: Kensington High Street)

Admission: Free

Hours: Daily dawn to dusk

When to Go: Any time, especially when Kensington Palace and the Orangery are open. In spring and summer there is the flower walk; great fall foliage

Description and Comments   Kensington Palace will probably be forever associated with the extraordinary event of public mourning for Princess Diana, when in the days after her death in Paris, people arrived and laid flowers in front of the palace that was her home. By week's end there was a sea of blooms and cellophane in front of the gates, and the trees nearby were festooned with pictures, poems, and flowers, and candles stood burning everywhere. We will probably never again see such a phenomenon, which no doubt is a source of great relief to the neighbors, who banded together to thwart a memorial garden to Diana that threatened to forever disturb the tranquility of these environs.

By the side of the palace is a lovely sunken garden that can be looked at, but not entered. Before the Orangery, which is a good place for tea, are topiary trees that recall the Restoration; and the Round Pond on which children have sailed toy boats for generations brings Mary Poppins vividly to mind. By the bridge over the Sepentine is a statue of Peter Pan; author J. M. Barrie lived right by the park and the island in the middle of the lake is clearly the model for the Island of the Lost Boys.

The Broad Walk is good for inline skating, as is the area in front of the Albert Memorial. And if you're in the mood for art, the Serpentine Gallery has changing exhibits and a good bookshop.

Kew Gardens (The Royal Botanic Gardens)

Type of Park: Botanical extravaganza with 30,000 different species of plants and flowers planted over 300 acres filled with follies, water features, and conservatories

Location: Southwest London on the Thames, Zone 12 (tube: Kew Gardens)

Admission: Adults £5, children age 5–16 £2.50, under age 5 free, family ticket £13

Hours: Daily 9:30 p.m.–5:30 in winter, open later in summer

When to Go: Any time of the year, although summer is best to get your money's worth

Description and Comments The Royal Botanical Gardens at Kew were begun in the eighteenth century, when wealthy and royal folks began to move out of smelly, crowded London. The Botanical Gardens, originally developed for the pleasure of the royal family, intersected nicely with the global travels of adventurers such as Captain Cook, who brought home never-before-seen specimens of plant life, such as the geranium. The gardens have gone from strength to strength since then as one of the world's most remarkable and serious centers of botanical research.

The enormous glass Palm House is a treasure trove of exotic tropical plants, with two levels on which to wander through the huge fronds and steamy atmosphere. There's a tropical aquarium in the basement that furthers the impression of being in a foreign clime. The Water Lily House is also interesting, and a testament to the wide-ranging journeys of the English explorers. The Temperate House is an even more impressive structure than the Palm House, twice as large, and containing plants from each and every continent, some of which were planted at Kew in the middle of the nineteenth century.

There are identifying plaques on the trees and signs on the flower beds, so that a visit to Kew can be a real education in botany. Two art galleries, Kew Palace, a Japanese pagoda, and numerous follies and conservatories make Kew an outing at which you can easily spend the whole day. There are a few cafes to choose from, and believe me, you'll need refreshment after a long day at plant-viewing. It's a shame that Kew is right in the path of Heathrow—the impression of stepping back in time is continually spoiled by the noise of overhead jets.

Regent's Park

Type of Park: Elegant, Nash-designed playground of 490 acres with 6,000 trees

Location: Marylebone, at end of Baker Street, Zone 3 (tube: Baker Street)

Admission: Free

Hours: Daily 5 a.m. to dusk

When to Go: Any time, flower gardens in spring and summer, autumn leaves

Description and Comments   Named for George IV, when he was mad King George's understudy monarch, Regent's Park was designed by John Nash as part of the grand plan for a garden city of terraced mansions with country-like views. Started in 1811, the scheme ultimately failed, with only a portion of the terrace houses sold (and those were said to be of substandard quality). However, in 1835, the park was flourishing and was opened to the public. Although the neighborhood may not have turned out as Nash planned, it's still gorgeous, and few can resist the grace and beauty of the classically inspired white mansions of Cumberland Terrace that look out on the magnificent landscape.

Within the park you will find the home of the American ambassador, donated by the heiress Barbara Hutton; a boating lake with ornamental bridges and an island; a lake by Queen Mary's Rose Gardens, which are quite extraordinary and include a waterfall and an open-air theater; a number of lodges; a mosque; Regent's Canal; and of course, the London Zoo. In the summer there are concerts on the Bandstand and plays at the theater, bird-watching walks, puppet shows, and outdoor refreshments. The Royal Horse Artillery can be seen occasionally on Cumberland Green. Primrose Hill, north of the zoo, is not officially part of Regent's Park, but can be accessed easily from there, and provides a lovely view of all London.

Richmond Park

Type of Park: London's largest park, featuring herds of deer and ancient oak trees

Location: Southwest London, Zone 12 (tube: Richmond Station, then take buses 72, 265, 371, or 415)

Admission: Free

Hours: Daily 7 a.m. to dusk

When to Go: Any time

Description and Comments   Richmond Park is a gargantuan 2,470-acre preserve in which 400 fallow deer and 250 red deer live and graze. It is an extraordinary place, a piece of rolling countryside a stone's thrown (seven miles from Charing Cross) from the center of a major metropolitan city, with wildlife still roaming freely. Richmond had its first royal connections when Henry VII rebuilt a fine old palace on the Thames; his granddaughter Elizabeth I died at the palace. In 1625, surrounding lands were seized and walled to give King Charles I a country asylum from the plague. His wall created much ill will among the neighbors, who had been used to grazing their animals on the land and using the common roads. The king tried to compensate by allowing foot traffic through the park and permitting the local poor to gather deadwood for their hearth fires. After the Civil War, the House of Commons voted to leave the park as undeveloped land, and so it has remained ever since. There were various skirmishes between the royals and the public over right of access, which were put to rest on the death of the last royal ranger, Edward VII in 1910. Today, Richmond Park is a testament to the admirable environmental protectionism of the British and provides for the visitor a wonderfully unchanged picture of a medieval hunting ground.

Be aware that the deer are not completely harmless and can be aggressive if they are bothered while tending young or during rutting season. There are refreshments found in the Pembroke Lodge Cafeteria from April through October, from 10 a.m. to 5:30 p.m. (7 p.m. on weekends). White Lodge houses the Royal Ballet School. There are a number of seasonal events that take place in Richmond Park — check a newspaper or *Time Out* to see when, what, and where. Pembroke Lodge often stages lunchtime concerts. The best time to see the wonders of Richmond Park may be during the height of the fall leaf change: The colors are incomparably fine.

St. James's Park

Type of Park: Oldest royal park in London, a must-see for sight-seers

Location: East of Buckingham Palace's gates, Zone 9 (tube: St. James's Park)

Admission: Free

Hours: Daily 5 a.m.–midnight

When to Go: Any time is excellent, but in summer it is the most floral, and there are concerts on the bandstand between May and August

Description and Comments St. James is certainly London's most royal of all parks, lying as it does between Buckingham and St. James's Palaces. There is a view from Buckingham Palace and from the bridge in the middle of the lake that is just magical — it looks like our fondest fantasy of an enchanted fairy-tale kingdom, with the turrets and steeples of Whitehall in the distance. St. James is the place to go see birds; the famous pelicans are there, as well as a huge assortment of unusual feathered friends. The Ornithological Society of London donated some birds in 1837 and started this particular feature of this beautiful park.

A leper hospital, called St. James, was erected here in the 1400s. The Tyburn River flowed through this area, so the land was marshy and unsuitable for much more than hunting until King James I drained and planted the area as a pleasure garden, filling it with pelicans and other rara avis. He also had an exotic menagerie there, with crocodiles and elephants, for his court's entertainment. When Charles II returned from exile in France, he redid the park in a more formal, French manner, and opened St. James's

Park to the public. It was embraced enthusiastically and began its long life as a favorite spot for Londoners to meet and stroll—although it did have its darker days when people hung laundry there, muggers prowled the bushes, and prostitutes conducted business. Its appeal was upgraded when George IV rebuilt Buckingham House to be a royal palace and had John Nash make the park a more beautiful and natural-looking place.

There is a children's playground on the southwest corner of the park, and The Cake House (open daily from 9:30 a.m. to 5:30 p.m.) is in the east end, north of the lake. There are concerts at the bandstand in summer, and the birds are there all year to be admired. Green-and-white striped deck chairs can be rented on an hourly basis between April and September.

Greenwich

In 1863, American author Nathaniel Hawthorne described the quiet town of Greenwich as "beautiful,—a spot where the art of man has conspired with Nature." No doubt he was thinking how the rolling hills of Greenwich Park create a glorious backdrop for Christopher Wren's splendid **Royal Naval College** and Inigo Jones's equally noble **Queen's House,** while Wren's other Greenwich project, the **Royal Observatory,** sits serenely on the park's highest hill. The streets of Greenwich are just perfect for strolling; whether you are wandering down historic Croom's Hill or over past St. Alfrege's near the town center, the area has retained much of its cozy village atmosphere. Weekends bring craft and antiques lovers of all kinds converging on the Greenwich Market or enjoying a boat ride on the Thames.

Like London, Greenwich is steeped in royal history. The park dates from 1433, and the Palace of Placentia once graced the riverside where the Royal Naval College now stands. Henry VIII and all three of his children, Mary I, Elizabeth I, and Edward IV were born here. In 1616, Jones began the Queen's House as a Palladian country home at the bottom of the park for Charles II's wife, Henrietta Maria; Wren followed this up with the hilltop Observatory and the Naval College, which elegantly frames the Queen's House today. With the fast approach of the year 2000, Greenwich has also begun to take on a new role as the starting point for the world's millennium celebrations. Just north of the town's center, the colossal Millennium Dome is quickly nearing completion and promises a diverse collection of exhibits and attractions with which to usher in the future.

Getting There

Located only a few miles downriver from London, Greenwich is easy to reach and makes a delightful day trip for visitors. The town center provides a wide variety of book, art, and nautical shops as well as a diverse selection of restaurants from Vietnamese to Mexican to good old English pub food. On weekends, the Greenwich Market is teeming with craft stalls and, combined with the nearby flea market and secondhand book market, can allow for hours of browsing.

There are three primary means by which you can arrive in Greenwich. A ten-minute train ride from Charing Cross will get you there with no more effort than that required to obtain a Zone 1–2 travel card. Although not a particularly scenic ride, it is the fastest. You can alight at Maze Hill Station, which places you just east of Greenwich Park, or at Greenwich Station, just west of the town center. Call National Rail Inquiries (phone (0345) 484-950) for train schedules. For a more enjoyable view you might opt to catch the Docklands Light Railway (DLR), a fully automated and electric overland tram car type of transport that leaves from Bank Street or Tower Hill. The trip is about 20 minutes from either station and in the summer includes a recording that guides you through the wharfs and docks of London's East End. In 1999, construction began on the DLR to extend its tracks, bringing you directly to Greenwich Pier. By the time you read this, all work should be completed. If you would like to confirm this however, you can call DLR at (0171) 363-9700. By far, the most picturesque journey comes from a guided riverboat ride down the Thames, past views of St. Paul's Cathedral, Tower Bridge, and the Docklands. Boats leave from Westminster, Charing Cross, and Tower Pier for Greenwich approximately every 45 minutes and take 40 minutes to an hour, depending on where you embark. Enquiries can be made by calling (0171) 930-4097 or (0171) 987-1185.

Finally, you can call the Greenwich Tourist Information Center at (0181) 858-6376, write them, or stop by their location at 46 Greenwich Church St., London SE10 9BL, for information on guided tours in Greenwich, special events, or any additional information you may need.

Part Ten
Children's London

London with Children

London is a wonderful city for children, even jet-lagged ones who can't quite figure out when to go to sleep. Before you go to London, get out some nursery rhymes, fairy tales, or Dickens (depending on the age of your children), and introduce them to the wonders of London in letters. It will make it that much more exciting when you get here. Rent some good kid's London's movies: *The Parent Trap, 101 Dalmations* (not the animated one), *Oliver!, Mary Poppins, A Little Princess* (Shirley Temple version), *The Prince and the Pauper, A Christmas Carol* (the Muppets version is good, less scary than the old Alistair Syms one), and *The Princess Carabou* are just a few that can get them thinking about and looking at London. A contributor to this book, Denise Knestaut, has devised an excellent Web site for her sixth-grade students in New Jersey that includes photos of major attractions, history, a travelogue, and links to the Museum of London and the Tower of London. Take your kids for a look at *web.ukonline.co.uk/D.Knestautindex.html;* It's entitled "An American Teacher in London."

London has an enormous selection of attractions for children of all ages. The museums are getting more interactive and attention-grabbing all the time. Even the staid old Victoria and Albert now features a fun cart on weekends to keep the kids busy, entertained, and actually learning something about the wonderful collection. Parents will enjoy the kids' attractions as much as the children will. Just maybe, if you give the kids a chance, they will find something great in the places that cater to a more mature palate, such as the National Portrait Gallery or the Globe Theatre. But don't count on it with the really little ones. With them it's just crowd control and riding on buses; they love the double deckers.

A "London Book"

A great idea to really get the kids paying attention and having fun is to start a "London book" before you even leave. Pick out a blank book, big enough to paste lots of things in, and write down the itinerary, paste in pictures of planes, get the stewardess to sign it, and so on. Then, everywhere you go, you can collect stubs and pamphlets and take plenty of photos. Get film developed at one- hour labs, and spend the evening helping with the scrapbook. Drawings, poems, thoughts, a leaf from Holland Park, a feather from the Serpentine—all these things can make a beautiful scrapbook that children will always love to look through. Get a disposable camera for your child to take his or her own photos; you'll be surprised at how much more they'll go in for sight-seeing when it has such a personal purpose.

Planning and Touring Tips

Here are a few ideas to bear in mind when planning a vacation with the little and not-so-little ones:

Age Although the wonderful park playgrounds and certain tourist attractions of London have much to offer toddlers and preschoolers, the bulk of London's attractions are generally oriented to older kids and adults. Children should be a fairly mature six years old to get the most out of popular attractions such as the Imperial War Museum, the HMS *Belfast*, possibly even the Tower of London, and a year or two older to get much out of the art museums, cathedrals, and palaces that London has in such grand abundance.

Time of Year to Visit If there is any way to swing it, avoid the crowded summer months. Try to go in late September through November or early April through mid-June. If you have children of varying ages and your school-age kids are good students, consider taking the older ones out of school so you can visit during the less expensive, less congested off-season. Arrange special study assignments relating to the many educational aspects of London. If your school-age children are not great students and cannot afford to miss any school, take your vacation as soon as the school year ends in June.

Building Naps and Rest into Your Itinerary London is huge and offers more attractions than you can possibly see in a whole week, so definitely don't try to see everything in one day. Tour in the early morning and return to your hotel midday for lunch and a nap. Go back and visit more attractions in the late afternoon and early evening; or take a bus tour that is easier on the legs. Don't pooh-pooh jet-lag; the children seem to suffer from it less than the adults, but they are definitely thrown off-kilter by the time change. Try to get them on the right time by getting plenty of sunlight and not letting them nap too long in the day.

Where to Stay   The best area to stay in when you're carting kids around is near a park—Hyde, Holland, or Kensington Gardens are good, and there are lots of inexpensive hotels around Paddington, which is an easy walk to the park. Kids who will complain about tired feet and hunger will perk up amazingly when they see a swing set, have some room to kick a soccer ball around, or can watch horses ride by. It's important to get small children off the tourist trail for a few hours to rest and recuperate. Neglecting to relax and unwind is the best way to get the whole family in a snit and ruin the day.

With small children, you will be glad to have planned ahead. Make sure you get a hotel within a few minutes' walk to a tube station. Naps and relief from the frenetic pace of touring London are indispensable. Even if you do get some good downtime in a park, there is no true substitute for returning to the familiarity and security of your own hotel for the little ones. Children too large to sleep in a stroller will relax and revive better if you get them back to your room.

Another factor in choosing a hotel is whether or not it has a swimming pool. A lot of visitors to London assume that, like those in so many American destinations, London hotels automatically come with a pool. Nothing could be further from the truth. There are a few expensive ones that do; more to the point, there are many hotels that can steer you to a public pool or who have some arrangement with a health club. Call ahead to find out if there are any age restrictions on swimming. A swimming pool can be a lifesaver for both you and your kids, keeping you all happily busy and healthily exercising for hours. It's also great for dealing with jet-lag.

Stay Loose   As every parent has discovered by day three of their first baby's life, flexibility is everything in parenting, and that goes double for sight-seeing with children. Remember that having fun is not necessarily the same as seeing everything. When you and your children start getting tired and irritable, call a time-out and regroup. Trust your instincts. What would really feel best right now? Another museum, a rest break with some ice cream, or going back to the room for a nap? The way to have a great vacation is to put the emphasis on being happy and having a good time, whatever that takes. You do not have to meet a quota for experiencing every museum or attraction, seeing every neighborhood and monument, or following every suggestion in the book. London has been here for a long time, and it's not going anywhere. Your kids' childhood, on the other hand, is a flash of lightning. Make sure their memories of London are happy ones, and they'll want to come back when they're grown up.

All for One and One for All   When you're traveling en famille, you are a moving unit made up of many differing tastes, abilities, and interests. It's inevitable that somebody is going to run out of steam first; when they do, the whole family will be affected. Sometimes a cold drink and a rest break will recharge the flagging member. Sometimes, however, you just have to strap on your parachute and bail out. Pushing the tired or discontented beyond their capacity is like driving on a flat tire: It may get you a few more miles down the road, but you will be sorry in the long run. Accept that energy levels vary among individuals and be prepared to respond to small children or other members of your group who poop out. Try not to let your own disappointment hurt the tired one's feelings. Maybe you can take turns with the other grown-up, if there is one with you, in bringing the walking wounded back to the hotel, so that one of you can continue sight-seeing.

Setting Limits and Making Plans   The best way to avoid arguments and disappointments is to develop a game plan before you go. Establish some general guidelines for each day and try to get everybody excited about the plans. Be sure to include:

1. Wake-up time and breakfast plans.
2. What time you need to depart for the part of London you plan to explore.
3. What you need to take with you.
4. A policy for splitting the group up or for staying together.
5. A plan for what to do if the group gets separated or someone is lost.
6. How long you intend to tour in the morning and what you want to see, including fall-back plans in the event an attraction is too crowded.
7. A policy on what you can afford for snacks, lunch, and refreshments. This is *very* important in London, the most expensive of cities.
8. A target time for returning to your hotel for a rest.
9. What time you will return to touring London and how late you will stay.
10. Plans for dinner.
11. A policy for shopping and buying souvenirs, including who pays (parents or kids).

Be Flexible   Having a game plan does not mean forgoing spontaneity or sticking rigidly to the itinerary. Once again, listen to your intuition. Alter the plan if the situation warrants. Be prepared to roll with the punches.

Rain, Sunburn, and Dehydration   London's weather is changeable. Although it's not often terribly hot, it can get quite warm in the sun, and you can get a beauty of a sunburn. Carry a small bottle of sunscreen, or smear it on before you go out. Remember a bottle of water to rehydrate the happy campers. Rain is the biggest surprise in London: You never know when it's going to come, but chances are it will, if only for a sprinkle. The best and lightest protection is a plastic rain poncho; you can carry a few and not have as much weight or bulk as with a couple of umbrellas.

Blisters   Blisters and sore feet are common for visitors of all ages, so wear comfortable, well-broken-in shoes and two pairs of thin socks (preferable to one pair of thick socks). If you or your children are unusually suscepti-ble to blisters, carry some precut Moleskin bandages; they offer the best pos-sible protection and won't sweat off. When you feel a hot spot, stop, air out your foot, and place a Moleskin over the area before a blister forms. You'll probably find some in London in a chemist's shop under a Dr. Scholl's dis-play, but bring some with you just in case. Sometimes small children won't tell their parents about a developing blister until it's too late. Check out your preschooler's feet a couple of times a day—this penny's worth of preven-tion will be worth many pounds of cure to you and them.

Health and Medical Care   If you have a child who requires medication, pack plenty and bring it on the plane in a carry-on bag. A bottle of liquid Dramamine will come in handy to fight off motion sickness, which can affect kids who are normally fine in a car but may get sick in a plane, train, or boat.

A small first-aid kit, available at most pharmacies, will handle most minor cuts, scrapes, and splinters and is easy to pack. Grown-up and children's-strength aspirin or Tylenol, a thermometer, cough syrup, baby wipes, a plas-tic spoon, a nightlight, and pacifiers will round out a small kit of health-related items for people traveling with children or infants. Again, bring it from home: It's much more expensive to get these items in London.

If You Become Separated   Before venturing out of your hotel room, sit down with your kids and discuss what they should do if they get separated from you while touring a museum or attraction. Tell them to find a uni-formed guard and ask for help. Point out that the main entrance of most London attractions has an information desk where they should go if they temporarily get separated.

It's not a bad idea to dress the smaller kids in distinctive colors so you can find them with a quick scanning. It is also considered prudent to sew a label into each child's shirt indicating his or her name, your name, and the name of your hotel. The same thing can be accomplished less elegantly by writing the information on a strip of masking tape: Hotel security professionals suggest that the information be printed in small letters and that the tape be affixed to the outside of the child's shirt five inches or so below the armpit.

Rainy Days   As you know, London is a pretty rainy place—certainly not as bad as its reputation (Rome actually has more inches per year), but it does come down. Museums and galleries are obvious solutions to the rainy-day blues; that old stand-by, the movies, is a good place to kick back. Whiteley's has an indoor ice-skating rink, and there are a few paint-your-own-pottery places that kids just love—see "Activities" below for names and numbers. You have to wait a day or two to pick up your finished pieces, so ask ahead how long it will take to fire your kids' work. There's also brass rubbing at St. Martin–in-the-Fields, a cheaper option, and the kids can bring them home on the spot. Look in *Time Out* under children's events— there may be a puppet show or story-time reading where you can stay dry. You can also get *Kids Out,* published monthly, for some bright ideas. There's a phone number, Kidsline (0171) 222-8070, that will give you details of events, shows, museums, attractions, and workshops for kids. Also, the London Tourist Board has a 24-hour recorded service of what's on for children in London, phone (0839) 123-404 or (0839) 123-436.

The lists below are very general; obviously some kids will be of a more appropriate age to enjoy some attractions than others. I've left out some of the attractions that one can see in any city, such as zoos, arcades, and amusement parks.

Please note the museums that charge have some free admission hours in the late afternoon—you'll only get an hour and a half, but that's about all many kids can take, and the savings are well worth it. These include the London, Victoria and Albert, Imperial War, Natural History, and Science museums.

The Top 10 Most Popular Sights for Children

1. Natural History Museum
2. Hampton Court Palace
3. Museum of London
4. Theatre Museum
5. Museum of the Moving Image
6. HMS *Belfast*
7. Tower of London
8. London Transport Museum
9. Science Museum
10. London Aquarium (toddlers and preschoolers are very entertained here, older ones might prefer something more Londonesque)

The Top 10 Least Popular Sights for Children

1. Queen's Gallery
2. Kenwood House
3. Design Museum
4. Buckingham Palace
5. Dickens' House
6. Parliament
7. Portobello Road
8. The Clink
9. Dr. Johnson's House
10. The Tate

Also See

- Imperial War Museum
- Madame Tussaud's and the London Planetarium
- The Rock Circus
- The London Balloon
- The Bank of England Museum
- London Dungeon (for gore-loving adolescents)
- All the military museums for children of that bent: Cabinet War Rooms, Imperial War Museum, Guards Museum, National Army Museum

Services for Families

RENTING EQUIPMENT

Chelsea Baby Hire, phone (0181) 540-8830; and **Nappy Express,** phone (0181) 361-4040, rent cribs, high chairs, double-strollers, or buggies, as they're known here.

CHILD CARE

With **Childminders,** phone (0171) 935-3000, you pay a joining fee, then an hourly rate. **Universal Aunts,** phone (0171) 386-5900, can deal with any domestic needs or crisis, like a good auntie should. **Hopes and Dreams,** EC1, phone (0171) 833-9388, is an alternative to agency baby-sitters—it's a five-star hotel for kids, complete with organic food and big fun. Big prices, too. **Pippa Pop-Ins Excursions and Activities**, phone (0171) 385-2458, is another children's hotel, where kids stay while the parents play (£100 a night).

Activities

PAINT YOUR OWN POTTERY

Kids can practice their creative skills at **Art 4 Fun,** W4, phone (0181) 994-4100, in the Creative Café. It serves food, and you can paint many different things. Also try **Bridgewater Pottery Café,** 735 Fulham Rd., SW6, phone (0171) 736-2157.

BRASS RUBBINGS

London Brass Rubbing Centre, St. Martin–in-the-Fields, Trafalgar Square, WC2, phone (0171) 481-2928, offers a wonderful treat for kids age six and up—they can make their own souvenirs. **All-Hallows-By-The-Tower,** Byward Street, EC3, phone (0171) 481-2928, is a little less expensive than St. Martin–in-the-Fields, but does not have so many choices of brasses.

SKATING

Queen's Ice-Skating Rink, 17 Queenway, W2, phone (0171) 229-0172, is a big ice skating rink. Minimum age is three years.

BOOKSTORES

Call the following to check on storytelling performances: **Books Etc.,** Whiteleys Center, W2, phone (0171) 229-3865, and **Children's Book Centre,** 237 Kensington High St., W8, phone (0171) 937-7497.

CLOTHING

Shopping may not be high on a kid's list of activities, but adults may not be able to resist some of the French- and English-made clothing you can get here. You'd be wise to get kids' clothing in the United States, but if you're looking for special items, check **Tibou,** 19 Harrington Rd., SW7, phone (0171) 581-3432, **Trotters**, 34 King's Rd., SW3, phone (0171) 259-9620, and **Young England,** 47 Elizabeth St., SW1, phone (0171) 259-9003.

PLAYGROUNDS

Battersea Park, SW11. All over fun, plus a zoo.

Coram Fields, WC1. Famous playground in which adults may not enter without an accompanying child—and they mean it. Animals on view.

Holland Park, W8. Multilevel adventure playground, with an area for kids under age eight. Peacocks, too!

Hyde Park, east of Princes Gate, SW1. Good swings and play stuff as well as paddle-boats in summer and Peter Pan all year.

Kensington Gardens, W8. Playground at end of Broad Walk and remote control model boats to watch in the Round Pond.

St. James's Park, SW1. Smallish playground by Birdcage Walk, plenty of pelicans and other birds to watch—3 p.m. feeding of pelicans is very popular.

THEATERS

Children's theaters feature plays of puppetry and fairy tales and other good things. Call the following theaters for schedules: **Little Angel Theatre,** 14 Dagmar Passage, Cross Street, N1, phone (0171) 226-1787; **Polka Theatre for Children,** 240 The Broadway, Wimbledon, SW19, phone (0181) 543-4888; and **Unicorn Theatre,** 6-7 Great Newport St., WC2, phone (0171) 836-3334.

TOYS

Daisy & Tom's, 81 King's Rd., Chelsea, SW3, phone (0171) 352-5000, is a great kids' store with toys, books, soda bar, carousel, and a very cool haircutting salon. **Davenport's Magic Shop,** 7 Charing Cross Underground Concourse, Strand, WC2, phone (0171) 836-0408, is still going strong after

100 years of selling magic. **Hamleys,** 188-96 Regent St., W1, phone (0171) 734-3161, has seven floors, which makes it the largest toy store in the world. You've been warned. **Harrods,** Knightsbridge, SW1, phone (0171) 730-1234, has a remarkable selection of dolls, but watch that wallet. **Tridias,** 25 Bute St., South Kensington, SW7, phone (0171) 584-2330, sell lots of interesting toys and small, inexpensive gimcracks.

TRANSPORTATION

The **Six 2 16 Car Club,** "London's First Children's Car Service," phone (0181) 830-2255, is really for kids who travel alone back and forth to school, but they do have a station wagon that can take your brood and you around London. The **Asquith Limousine,** phone (0181) 230-5412, is a 1930s classic cab, delightful to tour in, fun for the kids.

Where to Eat

Here are some kid-friendly places to eat:

Capitol Radio Café, Leicester Square, WC2, phone (0171) 484-8888, is attached to the big pop radio station in happening Leicester Square.

The Collection, 264 Brompton Rd., SW3, phone (0171) 225-1212, has a special Sunday brunch that pleases everyone. On Sunday morning the posh eatery features kids toys and a Norton-trained nanny to watch the sprites play while you eat in peace and splendor.

Daisy & Tom Soda Bar, 181 King's Rd., SW3, phone (0171) 352-5000, located in the kid's toy, book, and clothing store, has a Soda Bar featuring sandwiches and sundaes; it even has Beechnut natural baby food on hand.

Football Football, 57-60 Haymarket, SW1, phone (0171) 930-9970, is for the rabid soccer fan.

Luna Nuova, 22 Shorts Gardens, WC2, phone (0171) 836-4110, is a pizzeria where kids can make their own pizzas at a certain time. Sundays they have an entertainer. Call ahead.

Smollensky's Balloon, 1 Dover St., W1, phone (0171) 491-1199, is the perfect place for the American kid: puppet shows, magic tricks, everything to get a kid through the chore of eating. Book ahead. **Smollensky's on the Strand,** 105 The Strand, WC2, phone (0171) 497-2101, is also big fun: There's a special play area for the kids and a magic show.

Good Deals for Kids

Now here's a novel idea: free or reduced-price meals for kids. Call for details—it only applies on certain days, and it's wise to book ahead. The following restaurants offer such deals: **Big Easy**, 332-4 King's Rd., SW3, phone (0171) 352-40711, American crab shack; **El Metro,** 10-12 Effie Rd., SW6, phone (0171) 384-1264; **Meson Bilbao,** 33 Malvern Rd., NW6, phone (0171) 328-1744, Spanish cuisine; **Sahara,** 1 Devonshire St., W1, phone (0171) 436-4547, Lebanese food.

Part Eleven

Dining in London

Ten years ago, if you had said you were going to London for the food, your friends would have advised a long period of rest and perhaps a visit to your doctor. The idea simply seemed crazy. Food in London, and all of the United Kingdom, was famous for its brutally unyielding awfulness.

To say that things have changed is to make a gross understatement. London now boasts two restaurants with three Michelin stars (the highest accolade restaurateurs can receive) and has been described as one of the gastronomic capitals of the world. Well, you can argue that kind of point endlessly, and making comparisons with other cities is an academic exercise. But there's no denying that you can now eat better in London than at any time since the Romans arrived.

Asian and South Asian cuisines have always been a strong point in London, and they remain so—but they're even better now, especially Indian cooking. There's a bigger range than ever before, with more regional variety and a general emphasis on fresh ingredients cooked to order. The same can be said of Chinese food, another traditional area of strength. It's true also of French and Italian cooking. Even old-fashioned British food is taken with the greatest seriousness, again at every price level.

But if there's anything special about London's food at the moment, it's a phenomenon that's various called modern British, or (the term used here) modern European cooking. Nearly everyone who pays attention to gastronomic trends will use some version of this term. Defining it precisely . . . well, that's another matter. But here's a rough working definition: classic European techniques (especially French and Italian) applied to top-quality ingredients that may—but don't necessarily—come from any corner of the globe.

London is well suited to the development of this kind of eclecticism in cooking. The ingredients are there because of its proximity to Europe and longtime connections with Asia, and a widely traveled customer base provides a serious demand for good cooking. Some of the best chefs exploit their position with amazing results. Some borrow widely from Asia and the Americas, with the results bordering on so-called fusion cooking. Some remain deliberately French and Italian in orientation, whereas others emphasize the British source of ingredients and inspirations. This is the most interesting food being cooked in London now, and restaurants of this type feature prominently in these listings.

If eating out in London is better than ever, you should also be warned of the downside: It's *expensive*. Expensive even for Londoners, and especially expensive for Americans traveling with the dollar weak against the pound sterling. It is nearly impossible to find a good three-course meal with a bottle of wine for under £25 a head, and even fairly basic restaurants have an annoying tendency to cost twice that amount if you drink more than the house wine. We wish it weren't so, but there's nothing to be done unless exchange rates and pricing policies change.

In the meantime, those who seek high quality at low prices should pay special attention to the list of gastropubs in the "More Recommendations" section. These are old-fashioned pubs, refurbished in a simple style, that place the greatest emphasis on good food rather than beer and crisps (potato chips). The top gastropubs are usually off the beaten track (one reason they can charge lower prices), but you should seek them out if you don't mind a bit of extra traveling. They are one of London's best bets for budget eating in totally relaxed surroundings.

At the other restaurants, there are ways to cut costs. Lunch is likely to be considerably cheaper than dinner, and some places have pre- or post-theater offers with limited choice and lower prices. With drinks making up a large part of many bills, look for house wines or order by the glass if that's all you want. And don't feel obliged to order a bottle of water (almost always marked up heavily) if tap water will please you just as well. If you're traveling with children but don't see a children's menu, ask if they will do a child-size portion—many good restaurants will oblige.

The other big complaint about London restaurants is the quality of service, and there's a lot of merit in the complaint. Cooking skills have zoomed up, but there is a perennial shortage of well-trained, conscientious waiters. At expensive restaurants this should not be a problem, but in others—well, you may be lucky and you may not. Complain if you feel it's warranted. You'll be doing the restaurant a favor.

The Restaurants

RATING OUR FAVORITE LONDON RESTAURANTS

We have developed detailed profiles for the best and most interesting restaurants (in our opinion) in town. Each profile features an easily scanned heading that allows you, in just a second, to check out the restaurant's name, cuisine, star rating, cost, quality rating, and value rating.

Cuisine   This is actually less straightforward than it sounds. A couple of years ago, for example, "pan-Asian" restaurants in Washington, D.C. were serving what was then generally described as "fusion" food—Asian ingredients with European techniques, or vice versa. Since then, there has been a pan-Asian explosion, but nearly all specialize in what would be street food back home: noodles, skewers, dumplings, and soups. Once-general categories have become subdivided—French into bistro fare and even Provençal, "new continental" into regional American and "eclectic"—while others have broadened and fused: Middle Eastern and Provençal into Mediterranean, Spanish and South American into nuevo Latino, and so on. In some cases, we have used the broader terms (i.e., "French") but added descriptions to give a clearer idea of the fare. Again, though, experimentation and "fusion" is ever more common, so don't hold us, or the chefs, to too strict a style.

Star Rating   The star rating is a rating that encompasses the entire dining experience, including style, service, and ambience in addition to the taste, presentation, and quality of the food. Five stars is the highest rating possible and connotes the best of everything. Four-star restaurants are exceptional and three-star restaurants are well above average. Two-star restaurants are good. One star is used to indicate an average restaurant that demonstrates an unusual capability in some area of specialization—for example, an otherwise unmemorable place that has great barbecued chicken.

Cost   Our expense description provides a comparative sense of how much a complete meal will cost. A complete meal for our purposes consists of an appetizer, entrée, and dessert. Drinks and tips are excluded.

Inexpensive	Less than £20 per person
Moderate	£20–50 per person
Expensive	More than £50 per person

Quality Rating   On the far right of each heading appear a number and a letter. The number rates the food quality on a scale of 0 to 100; 100 is the best rating attainable. It is based expressly on the taste, freshness of ingredients, preparation, presentation, and creativity of food served. There is no consideration of price. If you are a person who wants the best food available and cost is not an issue, you need look no further than the quality ratings.

Value Rating - If, on the other hand, you are looking for both quality and value, then you should check the value rating, expressed in letters. The value ratings are defined as follows:

A Exceptional value; a real bargain
B Good value
C Fair value; you get exactly what you pay for
D Somewhat overpriced
F Significantly overpriced

Locating the Restaurant   Just below the heading is a designation for geographic zone. This zone description will give you a general idea of where the restaurant described is located. We've divided London into the following 15 geographic zones (see page 14 for detailed zone maps):

Zone 1 North London: Hampstead, Highgate (NW3, NW8, NW9)
Zone 2 Bloomsbury and Holborn (WC1, WC2)
Zone 3 The City, Clerkenwell, and Barbican (EC1, EC2, EC4)
Zone 4 East End: Spitalfields, White Chapel (E1)
Zone 5 South London: South Bank, Lambeth, Brixton
Zone 6 Greenwich and The Docklands
Zone 7 Soho and the West End (W1)
Zone 8 Mayfair and Piccadilly (W1, SW1)
Zone 9 Victoria and Westminster (SW1)
Zone 10 Knightsbridge and Belgravia (SW1, SW3)
Zone 11 Chelsea and South Kensington (SW3, SW7, SW10)
Zone 12 West London: Hammersmith, Chiswick, Richmond, Kew (W4)
Zone 13 Kensington, Holland Park, Notting Hill (W8, W11)
Zone 14 Bayswater, Marylebone, Little Venice, St. John's Wood (NW1, W1, W9, NW8)
Zone 15 Regent's Park and Camden Town (NW1, NW8)

Payment   We've listed the type of payment accepted at each restaurant using the following code: AMEX equals American Express (Optima), CB equals Carte Blanche, D equals Discover, DC equals Diners Club, MC equals Master-Card, and VISA is self-explanatory.

Who's Included   Restaurants in London open and close at an alarming rate. So, for the most part, we have tried to confine our list to establishments with a proven track record over a fairly long period of time. The exceptions here are the newer offspring of the demigods of the culinary world—these places are destined to last, at least until our next update. Also, the list is highly selective. Noninclusion of a particular place does not necessarily indicate that the restaurant is not good, only that it was not ranked among the best in its genre. Detailed profiles of individual restaurants follow in alphabetical order at the end of this chapter.

MORE RECOMMENDATIONS

Chinese

China City 25A Lisle St., WC2, (0171) 734-3388. Dim sum specialist by day, solid Cantonese menu in the evening; a good alternative if there's a long line at Chuen Cheng Ku (page 397).

Fung Shing 15 Lisle St., WC2, (0171) 437-1539. Similarly ambitious cooking to Mr. Kong (see page 414) and at its best capable of producing memorable dishes.

Harbour City 46 Gerrard St., WC2, (0171) 439-7859. Superb dim sum, very popular with the local Chinese community, and good in the evenings as well.

Hunan 51 Pimlico Rd., SW, (0171) 730-571. One of London's few Hunan specialists, and essential eating for devotees of that spicy cuisine.

Mandarin Kitchen 14–16 Queensway, W2. Just across the street from Royal China (see page 426); dreary in decor, but with wonderful dim sum and special dishes.

Fish and Chips

Upper Street Fish Shop 324 Upper St., N1, (0171) 359-1401. Upmarket F&C in a trendy area, popular with locals; great desserts in addition to sparkling-fresh fish.

Geales 2 Farmer St., W8, (0171) 727-7969. Long-established and recently given a makeover, this popular spot in fashionable Notting Hill is almost always crowded.

French

1 Lombard Street 1 Lombard St., EC3, (0171) 929-6611. A big brasserie and a smaller, pricier dining room in a building that began life as a bank; the cooking can be sensational, and the location is good if you're exploring the City (London's financial district).

L'Escargot   48 Greek St., W1(0171) 437-2679. The ground floor is cheaper and more informal than the upstairs dining room, but the French food here is generally good and the service professional; great Soho location.

Gordon Ramsay   68–69 Royal Hospital Rd., SW3, (0171) 352-4441. Two Michelin stars, an extraordinarily talented chef, and a small space that means tables are hard to come by; one of the best in London, but with dizzying prices outside the set lunch.

Pied à Terre   34 Charlotte St., W1, (0171) 636-1178. In a busy restaurant street, a source of modern European cooking that can sometimes rank with the best in London; decor a little clinical and dinner prices slightly scary, but serious food-lovers should try and get here at least for the inexpensive lunch.

Quo Vadis   26–29 Dean St., W1, (0171) 437-9585. Excellent modern French cooking in the restaurant downstairs, acutely trendy bar upstairs with decoration that will not appeal to vegetarians or animal-lovers (go and see what we mean); another good place from the omnipresent Marco Pierre White.

The Square   6–10 Bruton St., W1, (0171) 839-8787. Some people consider the modern European cooking here to be among the best in London, and their views are legitimate; only the pricey wine list and occasional wobbles of service excluded it from the main entries. But it should be a top choice for a special, expensive meal.

Gastropubs and Wine Bars

Cork & Bottle Wine Bar   44–46 Cranbourn St., WC2, (0171) 734-7807. Food is nothing special, but the wine list is amazing and the Leicester Square location is as central as you can get; this is why the cramped basement rooms are always packed. Good for a light bite and a drink before or after a movie or play.

The Cow   89 Westbourne Park Rd., W11, (0171) 221-5400. Prices are not especially low, but the quality is especially high at this popular place near Notting Hill.

The Eagle   159 Farringdon Rd., EC1, (0171) 837-1353. The first of the gastropubs and still one of the best, though its immense popularity means space is hard to come by; pop in if you're nearby for classy Italian/French cooking.

The Havelock Tavern   57 Masbro Rd., W14, (0171) 603-5374. A popular local pub in a nice residential area of Shepherd's Bush; great atmosphere and great food.

Odette's Wine Bar   130 Regent's Park Rd., NW1, (0171) 722-5388. One of London's better wine bars, and downstairs from an excellent, expensive neighborhood restaurant; a good spot when visiting Regent's Park, Camden Town, or Primrose Hill.

The Vine   86 Highgate Rd., NW5, (0171) 209-0038. The building doesn't look like much, but everything here is done fantastically well; not far from Parliament Hill Fields, the southeastern extension of Hampstead Heath.

Greek

Lemonia   89 Regent's Park Rd., NW1, (0171) 586-7454. London used to be famous for its Greek restaurants, but most are a shadow of their former glories. This is one of the exceptions, constantly packed and worth visiting if you're going to be sight-seeing in Regent's Park, Camden Town, or Primrose Hill. Reservations essential.

Italian and Pizza

Condotti   4 Mill St., W1, (0171) 499-1308. In an expensive area (Mayfair), this is a cheap source of good pizza in an attractive space; the proprietor was one of the founders of Pizza Express (see page 420).

Purple Sage   90–92 Wigmore St., Wl, (0171) 486-1912. A centrally located place for pizza that's sometimes inventive, sometimes classic, and always good; the changing roster of nonpizza dishes is also reliable and reasonably priced.

Riva   169 Church Rd., SW13, (0181) 708-0434. Riva is way, way out in quasi-suburban Barnes; but if you really love the finest Italian food and feel like a walk around one of London's loveliest neighborhoods, consider it a top destination.

Japanese

Kulu Kulu   76 Brewer St., W1, (0171) 734-7316. The first and best of London's kaiten sushi restaurants—where dishes are circulated on a conveyor belt and you pick what you want as it goes around; some of the best sushi in town and cheap, too.

Misato   11 Wardour St., W1, (0171) 734-0808. Small, simple place in Chinatown for a quick meal; don't expect anything astounding, but the quality is good and prices low.

Yoshino   3 Piccadilly Place, W1, (0171) 287-6622. The menu is all in Japanese, but the outstanding food (with good, cheap, set menus) makes it worth the difficulty; a surprise in every sense.

Midde Eastern and Turkish

Al Hamra   31–33 Shepherd Market, W1,(0171) 493-1954. Popular with tourists and locals alike, a Middle Eastern restaurant specializing in meze (assorted small dishes); it sometimes disappoints, but when it's good, it's very good.

Patogh   8 Crawford Place, W1, (0171) 262-4015. Simple in decor, but with exceptionally fine cooking—one of the better Middle Eastern restaurants in an area that's crowded with them.

Ranoush Juice Bar   43 Edgeware Rd., W2, (0171) 723-5929. London's first juice bar and still a source of excellent sandwiches, kebabs, and cakes—as well as a lovely range of delicious fruity drinks; great budget food.

Sofra Bistro   18 Shepherd Market, W1, (0171) 499-4099. Sofra is a large chain specializing in reasonably priced Turkish food; service doesn't always achieve the high standards set by the food, but this branch is better than most—and the others are worth considering if you want something cheap and tasty.

Thai

Patara   9 Beauchamp Place, SW3, (0171) 581-8820. One of the best Thai places in London, and with prices that aren't too painful considering the ritzy area (Knightsbridge).

Sri Siam   16 Old Compton St., W1, (0171) 434-3544. An old warhorse, very central, very popular, and still capable of doing good things when everything's working well.

ALFRED		★★
British	Inexpensive–Moderate	Quality 60
245 Shaftesbury Ave. (0171) 240-2566		Value C

Zone 7: Soho and the West End
(tube: Tottenham Court Road), WC2

Customers: Mostly locals
Reservations: Recommended
When to go: Lunch or dinner
Entrée range: £8.95–12.95
Payment: VISA, MC, AMEX, D, DC, CB
Service rating: ★★½

Friendliness rating: ★★★½
Bar: Yes
Wine selection: Adequate; beers are outstanding
Dress: Casual
Disabled access: Yes

Lunch: Monday–Friday noon–3:30 p.m.

Dinner: Monday–Saturday 6–11:30 p.m.

Atmosphere/setting: Plain decor, Formica tables, livelier by day.

House specialties: Soups, haggis and neeps, baked rock oysters, scallops in beer batter with black pudding, Welsh lamb cutlet with roasted vegetables and lentils, grilled rib-eye steak with Stilton butter.

Summary & comments: Alfred is owned by the same people who own RK Stanleys, and has the same policy of serving down-to-earth British food at relatively low prices. The room itself is nothing special, but the food is solid and dependably well produced, with an emphasis on regional ingredients and preparations. There's no fusion cooking here, unless you count the mixing of different parts of Britain and a bit of Ireland thrown in as well. Fish and meat are the top priorities, underpinned by filling side dishes and garnished by particularly delicious relishes and chutneys. Desserts are equally solid and traditional; bread is baked on the premises. Haggis, served as an appetizer, is Scotland's famous dish of meat and oatmeal cooked in a lamb's stomach and served with neeps (turnips)—it is better than it sounds! The set menu, £12.95/£15.90 for two or three courses, is a tremendous bargain.

ARKANSAS CAFÉ ★★

American	Inexpensive	Quality
		65
Spitalfield Market, E1		Value
(0171) 377-6999		B

Zone 4: East End: Spitalfields, Whitechapel
(tube: Liverpool Street)

Customers: Locals and American business community
Reservations: Not needed
When to go: Lunch
Entrée range: £3.75–11
Payment: VISA, MC, D, CB
Service rating: ★★★

Friendliness rating: ★★★★
Bar: Yes
Wine selection: Minimal, but inexpensive
Dress: "Shirt and shoes mandatory"
Disabled access: Main dining room only

Lunch: Monday–Friday noon–3 p.m., Sunday noon–4 p.m.

Atmosphere/setting: Roadhouse barbecue joint.

House specialties: Barbecued ribs, brisket, sliced pork, chicken, burgers.

Entertainment & amenities: Two-man rockabilly band, by arrangement only.

Summary & comments: If you are suffering withdrawal symptoms for top-quality American barbecue, come to the Arkansas. The proprietor is a prize-winning barbecue chef from Maryland, and his specially imported pit barbecues turn out what is, by a margin of several hundred miles, the best ribs in town. As a matter of fact, there's no competition: and if you don't believe us, ask the U.S. ambassador, who gets the Arkansas to cater parties at the embassy. Much of the meat comes from the United States, and the rest of it is from impeccably chosen sources (English, Irish, French). The atmosphere is totally laid-back, the welcome makes you feel at home. Vegetarians won't have much fun; everyone else will have loads of it.

BANK		★★★
Modern European	Moderate	Quality 75
1 Kingsway, WC2 (0171) 379-9797		Value C

Zone 2: Bloomsbury and Holborn (tube: Covent Garden or Holborn)

Customers: Mostly locals
Reservations: Recommended
When to go: Lunch or dinner
Entrée range: £8–26.50
Payment: VISA, MC, AMEX, D, DC, CB

Service rating: ★★★½
Friendliness rating: ★★★½
Bar: Yes
Wine selection: Good
Dress: "No code"
Disabled access: Yes

Breakfast: Monday–Friday 7–11:30 a.m.

Brunch: Saturday and Sunday 11:30 a.m.–3 p.m.

Lunch: Monday–Friday noon–3 p.m.

Dinner: Monday–Saturday 5:30–11.30 p.m., Sunday 5:30–10.30 p.m.

Atmosphere/setting: Big, ultramodern room, almost always packed in the evening both at the bar and in the restaurant.

House specialties: Seared tuna with ginger and dipping sauce, crab linguine with chili, sea bream with black bean salsa and caramelized lime butter, glazed belly of pork with Chinese cabbage, sausage and mashed potatoes with onion sauce.

Other recommendations: Pretheater prix-fixe menu, breakfast, fish and chips, steak and chips, desserts.

Summary & comments: Bank is one of London's big restaurants, occupying a huge site that was formerly a branch of one the national banks. Despite its size it manages to wear a human face, and its central location and extensive opening hours make it a very useful place to know about. Though the chef is French, the food takes on Italian, Asian, and ultratraditional British cooking— what's more, everything is done with consistent skill. Its size means that it's not necessarily a place to linger in, though you can if you want to. The low-cost prix-fixe menu (available at lunch and in the evening until 7 p.m.) offers two courses for just £13.90. The wine list offers ample choices under £20, service is friendly, and the bar would not be out of place in any big American city. If you like buzz and bustle, chances are you'll like Bank.

BELGO ★

Belgian	Inexpensive–Moderate	Quality
		50

		Value
50 Earlham St., WC2 (0171) 813-2233		B

72 Chalk Farm Rd., NW1
(0171) 267-0718

Zone 7: Soho and the West End (tube: Covent Garden)

Customers: Locals and tourists
Reservations: Recommended
When to go: Lunch or dinner
Entrée range: £5–16.95
Payment: VISA, MC, AMEX, D, DC, CB
Service rating: ★★

Friendliness rating: ★★★½
Bar: No
Wine selection: Adequate, but beers are outstanding
Dress: Casual
Disabled access: Yes

Open: Monday–Thursday noon–11:30 p.m., Friday–Saturday noon– midnight, Sunday noon–10:30 p.m.

Atmosphere/setting: Big, high-ceilinged subterranean room with view of the kitchen and a deliberately encouraged air of conviviality.

House specialties: Croquettes de fromage, salade Liègoise, tomato crevettes, Belgian braised meats, mussels in all guises, Belgian crêpes and waffles.

Other recommendations: The beer list.

Summary & comments: Belgo is an incredible success story—and one that's being told on the other side of the Atlantic, with an opening in New York. The formula is simple. Sell Belgian food and drink at low prices—with a helpful array of special offers to keep them even lower—and get the waiters to dress in monks' robes. Not everyone's a fan, and the food (especially more complicated dishes) can be of variable quality. But the simpler mussel dishes are usually just fine. What's more, you can wash them down with a truly stunning array of the great beers of Belgium, one of the world's great beer producers. Lunch is the best time for bargains, but pre-theater diners (this is theater-land) should take advantage of the "Beat the Clock" offer Monday through Friday: from 6 until 7:30 p.m., three main courses are charged according to the time shown on your food order—that is, order at 6:43 and you pay £6.43. Not the greatest food in town, but likely to be decent—and certainly a notable bargain.

BIBENDUM		★★★★
Modern	Expensive	Quality 85
Michelin House, 81 Fulham Rd., SW3 (0171) 581 5817		Value D

Zone 11: Chelsea and South Kensington (tube: South Kensington)

Customers: Locals, tourists, and gastronomes
Reservations: Recommended
When to go: Lunch for the cheapest option and lovely view, dinner for that special occasion
Entrée range: Lunch £14–22
Payment: VISA, MC, AMEX, D, DC

Service rating: ★★★★½
Friendliness rating: ★★★★½
Bar: No
Wine selection: Excellent, but expensive
Dress: Smart casual
Disabled access: Yes

Lunch: Monday–Friday noon–2:30 p.m., Saturday–Sunday 12:30–3 p.m.

Dinner: Monday–Saturday 7–11:30 p.m., Sunday 7–10:30 p.m.

Atmosphere/setting: A large, wonderfully high-ceilinged art deco room in what was formerly the headquarters of the Michelin Tire Company. The decor is simple and contemporary, but the setting is dominated by the huge stained-glass windows, which let in a shower of light by day and offer a fine view.

House specialties: Escargots de Bourgogne; crêpes Parmentier au caviar; fried frogs' legs with warm potato purée and fresh black truffles; fillet of sea bass with oyster sauce and fried oysters; poulet de Bresse à l'estragon; sautéed rabbit with anchovies, garlic, and rosemary; pithivier au chocolate; crème brûlée; passionfruit bavarois.

Other recommendations: Sautéed scallops with shellfish ravioli and chives, crab vinaigrette with herbs, Baltic herrings à la crème, soupe de poisson, fish and chips, grilled John Dory with spinach and ginger salad, roast pigeon with celeriac purée and apple, steak au poivre, tarte fine aux pommes with vanilla ice cream, cold creamed rice with lemon and rhubarb.

Summary & comments: Bibendum was the first restaurant in Sir Terence Conran's soon-to-be empire, and it remains one of the best exponents of modern cooking in London despite the departure of founding chef Simon Hopkinson. You can come here for lunch or dinner knowing that you'll get superbly cooked food from ingredients of the highest quality, served with consummate professionalism that still manages to be friendly. As you can see from the dishes listed above, the orientation is French and classic; but Asian influences appear as well, and so does solid Britishness (the fish and chips may be the best in London). This is what has brought food-fanatical Londoners back to Bibendum for years. There's only one complaint: cost. They're not ripping anyone off with the food prices (attention to detail is expensive, especially when success depends heavily on top-quality ingredients). But wine is marked up without mercy, making an evening meal here a very costly exercise. Is it worth it? Yes, for a rare and very special treat in exquisite surroundings.

THE BIRDCAGE ★★★

Oriental	Moderate	Quality
		75

		Value
10 Whitfield St., W1		C
(0171) 323-9655		

Zone 7: Soho and the West End (tube: Goodge Street or Warren Street)

Customers: Mostly locals
Reservations: Recommended
When to go: Lunch or dinner
Set Menus: Lunch £26.75/3 courses, dinner £36.50/3 courses
Payment: VISA, MC, AMEX, D, DC
Service rating: ★★★

Friendliness rating: ★★★★
Bar: Yes
Wine selection: Small, but good
Dress: Casual
Disabled access: Restaurant only, not toilets

Lunch: Monday–Friday noon–2:30 p.m.

Dinner: Monday–Friday 6 p.m.–12:30 a.m.; Monday–Saturday 6 p.m.–1 a.m.

Atmosphere/setting: Small, colorful room eclectically decorated with a Southeast Asian theme: brasses, Buddhas, and (of course) a birdcage; the effect will not please everyone but it is extraordinary and unusual.

House specialties: Menu changes frequently, but regular dishes include salmon in betel leaf with Israeli couscous, coconut and foie gras soup, pickled mackerel with Peruvian mash, sweetbreads, and jasmine-infused polenta.

Entertainment & amenities: Performances of various kinds, including poetry readings, musicians, and palm readers.

Summary & comments: In terms of geography, the Birdcage is centrally located, but slightly off the beaten track. In terms of cuisine and decor it is *totally* off the beaten track. The chef, Michael von Hruschka, formerly cooked at a big, fashionable restaurant (The Hempel) offering innovative fusion food at heart-stopping prices. Now he's doing the same kind of cooking, but for a tiny room (just 25 covers) and at much lower prices. Eccentricity abounds in every detail, from the tableware to the handmade paper on which menus and wine lists are presented. Cumulatively, the effect is decidedly camp, and the "Birdcage" here has a connection with *La Cage aux Folles*. But the cooking, though full of novelty, is also very serious and, when successful, works wonders with its diverse influences. The chef regards cooking as an adventure. If you agree with that view, you will not be disappointed by a visit here. The wine list offers good choices under or around £25.

BLUEPRINT CAFE		★★½

		Quality
Modern European	Moderate	75
		Value
28 Shad Thames, SE1		B
(0171) 378-7031		

Zone 5: South London: South Bank, Lambeth, Brixton (tube: London Bridge or Tower Bridge)

Customers: Mostly locals
Reservations: Recommended
When to go: Lunch or dinner
Entrée range: £10–16
Payment: VISA, MC, AMEX, D, DC, CB

Service rating: ★★★
Friendliness rating: ★★★★
Bar: Yes
Wine selection: Very good
Dress: Smart casual
Disabled access: Yes

Lunch: Daily noon–3 p.m.

Dinner: Monday–Saturday 6–11 p.m.

Atmosphere/setting: Attractive modern room with big windows overlooking the Thames, trendy clientele.

Summary & comments: The Blueprint is one of many restaurants in the Shad Thames area, and one of several in the empire of Sir Terence Conran (see Bibendum, page 386, and Quaglino's, page 422). It is also one of several with a sweeping view of the Thames, and for this reason alone it is worth a visit. But it's also cheaper than much of the local competition. The food is very good, modern in style, and with the emphasis heavily on the Mediterranean, especially Italy. The seasons and the market are king here, so the menu changes daily to reflect what's available. Fish, pasta, and home-curing are strong points; if there is a single principle tying every dish together, it's the desire to do justice to exemplary ingredients. The wine list is not huge, but it is carefully chosen and easily accommodates diners on a budget. In warm weather, beg for a table on the terrace.

BOISDALE RESTAURANT AND BAR		★★½
British	Moderate	Quality 70
15 Eccleston St., SW1 (0171) 730-6922		Value C

Zone 10: Knightsbridge and Belgravia (tube: Victoria)

Customers: Tourists and usually affluent locals
Reservations: Recommended
When to go: Lunch or dinner
Entrée Range: £8.50–25.90
Payment: VISA, MC, AMEX, D, DC, CB

Service rating: ★★★½
Friendliness rating: ★★★ ½
Bar: Yes
Wine selection: Good
Dress: Smart casual
Disabled access: No

Lunch: Monday–Friday noon–2:30 p.m.

Dinner: Monday–Saturday 7–10:30 p.m.

Atmosphere/setting: Dark wood and red paneling, "clublike" feel, garden at rear open in warm weather.

House specialties: Anything with a Scottish element, such as smoked salmon, smoked grouse, venison, Highland lamb, Aberdeen Angus beef.

Other recommendations: Set menus.

Entertainment & amenities: Late jazz bar, live music.

Summary & comments: Boisdale has established itself as London's most serious champion of the food and drink of Scotland. The emphasis is on getting great ingredients, whether raw or cured, and presenting them to their best advantage. You can go for the simplicity of an Aberdeen Angus steak, grilled and served with béarnaise sauce, or venture into more modern territory with dishes such as hand-dived Hebridean scallops with sesame-seed crust and star-of-anise jus. The kitchen does well with both approaches, and the cosy atmosphere makes a warmly attractive setting. And if you're game enough to try haggis, one of Scotland's national dishes, this is probably the place to do it. Whisky lovers should note that Boisdale's Back Bar, open throughout the day, has London's largest selection of single-malt scotch; the selection of cigars is also notable.

CACTUS BLUE ★★★

American	Moderate	Quality
		80
86 Fulham Rd.. SW3		Value
(0171) 823-7858		B

Zone 11: Chelsea and South Kensington (tube: South Kensington)

Customers: Mostly locals
Reservations: Recommended
When to go: Dinner is best
Entrée range: £9.95–13.95
Payment: VISA, MC, AMEX, D, DC, CB

Service rating: ★★★
Friendliness rating: ★★★★½
Bar: Yes
Wine selection: Small, but good
Dress: Smart casual
Disabled access: Yes

Open: Monday–Friday 5:30–11:45 p.m., Saturday noon–11:45 p.m., Sunday noon–11 p.m.

Atmosphere/setting: Nicely decorated with wrought iron and Southwestern U.S. artifacts, affluent, mostly young local crowd.

Entertainment & amenities: Live funk/jazz Sunday brunch and Tuesday evenings.

Summary & comments: Cactus Blue has lovely decor, good food, great drinks, and unusually low prices for this chi-chi part of town. The menu is modern Southwestern, with "appetizers and small plates" followed by a short group of quesadillas and a longer list of main courses. And though the format may not be out of the ordinary, the cooking is: a tortilla is wrapped around Peking duck and served with apricot and ginger jam, for instance. A quesadilla might contain Serrano ham, Taleggio cheese, and oven-dried tomatoes; yellowfin tuna is served with bourbon marmalade. All very modern and executed with skill. Sunday brunch is a popular event among local residents, but the evening's better if you want a drink with your meal. They make some of London's best margaritas, and have a good range of premium tequila by the shot. And the mostly American wine list tops out at £23 apart from champagne, so drinking here won't break the bank.

CAFÉ FISH   ★ ★

Fish	Inexpensive–Moderate	Quality
		55

36–40 Rupert St., W1	Value
(0171) 287-8989	C

Zone 7: Soho and the West End (tube: Leicester Square or Piccadilly Circus)

Customers: : Locals and tourists
Reservations: Not needed
When to go: Lunch or dinner
Entrée range: Lunch £8.75–19.90
Payment: VISA, MC, AMEX, D, DC, CB

Service rating: ★★½
Friendliness rating: ★★★★
Bar: Yes
Wine selection: Adequate
Dress: Casual
Disabled access: Limited

Lunch: Daily noon–3 p.m.

Dinner: Monday–Saturday 5:30–11:30 p.m.; Sunday 5:30–10:30 p.m.

Atmosphere/setting: Very casual in the Canteen downstairs, more formal in the Restaurant upstairs.

House specialties: Seafood platters.

Other recommendations: Regularly changing range of fish dishes, especially classic dishes such as seafood pie, fish and chips, and kedgeree.

Summary & comments: Café Fish is owned by the same group that owns Livebait and Chez Gérard (see pages 407 and 395), and it also reflects the group's skill at turning out good food at reasonable prices. This place, in the heart of the West End theater district, is on two floors: The more casual Canteen is open all day and the Restaurant at lunch and dinner. The food is mostly on the simple side and French or British in orientation, though you may also find blackened Cajun swordfish steak with Creole coleslaw or a warm salad of sautéed monkfish, chorizo sausage, red onion, and new potatoes. Or make life easy by ordering one of the shellfish platters. Prices are lower in the Canteen, and though service may slow down at hectic times, it is charming and friendly.

CAFÉ SPICE NAMASTE ★★★★

Indian	Moderate	Quality
		85

16 Prescot St., E1	Value
(0171) 488-9242	B

247 Lavender Hill
(0171) 738-1717

Zone 4: East End: Spitalfields, Whitechapel (tube: Aldgate, Aldgate East, Tower Hill)

Customers: Mostly locals, especially businesspeople and aficionados
Reservations: Recommended
When to go: Lunch or dinner
Entrée range: Lunch £5.95–14.75
Payment: VISA, MC, AMEX, D, DC, CB

Service rating: ★★★
Friendliness rating: ★★★★
Bar: No
Wine selection: Good
Dress: Casual
Disabled access: Yes

Lunch: Monday–Friday noon–3 p.m.

Dinner: Monday–Saturday 6:15–10:30 p.m.

Atmosphere/setting: High-ceilinged room in nineteenth-century building, nicely redecorated.

House specialties: Unusual curries from various Indian regions, tandoori dishes, breads, vegetarian dishes.

Other recommendations: Weekly changing specialty menus.

Summary & comments: Since 1995, chef Cyrus Todiwala has made Café Spice Namaste one of London's best places to find really serious Indian food. Indeed, he is one of the prime "modernizers" of this favorite British cuisine, raising standards in every aspect over the nondescript "curry houses" of the bad old days. The dishes on the regular menu cover nearly every area of the Indian subcontinent and are distinguished for their subtle, complex spicing and relative rarity on British menus. There is a weekly "speciality menu" as well, featuring a particular region, and the wine list is notable for its serious attention to matching every style of food on the menu. There are only two minor negative points to bear in mind. One is the location, which is out of the way. The other is an occasional problem with rowdy (affluent) clients, given the restaurant's proximity to London's financial center. Apart from that, there's no way to recommend Café Spice Namaste too highly. If you happen to be staying in south London, their Battersea branch is of equally high quality.

CAMBIO DE TERCIO ★★★

		Quality
Spanish	Moderate	80

	Value
163 Old Brompton Rd., SW5	B
(0171) 244-8970	

Zone 11: Chelsea and South Kensington (tube: Gloucester Road)

Customers: Locals
Reservations: Recommended
When to go: Lunch or dinner
Entrée range: Lunch £8.90–14.90
Payment: VISA, MC, AMEX, DC, CB
Service rating: ★★★★

Friendliness rating: ★★★★
Bar: No
Wine selection: Excellent, mostly Spanish
Dress: Casual
Disabled access: Restaurant only

Lunch: Daily noon–2:30 p.m.

Dinner: Monday–Saturday 7–11 p.m., Sunday 7–10:30 p.m.

Atmosphere/setting: Cozy, comfortable basement room decorated with bullfighting motifs.

House specialties: Oxtail, hake, suckling pig, tapas.

Summary & comments: Cambio is one of London's best Spanish restaurants. The kitchen is equally adept at staple dishes, using the best and most authentic imported ingredients, and at reinterpreting classics with a modern slant. Lovers of tapas, the "little dishes" with which Spanish people love to begin an evening's festivities, should note that the selection and quality here are excellent—and the choice of sherries, the perfect partner for this kind of eating, is similarly broad. There have been a few personnel changes in the kitchen in recent years, but standards seem to have been kept high. And though there have been grumbles about service from some quarters, they are neither numerous nor serious enough to keep Cambio off your list of possibilities. Dessert lovers should note that while Spain does not always excel in that department, Cambio de Tercio almost always *does*.

LE CAPRICE   ★★½

		Quality
Modern	Moderate	75

		Value
Arlington St., SW1		C
(0171) 629-2239		

Zone 9: Victoria and Westminster (tube: Green Park)

Customers: Celebrities, affluent locals
Reservations: Recommended
When to go: Dinner is best, or Sunday brunch
Entrée range: £9.75–21.75
Payment: VISA, MC, AMEX, D, DC

Service rating: ★★★
Friendliness rating: ★★★
Bar: Yes
Wine selection: Short, but good
Dress: "No dress code"
Disabled access: Yes, but not to toilets

Lunch: Monday–Saturday noon–3 p.m., Sunday noon–3:30 p.m.

Dinner: Monday–Saturday 5:30 p.m.–midnight, Sunday 6 p.m.–midnight

Atmosphere/setting: Lively, but low-key, modern room that is pleasant but of no great distinction.

House specialties: Nearly everything on the menu, especially simple dishes such as fish and chips, salmon fishcakes, and eggs Benedict.

Summary & comments: Le Caprice has a well deserved reputation for serving food that reaches a high standard pretty consistently. But that is not the main reason that Londoners come here, even if it helps. Le Caprice is a supremely fashionable restaurant in a low-key, understated kind of way. It's the kind of place where, if the next table is occupied by a princess, two movie stars, and a Nobel Prize–winning novelist, no one raises an eyebrow. Well, not in a way that you would notice, anyway. This is surely one of the reasons why the rich and fashionable and celebrated love the place so much, just as they love its sister restaurant, The Ivy (see page 404). For us mortals, the possibility of star-gazing might be a bonus. But I have paid three visits with not a star in sight and have loved the place anyway. It is comfortable and well run, and the food can be outstanding. And when it isn't outstanding, it's still very good. Dinners are buzzy, Sunday brunch more laid-back.

CHEZ GÉRARD   ★★

		Quality
French (bistro)	Inexpensive–Moderate	70

	Value
The Market, The Piazza, WC2	C
(0171) 379-0666	

Zone 7: Soho and the West End (tube: Covent Garden)

Customers: Locals and tourists
Reservations: Recommended
When to go: Lunch or dinner
(restaurant), any time (bar)
Entrée range: Lunch £9.90–16.40
Payment: VISA, MC, AMEX, D, DC, CB

Service rating: ★★½
Friendliness rating: ★★★½
Bar: Yes
Wine selection: Good
Dress: Casual
Disabled access: No

Lunch: Daily noon–3 p.m.

Dinner: Monday–Saturday 5:30–11:30 p.m., Sunday 5:30–10:30 p.m.

Atmosphere/setting: Conservatory overlooking Covent Garden market, open-air terrace in warm weather.

House specialties: Steak, especially Châteaubriand and *onglet* (hanger steak) served with pommes frites.

Other recommendations: Simple bistro-style dishes such as oysters, fish soup, snails, Bayonne ham with pickles.

Summary & comments: Groupe Chez Gérard, which has seven other branches in addition to this one, has a very simple formula: French-style steak, French-style pommes frites (better known as French fries), and French-style service. They usually do it very well, though there are variations from branch to branch, and prices are kept low enough to keep most people happy even if they run into occasional problems with cooking or service. Fish-eaters will always find at least one dish aimed at them, as will vegetarians; but these are the most variable options in terms of quality, and they are not—let's be frank— what Chez Gérard is about. Set menus can offer exceptionally good value for money: £15 for three courses at lunch or in the evening. Don't come here expecting the meal of a lifetime, but if you're a steak-lover then this is your home away from home.

CHEZ NICO AT 90 PARK LANE   ★★★★★

French (haute cuisine)	Expensive	Quality
		95

90 Park Lane, SWI	Value
(0171) 409-1290	C

Zone 10: Knightsbridge and Belgravia (tube: Marble Arch)

Customers: Tourists and locals
Reservations: Essential
When to go: Lunch or dinner
Set menus: Lunch £25 – 40; dinner, £53 for 2 courses or £65 for 3 courses
Payment: VISA, MC, AMEX, D, DC, CB

Service rating: ★★★★★
Friendliness rating: ★★★★½
Bar: Yes
Wine selection: Excellent
Dress: Smart casual
Disabled access: Yes

Lunch: Monday–Friday noon– 2 p.m.

Dinner: Monday–Saturday 7 – 11 p.m.

Atmosphere/setting: Formal, but comfortable, plush elegance.

House specialties: The menu changes with moderate frequency, but certain dishes (possibly with minor changes) are always featured. Terrine of foie gras, escalope of foie gras with brioche and caramelized orange, scallops both as appetizers and main course, noisettes of sweetbreads, grilled veal cutlet, Dover sole, glazed lemon tart, chocolate "Negus."

Other recommendations: Nothing here can specifically *not* be recommended. Particularly noteworthy are all fish dishes, all risotto, breast of duck with honey and peppercorns, all pastry.

Summary & comments: Nico Ladenis, of Greek origin and raised in East Africa, is a self-taught chef whose passion for French food has taken him through a succession of London restaurants, of which this is the fitting culmination: a grand setting in one of the city's most expensive hotels. Awarded a third Michelin star in 1997, he has maintained his high standards of cooking and service even as he increasingly turns over day-to-day running of the restaurant to staff and family. For those who love classic French food executed flawlessly and with the added dimension of well-judged innovation, this is one of London's top restaurants. Service is formal and precise, but not stiff or stuffy. The wine list is expensive, but you don't have to spend a fortune to get something worthy of the food. Just two warnings: Some find the setting charmless and the decor uninspired, and the prices are extremely high outside the set lunch. But those who like the restaurant just find it a comfortable place to indulge occasionally in world-class cooking. If everything's working smoothly, you may get a meal you'll remember your whole life.

CHUEN CHENG KU ★★

		Quality
Chinese	Inexpensive–Moderate	65

	Value
17 Wardour St., W1 (0171) 734-3281	B

Zone 7: Soho and the West End (tube: Leicester Square or Piccadilly Circus)

Customers: Locals and tourists
Reservations: Not needed
When to go: Lunch is best
Entrée range: Lunch £6.30–16.80
Payment: VISA, MC, AMEX, DC, CB
Service rating: ★★½

Friendliness rating: ★★½
Bar: No
Wine selection: Adequate
Dress: Casual
Disabled access: Restaurant only

Open: Daily 11 a.m.–midnight

Atmosphere/setting: Huge, very busy at lunch (especially weekends) and mostly quieter in the evening.

House specialties: Dim sum, rice and noodles, fish, and shellfish.

Other recommendations: Standard Cantonese dishes.

Summary & comments: Chuen Cheng Ku has been packing happy eaters into its capacious rooms for a couple of decades now and shows no sign of flagging in popularity. The best thing here, without a doubt, is the dim sum: Served daily until 5:45 p.m., it comes around on trolleys and offers a huge choice with more or less consistent quality. Weekends are the busiest time. You can expect a line of between 1 and 20 parties, but the crowd is well managed and the waits are rarely longer than about 20 minutes. The large numbers of Chinese families show that the place is appreciated by those who know quality when they see it. Dinner is usually less busy and of solid rather than exciting quality—but certainly good enough to make CCK a top choice when you're in the area, as you're sure to be, at some point. If there are six or more of you eating, the nine-dish set menus (£13–30) offer excellent value and a simplified choice.

CLARKE'S   ★★★★

		Quality
Modern European	Moderate–Expensive	85

	Value
124 Kensington Church St., W8	C
(0171) 221-9225	

Zone 13: Kensington, Holland Park, Notting Hill (tube: Notting Hill Gate)

Customers: Mostly locals
Reservations: Essential
When to go: Lunch or dinner
Entrée range: Lunch £14; Dinner set menu £42 for 4 courses
Payment: VISA, MC, AMEX, D, DC
Service rating: ★★★★½

Friendliness rating: ★★★★½
Bar: No
Wine selection: Outstanding
Dress: Casual
Disabled access: Restaurant yes, toilets no

Lunch: Monday–Friday 12:30–2 p.m.

Dinner: Monday–Friday 7–10 p.m.

Atmosphere/setting: Upstairs room is tiny and intimate, downstairs is big and bustling, with a view of the kitchen.

House specialties: Menu changes daily.

Summary & comments: No one in Britain understands Californian cooking better than Sally Clarke, who worked there years ago (at Chez Panisse and elsewhere) before moving back to London and opening her own place. She bases her cooking on the seasons and on what's available in the market on a given day. Thus, menus change every day, with a short carte at lunchtime and fixed menus (following the example of Chez Panisse) at dinner. The cooking is strong in baking (including some of the best bread in London), roasting, and char-grilling. Combinations are simple, but they never fail to impress, partly because the execution is so skilled and especially because the ingredients are as good as money can buy. The lack of choice at dinner may be somewhat irritating. You can phone in advance to find out what's on the menu, however, and given enough warning they will happily provide alternatives if possible. The wine list is superb, and not especially high-priced. Clarke's is not cheap, but at its price level it is one of the best restaurants in London.

CONNAUGHT RESTAURANT ★★★★

French (haute cuisine)	Expensive	Quality
		90

Carlos Place, WI	Value
(0171) 499-7070	C

Zone 8: Mayfair and Piccadilly (tube: Green Park)

Customers: Hotel guests, affluent tourists, and locals
Reservations: Essential
When to go: Lunch or dinner
Entrée range: Lunch £12–37.50
Payment: VISA, MC, AMEX, D, DC, CB
Service rating: ★★★★★

Friendliness rating: ★★★★½
Bar: Yes
Wine selection: Excellent, but expensive
Dress: Formal, jacket and tie for men
Disabled access: Limited

Lunch: Daily 12:30–2:30 p.m.

Dinner: Daily 6:30–10:45 p.m.

Atmosphere/setting: Chandeliers, wood paneling, luxury, unsurpassable comfort, formal but not intimidating.

House specialties: Classic French and British cooking, roasts from the trolley, game (in season).

Summary & comments: Eating at the Connaught is not just a meal, it's an experience. The hotel dates back to Edwardian times and is accustomed to catering for royalty—the menu has a special symbol for dishes created by chef Michel Bourdin for the queen's silver jubilee (1977). This is about as indiscreet as they get at the Connaught, a place where the high and mighty come to eat, but everyone is treated like an honored guest. There are two places to eat, the Restaurant and the smaller, more intimate Grill with slightly different hours. It's a matter of personal preference, but one of the banquettes in the Restaurant is a perfect place to get a taste of Connaught-style luxury. The food is mostly old-fashioned, a combination of English and French presented side by side in a mixture of the two languages: filet de boeuf en croûte légère "Strasbourgeoise" and croustade d'oeufs de caille maintenon alongside Cornish crab bisque and bread and butter pudding. The cooking is never less than assured and can sometimes reach dazzling heights, and the service is as good as service ever gets. Let's be blunt: Outside the limited-choice set menus (£27.50 at lunch, £37.50 at dinner), the Connaught is very, very expensive unless you order the cheapest things on the menu. The wine list doesn't help in the matter of budgetary restraint. But this is a unique restaurant, the likes of which you will not find anywhere in the United States. For this reason alone it's worth a visit.

CORNEY & BARROW   ★★

Modern European	Moderate	Quality
		65

116 St. Martin's Lane, E1	Value
(0171) 655-9800	C

44 Cannon St., WC2
(0171) 248-1700

Zone 4: East End: Spitalsfield, White Chapel

Customers: Mostly locals
Reservations: Not needed
When to go: Lunch or dinner
Entrée range: £9.75–16
Payment: VISA, MC, AMEX, DC, CB

Service rating: ★★½
Friendliness rating: ★★★
Bar: Yes
Wine selection: Excellent
Dress: Casual
Disabled access: No

Open: Monday–Saturday noon–11:15 p.m.

Atmosphere/setting: Bar with high stools on ground floor, more comfortable brasserie upstairs, lively and casual.

Summary & comments: If location is everything in retail, this branch of Corney & Barrow has got it made. It's across the street from the English National Opera, one minute from Trafalgar Square and its galleries, and five minutes from the theaters and cinemas around Leicester Square. Corney & Barrow is a group of wine bars, backed up by a retail and wholesale wine merchant of great distinction, so the wine list is predictably strong: plenty of choices under £20, a rarity for London, and interesting bottles from all over. But the food is serious, too. Crab soup, aubergine (eggplant) and roast garlic tortellini, poached sea bass with new season vegetables and green-peppercorn aïoli, pan-fried duck with potato gnocchi and artichokes, attractive desserts — these are all worthy companions for the wine. The set menus (lunchtime and 5–7:30 p.m.) are a major bargain at £10.95 for two courses or £12.95 for three. There are eight other branches, mostly in Zone 3 (The City, Clerkenwell, and Barbican), in addition to the one listed above. Worth bearing in mind when you're doing the sights.

FIFTH FLOOR ★★★½

Modern European	Moderate	Quality
		75

Harvey Nichols, 109 Knightsbridge, SW1	Value
(0171) 235-5250	C

Zone 10: Knightsbridge and Belgravia (tube: Knightsbridge)

Customers: Locals, tourists, and shoppers
Reservations: Recommended
When to go: Lunch or dinner
Entrée range: Lunch £11–35
Payment: VISA, MC, AMEX, D, DC, CB

Service rating: ★★★½
Friendliness rating: ★★★½
Bar: Yes
Wine selection: Excellent
Dress: "No dress code"
Disabled access: Yes

Lunch: Monday–Friday noon–3 p.m., Saturday–Sunday noon–3:30 p.m.

Dinner: Monday–Saturday 6:30–11:30 p.m.

Atmosphere/setting: Smart, contemporary decor in the ultrachic Harvey Nichols department store, attracting fashion-conscious clientele at both lunch and dinner.

House specialties: Black bean soup, poached egg and salt cod crostini; Bismarck herrings with marinated beet and horseradish Chantilly; deep-fried oysters and belly pork; rabbit with spinach, chickpeas, paprika-cured bacon, and mustard sauce; fillet of brill with green beans braised with chorizo and clams.

Summary & comments: In-store eating does not get any better than the Fifth Floor. It's not just a pit stop after doing the rounds of Harvey Nichols but a destination in its own right, and very popular with discerning Londoners who love Henry Harris's superb take on contemporary cooking. Good design means that you don't even notice you're in a store when you're eating here—not that there are many complaints about that. The prices are as serious as the cooking, though the entrée range is distorted by the expense of roast lobster: Most main dishes are in the £13–16 range. At lunchtime, two appetizers (a popular option) will cost little more than £15. Or take advantage of the prix-fixe lunch at £23.50 for three courses, a real bargain. Wine lovers are particularly well served by a list that includes all the bottles from the nearby HN wine shop. It's absolutely *endless,* as you can guess from the fact that the helpful "Little List" and "House Selection" contain over 40 bottles.

LE GAVROCHE   ★★★★½

French (haute cuisine)	Expensive	Quality
		90

43 Upper Brook St., W1	Value
(0171) 408-0881	C

Zone 8: Mayfair and Piccadilly (tube: Marble Arch)

Customers: Locals and tourists
Reservations: Essential
When to go: Lunch or dinner
Entrée range: £27.40–36.80
Payment: VISA, MC, AMEX, DC, CB
Service rating: ★★★★★
Friendliness rating: ★★★★½

Bar: Yes, for diners only
Wine selection: Excellent
Dress: Formal, jacket and tie for men
Disabled access: No

Lunch: Monday–Friday noon–2 p.m.

Dinner: Monday–Friday 7–11 p.m.

Atmosphere/setting: A downstairs room offering intimate comfort at both lunch and dinner; indisputably grand, but with the kind of ultraprofessional service that pampers without being intimidating.

House specialties: Foie gras chaud et pastilla de canard à la canelle; Rable de lapin et galette au Parmesan; Le Palet de chocolat amer et praline croustillant.

Other recommendations: Soufflé Suissesse, ragoût de langoustines parfumé au gingembre, agneau de lait rôti, le caneton Gavroche en pot-au-feu, set lunch.

Summary & comments: Le Gavroche is one of London's most famous and most expensive restaurants. It is classic in every sense, even though the menu has been "modernized" in recent years. The service is among the best in London, priding itself on knowing what the customers want before they themselves know they want it, and the care taken with every detail is astonishing. All this comes at a truly frightening price outside the set lunch, which at £40 per person includes three courses, half a bottle of wine, water and coffee, and service. Sure, that's pretty expensive, too. But with main courses alone costing £30 on average, lunch is the only way most people can afford Le Gavroche. It's worth that one splash-out, because this is a great restaurant of the old-fashioned, perfectionist kind. Bread, ice creams and sorbets, premeal tidbits—they're all outstanding. And the all-French cheese board is probably the best in London. Come here if you want to treat yourself.

IBLA		★★
Italian	Moderate	Quality 80
89 Marylebone High St., W1 (0171) 224-3799		Value B

Zone 14: Bayswater, Marylebone, Little Venice, St. John's Wood (tube: Bond Street)

Customers: Mostly locals, including many Italians
Reservations: Recommended
When to go: Lunch or dinner
Set Menus: Lunch £15 for 2 courses, £18 for 3 courses; Dinner: £22 or £25

Payment: VISA, MC, AMEX, CB
Service rating: ★★★
Friendliness rating: ★★★★★
Bar: Yes
Wine selection: Very good
Dress: Casual
Disabled access: Restaurant only

Lunch: Monday–Saturday noon–2:30 p.m.

Dinner: Monday–Saturday 7–10:30 p.m.

Atmosphere/setting: Delicatessen items on sale in front room; attractive, simply decorated dining room at the back, exceptionally pleasant.

Summary & comments: Ibla is a quiet, unassuming treasure. One of its many good points is that it attracts (in my experience anyway) more Italians than "foreigners"—which is always a good sign. Another good point is the charming service. And the main good point: modern Italian food that's imaginative but never contrived, all the more enticing because the prices are exceptionally low for this level of excellence. The dishes are identifiably Italian, but often with French touches, and they rarely sound familiar. Monkfish and sweetbread *involtini* with morels; roast quail stuffed with salmon, raisins, and pine nuts; pineapple and semolina raviolo with chocolate sauce—these items from a recent menu should convey the idea. The wine list is mostly Italian and extremely well priced. Set lunch offers fewer choices than dinner, and somewhat simpler cooking. Diners on a budget who want one really special meal should consider Ibla.

THE IVY ★★★★

Modern European	Moderate	Quality
		85

1 West St., WC2	Value
(0171) 836-4751	C

Zone 7: Soho and the West End (tube: Leicester Square)

Customers: Mostly locals
Reservations: Essential
When to go: Lunch or dinner
Entrée range: Lunch £8.75–18.75
Payment: VISA, MC, AMEX, D, DC
Service rating: ★★★★

Friendliness rating: ★★★
Bar: For diners only
Wine selection: Good
Dress: "No dress code"
Disabled access: Restaurant only

Lunch: Monday–Saturday noon–3 p.m., Sunday noon–3:30 p.m.

Dinner: Daily 5:30 p.m.–midnight

Atmosphere/setting: Exceptionally comfortable wood-paneled room with stained-glass windows, discreet and refined.

House specialties: Simple classics such as steak tartare, calves liver, smoked salmon with scrambled eggs, shepherd's pie, eggs Benedict, grilled or fried fish.

Other recommendations: Salads, desserts, Oriental dishes.

Summary & comments: Let's get the bad news out of the way first. Getting a table at The Ivy is famously difficult. If you're planning a trip and are dying to eat here, it's advisable to reserve at least a month in advance. Why should this be? Here's the good news: The Ivy is a supremely wonderful place. The food is mostly simple, but always executed with skill. Service is professional and efficient, though there are sometimes complaints about off-handedness. But The Ivy isn't just a place to eat and drink. It is also, for most people, a spot to do a bit of star-gazing. The rich and famous love it, and chances are reasonable that you'll spot a familiar face while enjoying your eggs Benedict or fish and chips. But don't stare, please. That wouldn't be in keeping with Ivy etiquette.

JOE ALLEN ★★½

		Quality
American	Inexpensive–Moderate	70

	Value
13 Exeter St., WC2	C
(0171) 836-0651	

Zone 2: Bloomsbury and Holborn (tube: Covent Garden)

Customers: Varied, locals and tourists
Reservations: Recommended
When to go: Any time
Entrée range: Lunch £7–13.50
Payment: VISA, MC, AMEX

Service rating: ★★★½
Friendliness rating: ★★★★
Bar: Yes
Wine selection: Small, but good
Dress: Casual
Disabled access: No

Open: Monday–Friday noon–1 a.m., Saturday 11:30 a.m.–1 a.m., Sunday 11:30 a.m.–midnight.

Atmosphere/setting: Think of your favorite local bar/restaurant, the kind of place you go for a cheerful, noisy night out with friends.

House specialties: Black bean soup; chopped chicken liver; Caesar salad; eggs Benedict or eggs Joe Allen; grilled tuna with sautéed new potatoes, black olives, chopped tomatoes, and coriander; grilled chicken with marinated roast peppers, herb roast potatoes, and pesto; grilled sirloin steak with steak fries; brownies; cheesecake.

Other recommendations: Anything cooked simply (which means just about everything on the menu), especially the hamburgers, sandwiches, and salads.

Entertainment & amenities: Piano player Monday–Saturday 9 p.m.–1 a.m., jazz Sunday 8 p.m.–1 a.m.

Summary & comments: Like its two other branches in Paris and New York, the London Joe Allen is a place to go for unpretentious, American-style food in a lively atmosphere. It's set in the heart of theaterland, and its theatrical connections are firmly cemented in the cheap precurtain menus (£12 for two courses, £14 for three courses) and the late opening hour. Actors come in from the nearby theaters after their performance, and if you're lucky you may find yourself eating Caesar salad next to someone you watched on stage an hour earlier. It's the spirited buzz that brings Londoners in, rather than any fancy fireworks in the food. But the food itself is solid, rarely disappointing those who like simple classics done well, and the drinks list, though short, is enticing at every level from £13 and up (Dom Perignon sells for barely 20% more than its shop price).

LINDSAY HOUSE   ★★★½

British	Moderate–Expensive	Quality
		80

21 Romilly St., W1	Value
(0171) 439-0450	D

Zone 7: Soho and the West End (tube: Leicester Square or Piccadilly Circus)

Customers: Mostly locals
Reservations: Recommended
When to go: Lunch or dinner
Entrée range: Lunch only, £17–21; set menus £23 (lunch), £38 (dinner)
Payment: VISA, MC, AMEX, D, CB
Service rating: ★★★★

Friendliness rating: ★★★★
Bar: No
Wine selection: Excellent, but expensive
Dress: Smart casual
Disabled access: No

Lunch: Monday–Friday noon–2:30 p.m.

Dinner: Monday–Saturday 6–11 p.m.

Atmosphere/setting: Two stories of a townhouse decorated with quiet elegance; cozy and subdued, but not stuffy.

House specialties: Menu changes daily, meat is the strong point.

Summary & comments: Richard Corrigan, the chef at Lindsay House, has long had devoted followers for his robust, sophisticated approach to modern cooking. After moving around a slew of London restaurants, he seems to have settled in here, giving his fans the kind of hearty eating that they've come to expect from him. Corrigan is Irish, and his native tradition shows through in a love of pork, offal, and Irish ingredients such as black pudding. Veal tongue, pigeon, belly of pork, sweetbreads—this is the sort of thing you can expect to find on the daily changing menu. There's a lot of fish, too, perhaps not always as reliable as the meat, and desserts are a strong point. Prices are not low, on the menu or (especially) the wine list; this is a restaurant for a special occasion. But if you like hearty cooking, chances are you'll like the Lindsay House a lot. They'll cook specially for vegetarians if asked.

LIVEBAIT	★★★½

Seafood	Inexpensive–Moderate	Quality
		75

	Value
21 Wellington St., WC2	C
(0171) 836-7161	

43 The Cut, SE1
(0171) 928-7211

Zone 7: Soho and the West End (tube: Covent Garden)

Zone 5: South Bank (tube: Waterloo)

Customers: Locals and tourists	**Service rating:** ★★½
Reservations: Recommended	**Friendliness rating:** ★★★½
When to go: Lunch or dinner	**Bar:** Yes
Entrée range: Lunch £12.50–20.75	**Wine selection:** Good
Payment: VISA, MC, AMEX, D,	**Dress:** Casual
DC, CB	**Disabled access:** No

Lunch: Monday–Saturday noon–3:30 p.m.; Sunday noon–3 p.m.

Dinner: Monday–Saturday 5:30–11:30 p.m.

Atmosphere/setting: Black and white tiles, minimal decor, brash and fun and noisy.

House specialties: Ever-changing selection of fish dishes and shellfish platters.

Summary & comments: The original Livebait, in SE1, took London by storm when it opened in 1997. The Covent Garden branch is centrally located and duplicates the formula—a simple setting with fairly elaborate cooking—very successfully. The secret lies in wonderfully fresh fish, some from exotic sources and some local to the United Kingdom, which you will find cooked in exceptionally innovative ways (such as grilled bluefin tuna with celeriac and foie gras purée, pousse spinach, port and thyme sauce) and in classic presentations such as sumptuous shellfish platters of oysters, clams, crevettes, cockles, winkles, whelks, prawns, and crab. Service can slow down as the kitchen gets busy (especially in the evening), but it never fails in the friendliness department. Prices à la carte are not exactly cheap, but it's worth noting the set menu (from £15.50) available at lunch and both pre- and post-theater, the daily set dinner menu for £19.50–24.50, and the "café express menu" (in and out in 45 minutes) for £10.

LOLA'S   ★★★½

Modern European	Moderate	Quality
		85

The Mall, 359 Upper St., N1	Value
(0171) 359-1932	B

Zone 1: North London (tube: Angel)

Customers: Locals, all ages
Reservations: Recommended
When to go: Weekend lunch or
dinner any day
Entrée range: £10–16
Payment: VISA, MC, AMEX, D

Service rating: ★★★½
Friendliness rating: ★★★★★
Bar: Yes
Wine selection: Good
Dress: Casual to all dressed up
Disabled access: No

Lunch: Monday–Friday noon–3:30 p.m.; Saturday and Sunday (brunch) noon–3 p.m.

Dinner: Monday–Saturday 6:30–11 p.m.; Sunday 7–10 p.m.

Atmosphere/setting: Simply decorated upstairs room with skylight, nice and relaxed.

House specialties: Menu changes daily, but dishes that appear regularly include chicken or fish harira, spinach soup with split-pea dhal, potato pancake with smoked salmon, crème fraîche and salmon caviar, calzones and pizzas, homemade breads and ice creams.

Other recommendations: Baked desserts, fish, pasta.

Summary & comments: Lola's is perfectly situated for a visit to the Camden Passage Antiques Market: The ground floor of the building it occupies is part of the market, and the rest is just a minute away. The area has other attractions as well, including the Sadler Wells theater. Even without those other attractions, however, Lola's would be worth visiting for exceptionally good modern-style cooking in very pleasant surroundings and at reasonable prices. You can eat three courses here for little more than £20. Occasionally, one hears of dishes that didn't quite set the tastebuds alight, but most reports have nothing but praise for chef Juliet Peston's cooking. She uses ideas from all over the world, though the most precise description would probably be pan-European with a Middle Eastern accent. Flavors are big, combinations unfailingly well judged; this is intelligent cooking of a quiet, unostentatious kind. All in all, a firm favorite and a bargain given the quality.

MANGO ROOM ★★½

		Quality
Caribbean	Inexpensive	70

	Value
10 Kentish Town Rd., NW1	B
(0171) 482-5065	

Zone 15: Regent's Park and Camden Town (tube: Camden Town)

Customers: Locals, fairly young
Reservations: Recommended
When to go: Dinner is livlier
Entrée range: £7.50–9.50
Payment: VISA, MC, CB
Service rating: ★★★

Friendliness rating: ★★★★★
Bar: Yes
Wine selection: Minimal
Dress: "As you wish"
Disabled access: Yes

Lunch: Tuesday–Sunday noon–3 p.m.

Dinner: Daily 6 p.m.– midnight

Atmosphere/setting: Colorful decor with a handmade look; mostly young, trendy crowd.

House specialties: Ebony chicken wings, marinated in chile, pepper, garlic, and soya; curry goat with hot pepper, scallions, garlic, pimiento, and spices; mango and banana brûlée.

Other recommendations: Steamed green-lip mussels with ginger, scallions, garlic, and coconut; ackee and avocado with spinach, plantains, tomatoes, and olives; grilled barracuda with courgettes and coconut sauce.

Entertainment & amenities: Great ska, reggae, and "jazz Jamaica" background music.

Summary & comments: Camden Town is one of London's hip, casual areas. With the popular Camden Lock market nearby and Regent's Park not much farther away, it gets incredibly crowded, especially on weekends. A host of establishments cater for the crowds, but few match the Mango Room for quality. Being here is just a pleasure: The music is wonderful, the staff is really friendly, and the food is good, filling, and cheap. Based in Caribbean cooking, it offers both traditional classics and modern variations in the spirit of gastronomic globalism. There's a bar next door with comfortable chairs and sofas. If you're in the area, the Mango Room is a great place to eat and/or drink after sight-seeing and shopping. Consider beer or a fruit punch rather than wine from the short list, and get set to enjoy yourself in laid-back surroundings.

MASH   ★★

Modern European	Inexpensive–Moderate	Quality
		70

19–21 Great Portland St., W1	Value
(0171) 637-5555	C

Zone 7: Soho and the West End (tube: Oxford Circus)

Customers: Mostly young locals
Reservations: Recommended
When to go: Lunch or dinner or weekend brunch
Entrée range: Lunch £7–14.50
Payment: VISA, MC, AMEX, D, DC

Service rating: ★★½
Friendliness rating: ★★★½
Bar: Yes
Wine selection: Very good
Dress: "No dress code"
Disabled access: Ground floor only

Lunch: Monday–Friday noon–3 p.m., Saturday and Sunday noon–4 p.m.

Dinner: Monday–Saturday 6–11:30 p.m.

Bar: Monday–Saturday 11 a.m.–1 a.m., Sunday noon–4 p.m.

Atmosphere/setting: Futuristic/modern decor, high ceilings, microbrewery in the ground floor bar; fairly noisy when crowded.

House specialties: Char-grilled squid with chili jam and rocket (arugula); wood-roasted asparagus with citrus salsa; pizzas; swordfish with cavolo nero, shallots, garlic, and grilled polenta; char-grilled rib-eye; rosemary focaccia with fennel and pancetta.

Other recommendations: Fresh fruit drinks, microbrewed beer.

Summary & comments: Mash is lively and boisterous and ultracool. And very popular with a mostly young clientele, who crowd into the ground-floor bar and the upstairs restaurant by day and night. Some come for the excellent beers brewed on the premises, and you can join a lunchtime tour on Saturday (12:30 p.m.) for a tour, tasting, and two-course lunch. Or you can just come in to eat and drink without the educational angle. Grilling over wood and pizzas baked in a wood oven are strong points of the hip, usually well-judged cooking, from a short menu that does pretty well by vegetarians. The bar is a good place for a quick lunch, and there's also a deli counter where you can get meals to take out. Noise-phobics should avoid the restaurant in the evening, but everyone else will enjoy the good buzz and decent food.

MATSURI

★★★½

		Quality
Japanese	Moderate–Expensive	75

	Value
15 Bury St., SW1	D
(0171) 839-1101	

Zone 9: Victoria and Westminster (tube: Green Park)

Customers: Locals and tourists
Reservations: Recommended
When to go: Lunch or dinner
Entrée range: Lunch £13–30
Payment: VISA, MC, AMEX, DC, CB
Service rating: ★★★½

Friendliness rating: ★★★½
Bar: Yes
Wine selection: Adequate, beer and sake better
Dress: Casual
Disabled access: Yes

Lunch: Monday–Saturday noon–2:30 p.m.

Dinner: Monday–Saturday 6–10:30 p.m.

Atmosphere/setting: Big, spacious main dining room, smaller sushi bar; elegant but relaxed.

House specialties: Sushi and teppanyaki.

Summary & comments: London has its full share of big Japanese restaurants catering to businessmen with expense accounts as big as the Grand Canyon. You'll find a few of them in the "More Recommendations" section, along with some smaller places at significantly lower prices. This is a big place, but the prices are relatively reasonable and the quality is high. Sushi and sashimi are expertly prepared and can be ordered either à la carte at the bar or in various permutations of a set meal (from £12 and up). Most of the space is given over to teppanyaki tables, where your choice of fish, meat, and vegetables is prepared and cooked for you on a sizzling hot plate. Very theatrical, but also good food. There's even a nod toward fusion cooking, in the form of Japanese pizza and little dishes such as deep-fried chicken. The list of specialty brand sakes is intriguing, though not cheap. But then, top-quality Japanese *never* comes cheap.

MIRABELLE   ★★★★

French	Moderate	Quality
		90
56 Curzon St., W1		Value
(0171) 499-4636		C

Zone 8: Mayfair and Piccadilly (tube: Green Park)

Customers: Locals and tourists
Reservations: Recommended
When to go: Lunch or dinner
Entrée range: £12.95–24.95
Payment: VISA, MC, AMEX, D, DC, CB
Service rating: ★★★★

Friendliness rating: ★★★½
Bar: Yes
Wine selection: Good
Dress: Casual
Disabled access: No

Lunch: Monday–Friday noon–2:30 p.m., Saturday and Sunday noon–3p.m.

Dinner: Monday–Saturday 6–11:30 p.m., Sunday 6–10:30 p.m.

Atmosphere/setting: Spacious modern rooms with a garden at the back; lively and busy.

House specialties: Omelette "Arnold Bennett," salmon ballottine, truffled parsley soup with a poached egg, aspic of oysters, roast seabass with citrus fruits, braised pork cheeks with spices and fresh ginger, calves liver with bacon and sage, daube of beef "à l'ancienne," prune and Armagnac soufflé, lemon tart.

Other recommendations: Tarte tatin of endive with caramelized sea scallops; foie gras parfait en gelée; tuna with aubergines, basil, and tomato; caramelized skate with beurre noisette; smoked haddock with bubble and squeak and beurre blanc; biscuit glacé; crème brûlée.

Entertainment & amenities: Pianist Monday through Saturday in the back of the restaurant.

Summary & comments: This is the most recent of Marco Pierre White's restaurants (see The Oak Room, page 417). It's also one of the most successful as well as one of the best. There has been a Mirabelle restaurant on this site for many years, but none was as brilliant as its most recent incarnation, and there are people of good taste who regard it as one of the very best restaurants in London. Everything on the menu is good. The prices are *very* reasonable considering the quality and the area. The cooking combines classic French with old-fashioned British, with White's own original take enlivening them all. It's worth noting two things about the Mirabelle. One, it has a garden, which is almost unheard of in this very expensive part of town. Two, some of the dishes appear (at far, far greater cost) on the menu of The Oak Room.

MORO ★★★★

Spanish/Middle Eastern	Moderate	Quality
		80

34–36 Exmouth Market, EC1	Value
(0171) 833-8336	B

Zone 3: The City, Clerkenwell, and Barbican
(tube: Farringdon or Angel)

Customers: Locals both young and old
Reservations: Recommended
When to go: Any time
Entrée range: £10–14
Payment: VISA, MC, AMEX, D

Service rating: ★★★
Friendliness rating: ★★★★½
Bar: Yes; with tapas menu
Wine selection: Very good
Dress: Casual
Disabled access: Yes

Lunch: Monday–Friday 12:30–2:30 p.m.

Dinner: Monday–Friday 7–10:30 p.m.

Drinks and tapas: Monday–Friday 12:30–10:30 p.m.

Atmosphere/setting: Casual, lively; high-ceilinged room with simple decor.

House specialties: Everything cooked in the wood-fired oven, such as cod with Saffron rice, caramelized onions, and tahini; charcoal-grilled dishes like lamb kebab with egg and mint salad and bulgur; homemade breads and yogurt; tarts and other desserts.

Other recommendations: Vegetarian dishes, well-chosen Spanish cheeses, braised dishes.

Summary & comments: Since opening in 1998, Moro has become one of the hottest, coolest, and most popular restaurants in London. The area is off the beaten track as far as sight-seeing is concerned, apart from Sadler's Wells Theatre, but it is also increasingly trendy in a nicely bohemian way. Moro has played a part in this. But it is popular because the food is really outstanding: If anyone has ever had a bad time there, we haven't heard about it. The prices are very reasonable for cooking of this quality. Based on the cuisine and culture of Moorish Spain, when the country was under Islamic rule, it's full of big, bold flavors and generous spicing. You can never tell what you'll find there because the menu changes weekly, but it doesn't matter: Everything's delicious. Not a place for a quiet evening. *Definitely* a place for a memorable meal, in a bustling restaurant that shows why people enthuse about London's gastronomic renaissance.

MR. KONG ★★★½

Chinese	Inexpensive–Moderate	Quality
		75

21 Lisle St., WC2	Value
(0171) 437-7341	B

Zone 7: Soho and the West End (tube: Leicester Square)

Customers: Mostly locals
Reservations: Recommended
When to go: Lunch or dinner
Entrée range: Lunch £6–25
Payment: VISA, MC, AMEX, D, DC, CB
Service rating: ★★★

Friendliness rating: ★★½
Bar: No
Wine selection: Adequate
Dress: Casual
Disabled access: Restaurant

Open: Daily, noon–3 a.m.

Atmosphere/setting: Unexceptional if well-appointed Chinese decor, usually very busy.

House specialties: Chef's specials, especially shellfish and hot-pot dishes.

Other recommendations: Standard Cantonese dishes.

Summary & comments: In an area that's crowded with Chinese restaurants, Mr. Kong stands out by virtue of its interesting and innovative cooking. The menu is long, but you don't need to look any further than the "Chef's Special" page—over 50 dishes, some of them found nowhere else. They seldom climb beyond the £12 mark, and there's enough to keep you happy and interested for a good half-dozen mealtimes. Adventurous eaters can sample baked frogs' legs, fish maw, or pig's intestines; seafood fans should have soft-shell crabs (an occasional special), clams in various guises, or steamed crab with rice wine. Even if you stick with more conventional dishes, you will be well fed. Though Mr. Kong is somewhat more expensive than most restaurants in the area, it's worth the money.

NOBU ★★★★

"New-style" Japanese	Expensive	**Quality** 85
19 Old Park Lane, W1 (0171) 447-4747		**Value** D

Zone 8: Mayfair and Piccadilly (tube: Hyde Park Corner)

Customers: Business people, tourists, the occasional celebrity
Reservations: Essential
When to go: Lunch or dinner
Entrée range: £11.75–27.50
Payment: VISA, MC, AMEX, DC, CB

Service rating: ★★★½
Friendliness rating: ★★★★
Bar: Yes
Wine selection: Very good
Dress: Fashionable
Disabled access: Yes

Lunch: Monday–Friday noon–2:15 p.m.

Dinner: Monday–Saturday 6–10:30 p.m., Sunday 6–9:45 p.m.

Atmosphere/setting: Ultraminimalist decor for an ultrachic clientele.

House specialties: "Special appetizers" such as yellowtail sashimi with jalapeño and tomato rock shrimp ceviche, all traditional sushi and sashimi.

Other recommendations: "Special dishes" such as black cod with miso and Inaniwa pasta salad with lobster.

Summary & comments: Nobu is one-of-a-kind, even though there are two other branches (in New York City and Beverly Hills). If you know about those outlets for Matsuhisu Nobuyuki's extraordinary reworking of Japanese cuisine, then you know what to expect here. There are three things that come to mind, and the most important is startling innovation that almost invariably sends diners into raptures. This is like no other Japanese food, taking in influences from every corner of the globe, especially South America. But it's innovation that *works,* which is what counts. The second thing is chic: Nobu attracts entertainment people, and you may get to see one or two when you eat here. The third thing is the daunting expense. If you order a full meal, it's hard to come away without spending £50 or more on food alone, and that won't even fill you up. This means Nobu doesn't rate well for value. But it is an amazing place which everyone should visit once: Consider going for a sushi lunch, which shouldn't set you back more than £15 a head as long as you avoid alcohol.

NORTH SEA FISH RESTAURANT   ★½

Fish and chips	Inexpensive	Quality
		60

7–8 Leigh St., WC1	Value
(0171) 387-5892	A

Zone 2: Bloomsbury and Holborn (tube: Holborn or King's Cross)

Customers: Mostly locals
Reservations: Not needed
When to go: Lunch or dinner
Entrée range: £6.50–13.50
Payment: VISA, MC, AMEX, DC
Service rating: ★★★

Friendliness rating: ★★★★
Bar: Yes
Wine selection: Adequate
Dress: Casual
Disabled access: Limited

Lunch: Monday–Saturday noon–2:30 p.m.

Dinner: Monday–Saturday 5:30–10:30 p.m.

Atmosphere/setting: Charmingly old-fashioned room with wooden beams, lively buzz.

House specialties: Fish and chips, avocado prawn, seafood platter, scampi, salmon, Dover sole.

Other recommendations: Traditional desserts.

Summary & comments: Everyone visiting London should eat fish and chips at least once. And if they eat it here, they'll see why it's one of the national dishes. To succeed, a cook needs top-quality fish and potatoes, good batter and oil, and an intimate knowledge of the art of deep-frying. At North Sea, they have all the requirements. You can have your choice of fish either fried in batter or matzo meal, or plainly grilled. Don't be put off by the fear of frying (even if it's supposedly "bad for you"). Batter-fried cod at the North Sea is absolutely delicious, not leaden or greasy like some fried foods. If you want to be authentic, have a side order of pickled onion to go with it. Service is decorous and efficient, the wine list is short but good, and the homemade desserts are wonderful. If you have room for them, that is.

THE OAK ROOM ★★★★★

| French (haute cuisine) | Expensive | Quality |
| | | 95 |

| Meridien Hotel, 21 Piccadilly, W1 | Value |
| (0171) 437-0202 | D |

Zone 8: Mayfair and Piccadilly (tube: Piccadilly Circus)

Customers: Locals and tourists
Reservations: Essential
When to go: Lunch or dinner
Set Menus: £29.50 (lunch only);
dinner £55–90
Payment: VISA, MC, AMEX, D
Service rating: ★★★★½

Friendliness rating: ★★★½
Bar: No
Wine selection: Expensive and
extensive
Dress: "No code"
Disabled access: Yes

Lunch: Monday–Friday noon–2:15 p.m.

Dinner: Monday–Saturday 7–11:15 p.m.

Atmosphere/setting: Beautiful, spacious, high-ceilinged room with gilt, mirrors, and chandeliers; formal but not stuffy.

House specialties: Tarte tatin of endive with sea scallops and vinaigrette of red peppers; escalope of brill Viennoise, young spinach, sabayon of chives; oeufs à la neige.

Other recommendations: Mosaic of Bresse chicken, sweetbread, and foie gras; Bresse pigeon à la brioche, petit pain of foie gras, braised cabbage in champagne, lemon tart, feuillantine of raspberries, sauce Cardinale; set lunch.

Summary & comments: This is one of London's two restaurants with three Michelin stars, and it offers everything you would expect from that: superb quality at high prices. The man behind the scenes is Marco Pierre White, whose mini-empire of London restaurants also takes in Mirabelle (see page 412) among others. But the second in command here is Robert Reid, and he runs things well. The set lunch is the affordable option. At dinner you can't spend less than £110 for two before service, and if you really want to indulge yourself you'll have trouble spending less than £100–120 *per person*. Especially because the wine list is notable for ignoring the needs of non-millionaires, and the menu throws in several dishes with supplemental charges even though the basic cost is already high. Don't say we didn't warn you. But having issued the warning, we have to add that the Oak Room sets itself world-class standards—and usually attains them. It is a place you have to consider if you love great French food.

OCEANA   ★★★

		Quality
Modern European	Inexpensive–Moderate	75

		Value
Jason Court, 76 Wigmore St., W1 (0171) 224-2992		C

Sonata, 36 Wigmore St., W1
(0171) 486-1111

Zone 14: Bayswater, Marylebone, Little Venice, St. John's Wood (tube: Bond Street)

Customers: Mostly locals
Reservations: Recommended
When to go: Lunch or dinner
Entrée range: £8.25–14.50
Payment: VISA, MC, AMEX, DC, CB
Service rating: ★★★

Friendliness rating: ★★★★
Bar: Yes
Wine selection: Good
Dress: Smart casual
Disabled access: Yes

Lunch: Monday–Friday noon–3 p.m.

Dinner: Monday–Saturday 6–11:15 p.m.

Atmosphere/setting: Attractive basement room with small bar, quiet but friendly.

House specialties: Cold salad of lamb with marinated aubergine (eggplant) and feta cheese; roast seabass with anchovies, thyme, and chile.

Other recommendations: Any fish dish, soups, set lunch.

Summary & comments: Oceana is as pretty as a basement can be, with vivid Mediterranean colors and daylight streaming in from skylights covering almost a whole wall of the restaurant. But you might ignore your surroundings completely when the food appears on the table, because food is the undisputed star here. It doesn't sound like much on the menu, as descriptions are fashionably minimal. But there's nothing minimal about the flavors, which are zingy and exciting, or about the skill with which they're combined. Vegetarians are presented with at least one choice of both appetizer and main course, and for the rest of us, fish is a particular strength. The wine list is not long, but it doesn't contain a duff bottle. Though prices are fair on the carte, the set menu (lunchtime and 6–7:15 p.m.) is an astonishing bargain at £12.50 for two courses. Only complaint: The background music can be slightly intrusive.

PELHAM STREET   ★★★½

Modern	Moderate	Quality
		75

93 Pelham St., SW7
(0171) 584-4788

	Value
	B

Zone 11: Chelsea and South Kensington (tube: South Kensington)

Customers: Locals
Reservations: Recommended
When to go: Lunch or dinner, or for an afternoon snack on weekends
Entrée range: £8.95–14.95
Payment: VISA, MC, AMEX, D, DC, CB

Service rating: ★★★½
Friendliness rating: ★★★★½
Bar: Yes
Wine selection: Small, but good
Dress: Casual
Disabled access: Yes

Lunch: Daily noon–3 p.m.

Dinner: Daily 7–11 p.m.

Café menu: Saturday–Sunday noon–7 p.m.

Atmosphere/setting: Very informal, simple decoration, plain but comfortable.

House specialties: Swiss cheese soufflé with garlic and parsley cream, rump of lamb with spiced aubergine (eggplant) and goat cheese cannelloni, chocolate fondant with passion fruit sorbet.

Other recommendations: Thai crab cakes, sesame-crusted John Dory with salsify and saffron mash, lemon tart.

Entertainment & amenities: Live music in the evening.

Summary & comments: Pelham Street is just a stone's throw from Bibendum (page 386), which is more famous and more glamorous, and serves roughly similar food. But this smaller place is still worth recommending because it is cheap for the area—and for the level of quality. The menu changes daily, so it's impossible to tell what will be on it if you pay a visit, but the cooking is skilled and the assembly of flavors intelligent. Pelham Street is also worth keeping in mind on weekend visits to the nearby Victoria and Albert, Science, and Natural History Museums: Its all-day policy is nicely flexible, with light dishes, sandwiches, and burgers served from lunch until the beginning of dinner service. Children are made welcome with a set menu of pasta, ice cream, and a drink (£5.95) and adults can enjoy a prix-fixe lunch (£10.95–13.95, two or three courses), which is a real bargain. A serious place at unserious prices.

PIZZA EXPRESS ★

		Quality
Pizza	Inexpensive	50
70 Heath St., NW3		Value
(0171) 433-1600		B

Zone 1: North London: Hampstead, Highgate (tube: Hampstead)

Customers: Locals and tourists
Reservations: Not needed
When to go: Any time
Entrée range: £4.05–7.20
Payment: VISA, MC, AMEX, DC
Service rating: ★★

Friendliness rating: ★★★½
Bar: No
Wine selection: Minimal
Dress: Casual
Disabled access: Yes

Open: Daily 11 a.m.–midnight

Atmosphere/setting: Relaxed, unpretentious, notably child-friendly.

Summary & comments: This branch is just one of dozens: There are over 200 branches nationwide. Its formula is very simple. There are 16 types of pizza, a couple of baked pasta dishes and salads, and a few side dishes. The thin-crust pizzas are smallish by American standards, but good; the pasta dishes are acceptable if not exciting; main-course salads are so-so. In short, not a place to come for a special meal, but when you want something cheap and fast. It is especially good for children, who are always made welcome. Art-lovers should note that they contribute 25p to the Veneziana Fund, formerly Venice in Peril, whenever they order a Veneziana pizza (onions, capers, olives, pine nuts, sultanas, mozzarella, tomato, £4.55).

POLLO ★

		Quality
Italian	Inexpensive	50
20 Old Compton St., W1		Value
(0171) 734-5917		A

Zone 7: Soho and the West End (tube: Leicester Square or Tottenham Court Road)

Customers: Locals
Reservations: Not needed
When to go: Lunch or dinner
Entrée range: £3.20–4
Payment: Cash or sterling travelers checks

Service rating: ★★
Friendliness rating: ★★★★
Bar: No
Wine selection: Minimal
Dress: Casual
Disabled access: No

Open: Daily noon–midnight

Atmosphere/setting: Old-fashioned 1950s decor, charmingly run-down, very lively at all hours.

House specialties: Pasta.

Summary & comments: The reasons for including Pollo in this book can be summed up in three words: pasta, price, and character. The prices are so low they're almost surreal, especially in a city where nothing comes cheap. The pasta is consistently good, whether sauced or baked. And the character is just great, made equally by the cheerful staff and the customers who pile in for cheap eats at any time of day. It's a glimpse of a London that has nearly disappeared from most areas frequented by tourists, and it's worth a visit for that reason alone. If you think of it as an Anglo-Italian diner, you'll have the right idea. One of a kind, and useful for budget-watchers.

PRET À MANGER ★

		Quality
Sandwiches, etc.	Inexpensive	50
The Tower of London, EC3		Value
		B

Zone 3: The City, Clerkenwell, and Barbican (tube: Leicester Square)

Customers: Locals and tourists
Reservations: Not needed
When to go: Breakfast, lunch, or snack
Entrée range: 99p–£4.75
Payment: VISA, MC, AMEX, D, DC, CB

Service rating: ★★★
Friendliness rating: ★★★½
Bar: No
Wine selection: None
Dress: Casual
Disabled access: Yes

Open: 8:30 a.m.–6 p.m. daily

Atmosphere/setting: Sandwich shop.

Summary & comments: Pret à Manger isn't a restaurant but an outlet for fast food, mostly sandwiches, and part of a chain of over 75 in the capital. Sandwiches range from ultrasimple egg salad (called "egg mayonnaise" in Britain, 99p) to wraps filled with hummus and red pepper salad (£2.10) and even vegetarian sushi (£2.70) or deluxe sushi (£4.95). Cakes and desserts are decent, coffee could be a lot better. In short, nothing to set the heart racing—but it's good, it's cheap, it's quick, and it's everywhere. If you just want a light, quick refueling session, this is one place to get it.

QUAGLINO'S   ★★½

Modern European	Moderate	Quality
		70

16 Bury St., SW1	Value
(0171) 930-6767	C

Zone 9: Victoria and Westminster (tube: Green Park)

Customers: Locals and tourists
Reservations: Recommended
When to go: Lunch or dinner
Entrée range: £11–28.50
Payment: VISA, MC, AMEX, D, DC, CB
Service rating: ★★½

Friendliness rating: ★★
Bar: Yes
Wine selection: Good
Dress: Smart casual
Disabled access: Yes

Lunch: Daily 12 noon–3 p.m.

Dinner: Monday–Thursday 5:30 p.m.–midnight, Friday and Saturday 5:30 p.m.–1 a.m., Sunday 5:30–11 p.m.

Atmosphere/setting: Massive interior, with a street-level mezzanine bar (very popular) overlooking the sunken dining room; very noisy.

House specialties: Plateau de fruits de mer (and all shellfish), grilled meats such as Châteaubriand.

Other recommendations: Prix-fixe menus.

Entertainment & amenities: Jazz every night from 9 p.m.

Summary & comments: Quaglino's was a famous bar/restaurant in the 1930s. On its reopening by Sir Terence Conran in the late 1980s, it started a fad for really huge London restaurants—several of them owned by Conran himself. Many people, however, think this is still the best of them. The kitchen is on view behind glass, and so are banks of the fresh seafood which is one of the restaurant's strengths. Because it's so huge, this is not a place for quiet conversation. It's buzzy, boisterous, and brash. Some people love this kind of place, others do not. But even if this is not your usual style of restaurant, Quaglino's is worth considering to see a style of eating that London has taken to its heart. The prix-fixe menus (lunchtime, and pre- and post-theater) are the best choice if you're on a limited budget. Service can also slow down at busy times.

RANSOME'S DOCK ★★★

		Quality
Modern	Moderate	80

	Value
35-37 Parkgate Rd., SW1	B
(0171) 223-1611 or (0171) 924-2462	

Zone 11: Chelsea and South Kensington

Customers: Locals and wine fanatics
Reservations: Recommended
When to go: Dinner, so you can enjoy the wine list
Entrée range: £9.50–17.50
Payment: VISA, MC, AMEX, D, CB

Service rating: ★★★½
Friendliness rating: ★★★★★
Bar: Yes
Wine selection: Outstanding
Dress: Casual
Disabled access: Yes

Open: Monday–Friday 11 a.m.–11 p.m., Saturday 11 a.m.–midnight, Sunday 11:30 a.m.–3:30 p.m.

Atmosphere/setting: Lively, casual, and friendly, dockside views of the Thames.

House specialties: Seared scallops with celeriac purée and chorizo; Norfolk smoked eel with buckwheat pancakes and crème fraîche; "Shorthorn" sirloin steak with mustard and tarragon sauce; hot prune and Armagnac soufflé with Armagnac custard.

Other recommendations: Hot hors d'oeuvres plate; Morecambe Bay potted shrimps; Trelough duck breast with Oloroso sherry and figs, fondant potato, and snap peas; baked banana with dark rum, orange, cream, and cardamom; passion fruit and blood orange jelly with fresh fruits.

Entertainment & amenities: Dockside terrace open in warm weather.

Summary & comments: Ransome's Dock is a bit out of the way: south of the river in the Battersea area. But it's a short cab ride from King's Road and other shopping areas of Chelsea, and well worth a special trip for its nice views, good food, and (most of all) its outstanding wine list. The emphasis is on good ingredients, especially distinctive foods unique to the area of production. Origins are announced on the menu when possible, to show that they take pride in the best of British. They also take pride in their wines, which come from all over the world and sometimes include mature bottles that you are unlikely to find in other restaurants. Ransome's Dock is up to the minute in its cooking, but not flashy or pretentious. Very popular, and with good reason.

RASA		★★★½
Indian	Moderate	Quality
		75
6 Dering St., W1		Value
(0171) 629-1346		B

55 Stoke Newington Church St., N1
(0171) 249-0344

Zone 8: Mayfair and Piccadilly (tube: Oxford Circus)

Customers: Locals and aficionados
Reservations: Recommended
When to go: Lunch or dinner
Entrée range: £6–10.95
Payment: VISA, MC, AMEX, D, DC, CB
Service rating: ★★★½

Friendliness rating: ★★★
Bar: Yes
Wine selection: Small, but good
Dress: Casual
Disabled access: Restaurant only

Lunch: Monday–Saturday noon–3 p.m.

Dinner: Monday–Saturday 6–11 p.m.

Atmosphere/setting: Pleasant modern interior, simply decorated, friendly and informal.

House specialties: Southern Indian vegetarian dishes.

Other recommendations: Breads, pickles, and chutneys.

Summary & comments: The original Rasa, in out-of-the-way Stoke Newington, has educated thousands of Londoners about the beauties of Keralan (southern Indian) vegetarian cuisine. This is the second branch, more centrally located, and it deserves a visit if you have the slightest interest in Indian food. For £22.50 you can ask them to put together a Kerala Feast, which will give a good balance and range of dishes featuring different flavors and textures. Or choose for yourself among the dosas (filled pancakes), curries, and side dishes of rice, vegetables, and exquisite bread. The food is filling but not stodgy, and no one who eats it comes away unimpressed. If you like the idea but don't like vegetarian meals, there's a branch called Rasa Samudra (5 Charlotte St., W1, phone (0171) 637 0222) specializing in Southern Indian fish and shellfish. The Stoke Newington restaurant has humbler decor, far lower prices, and a huge local fan club that can cause a long wait for tables.

RK STANLEY'S ★★

		Quality
British	Inexpensive	70

	Value
6 Little Portland St., W1	B
(0171) 462-0099	

Zone 7: Soho and the West End (tube: Oxford Circus)

Customers: Mostly locals
Reservations: Not needed
When to go: Lunch or dinner
Entrée range: £7.25–11.95
Payment: VISA, MC, AMEX, D, CB
Service rating: ★★½

Friendliness rating: ★★★★
Bar: Yes
Wine selection: Adequate; beers are outstanding
Dress: Casual
Disabled access: Yes

Open: Monday–Saturday noon–midnight

Atmosphere/setting: Jolly and very informal.

House specialties: "The Magnificent Seven" sausages, spit roast Welsh beef, saddle of lamb.

Other recommendations: House "savouries," desserts.

Summary & comments: RK Stanleys is known to Londoners as the place to eat sausages—seven varieties, ranging from plain pork through Caribbean-style, Thai-style, game, chicken, bratwurst, and even a vegetarian Glamorgan sausage. They're served up by friendly and skilled staff in a simple room that's also pleasing to the eye, with its red banquettes and booths. And the sausages are reason enough to go here. But the rest of the food is also worth a look—simple, using top ingredients, and consistently well prepared. The wine list is dominated by English wines (which will surprise you with their quality). You'd be much better off, however, drinking one or more of the outstanding beers from the United Kingdom or Europe. RK Stanleys is a low-priced star, one of the best in the West End. Please note one of the best bargain offers anywhere in London: at Saturday lunchtime, children eat for free.

ROYAL CHINA   ★★★

Chinese	Inexpensive	Quality
		70

	Value
13 Queensway, W2	B
(0171) 221-2535	

40 Baker St., W2
(0171) 487-4688

Zone 14: Bayswater, Marylebone, Little Venice, St. John's Wood (tube:
Bayswater or Queensway)

Customers: Locals and tourists, many Chinese
Reservations: Not needed
When to go: Weekend lunch or dinner
Entrée range: £5.50–40
Payment: VISA, MC, AMEX, D

Service rating: ★★
Friendliness rating: ★★½
Bar: Yes
Wine selection: Excellent for a Chinese restaurant
Dress: Casual
Disabled access: Restaurant only

Open: Monday–Thursday noon–11 p.m., Friday and Saturday noon–11:30 p.m., Sunday 11 a.m.–10:30 p.m.

Atmosphere/setting: Plush Chinese decor with lots of black lacquer and gold, comfortable seating; can be quite hectic when there's a crowd.

House specialties: All shellfish, especially lobster (cooked in six different ways), scallops, and prawns; dim sum.

Other recommendations: Chicken with cashews, sautéed chicken with black beans and chili, fillet steak with black pepper, hot and spicy veal, Royal China Dover sole, Royal China lotus leaf rice, chilled mango pudding.

Summary & comments: Probably the best restaurant in this Chinese restaurant–crowded street, Royal China is also a cut above in comfort, and care has been taken with the decor, even if it is not to everyone's taste. But the food *is* to everyone's taste, as you'll see if you go along for dim sum. There are the usual dumplings and rolls, as well as special dishes rarely found elsewhere, and the quality is exceptional. The only problem is the crowds, which on weekends (especially Sunday) can lead to enormous lines outside. Go during the week for a more leisurely affair, and for dinner as well as lunch. Seafood is exquisite, and even the set meals (normally a no-go area) are good. Service can be a little abrupt, but is better than at many comparable places. And the wine list is a surprise, as good as some upper-echelon European restaurants—and much cheaper!

RULES ★★★

		Quality
British	Moderate–Expensive	80

	Value
35 Maiden Lane, WC2	D
(0171) 836-5314	

Zone 5: Regents Park and Camden Town

Customers: More tourists than locals
Reservations: Recommended
When to go: Dinner is best
Entrée range: £14.95–27.95
Payment: VISA, MC, AMEX, D, DC

Service rating: ★★★
Friendliness rating: ★★★
Bar: No
Wine selection: Small, but good
Dress: Casual
Disabled access: No

Open: Monday–Saturday noon–midnight, Sunday noon–10:30 p.m.

Atmosphere/setting: Ornate old-fashioned decor with antique prints and statues, but lively bustle at busy times.

House specialties: Game dishes, Aberdeen Angus beef.

Other recommendations: Twice-baked wild mushroom and goat cheese soufflé; terrine of foie gras and pigeon; whole roast guinea fowl with onions, mushrooms, and crispy bacon; braised shank of venison with spiced roasted vegetables; roast rib of beef; roast rack of lamb with creamed leeks and dauphine potatoes.

Summary & comments: Rules has been serving food from this location since 1798. That by itself is not a reason to recommend it, and for years the restaurant served indifferent food to tourists who didn't know any better. But now it has a French-trained chef of high quality who's combining classic game and meat cookery with modern touches—all of them handled with skill. You may not wish to start with lobster and asparagus salad with mango dressing, but you can. Or just dive headlong into the comforting waters of tradition. The selection of "feathered and furred game" is as good as you'll find anywhere in London, and lamb and beef are first-rate. Vegetarians should probably not bother, but fish eaters will find several salmon dishes in a six-strong list. If you want to try real old-fashioned English food of the highest standard, Rules is probably one of your best bets.

SILKS & SPICE   ★★

Oriental	Inexpensive–Moderate	Quality
		70

23 Foley St., W1	Value
(0171) 636-2718	B

95 Chiswick High Rd., W4
(0181) 995-7991

Zone 14: Bayswater, Marylebone, Little Venice, St. John's Wood (tube: Oxford Circus or Great Portland Street)

Customers: Locals
Reservations: Recommended
When to go: Any time
Entrée range: £5.50–12.50
Payment: VISA, MC, AMEX, D, DC
Service rating: ★★½

Friendliness rating: ★★★★
Bar: No
Wine selection: Cheap and adequate
Dress: Casual
Disabled access: Ground floor only

Open: Monday–Friday noon–11 p.m., Saturday 5:30–11 p.m., Sunday 5:30–10:30 p.m.

Atmosphere/setting: Pleasantly scruffy decor with Southeast Asian ornaments, noisy and lively.

House specialties: Lobster noodles, salmon salad, grilled prawns.

Other recommendations: All noodles, all char-grilled dishes, dim sum, curries.

Summary & comments: Silks & Spice began here and now has two other branches in addition to the one listed above. It deserves its success. The feel is slightly student-y, with jazz/funk playing on the stereo, but customers are of all ages. They come for well-priced and delicious Asian food, mostly Thai and Malaysian with bits of China and Japan. Comfort is not a selling point: Tables are close, and chairs won't make you feel sleepy. But as long as you don't expect luxury you will enjoy their long, varied menu. Most dishes are classified according to chile-heat, which is useful, and although portions aren't huge, you can easily eat a filling meal for under £15 before drinks. On the minus side, note that the large basement is the smoking area and gets *very* smoky when busy. On the plus side, the Oriental Express Menu (noon–7 p.m.) offers smaller servings at lower prices for people in a rush. If Silks & Spice is full, there's an excellent, moderately priced fish restaurant next door called Back to Basics.

SPAGHETTI HOUSE ★★

Italian	Inexpensive	Quality
		65

71 Haymarket, W1	Value
(0171) 839-3939	B

Zone 7: Soho and the West End (tube: Piccadilly Circus)

Customers: Locals and tourists, families especially welcome
Reservations: Not needed
When to go: Lunch or dinner
Entrée range: £5.95–10.95
Payment: VISA, MC, AMEX, D, DC, CB
Service rating: ★★★

Friendliness rating: ★★★★
Bar: Yes
Wine selection: Minimal, but good
Dress: Casual
Disabled access: Yes

Open: Monday–Saturday 11 a.m.–11 p.m., Sunday 11 a.m.–10 p.m.

Atmosphere/setting: Understated modern decor, friendly, informal atmosphere.

House specialties: Malfatti pomodoro e peperoncino, lasagna, cannelloni, melanzane parmigiana.

Other recommendations: Antipasti, salads, standard pasta dishes.

Summary & comments: The Spaghetti House is part of a long-established chain (consult phone book for other branches) that anticipated London's love affair with Italian food but then fell behind in terms of decor and cooking. This flagship branch is the company's attempt to catch up, and it is a huge success. The food is good, the feeling is pleasant, and its prime location near Piccadilly Circus makes it a perfect spot before, during, or after sight-seeing in the West End. What's more, it is a perfect place to bring children, who have always been one of the most important parts of the company's core constituency. And the prices are low.

SPIGA ★★

Italian	Inexpensive	Quality
		65
84/86 Wardour St., W1		Value
(0171) 734-3444		C

Spighetta, 43 Blandford St., W1
(0171) 486-7340

Zone 7: Soho and the West End (tube: Tottenham Court Road)

Customers: Mostly locals, mostly young
Reservations: Recommended
When to go: Lunch or dinner
Entrée range: £5.50–14
Payment: VISA, MC, AMEX, D, DC, CB
Service rating: ★★½

Friendliness rating: ★★★
Bar: No
Wine selection: Small, but adequate
Dress: Casual
Disabled access: Yes

Lunch: Daily noon–3 p.m.

Dinner: Sunday–Tuesday 6:30–11 p.m., Wednesday–Saturday 6:30–midnight

Atmosphere/setting: Sleek, modern decor with view of the kitchen, informal and friendly.

House specialties: Pizzas; angel hair pasta with prawns, rocket (arugula) salad, garlic, and chiles; char-grilled chicken breast with spinach and roasted potatoes.

Summary & comments: Spiga, like its cousin Spighetta, is a friendly, low-priced outlet for top-quality pizzas baked in wood-burning ovens. And these are some of the best pizzas in town, whether a simple Margherita or topped with prosciutto and wild mushrooms. They make Spiga a top choice in this part of town when you want good, simple food in informal surroundings. But there's more to the place than pizza: Pasta dishes in particular also excel, and appetizers, fish, and meat are simple, but well executed. Friendly service, good coffee, and ample choice in cheap wines completes the picture. The only complaint is a tendency for service to flag when the place is busy. For outstanding (and more expensive) cooking from the same group, see the entry for Zafferano (page 438).

STEFANO CAVALLINI AT THE HALKIN ★★★★½

Italian	Expensive	**Quality** 90
Halkin Hotel, 5 Halkin St., SW1 (0171) 333-1234		**Value** C

Zone 10: Knightsbridge and Belgravia (tube: Hyde Park Corner)

Customers: Hotel guests, business-men, locals, tourists
Reservations: Recommended
When to go: Lunch or dinner
Entrée range: £23–28
Payment: VISA, MC, AMEX, DC, CB

Service rating: ★★★★★
Friendliness rating: ★★★★★
Bar: Yes
Wine selection: Outstanding
Dress: Smart casual
Disabled access: Yes

Lunch: Monday–Friday 12:30–2:30 p.m.

Dinner: Monday–Saturday 7:30–11 p.m., Sunday 7–10 p.m.

Atmosphere/setting: Elegant, modern room, bright in the day and candlelit in the evening.

House specialties: Salad of rabbit with Belgian endive, celery, and green olives; duck ravioli with Savoy cabbage and foie gras; panettone soufflé.

Other recommendations: Set lunch.

Entertainment & amenities: Guitarist or harpist in the evening.

Summary & comments: Along with Zafferano (see page 438), Stefano Cavallini probably serves the best Italian food in London—at a serious price. The restaurant is located in one of the capital's grandest hotels, and it occupies a beautiful modern room overlooking the gardens. Cavallini starts from the fundamental Italian principles of simplicity, directness, and respect for good ingredients, and some dishes (such as veal cutlet à la Milanese) are essentially traditional. But elsewhere he is modern in his adventurousness, with happy results. Fish is a specialty; pasta, risotto, and desserts are sublime. The exceptional wine list includes great Italian classics at stupendous prices, but also a few cheaper bottles of uniformly high quality. Service is among the best in London, flawless but smiling. Unless you're out for a special evening, the set lunch (£25 for three courses) is definitely the way to go. But if you really love Italian food and want one evening of luxury—complete with discreet live music—this is as good a place as any to have it.

STEPHEN BULL   ★★★½

Modern European	Moderate	Quality
		75

		Value
5–7 Blandford St., W1		C
(0171) 486-9696		

71 St. John St., EC1
(0171) 490-1750

Zone 14: Bayswater, Marylebone, Little Venice, St. John's Wood
(tube: Bond Street)

Customers: Mostly locals
Reservations: Recommended
When to go: Lunch or dinner
Entrée range: £10.50–16.50
Payment: VISA, MC, AMEX, DC
Service rating: ★★★½

Friendliness rating: ★★★
Bar: No
Wine selection: Excellent
Dress: "Anything"
Disabled access: Restaurant only

Lunch: Monday–Friday noon–3 p.m.

Dinner: Monday–Saturday 6:30–10:30 p.m.

Atmosphere/setting: Minimal decor, small, bright, and comfortable.

Other recommendations: Twice-baked goat cheese soufflé with beet salad, all fish dishes, vegetarian dishes, desserts.

Summary & comments: Stephen Bull has long been one of the leading proponents of modern cooking in Britain, and this, his original restaurant, continues to maintain high standards. It's not flashy in any sense; there are no gimmicks. They simply aim to give your tastebuds a thrill in pleasant surroundings and with competent service. The wine list is particularly memorable for its international scope, fair prices, and helpful, user-friendly organization by style (such as, "Cruiserweights—lighter Cabs and medium Merlots"). And there is something to complement every style of cooking on a menu that might include both boeuf bourguignonne and poached skate with new potatoes, capers, and beet and horseradish relish. Vegetarians have two choices of appetizer and main course. The set dinner (£27.50 for three courses) is a mega-bargain.

TAMARIND ★★★½

Indian	Moderate	Quality
		75

20 Queen St., W1	Value
(0171) 629-3561	C

Zone 8: Mayfair and Piccadilly (tube: Green Park)

Customers: Locals and tourists
Reservations: Recommended
When to go: Lunch or dinner
Entrée range: £10–17
Payment: VISA, MC, AMEX, D, DC, CB
Service rating: ★★★

Friendliness rating: ★★★
Bar: Yes
Wine selection: Good
Dress: Smart
Disabled access: No

Lunch: Sunday–Friday noon–3 p.m.

Dinner: Monday–Saturday 6–11:30 p.m., Sunday 6–10:30 p.m.

Atmosphere/setting: Chic, stylish decor sets the tone.

Summary & comments: There are no specialties or recommendations listed here because this is one of those rare restaurants where you'll be hard-pressed to order a bad dish. Tamarind produces fireworks in every department, from chutneys and pickles (available for sale in jars) through breads and rice, and on to the meat, fish, and vegetable dishes that make this one of the best Indian eateries in London (vegetarians could do very well just ordering rice, bread, and a selection of side dishes). Mind you, it's also one of the most expensive. A three-course meal with all the right side dishes can easily cost £30 before drinks. Part of that is paying for the setting, for a large and polished team of waiters, and for rent in one of London's most exclusive areas. But it's also paying for the best ingredients, cooked with exceptional skill and attention. If you want to find out how good Indian restaurant cooking can be, and don't mind paying "European" prices for the pleasure, this is one of the three or four best places to do it.

TEATRO		★★★½

Modern European	Moderate	Quality
		80

93–107 Shaftesbury Ave., W1	Value
(0171) 494-3040	C

Zone 7: Soho and the West End (tube: Leicester Square or Tottenham Court Road)

Customers: Mostly locals
Reservations: Recommended
When to go: Dinner is best
Entrée range: £13.50–19.75
Payment: VISA, MC, AMEX, D, DC
Service rating: ★★★★

Friendliness rating: ★★★★
Bar: Yes
Wine selection: Very good
Dress: "No dress code"
Disabled access: Yes

Lunch: Monday–Friday noon–3 p.m.

Dinner: Monday–Saturday 6–11:45 p.m.

Atmosphere/setting: Modern interior of exceptional elegance, fairly chic clientele.

House specialties: Roasted shallot and tomato tatin, Teatro salade Niçoise, grilled bluefin tuna with creamed parsnip and sweet-and-sour shallots, roast rump of lamb with pommes boulangeres and jus Niçoise, warm chocolate cake with chocolate sauce and a mandarin sorbet, treacle tart with fromage-frais sorbet.

Other recommendations: Foie gras du jour, velouté of Jerusalem artichokes and truffle oil, roasted poulet noir on Parmesan risotto with a thyme jus and crisp shallots, rhubarb crème brûlée with poached rhubarb and rhubarb jus.

Summary & comments: Teatro opened in 1998, turning a 1960s building of no great distinction into one of the West End's smartest and most elegant showcases for modern cooking. The room is low-ceilinged and understated, service eager and almost invariably efficient. Everything lets you focus on the food, which at its best is stunningly good. Ingredients are top-class and assembled in a way that lets strong flavors shine through from every component of the dish. Though vegetarians are catered to with only one main course, there are usually a few choices among appetizers that can complete the meal without meat. Meat and fish eaters, by contrast, are spoiled for choice. Save room for dessert, which is a high point here—with or without a glass of dessert wine (several good choices) to accompany it.

VEERASWAMY ★★★½

		Quality
Indian	Moderate	80

	Value
Mezzanine Floor, Victory House, 99 Regent St. (0171) 734-1401	B

Chutney Mary, 535 Kings Rd., W1
(0171) 351-3113

Zone 7: Soho and the West End (tube: Piccadilly Circus)

Customers: Mostly locals
Reservations: Recommended
When to go: Lunch or dinner
Entrée range: £9–13.50
Payment: VISA, MC, AMEX, DC, CB
Service rating: ★★★★

Friendliness rating: ★★★★
Bar: No
Wine selection: Very good
Dress: No code
Disabled access: Yes

Lunch: Monday–Friday noon–2:30 p.m., Saturday and Sunday 12:30–2:30 p.m.

Dinner: Monday–Saturday 5:30–11:30 p.m., Sunday 6–10 p.m.

Atmosphere/setting: Stylish, colorful room overlooking Regent Street; mostly young, fashionable crowd.

House specialties: Fresh mussels in an aromatic coconut and ginger sauce; pan-fried lamb kebabs with roasted spices; spicy grilled chicken; Mangalorean chicken curry; Karwari red fish curry; white chicken curry flavored with almonds, cinnamon, cinnamon leaf, cardamom, and green chiles; fresh pineapple curry with spices, green chile and coconut.

Other recommendations: Breads, condiments, set meals, special diabetic menu according to Ayurvedic principles.

Summary & comments: Veeraswamy has been on this site for decades, but the quality-conscious Chutney Mary group took over and revamped it in 1998. They modernized everything from decor to menu to wine list, and the result is one of London's better Indian restaurants. The room is unusually attractive in the way it contrasts pale wood with deep, well-chosen color. Service is from a young, multiethnic crew, and the kitchen is staffed by specialists cooking the dishes of their own region. This means that any dish, whatever part of India it's from, is likely to be authentic. Vegetable and fish/meat/chicken dishes are given equal prominence and cooked with equal care, making Veeraswamy a particularly good place to come with a mixed group of vegetarians and meat eaters. Prices are reasonable compared with other Indian restaurants at this level, and set-price offerings make them even better. If your time is limited and you can only eat at one Indian place, this is a good candidate.

WAGAMAMA   ★

Oriental	Inexpensive	Quality
		55

4A Streatham St., WC1	Value
(0171) 323-9223	B

10A Lexington St.
(0171) 292-0990

Zone 2: Bloomsbury and Holborn (tube: Tottenham Court Road)

Customers: Mostly locals
Reservations: None taken
When to go: Any time
Entrée range: £4.70–7.25
Payment: VISA, MC, AMEX
Service rating: ★

Friendliness rating: ★★
Bar: No
Wine selection: Minimal
Dress: Casual
Disabled access: No

Open: Monday–Saturday noon–11 p.m., Sunday 12:30–10:30 p.m.

Atmosphere/setting: Spartan room with seating at long tables.

House specialties: Soup noodles, fried noodles, dumplings.

Summary & comments: This is the original branch of Wagamama; there are two others, and more were planned as this book went to press. The expansion tells the story of a phenomenal success based on a simple idea. Produce a menu that focuses on just a few things, make them consistently well, and cut out all the frills so you can sell them cheap. The focus is on noodles, mostly Japanese varieties such as ramen and udon. The frills that disappear are personal space (you sit at long tables with other diners) and flexibility. You're in a machine at Wagamama, and it's not a place to dawdle. But the meals are cheap and filling, and you can be in and out very quickly when you're on the go. Complaints usually deal with service, which has little to do with personalized attention and much more with keeping the machine working smoothly. The places can't be ignored for their quality and speed; just don't expect to feel pampered.

WÓDKA ★★½

Polish	Moderate	Quality 70

		Value C

12 St. Albans Grove, W8
(0171) 937-6513

Zone 11: Chelsea and South Kensington

Customers: Mostly locals and fans
Reservations: Recommended
When to go: Lunch or dinner
Entrée range: £9.90–13.50
Payment: VISA, MC, AMEX, DC
Service rating: ★★★

Friendliness rating: ★★★★½
Bar: Yes
Wine selection: Small, but good and very reasonable
Dress: Casual
Disabled access: Yes

Lunch: Monday–Friday 12:30–2:30 p.m.

Dinner: Daily 7–11:15 p.m.

Atmosphere/setting: Small rooms, plain decor; popular at both lunch and dinner, and very welcoming.

House specialties: Traditional Polish dishes such as blinis, dumplings, and herring; extensive vodka list.

Other recommendations: Cheap lunch menu (£10.90 for two courses, £13.50 for three courses), roast and grilled meats, daily specials.

Summary & comments: London has a long tradition of hosting emigrés from Eastern and Central Europe, who have brought with them the richness of their national cuisines. Wódka is part of that tradition, but it is not a traditional restaurant: The setting is modern and so is the food, despite paying due respect to classic Polish fare. Thus, you'll find blinis alongside risotto, and pierogis alongside grilled swordfish; unusual ingredients such as foie gras and oysters are there with kasha and dill. This gives a meal at Wódka a welcome element of surprise, and also means you can eat more lightly here than at many restaurants serving this type of cuisine. The area is affluent, but Wódka is unpretentious and very well priced, both at lunch and at dinner. Wine is priced to match the food, but aficionados will not be able to resist the vodkas that give the restaurant its name. There are around 25 on the list, including vodkas that are flavored on the premises (such as vanilla or pear).

ZAFFERANO		★★★★
Italian	Moderate–Expensive	Quality 90
15 Lowndes St., SW1 (0171) 235-5800		Value C

Zone 10: Knightsbridge and Belgravia (tube: Knightsbridge)

Customers: Food-loving locals
Reservations: Recommended
When to go: Lunch or dinner
Set menus: £17.50–20.50 (lunch only). £26.50–36.50 (dinner)
Payment: VISA, MC, AMEX, D, DC, CB
Service rating: ★★★★

Friendliness rating: ★★★★
Bar: Yes
Wine selection: Very good
Dress: Smart casual
Disabled access: Restaurant yes, toilets no

Lunch: Monday–Saturday noon–2:30 p.m.

Dinner: Monday–Saturday 7–11 p.m.

Atmosphere/setting: Simple modern decor, subdued but not stuffy.

House specialties: Roast rabbit with Parma ham and polenta, pan-fried sea bream with balsamic vinegar, ravioli of osso buco, potato and mint tortelli, tiramisu.

Summary & comments: Many people think Zafferano is the best Italian restaurant in London. Even those who quibble with that assessment agree that it's right up there—and that it offers a pretty good bargain for cooking on such an exalted level. Chef Giorgio Locatelli turns out dishes that impress again and again, even when you've eaten them a dozen times before. The cooking combines tradition with invention, ingredients are always first-rate, and the total effect is of simplicity—big, fresh flavors artfully combined. You'll find dishes here that are unlikely to appear on menus elsewhere, and even when they're familiar they are rarely better. Service is skilled and friendly. On the long wine list, almost all Italian, little is explained; ask for guidance if you're not sure about the unfamiliar names. Note: The same group is behind Spiga (see page 430).

Index

Unofficial Guide **Reader Survey**

If you would like to express your opinion about London or this guide-book, complete the following survey and mail it to:

> *Unofficial Guide* Reader Survey
> PO Box 43673
> Birmingham AL 35243

Inclusive dates of your visit: _____

Members of
your party: Person 1 Person 2 Person 3 Person 4 Person 5
Gender: M F   M F   M F   M F   M F
Age: _____

Have you ever been to Europe before? _____
Was this your first trip to London? _____
On your most recent trip, where did you stay? _____

Concerning your accommodations, on a scale of 100 as best and 0 as worst, how would you rate:

The quality of your room?   ____   The value of your room?   ____
The quietness of your room?   ____   The reservation process?   ____
Staff's relations with foreigners? ____   Overall hotel satisfaction?   ____

Did you use public transportation? _____   What kind? _____

Concerning public transportation, on a scale of 100 as best and 0 as worst, how would you rate:

Ease of use?   ____   Value vs. rental cars?   ____
Cleanliness?   ____   Hours and areas serviced?   ____
Airport shuttle efficiency? ____

Concerning your dining experiences:

Estimate the number of meals eaten in restaurants per day. _____
Approximately how much did your party spend on meals per day? _____
Favorite restaurants in London: _____
_____

Did you buy this guide before leaving? ☐   while on your trip? ☐

How did you hear about this guide? (check all that apply)

Loaned or recommended by a friend ☐   Radio or TV ☐
Newspaper or magazine ☐   Bookstore salesperson ☐
Just picked it out on my own ☐   Library ☐
Internet ☐

What other guidebooks did you use on this trip? _____

_____

_____

On a scale of 100 as best and 0 as worst, how would you rate them?

_____

_____

_____

Using the same scale, how would you rate *The Unofficial Guide(s)?*

_____

Are *Unofficial Guides* readily available at bookstores in your area? _____

Have you used other *Unofficial Guides?* _____

Which one(s)? _____

_____

_____

_____

_____

Comments about your London trip or *The Unofficial Guide(s):*

_____

_____

_____

_____

_____

_____

_____

_____

_____

_____

_____

_____

_____